Houghton
Mifflin
Harcourt

GO MATH!

Volume 2

Made in the United States
Text printed on 100%
recycled paper

Houghton
Mifflin
Harcourt

Printed in the U.S.A.

ISBN 978-0-544-43280-2

11 12 13 14 15 0029 22 21 20 19 18

4500713599   D E F G

Dear Students and Families,

Welcome to **Go Math!**, Grade 5! In this exciting mathematics program, there are hands-on activities to do and real-world problems to solve. Best of all, you will write your ideas and answers right in your book. In **Go Math!**, writing and drawing on the pages helps you think deeply about what you are learning, and you will really understand math!

By the way, all of the pages in your **Go Math!** book are made using recycled paper. We wanted you to know that you can Go Green with **Go Math!**

Sincerely,

The Authors

© Houghton Mifflin Harcourt Publishing Company • Image Credits: (bg) ©Sankar Salvady/Flickr/Getty Images; (t) ©Blaine Harrington III/Alamy Images; (c) ©Don Johnston/All Canada Photos/Getty Images; (b) ©Erich Kuchling/Westend61/Corbis

GO MATH!

Authors

Juli K. Dixon, Ph.D.
Professor, Mathematics Education
University of Central Florida
Orlando, Florida

Edward B. Burger, Ph.D.
President, Southwestern University
Georgetown, Texas

Steven J. Leinwand
Principal Research Analyst
American Institutes for
    Research (AIR)
Washington, D.C.

Contributor

Rena Petrello
Professor, Mathematics
Moorpark College
Moorpark, CA

Matthew R. Larson, Ph.D.
K-12 Curriculum Specialist for
    Mathematics
Lincoln Public Schools
Lincoln, Nebraska

Martha E. Sandoval-Martinez
Math Instructor
El Camino College
Torrance, California

English Language Learners Consultant

Elizabeth Jiménez
CEO, GEMAS Consulting
Professional Expert on English
    Learner Education
Bilingual Education and
    Dual Language
Pomona, California

Fluency with Whole Numbers and Decimals

Critical Area

 Critical Area Extending division to 2-digit divisors, integrating decimal fractions into the place value system and developing understanding of operations with decimals to hundredths, and developing fluency with whole number and decimal operations

Real World Project In the Chef's Kitchen 2

1 Place Value, Multiplication, and Expressions   3

Domains Operations and Algebraic Thinking
Number and Operations in Base Ten
COMMON CORE STATE STANDARDS
5.OA.A.1, 5.OA.A.2, 5.NBT.A.1, 5.NBT.A.2, 5.NBT.B.5, 5.NBT.B.6

✔ Show What You Know 3
Vocabulary Builder 4
Chapter Vocabulary Cards
Vocabulary Game 4A
1 Investigate • Place Value and Patterns 5
2 Place Value of Whole Numbers 11
3 Algebra • Properties. 17
4 Algebra • Powers of 10 and Exponents 23
5 Algebra • Multiplication Patterns 29
✔ Mid-Chapter Checkpoint .35
6 Multiply by 1-Digit Numbers 37
7 Multiply by Multi-Digit Numbers. 43
8 Relate Multiplication to Division 49
9 Problem Solving • Multiplication and Division 55
10 Algebra • Numerical Expressions 61
11 Algebra • Evaluate Numerical Expressions. 67
12 Algebra • Grouping Symbols 73
✔ Chapter 1 Review/Test. .79

GO DIGITAL

Go online! Your math lessons are interactive. Use *i*Tools, Animated Math Models, the Multimedia eGlossary, and more.

Chapter 1 Overview

In this chapter, you will explore and discover answers to the following **Essential Questions**:

• How can you use place value, multiplication, and expressions to represent and solve problems?

• How can you read, write, and represent whole numbers through millions?

• How can you use properties and multiplication to solve problems?

• How can you use expressions to represent and solve a problem?

Personal Math Trainer
Online Assessment and Intervention

Divide Whole Numbers 85

Domains Number and Operations in Base Ten
Number and Operations–Fractions
COMMON CORE STATE STANDARDS
5.NBT.B.6, 5.NF.B.3

✓ Show What You Know 85
  Vocabulary Builder 86
  Chapter Vocabulary Cards
  Vocabulary Game 86A
1 Place the First Digit 87
2 Divide by 1-Digit Divisors 93
3 Investigate • Division with 2-Digit Divisors 99
4 Partial Quotients 105
✓ Mid-Chapter Checkpoint 111
5 Estimate with 2-Digit Divisors. 113
6 Divide by 2-Digit Divisors 119
7 Interpret the Remainder 125
8 Adjust Quotients 131
9 Problem Solving • Division 137
✓ Chapter 2 Review/Test 143

Add and Subtract Decimals 149

Domain Number and Operations in Base Ten
COMMON CORE STATE STANDARDS
5.NBT.A.1, 5.NBT.A.3a, 5.NBT.A.3b, 5.NBT.A.4, 5.NBT.B.7

✓ Show What You Know 149
  Vocabulary Builder 150
  Chapter Vocabulary Cards
  Vocabulary Game 150A
1 Investigate • Thousandths 151
2 Place Value of Decimals 157
3 Compare and Order Decimals 163
4 Round Decimals 169
5 Investigate • Decimal Addition 175
6 Investigate • Decimal Subtraction 181
✓ Mid-Chapter Checkpoint 187
7 Estimate Decimal Sums and Differences 189
8 Add Decimals 195
9 Subtract Decimals 201
10 Algebra • Patterns with Decimals 207
11 Problem Solving • Add and Subtract Money 213
12 Choose a Method 219
✓ Chapter 3 Review/Test 225

Chapter 2 Overview

In this chapter, you will explore and discover answers to the following **Essential Questions**:

• How can you divide whole numbers?
• What strategies have you used to place the first digit in the quotient?
• How can you use estimation to help you divide?
• How do you know when to use division to solve a problem?

Practice and Homework

Lesson Check and Spiral Review in every lesson

Chapter 3 Overview

In this chapter, you will explore and discover answers to the following **Essential Questions**:

• How can you add and subtract decimals?
• What methods can you use to find decimal sums and differences?
• How does using place value help you add and subtract decimals?

4 Multiply Decimals — 231

Domain Number and Operations in Base Ten
COMMON CORE STATE STANDARDS
5.NBT.A.2, 5.NBT.B.7

✓ Show What You Know 231
Vocabulary Builder 232
Chapter Vocabulary Cards
Vocabulary Game 232A
1 **Algebra** • Multiplication Patterns with Decimals 233
2 Investigate • Multiply Decimals and Whole Numbers 239
3 Multiplication with Decimals and Whole Numbers 245
4 Multiply Using Expanded Form 251
5 **Problem Solving** • Multiply Money 257
✓ Mid-Chapter Checkpoint 263
6 Investigate • Decimal Multiplication 265
7 Multiply Decimals 271
8 Zeros in the Product 277
✓ Chapter 4 Review/Test 283

Chapter 4 Overview

In this chapter, you will explore and discover answers to the following **Essential Questions**:

- How can you solve decimal multiplication problems?
- How is multiplying with decimals similar to multiplying with whole numbers?
- How can patterns, models, and drawings help you solve decimal multiplication problems?
- How do you know where to place a decimal point in a product?
- How do you know the correct number of decimal places in a product?

5 Divide Decimals — 289

Domain Number and Operations in Base Ten
COMMON CORE STATE STANDARDS
5.NBT.A.2, 5.NBT.B.7

✓ Show What You Know 289
Vocabulary Builder 290
Chapter Vocabulary Cards
Vocabulary Game 290A
1 **Algebra** • Division Patterns with Decimals 291
2 Investigate • Divide Decimals by Whole Numbers 297
3 Estimate Quotients 303
4 Division of Decimals by Whole Numbers 309
✓ Mid-Chapter Checkpoint 315
5 Investigate • Decimal Division 317
6 Divide Decimals 323
7 Write Zeros in the Dividend 329
8 **Problem Solving** • Decimal Operations 335
✓ Chapter 5 Review/Test 341

Chapter 5 Overview

In this chapter, you will explore and discover answers to the following **Essential Questions**:

- How can you solve decimal division problems?
- How is dividing with decimals similar to dividing with whole numbers?
- How can patterns, models, and drawings help you solve decimal division problems?
- How do you know where to place a decimal point in a quotient?
- How do you know the correct number of decimal places in a quotient?

Critical Area

Chapter 6 Overview

In this chapter, you will explore and discover answers to the following **Essential Questions**:

- How can you add and subtract fractions with unlike denominators?
- How do models help you find sums and differences of fractions?
- When you add and subtract fractions, when do you use the least common denominator?

Personal Math Trainer
Online Assessment and Intervention

VOLUME 2
Operations with Fractions

Common Core **Critical Area** Developing fluency with addition and subtraction of fractions, and developing understanding of the multiplication of fractions and of division of fractions in limited cases (unit fractions divided by whole numbers and whole numbers divided by unit fractions)

Real World Project The Rhythm Track 348

6 Add and Subtract Fractions with Unlike Denominators 349

Domains Operations and Algebraic Thinking
Number and Operations–Fractions
COMMON CORE STATE STANDARDS
5.OA.A.2, 5.NF.A.1, 5.NF.A.2

✔ Show What You Know 349
Vocabulary Builder 350
Chapter Vocabulary Cards
Vocabulary Game 350A
1 Investigate • Addition with Unlike Denominators 351
2 Investigate • Subtraction with Unlike Denominators 357
3 Estimate Fraction Sums and Differences 363
4 Common Denominators and Equivalent Fractions 369
5 Add and Subtract Fractions 375
✔ Mid-Chapter Checkpoint 381
6 Add and Subtract Mixed Numbers 383
7 Subtraction with Renaming 389
8 Algebra • Patterns with Fractions 395
9 Problem Solving • Practice Addition and Subtraction 401
10 Algebra • Use Properties of Addition 407
✔ Chapter 6 Review/Test 413

Multiply Fractions 419

Domain Number and Operations–Fractions
COMMON CORE STATE STANDARDS
5.NF.B.4a, 5.NF.B.4b, 5.NF.B.5a, 5.NF.B.5b, 5.NF.B.6

✓ **Show What You Know** 419
Vocabulary Builder 420
Chapter Vocabulary Cards
Vocabulary Game 420A
1 Find Part of a Group. 421
2 Investigate • Multiply Fractions
and Whole Numbers 427
3 Fraction and Whole Number Multiplication 433
4 Investigate • Multiply Fractions 439
5 Compare Fraction Factors and Products 445
6 Fraction Multiplication 451
✓ **Mid-Chapter Checkpoint** 457
7 Investigate • Area and Mixed Numbers 459
8 Compare Mixed Number Factors and Products 465
9 Multiply Mixed Numbers. 471
10 Problem Solving • Find Unknown Lengths 477
✓ **Chapter 7 Review/Test** 483

Divide Fractions 489

Domain Number and Operations–Fractions
COMMON CORE STATE STANDARDS
5.NF.B.3, 5.NF.B.7a, 5.NF.B.7b, 5.NF.B.7c

✓ **Show What You Know** 489
Vocabulary Builder 490
Chapter Vocabulary Cards
Vocabulary Game 490A
1 Investigate • Divide Fractions and
Whole Numbers 491
2 Problem Solving • Use Multiplication 497
3 Connect Fractions to Division. 503
✓ **Mid-Chapter Checkpoint** 509
4 Fraction and Whole-Number Division 511
5 Interpret Division with Fractions 517
✓ **Chapter 8 Review/Test** 523

Chapter 7 Overview

In this chapter, you will explore and discover answers to the following **Essential Questions**:

- How do you multiply fractions?
- How can you model fraction multiplication?
- How can you compare fraction factors and products?

Practice and Homework

Lesson Check and Spiral Review in every lesson

Chapter 8 Overview

In this chapter, you will explore and discover answers to the following **Essential Questions**:

- What strategies can you use to solve division problems involving fractions?
- What is the relationship between multiplication and division, and how can you use it to solve division problems?
- How can you use fractions, diagrams, equations, and story problems to represent division?
- When you divide a whole number by a fraction or a fraction by a whole number, how do the dividend, the divisor, and the quotient compare?

© Houghton Mifflin Harcourt Publishing Company

Geometry and Measurement

 Common Core Critical Area Developing understanding of volume

Real World Project Space Architecture **530**

9 Algebra: Patterns and Graphing   **531**

Domains Operations and Algebraic Thinking
Measurement and Data
Geometry

COMMON CORE STATE STANDARDS
5.OA.B.3, 5.MD.B.2, 5.G.A.1, 5.G.A.2

✓ Show What You Know **531**
  Vocabulary Builder **532**
  Chapter Vocabulary Cards
  Vocabulary Game **532A**
1 Line Plots **533**
2 Ordered Pairs **539**
3 Investigate • Graph Data **545**
4 Line Graphs **551**
✓ Mid-Chapter Checkpoint **557**
5 Numerical Patterns **559**
6 Problem Solving • Find a Rule **565**
7 Graph and Analyze Relationships **571**
✓ Chapter 9 Review/Test **577**

GO DIGITAL

Go online! Your math lessons are interactive. Use *i*Tools, Animated Math Models, the Multimedia eGlossary, and more.

Chapter 9 Overview

In this chapter, you will explore and discover answers to the following **Essential Questions**:

• How can you use line plots, coordinate grids, and patterns to help you graph and interpret data?

• How can a line plot help you find an average with data given in fractions?

• How can a coordinate grid help you interpret experimental and real-world data?

• How can you write and graph ordered pairs on a coordinate grid using two numerical patterns?

Personal Math Trainer
Online Assessment and Intervention

10 Convert Units of Measure 583

Domain Measurement and Data
COMMON CORE STATE STANDARD
5.MD.A.1

✓ Show What You Know 583
  Vocabulary Builder 584
  Chapter Vocabulary Cards
  Vocabulary Game 584A
1 Customary Length 585
2 Customary Capacity 591
3 Weight 597
4 Multistep Measurement Problems 603
✓ Mid-Chapter Checkpoint 609
5 Metric Measures 611
6 **Problem Solving** • Customary and
  Metric Conversions 617
7 Elapsed Time 623
✓ Chapter 10 Review/Test 629

Chapter 10 Overview

In this chapter, you will explore and discover answers to the following **Essential Questions**:

• What strategies can you use to compare and convert measurements?

• How can you decide whether to multiply or divide when you are converting measurements?

• How can you organize your solution when you are solving a multistep measurement problem?

• How is converting metric measurements different from converting customary measurements?

Practice and Homework

Lesson Check and Spiral Review in every lesson

Chapter 11 Overview

In this chapter, you will explore and discover answers to the following **Essential Questions**:

• How do unit cubes help you build solid figures and understand the volume of a rectangular prism?

• How can you identify, describe, and classify three-dimensional figures?

• How can you find the volume of a rectangular prism?

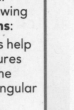

Geometry and Volume 635

Domains Measurement and Data
Geometry

COMMON CORE STATE STANDARDS
5.MD.C.3, 5.MD.C.3a, 5.MD.C.3b, 5.MD.C.4, 5.MD.C.5a, 5.MD.C.5b, 5.MD.C.5c, 5.G.B.3, 5.G.B.4

✔ **Show What You Know** 635
Vocabulary Builder 636
Chapter Vocabulary Cards
Vocabulary Game 636A
1 Polygons 637
2 Triangles 643
3 Quadrilaterals 649
4 Three-Dimensional Figures 655
✔ **Mid-Chapter Checkpoint** 661
5 **Investigate** • Unit Cubes and Solid Figures 663
6 **Investigate** • Understand Volume 669
7 **Investigate** • Estimate Volume 675
8 Volume of Rectangular Prisms 681
9 **Algebra** • Apply Volume Formulas 687
10 **Problem Solving** • Compare Volumes 693
11 Find Volume of Composed Figures 699
✔ **Chapter 11 Review/Test** 705

Glossary H1
Common Core State Standards for
Mathematics Correlations H14
Index H24
Table of Measures H37

Critical Area Operations with Fractions

CRITICAL AREA Developing fluency with addition and subtraction of fractions, and developing understanding of the multiplication of fractions and of division of fractions in limited cases (unit fractions divided by whole numbers and whole numbers divided by unit fractions)

Board operator at a recording studio ▶

The Rhythm Track

Math and music both involve numbers and patterns of change. In music, these patterns are called rhythm. We hear rhythm as a number of beats.

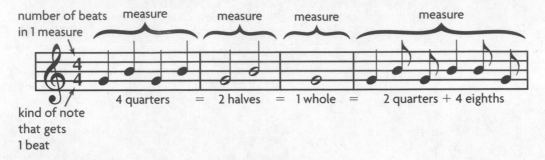

number of beats in 1 measure

measure   measure   measure   measure

kind of note that gets 1 beat

4 quarters = 2 halves = 1 whole = 2 quarters + 4 eighths

Get Started

WRITE ▸ Math

The time signature at the beginning of a line of music looks like a fraction. It tells the number of beats in each measure and the kind of note that fills 1 beat. When the time signature is $\frac{4}{4}$, each $\frac{1}{4}$ note or quarter note is 1 beat.

In the music below, different kinds of notes make up each measure. The measures are not marked. Check the time signature. Then draw lines to mark each measure.

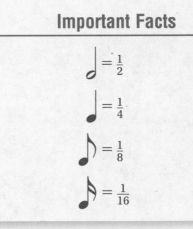

Important Facts

$\stackrel{\circ}{} = \frac{1}{2}$

$\stackrel{\bullet}{} = \frac{1}{4}$

$\stackrel{\bullet}{} = \frac{1}{8}$

$\stackrel{\bullet}{} = \frac{1}{16}$

Add and Subtract Fractions with Unlike Denominators

Show What You Know

Personal Math Trainer
Online Assessment and Intervention

Check your understanding of important skills.

Name _____

▶ **Part of a Whole** Write a fraction to name the shaded part. (3.NF.A.1)

1. number of shaded parts _____

   number of total parts _____

   fraction _____

2. number of shaded parts _____

   number of total parts _____

   fraction _____

▶ **Add and Subtract Fractions** Write the sum or difference in simplest form. (4.NF.B.3d)

3. $\frac{3}{6} + \frac{1}{6} =$ _____

4. $\frac{4}{10} + \frac{1}{10} =$ _____

5. $\frac{7}{8} - \frac{3}{8} =$ _____

6. $\frac{9}{12} - \frac{2}{12} =$ _____

▶ **Multiples** Write the first six nonzero multiples. (4.OA.B.4)

7. 5 _____

8. 3 _____

9. 7 _____

Math in the Real World

There are 30 senators and 60 members of the House of Representatives in the Arizona Legislature. Suppose 20 senators and 25 representatives came to a committee meeting. Write a fraction that compares the number of legislators that attended to the total number of legislators.

Vocabulary Builder

▶ **Visualize It** •

Use the ✓ words to complete the H-diagram.

```
┌─────────────────┐        ┌─────────────────┐
│ Add and Subtract│        │ Add and Subtract│
│ Fractions with  │        │ Fractions with  │
│ Like            │        │ Unlike          │
│ _____        │━━━━━━━━│ _____        │
│                 │        │                 │
│                 │        │                 │
└─────────────────┘        └─────────────────┘
```

▶ **Understand Vocabulary** • • • • • • • • • • • • • • • • • • •

Draw a line to match the word with its definition.

1. common multiple

2. benchmark

3. simplest form

4. mixed number

5. common denominator

6. equivalent fractions

• a number that is made up of a whole number and a fraction

• a number that is a multiple of two or more numbers

• a common multiple of two or more denominators

• the form of a fraction in which the numerator and denominator have only 1 as their common factor

• a familiar number used as a point of reference

• fractions that name the same amount or part

© Houghton Mifflin Harcourt Publishing Company

• Interactive Student Edition
• Multimedia eGlossary

Chapter 6 Vocabulary

common denominator

denominador común

4

common multiple

múltiplo común

6

denominator

denominador

15

difference

diferencia

16

equivalent fractions

fracciones equivalentes

22

mixed number

número mixto

40

numerator

numerador

42

simplest form

mínima expresión

64

A number that is a multiple of two or more numbers

Example: $4 \times 3 = \boxed{12}$
$6 \times 2 = \boxed{12}$

A common multiple of two or more denominators

Example: $\frac{3}{8}$ ⟵ common denominator ⟶ $\frac{7}{8}$

The answer to a subtraction problem

Example:

$75 - 13 = 62$

$\begin{array}{r} 75 \\ -13 \\ \hline 62 \end{array}$

difference ⟶ 62

The number below the bar in a fraction that tells how many equal parts are in the whole or in the group.

Example: $\frac{3}{4}$ ⟵ denominator

A number that is made up of a whole number and a fraction

Example:

whole number part ⟶ $4\frac{1}{2}$ ⟵ fraction part

Fractions that name the same amount or part

Example: $\frac{1}{2}$ and $\frac{4}{8}$ are equivalent.

A fraction is in simplest form when the numerator and denominator have only 1 as a common factor

Examples: $\frac{1}{2}$, $\frac{2}{3}$, $\frac{8}{15}$

The number above the bar in a fraction that tells how many equal parts of the whole or group are being considered

Example: $\frac{3}{4}$ ⟵ numerator

Going to Chicago

For 2 to 4 players

Materials

- 1 each as needed: red, blue, green, and yellow playing pieces
- 1 number cube
- Clue Cards

How to Play

1. Each player puts a playing piece on START.
2. To take a turn, toss the number cube. Move that many spaces.
3. If you land on these spaces:

   Green Space Follow the directions in the space.

   Yellow Space State the simplest form of the fraction. If you are correct, move ahead 1 space.

   Blue Space Use a math term to name what is shown. If you are correct, move ahead 1 space.

   Red Space The player to your right draws a Clue Card and reads you the question. If you answer correctly, move ahead 1 space. Return the Clue Card to the bottom of the pile.

4. The first player to reach FINISH wins.

Word Box

common
 denominator
common multiple
denominator
difference
equivalent
 fractions
mixed number
numerators
simplest form

Game

START

DIRECTIONS Each player puts a playing piece on START. • To take a turn, toss the number cube. Move that many spaces. • If you land on these spaces: Green Space: Follow the directions in the space. • Yellow Space: State the simplest form of the fraction. If you are correct, move ahead 1 space. • Blue Space: Use a math term to name what is shown. If you are correct, move ahead 1 space. • Red Space: The player to your right draws a Clue Card and reads you the question. If you answer correctly, move ahead 1 space. Return the Clue Card to the bottom of the pile. • The first player to reach FINISH wins.

Ride the 'L' train. Move ahead 1.

$\frac{4}{6}$

CLUE CARD

$\frac{3}{5}$ ←

Visit Willis Tower. Go back 1.

$\frac{5}{10}$

CLUE CARD

Watch a baseball game at Wrigley Field. Lose 1 turn.

$\frac{9}{14}$ ←

CLUE CARD

FINISH

$\frac{16}{20}$

$\frac{1}{8} = \frac{4}{32}$

CLUE CARD

$\frac{20}{100}$

Ride the Ferris wheel at Navy Pier. Take another turn.

Visit the Shedd Aquarium. Trade places with another player.

$\frac{6}{24}$

CLUE CARD

$8\frac{2}{3}$

The Write Way

Reflect

Choose one idea. Write about it.

- Write a paragraph that uses at least three of these words or phrases.

  denominator   **mixed number**   **numerator**   **simplest form**

- A family ate 6 out of 8 pieces of a pizza. Tell how to express the amount they ate and the amount leftover as two fractions. Be sure to write the fractions in simplest form.

- Rico needs to combine $\frac{2}{3}$ cup of strawberries, $\frac{1}{4}$ cup of raspberries, and $\frac{1}{2}$ cup of blueberries for a smoothie recipe. Explain how Rico can figure out the total amount of fruit he needs.

- Tell how to find the difference: $10\frac{4}{5} - 8\frac{1}{2}$

Addition with Unlike Denominators

Essential Question How can you use models to add fractions that have different denominators?

Common Core Number and Operations—
Fractions—5.NF.A.1, 5.NF.A.2
MATHEMATICAL PRACTICES
MP4, MP5, MP6

Investigate

Hands On

Hilary is making a tote bag for her friend. She uses $\frac{1}{2}$ yard of blue fabric and $\frac{1}{4}$ yard of red fabric. How much fabric does Hilary use?

Materials ■ fraction strips ■ MathBoard

A. Find $\frac{1}{2} + \frac{1}{4}$. Place a $\frac{1}{2}$ strip and a $\frac{1}{4}$ strip under the 1-whole strip on your MathBoard.

B. Find fraction strips, all with the same denominator, that are equivalent to $\frac{1}{2}$ and $\frac{1}{4}$ and fit exactly under the sum $\frac{1}{2} + \frac{1}{4}$. Record the addends, using like denominators.

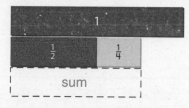

	+

C. Record the sum in simplest form. $\frac{1}{2} + \frac{1}{4} =$ _____

So, Hilary uses _____ yard of fabric.

Draw Conclusions

Math Talk **MATHEMATICAL PRACTICES ④**
Use Models How can you tell if the sum of the fractions is less than 1?

1. Describe how you would determine what fraction strips, all with the same denominator, would fit exactly under $\frac{1}{2} + \frac{1}{3}$. What are they?

_____

_____

_____

2. **MATHEMATICAL PRACTICE ⑤ Use Concrete Models** Explain the difference between finding fraction strips with the same denominator for $\frac{1}{2} + \frac{1}{3}$ and $\frac{1}{2} + \frac{1}{4}$.

_____

_____

_____

Make Connections

Sometimes, the sum of two fractions is greater than 1. When adding fractions with unlike denominators, you can use the 1-whole strip to help determine if a sum is greater than 1 or less than 1.

Use fraction strips to solve. $\frac{3}{5} + \frac{1}{2}$

STEP 1

Work with another student. Place three $\frac{1}{5}$ fraction strips under the 1-whole strip on your MathBoard. Then place a $\frac{1}{2}$ fraction strip beside the three $\frac{1}{5}$ strips.

STEP 2

Find fraction strips, all with the same denominator, that are equivalent to $\frac{3}{5}$ and $\frac{1}{2}$. Place the fraction strips under the sum. At the right, draw a picture of the model and write the equivalent fractions.

$$\frac{3}{5} = \underline{\qquad} \qquad \frac{1}{2} = \underline{\qquad}$$

STEP 3

Add the fractions with like denominators. Use the 1-whole strip to rename the sum in simplest form.

Think: How many fraction strips with the same denominator are equal to 1 whole?

$$\frac{3}{5} + \frac{1}{2} = \underline{\qquad} + \underline{\qquad}$$

$$= \underline{\qquad}, \text{ or } \underline{\qquad}$$

Math Talk MATHEMATICAL PRACTICES ⑥

In what step did you find out that the answer is greater than 1? Explain.

Share and Show MATH BOARD

Use fraction strips or *iTools* to find the sum. Write your answer in simplest form.

1.

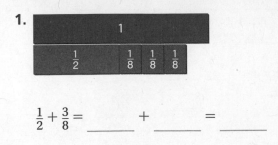

$$\frac{1}{2} + \frac{3}{8} = \underline{\qquad} + \underline{\qquad} = \underline{\qquad}$$

2.

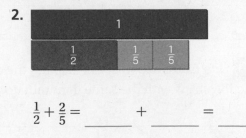

$$\frac{1}{2} + \frac{2}{5} = \underline{\qquad} + \underline{\qquad} = \underline{\qquad}$$

Name _____

Use fraction strips or *i*Tools to find the sum. Write your answer in simplest form.

3.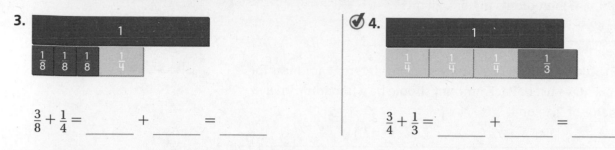

$\frac{3}{8} + \frac{1}{4} =$ _____ + _____ = _____

4.

$\frac{3}{4} + \frac{1}{3} =$ _____ + _____ = _____

Use fraction strips to find the sum. Write your answer in simplest form.

5. $\frac{2}{5} + \frac{3}{10} =$ _____

6. $\frac{1}{4} + \frac{1}{12} =$ _____

7. $\frac{1}{2} + \frac{3}{10} =$ _____

8. $\frac{2}{3} + \frac{1}{6} =$ _____

9. $\frac{5}{8} + \frac{1}{4} =$ _____

10. $\frac{1}{2} + \frac{1}{5} =$ _____

Problem Solving • Applications

11. **WRITE** ▸*Math* Explain how using fraction strips with like denominators makes it possible to add fractions with unlike denominators.

_____

_____

12. **GO DEEPER** Luis is making two batches of muffins for a school picnic. One batch of muffins uses $\frac{1}{4}$ cup of oats and $\frac{1}{3}$ cup of flour. What is the total number of cups of oats and flour needed for two batches? Explain how you use fraction strips to solve the problem.

_____

_____

_____

_____

13. **THINK SMARTER** Maya makes trail mix by combining $\frac{1}{3}$ cup of mixed nuts, $\frac{1}{4}$ cup of dried fruit, and $\frac{1}{6}$ cup of chocolate morsels. What is the total amount of ingredients in her trail mix?

_____

14. **Pose a Problem** Write a new problem using different amounts for ingredients Maya used. Each amount should be a fraction with a denominator of 2, 3, or 4.

_____

_____

_____

15. **MATHEMATICAL PRACTICE ④ Use Diagrams** Solve the problem you wrote. Draw a picture of the fractions strips you use to solve your problem.

_____

16. Explain why you chose the amounts you did for your problem.

_____

_____

_____

_____

Personal Math Trainer

17. **THINK SMARTER** Alexandria used $\frac{1}{2}$ cup of grapes and $\frac{2}{3}$ cup of raisins combined to make a fruit snack. How many cups of grapes and raisins did she use? Use the tiles to complete the fraction strip model to show how you found your answer. The fractions may be used more than once or not at all.

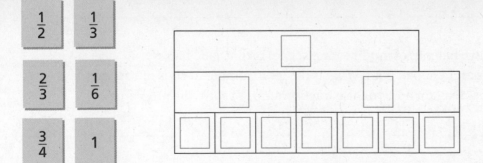

_____ cups of grapes and raisins

Name _____

Addition with Unlike Denominators

Common Core **COMMON CORE STANDARD—5.NF.A.1,**
5.NF.A.2 *Use equivalent fractions as a strategy to add and subtract fractions.*

Use fraction strips to find the sum. Write your answer in simplest form.

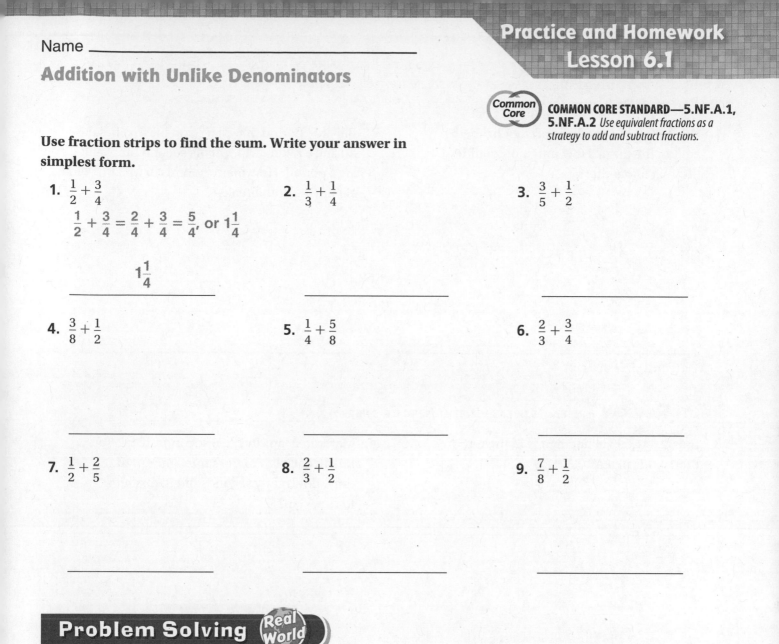

1. $\frac{1}{2} + \frac{3}{4}$

   $\frac{1}{2} + \frac{3}{4} = \frac{2}{4} + \frac{3}{4} = \frac{5}{4}$, or $1\frac{1}{4}$

   $1\frac{1}{4}$ _____

2. $\frac{1}{3} + \frac{1}{4}$

   _____

3. $\frac{3}{5} + \frac{1}{2}$

   _____

4. $\frac{3}{8} + \frac{1}{2}$

   _____

5. $\frac{1}{4} + \frac{5}{8}$

   _____

6. $\frac{2}{3} + \frac{3}{4}$

   _____

7. $\frac{1}{2} + \frac{2}{5}$

   _____

8. $\frac{2}{3} + \frac{1}{2}$

   _____

9. $\frac{7}{8} + \frac{1}{2}$

   _____

Problem Solving Real World

10. Brandus bought $\frac{1}{3}$ pound of ground turkey and $\frac{3}{4}$ pound of ground beef to make sausages. How many pounds of meat did he buy?

    _____

11. To make a ribbon and bow for a hat, Stacey needs $\frac{5}{6}$ yard of black ribbon and $\frac{2}{3}$ yard of red ribbon. How much total ribbon does she need?

    _____

12. **WRITE** *Math* Write a story problem that involves adding fractions with unlike denominators. Include the solution.

    _____

    _____

Lesson Check (5.NF.A.2)

1. Hirva ate $\frac{5}{8}$ of a medium pizza. Elizabeth ate $\frac{1}{4}$ of the pizza. How much pizza did they eat altogether?

2. Bill ate $\frac{1}{4}$ pound of trail mix on his first break during a hiking trip. On his second break, he ate $\frac{1}{6}$ pound. How many pounds of trail mix did he eat during both breaks?

Spiral Review (5.NBT.A.1, 5.NBT.A.2, 5.NBT.B.5, 5.NBT.B.6, 5.NBT.B.7)

3. In 782,341,693, what digit is in the ten thousands place?

4. Matt ran 8 laps in 1,256 seconds. If he ran each lap in the same amount of time, how many seconds did it take him to run 1 lap?

5. Gilbert bought 3 shirts for $15.90 each, including tax. How much did he spend?

6. Julia has 14 pounds of nuts. There are 16 ounces in one pound. How many ounces of nuts does she have?

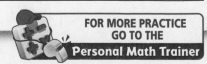

FOR MORE PRACTICE GO TO THE Personal Math Trainer

Name _____

Subtraction with Unlike Denominators

Essential Question How can you use models to subtract fractions that have different denominators?

Common Core Number and Operations—Fractions—5.NF.A.2
MATHEMATICAL PRACTICES
MP2, MP3, MP4, MP5

Investigate

Mario fills a hummingbird feeder with $\frac{3}{4}$ cup of sugar water on Friday. On Monday, Mario sees that $\frac{1}{8}$ cup of sugar water is left. How much sugar water did the hummingbirds drink?

Materials ■ fraction strips ■ MathBoard

A. Find $\frac{3}{4} - \frac{1}{8}$. Place three $\frac{1}{4}$ strips under the 1-whole strip on your MathBoard. Then place a $\frac{1}{8}$ strip under the $\frac{1}{4}$ strips.

B. Find fraction strips, all with the same denominator, that fit exactly under the difference $\frac{3}{4} - \frac{1}{8}$.

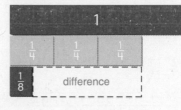

C. Record the difference. $\frac{3}{4} - \frac{1}{8} =$ _____

So, the hummingbirds drank _____ cup of sugar water.

Math Talk MATHEMATICAL PRACTICES ②
Reason Quantitatively How can you tell if the difference of the fractions is less than 1? Explain.

Draw Conclusions

1. Describe how you determined what fraction strips, all with the same denominator, would fit exactly under the difference. What are they?

_____

_____

_____

2. **MATHEMATICAL PRACTICE ⑤** Use Appropriate Tools Explain whether you could have used fraction strips with any other denominator to find the difference. If so, what is the denominator?

_____

_____

Make Connections

Sometimes you can use different sets of same-denominator fraction strips to find the difference. All of the answers will be correct.

Solve. $\frac{2}{3} - \frac{1}{6}$

A Find fraction strips, all with the same denominator, that fit exactly under the difference $\frac{2}{3} - \frac{1}{6}$.

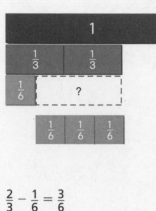

$\frac{2}{3} - \frac{1}{6} = \frac{3}{6}$

B Find another set of fraction strips, all with the same denominator, that fit exactly under the difference $\frac{2}{3} - \frac{1}{6}$. Draw the fraction strips you used.

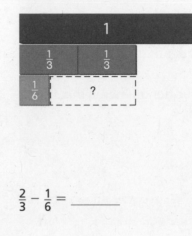

$\frac{2}{3} - \frac{1}{6} = $ _____

C Find other fraction strips, all with the same denominator, that fit exactly under the difference $\frac{2}{3} - \frac{1}{6}$. Draw the fraction strips you used.

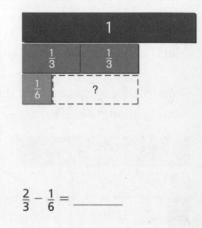

$\frac{2}{3} - \frac{1}{6} = $ _____

While each answer appears different, all of the answers

can be simplified to _____ .

Share and Show

MATH BOARD

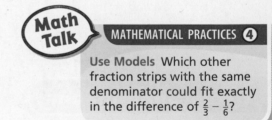

Math Talk

MATHEMATICAL PRACTICES **4**

Use Models Which other fraction strips with the same denominator could fit exactly in the difference of $\frac{2}{3} - \frac{1}{6}$?

Use fraction strips to find the difference. Write your answer in simplest form.

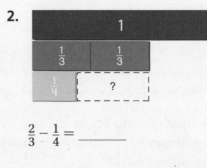

1.

$\frac{7}{10} - \frac{2}{5} = $ _____

2.

$\frac{2}{3} - \frac{1}{4} = $ _____

Name _____

Use fraction strips or *i*Tools to find the difference. Write your answer in simplest form.

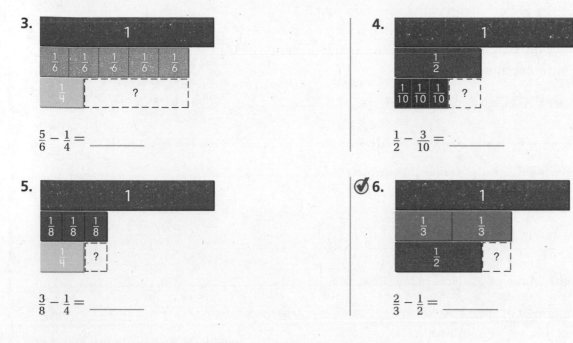

3.

$$\frac{5}{6} - \frac{1}{4} = \text{_____}$$

4.

$$\frac{1}{2} - \frac{3}{10} = \text{_____}$$

5.

$$\frac{3}{8} - \frac{1}{4} = \text{_____}$$

6.

$$\frac{2}{3} - \frac{1}{2} = \text{_____}$$

Use fraction strips to find the difference. Write your answer in simplest form.

7. $\frac{3}{5} - \frac{3}{10} = $ _____

8. $\frac{5}{12} - \frac{1}{3} = $ _____

9. $\frac{3}{5} - \frac{1}{2} = $ _____

Problem Solving • Applications

10. **MATHEMATICAL PRACTICE ③ Compare Representations** Explain how your model for $\frac{3}{5} - \frac{1}{2}$ is different from your model for $\frac{3}{5} - \frac{3}{10}$.

_____

_____

11. **GO DEEPER** The shaded part of the diagram shows what Tina had left from a yard of fabric. She now uses $\frac{1}{3}$ yard of fabric for one project and $\frac{1}{6}$ yard for a second project. How much of the original yard of fabric does Tina have left after the two projects? Write the answer in simplest form.

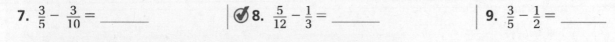

1 yard

_____

Unlock the Problem — Real World

12. **THINK SMARTER** The picture at the right shows how much pizza was left over from lunch. Jason eats $\frac{1}{4}$ of the whole pizza for dinner. Write a fraction that represents the amount of pizza that is remaining after dinner.

a. What problem are you being asked to solve? _____

_____

b. How will you use the diagram to solve the problem? _____

_____

_____

c. Jason eats $\frac{1}{4}$ of the whole pizza. How many slices does he eat? _____

d. Redraw the diagram of the pizza. Shade the sections of pizza that are remaining after Jason eats his dinner.

e. Complete the sentence.

There is _____ of the pizza remaining after dinner.

13. **THINK SMARTER** The shaded part of the diagram shows what Margie had left over from a roll of construction paper that measured one yard. She will use $\frac{3}{4}$ yard of paper to make a poster. She wants to determine how much paper she will have remaining after making the poster. For 13a–13c, select True or False for each statement.

1 yd

13a. To determine how much paper will be left after making the poster, Margie must find $1 - \frac{3}{4}$. ○ True ○ False

13b. The fractions $\frac{3}{4}$ and $\frac{6}{8}$ are equivalent. ○ True ○ False

13c. Margie will have $\frac{1}{8}$ yard of paper remaining. ○ True ○ False

Subtraction with Unlike Denominators

Common Core   **COMMON CORE STANDARD—5.NF.A.2**
Use equivalent fractions as a strategy to add and subtract fractions.

Use fraction strips to find the difference. Write your answer in simplest form.

1. $\frac{1}{2} - \frac{1}{3}$

$\frac{1}{2} - \frac{1}{3} = \frac{3}{6} - \frac{2}{6} - \frac{1}{6}$

$\frac{1}{6}$
_____

2. $\frac{3}{4} - \frac{3}{8}$
_____

3. $\frac{7}{8} - \frac{1}{2}$
_____

4. $\frac{1}{2} - \frac{1}{5}$
_____

5. $\frac{2}{3} - \frac{1}{4}$
_____

6. $\frac{4}{5} - \frac{1}{2}$
_____

7. $\frac{3}{4} - \frac{1}{3}$
_____

8. $\frac{5}{8} - \frac{1}{2}$
_____

9. $\frac{7}{10} - \frac{1}{2}$
_____

Problem Solving *Real World*

10. Amber had $\frac{3}{8}$ of a cake left after her party. She wrapped a piece that was $\frac{1}{4}$ of the original cake for her best friend. What fractional part did she have left for herself?

_____

11. Wesley bought $\frac{1}{2}$ pound of nails for a project. When he finished the project, he had $\frac{1}{4}$ pound of nails left. How many pounds of nails did he use?

_____

12. **WRITE** ▸*Math* Explain how modeling subtraction with fraction strips is different from modeling addition with fraction strips.

_____

_____

Lesson Check

1. A meatloaf recipe calls for $\frac{7}{8}$ cup of bread crumbs for the loaf and the topping. If $\frac{3}{4}$ cup is used for the loaf, what fraction of a cup is used for the topping?

2. Hannah bought $\frac{3}{4}$ yard of felt for a project. She used $\frac{1}{8}$ yard. What fraction of a yard of felt did she have left over?

Spiral Review

3. Jasmine's race time was 34.287 minutes. Round her race time to the nearest tenth of a minute.

4. The Art Club is having a fundraiser, and 198 people are attending. If 12 people can sit at each table, what is the least number of tables needed?

5. During the day, Sam spent $4.85 on lunch. He also bought 2 books for $7.95 each. At the end of the day, he had $8.20 left. How much money did he start with?

6. What is the product of 7.5 and 1,000?

FOR MORE PRACTICE
GO TO THE
Personal Math Trainer

Name _____

Estimate Fraction Sums and Differences

Essential Question How can you make reasonable estimates of fraction sums and differences?

Common Core
Number and Operations—Fractions—5.NF.A.2
MATHEMATICAL PRACTICES
MP2, MP3, MP6

Unlock the Problem Real World

Kimberly will be riding her bike to school this year. The distance from her house to the end of the street is $\frac{1}{6}$ mile. The distance from the end of the street to the school is $\frac{3}{8}$ mile. About how far is Kimberly's house from school?

You can use benchmarks to find reasonable estimates by rounding fractions to 0, $\frac{1}{2}$, or 1.

One Way Use a number line.

Estimate. $\frac{1}{6} + \frac{3}{8}$

STEP 1 Place a point at $\frac{1}{6}$ on the number line.

The fraction is between _____ and _____.

The fraction $\frac{1}{6}$ is closer to the benchmark _____.

Round to _____.

$$\frac{0}{6} \quad \frac{1}{6} \quad \frac{2}{6} \quad \frac{3}{6} \quad \frac{4}{6} \quad \frac{5}{6} \quad \frac{6}{6}$$
$$0 \qquad\qquad\qquad \frac{1}{2} \qquad\qquad\qquad 1$$

STEP 2 Place a point at $\frac{3}{8}$ on the number line.

The fraction is between _____ and _____.

The fraction $\frac{3}{8}$ is closer to the benchmark _____.

Round to _____.

$$\frac{0}{8} \quad \frac{1}{8} \quad \frac{2}{8} \quad \frac{3}{8} \quad \frac{4}{8} \quad \frac{5}{8} \quad \frac{6}{8} \quad \frac{7}{8} \quad \frac{8}{8}$$
$$0 \qquad\qquad\qquad\quad \frac{1}{2} \qquad\qquad\qquad\quad 1$$

STEP 3 Add the rounded fractions.

$$\frac{1}{6} \quad \rightarrow \quad $$

$$+ \frac{3}{8} \quad \rightarrow \quad + $$

So, Kimberly's house is about _____ mile from the school.

🔒 Another Way Use mental math.

You can compare the numerator and the denominator to round a fraction and find a reasonable estimate.

Estimate. $\frac{9}{10} - \frac{5}{8}$

STEP 1 Round $\frac{9}{10}$. **Think:** The numerator is about the same as the denominator.

Round the fraction $\frac{9}{10}$ to _____.

STEP 2 Round $\frac{5}{8}$. **Think:** The numerator is about half the denominator.

Round the fraction $\frac{5}{8}$ to _____.

STEP 3 Subtract.

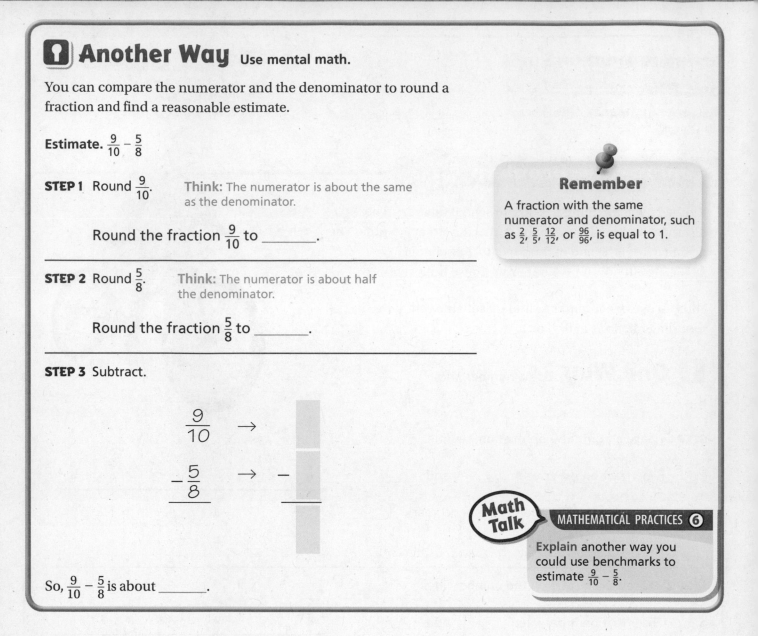

So, $\frac{9}{10} - \frac{5}{8}$ is about _____.

Math Talk MATHEMATICAL PRACTICES ⑥

Explain another way you could use benchmarks to estimate $\frac{9}{10} - \frac{5}{8}$.

Try This! **Estimate.**

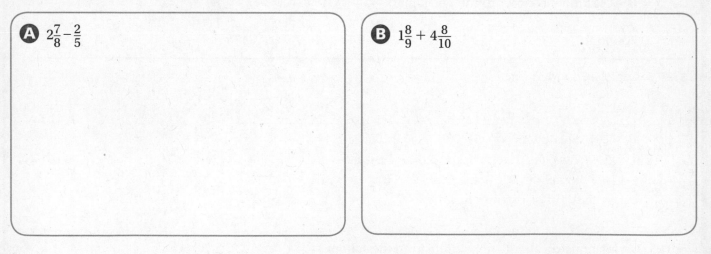

A $2\frac{7}{8} - \frac{2}{5}$

B $1\frac{8}{9} + 4\frac{8}{10}$

Name _____

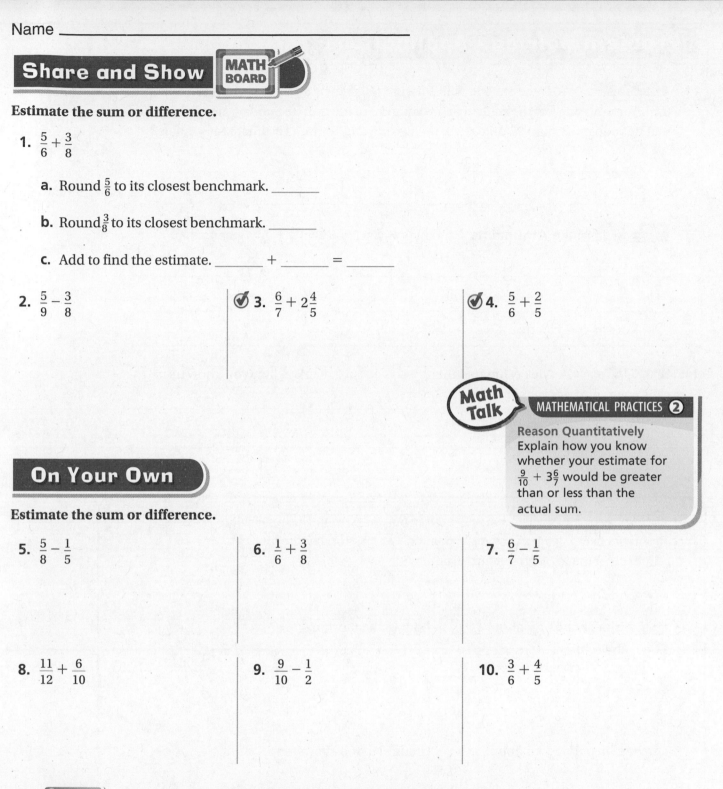

Share and Show MATH BOARD

Estimate the sum or difference.

1. $\frac{5}{6} + \frac{3}{8}$

    a. Round $\frac{5}{6}$ to its closest benchmark. _____

    b. Round $\frac{3}{8}$ to its closest benchmark. _____

    c. Add to find the estimate. _____ + _____ = _____

2. $\frac{5}{9} - \frac{3}{8}$ ☑ **3.** $\frac{6}{7} + 2\frac{4}{5}$ ☑ **4.** $\frac{5}{6} + \frac{2}{5}$

Math Talk MATHEMATICAL PRACTICES ②

Reason Quantitatively
Explain how you know whether your estimate for $\frac{9}{10} + 3\frac{6}{7}$ would be greater than or less than the actual sum.

On Your Own

Estimate the sum or difference.

5. $\frac{5}{8} - \frac{1}{5}$ **6.** $\frac{1}{6} + \frac{3}{8}$ **7.** $\frac{6}{7} - \frac{1}{5}$

8. $\frac{11}{12} + \frac{6}{10}$ **9.** $\frac{9}{10} - \frac{1}{2}$ **10.** $\frac{3}{6} + \frac{4}{5}$

11. **GO DEEPER** Lisa and Valerie are picnicking in Trough Creek State Park in Pennsylvania. Lisa has brought a salad that she made with $\frac{3}{4}$ cup of strawberries, $\frac{7}{8}$ cup of peaches, and $\frac{1}{6}$ cup of blueberries. They ate $\frac{11}{12}$ cup of salad. About how many cups of fruit salad are left?

_____

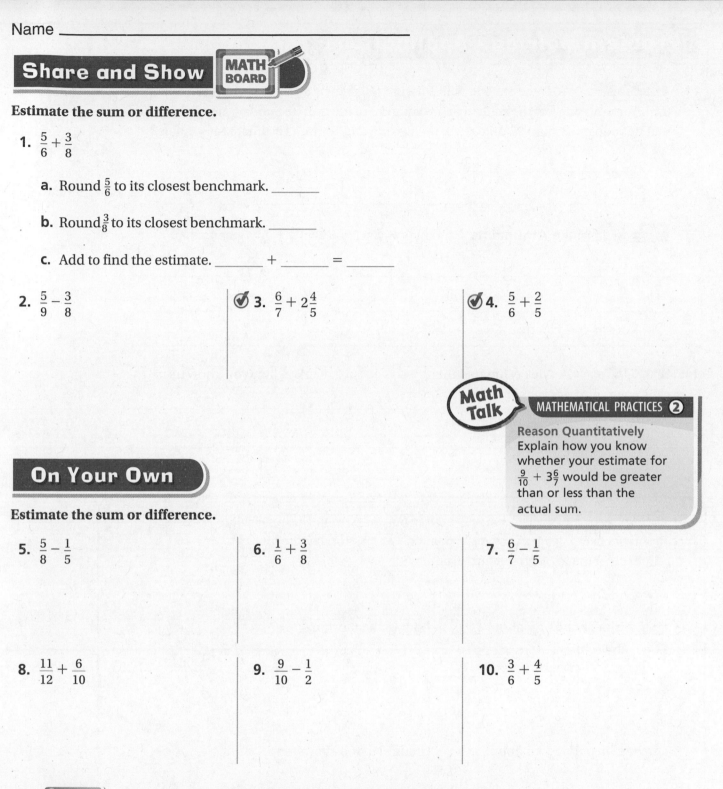

Problem Solving · Applications

12. **THINK SMARTER** At Trace State Park in Mississippi, there is a 40-mile mountain bike trail. Tommy rode $\frac{1}{2}$ of the trail on Saturday and $\frac{1}{5}$ of the trail on Sunday. He estimates that he rode more than 22 miles over the two days. Is Tommy's estimate reasonable?

_____

_____

13. **MATHEMATICAL PRACTICE ③** **Make Arguments** Explain how you know that $\frac{5}{8} + \frac{6}{10}$ is greater than 1.

_____

_____

_____

14. **WRITE** ▸Math Nick estimated that $\frac{5}{8} + \frac{4}{7}$ is about 2. Explain how you know his estimate is not reasonable.

_____

_____

15. **THINK SMARTER** Aisha painted for $\frac{5}{6}$ hour in the morning and $2\frac{1}{5}$ hours in the afternoon. Estimate how long Aisha painted. For 15a–15c, choose the number that makes each sentence true.

15a. Aisha painted for about
| 0 |
| $\frac{1}{2}$ |
| 1 |
hour in the morning.

15b. Aisha painted for about
| 1 |
| 2 |
| $2\frac{1}{2}$ |
| 3 |
hour(s) in the afternoon.

15c. Aisha painted for about
| 1 |
| 2 |
| $2\frac{1}{2}$ |
| 3 |
hours in the morning and afternoon combined.

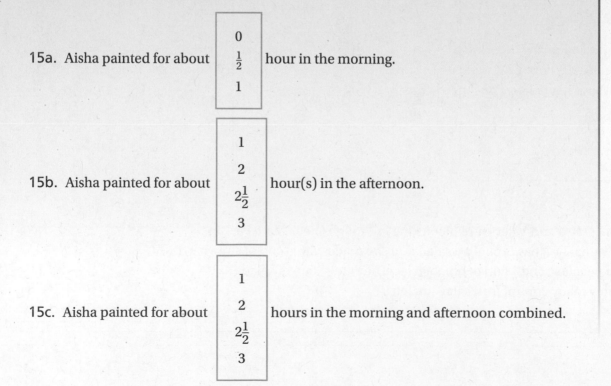

366

© Houghton Mifflin Harcourt Publishing Company

Name _____

Estimate Fraction Sums and Differences

Common Core
COMMON CORE STANDARD—5.NF.A.2
Use equivalent fractions as a strategy to add and subtract fractions.

Estimate the sum or difference.

1. $\frac{1}{2} - \frac{1}{3}$

Think: $\frac{1}{3}$ is closer to $\frac{1}{2}$ than to 0.

Estimate: ____0____

2. $\frac{1}{8} + \frac{1}{4}$

Estimate: _____

3. $\frac{4}{5} - \frac{1}{2}$

Estimate: _____

4. $2\frac{3}{5} - 1\frac{3}{8}$

Estimate: _____

5. $\frac{1}{5} + \frac{3}{7}$

Estimate: _____

6. $\frac{2}{5} + \frac{2}{3}$

Estimate: _____

7. $2\frac{2}{3} + \frac{3}{4}$

Estimate: _____

8. $1\frac{7}{8} - 1\frac{1}{2}$

Estimate: _____

9. $4\frac{1}{8} - \frac{3}{4}$

Estimate: _____

Problem Solving *Real World*

10. For a fruit salad recipe, Jenna combined $\frac{3}{8}$ cup of raisins, $\frac{7}{8}$ cup of oranges, and $\frac{3}{4}$ cup of apples. About how many cups of fruit are in the salad?

_____

_____

11. Tyler had $2\frac{7}{16}$ yards of fabric. He used $\frac{3}{4}$ yard to make a vest. About how much fabric did he have left?

_____

_____

12. **WRITE** *Math* What is an instance when you might want to find an estimate for fraction sums or differences rather than an exact answer?

_____

_____

Lesson Check (5.NF.A.2)

1. Helen's house is located on a rectangular lot that is $1\frac{1}{8}$ miles by $\frac{9}{10}$ mile. Estimate the distance around the lot.

2. Keith bought a package with $2\frac{9}{16}$ pounds of ground meat to make hamburgers. He has $\frac{2}{5}$ pound of ground meat left. About how many pounds of ground meat did he use for the hamburgers?

Spiral Review (5.NBT.B.5, 5.NBT.B.7, 5.NF.B.3)

3. Jason bought two identical boxes of nails. One box weighs 168 ounces. What is the total weight in ounces of the nails Jason bought?

4. Hank wants to divide 345 pieces of construction paper evenly among his 23 classmates. How many pieces will be left over?

5. What is the most reasonable estimate for $23.63 \div 6$?

6. What is a rule for the sequence below?

1.8, 2.85, 3.90, 4.95, 6

FOR MORE PRACTICE
GO TO THE
Personal Math Trainer

Common Denominators and Equivalent Fractions

Essential Question How can you rewrite a pair of fractions so that they have a common denominator?

Common Core
Number and Operations—Fractions— 5.NF.A.1 *Also 5.OA.A.2*
MATHEMATICAL PRACTICES
MP2, MP4, MP6

🔑 Unlock the Problem *Real World*

Sarah planted two 1-acre gardens. One had three sections of flowers and the other had 4 sections of flowers. She plans to divide both gardens into more sections so that they have the same number of equal-sized sections. How many sections will each garden have?

You can use a **common denominator** or a common multiple of two or more denominators to write fractions that name the same part of a whole.

🔒 One Way Multiply the denominators.

THINK

Divide each $\frac{1}{3}$ into fourths and divide each $\frac{1}{4}$ into thirds, each of the wholes will be divided into the same size parts, twelfths.

So, both gardens will have _____ sections.

RECORD

• Multiply the denominators to find a common denominator.

  A common denominator of $\frac{1}{3}$ and $\frac{1}{4}$ is _____.

• Write $\frac{1}{3}$ and $\frac{1}{4}$ as equivalent fractions using the common denominator.

$$\frac{1}{3} = \boxed{} \qquad \frac{1}{4} = \boxed{}$$

🔒 Another Way Use a list.

• Make a list of the first eight nonzero multiples of 3 and 4.

  Multiples of 3: 3, 6, 9, _____, _____, _____, _____, _____

  Multiples of 4: 4, 8, _____, _____, _____, _____, _____, _____

• Circle the common multiples.

• Use one of the common multiples as a common denominator to write equivalent fractions for $\frac{1}{3}$ and $\frac{1}{4}$.

$$\frac{1}{3} = \frac{}{} \qquad \frac{1}{4} = \frac{}{}$$

So, both gardens can have _____ , or _____ sections.

 *Math Talk*

MATHEMATICAL PRACTICES ⑥

Use Math Vocabulary
Explain what a common denominator of two fractions represents.

Least Common Denominator Find the least common denominator of two or more fractions by finding the least common multiple of two or more numbers.

🔑 Example Use the least common denominator.

Find the least common denominator of $\frac{3}{4}$ and $\frac{1}{6}$. Use the least common denominator to write an equivalent fraction for each fraction.

STEP 1 List nonzero multiples of the denominators. Find the least common multiple.

Multiples of 4: _____

Multiples of 6: _____

So, the least common denominator of $\frac{3}{4}$ and $\frac{1}{6}$ is _____.

STEP 2 Using the least common denominator, write an equivalent fraction for each fraction.

Think: What number multiplied by the denominator of the fraction will result in the least common denominator?

$\frac{3}{4} = \frac{?}{12} = \frac{3 \times 3}{4 \times 3} = \frac{\ }{\ }$ ← least common denominator

$\frac{1}{6} = \frac{?}{12} = \frac{1 \times \ }{6 \times \ } = \frac{\ }{\ }$ ← least common denominator

$\frac{3}{4}$ can be rewritten as _____ and $\frac{1}{6}$ can be rewritten as _____.

Share and Show 🖊 MATH BOARD

Math Talk MATHEMATICAL PRACTICES ⑥

Explain two methods for finding a common denominator of two fractions.

1. Find a common denominator of $\frac{1}{6}$ and $\frac{1}{9}$. Rewrite the pair of fractions using the common denominator.

   • Multiply the denominators.
     A common denominator of $\frac{1}{6}$ and $\frac{1}{9}$ is _____.

   • Rewrite the pair of fractions using the common denominator.

     $\frac{1}{6} = \frac{\ }{\ }$ $\frac{1}{9} = \frac{\ }{\ }$

Use a common denominator to write an equivalent fraction for each fraction.

✅ 2. $\frac{1}{3}, \frac{1}{5}$ common
     denominator: _____

_____

3. $\frac{2}{3}, \frac{5}{9}$ common
     denominator: _____

_____

✅ 4. $\frac{2}{9}, \frac{1}{15}$ common
     denominator: _____

_____

Name _____

On Your Own

Practice: Copy and Solve Use the least common denominator to write an equivalent fraction for each fraction.

5. $\frac{5}{9}, \frac{4}{15}$

6. $\frac{1}{6}, \frac{4}{21}$

7. $\frac{5}{14}, \frac{8}{42}$

8. $\frac{7}{12}, \frac{5}{18}$

MATHEMATICAL PRACTICE ② **Use Reasoning** **Algebra** Write the unknown number for each ▥.

9. $\frac{1}{5}, \frac{1}{8}$ least common

denominator: ▥

▥ = _____

10. $\frac{2}{5}, \frac{1}{▥}$ least common

denominator: 15

▥ = _____

11. $\frac{3}{▥}, \frac{5}{6}$ least common

denominator: 42

▥ = _____

12. **THINK SMARTER** Arnold had three pieces of different colored strings that are all the same length. Arnold cut the blue string into 2 equal-size lengths. He cut the red string into 3 equal-size lengths, and the green string into 6 equal-size lengths. He needs to cut the strings so each color has the same number of equal-size lengths. What is the least number of equal-sized lengths each color string could have?

13. **GO DEEPER** One tray of granola bars was cut into 4 equal-size pieces. A second tray was cut into 12 equal-size pieces, and a third was cut into 8 equal-size pieces. Jan wants to continue cutting until all three trays have the same number of pieces. How many pieces will there be on each tray?

14. **GO DEEPER** Mr. Nickelson tells the class that they double the least common denominator for $\frac{1}{2}$, $\frac{3}{5}$, and $\frac{9}{15}$ to find the number of the day. What number is the number of the day?

🔑 Unlock the Problem Real World

15. Katie made two pies for the bake sale. One was cut into three equal slices and the other into 5 equal slices. She will continue to cut the pies so each one has the same number of equal-sized slices. What is the least number of equal-sized slices each pie could have?

a. What information are you given? _____

_____

b. What problem are you being asked to solve? _____

_____

c. When Katie cuts the pies more, can she cut each pie the same number

of times and have all the slices the same size? Explain. _____

_____

_____

d. Use the diagram to show the steps you use to solve the problem.

e. Complete the sentences.

The least common denominator of $\frac{1}{3}$ and $\frac{1}{5}$

is _____.

Katie can cut each piece of the first pie into

_____ and each piece of the second pie

into _____.

That means that Katie can cut each pie into

pieces that are _____ of the whole pie.

---

16. THINK SMARTER Mindy bought $\frac{5}{8}$ pound of almonds and $\frac{3}{4}$ pound of walnuts. Select the pairs of fractions that are equivalent to the amounts that Mindy bought. Mark all that apply.

(A) $\frac{5}{8}$ and $\frac{6}{8}$ (B) $\frac{10}{16}$ and $\frac{14}{16}$ (C) $\frac{20}{32}$ and $\frac{23}{32}$ (D) $\frac{15}{24}$ and $\frac{18}{24}$

Name _____

Common Denominators and Equivalent Fractions

COMMON CORE STANDARD—5.NF.A.1
Use equivalent fractions as a strategy to add and subtract fractions.

Use a common denominator to write an equivalent fraction for each fraction.

1. $\frac{1}{5}, \frac{1}{2}$ common denominator: __10__

Think: 10 is a multiple of 5 and 2. Find equivalent fractions with a denominator of 10.

$\frac{2}{10}, \frac{5}{10}$
_____

2. $\frac{1}{4}, \frac{2}{3}$ common denominator: _____

_____

3. $\frac{5}{6}, \frac{1}{3}$ common denominator: _____

_____

4. $\frac{3}{5}, \frac{1}{3}$ common denominator: _____

_____

5. $\frac{1}{2}, \frac{3}{8}$ common denominator: _____

_____

6. $\frac{1}{6}, \frac{1}{4}$ common denominator: _____

_____

Use the least common denominator to write an equivalent fraction for each fraction.

7. $\frac{5}{6}, \frac{2}{9}$

_____

8. $\frac{1}{12}, \frac{3}{8}$

_____

9. $\frac{5}{9}, \frac{2}{15}$

_____

Problem Solving · Real World

10. Ella spends $\frac{2}{3}$ hour practicing the piano each day. She also spends $\frac{1}{2}$ hour jogging. What is the least common denominator of the fractions?

_____

11. In a science experiment, a plant grew $\frac{3}{4}$ inch one week and $\frac{1}{2}$ inch the next week. Use a common denominator to write an equivalent fraction for each fraction.

_____

12. **WRITE** *Math* Describe how you would rewrite the fractions $\frac{1}{6}$ and $\frac{1}{4}$ with their least common denominator.

_____

_____

Lesson Check (5.NF.A.1)

1. Name a pair of fractions that use the least common denominator and are equivalent to $\frac{9}{10}$ and $\frac{5}{6}$.

2. Joseph says that there is $\frac{5}{8}$ of a ham sandwich left and $\frac{1}{2}$ of a turkey sandwich left. What is NOT a pair of equivalent fractions for $\frac{5}{8}$ and $\frac{1}{2}$?

Spiral Review (5.OA.A.1, , 5.NBT.A.3b, 5.NBT.B.6, 5.NBT.B.7)

3. Matthew had the following times in two races: 3.032 minutes and 3.023 minutes. Use $>$, $<$, or $=$ to make the sentence true.

   3.032 $\bigcirc$ 3.023

4. Olivia's class collected 3,591 bottle caps in 57 days. The same number of bottle caps were collected each day. How many bottle caps did the class collect per day?

5. Elizabeth multiplied 0.63 by 1.8. What is the correct product?

6. What is the value of $(17 + 8) - 6 \times 2$?

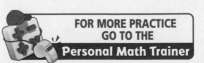

FOR MORE PRACTICE
GO TO THE
Personal Math Trainer

Name _____

Add and Subtract Fractions

Essential Question How can you use a common denominator to add and subtract fractions with unlike denominators?

Common Core — Number and Operations—Fractions—5.NF.A.1 Also 5.NF.A.2
MATHEMATICAL PRACTICES
MP1, MP2, MP3

CONNECT You can use what you have learned about common denominators to add or subtract fractions with unlike denominators.

Unlock the Problem

Malia bought shell beads and glass beads to weave into designs in her baskets. She bought $\frac{1}{4}$ pound of shell beads and $\frac{3}{8}$ pound of glass beads. How many pounds of beads did she buy?

- Underline the question you need to answer.
- Draw a circle around the information you will use.

Add. $\frac{1}{4} + \frac{3}{8}$ Write your answer in simplest form.

One Way

Find a common denominator by multiplying the denominators.

$4 \times 8 = $ _____ ← common denominator

Use the common denominator to write equivalent fractions with like denominators. Then add, and write your answer in simplest form.

$\frac{1}{4} = \frac{1 \times}{4 \times} = $

$+ \frac{3}{8} = + \frac{3 \times}{8 \times} = +$

$=$

Another Way

Find the least common denominator.

The least common denominator of $\frac{1}{4}$ and $\frac{3}{8}$ is _____.

$\frac{1}{4} = \frac{1 \times}{4 \times} = $

$+ \frac{3}{8} \qquad +$

So, Malia bought _____ pound of beads.

1. **MATHEMATICAL PRACTICE 1 Evaluate Reasonableness** Explain how you know whether your answer is reasonable.

_____

_____

🔓 Example

When subtracting two fractions with unlike denominators, follow the same steps you follow when adding two fractions. However, instead of adding the fractions, subtract.

Subtract. $\frac{9}{10} - \frac{2}{5}$ **Write your answer in simplest form.**

$$\frac{9}{10} =$$

$$-\frac{2}{5} =$$

_____

Describe the steps you took to solve the problem.

_____

_____

_____

_____

2. 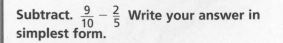 **Evaluate Reasonableness** Explain how you know whether your answer is reasonable.

_____

_____

Share and Show MATH BOARD

Find the sum or difference. Write your answer in simplest form.

1. $\frac{5}{12} + \frac{1}{3}$

2. $\frac{2}{5} + \frac{3}{7}$

✅3. $\frac{1}{6} + \frac{3}{4}$

4. $\frac{3}{4} - \frac{1}{8}$

5. $\frac{1}{4} - \frac{1}{7}$

✅6. $\frac{9}{10} - \frac{1}{4}$

$$\frac{2}{3} - \frac{2}{7} = \frac{8}{18} = \frac{4}{9}$$

Math Talk MATHEMATICAL PRACTICES ②

Use Reasoning Why is it important to check your answer for reasonableness?

Name _____

On Your Own

Practice: Copy and Solve Find the sum or difference. Write your answer in simplest form.

7. $\frac{1}{3} + \frac{4}{18}$

8. $\frac{3}{5} + \frac{1}{3}$

9. $\frac{3}{10} + \frac{1}{6}$

10. $\frac{1}{2} + \frac{4}{9}$

11. $\frac{1}{2} - \frac{3}{8}$

12. $\frac{5}{7} - \frac{2}{3}$

13. $\frac{4}{9} - \frac{1}{6}$

14. $\frac{11}{12} - \frac{7}{15}$

MATHEMATICAL PRACTICE ② Use Reasoning **Algebra** Find the unknown number.

15. $\frac{9}{10} - \blacksquare = \frac{1}{5}$

$\blacksquare = $ _____

16. $\frac{5}{12} + \blacksquare = \frac{1}{2}$

$\blacksquare = $ _____

Problem Solving • Applications Real World

Use the picture for 17–18.

17. Sara is making a key chain using the bead design shown. What fraction of the beads in her design are either blue or red?

_____

18. **THINK SMARTER** In making the key chain, Sara uses the pattern of beads 3 times. After the key chain is complete, what fraction of the beads in the key chain are either white or blue?

_____

19. **GO DEEPER** Tom has $\frac{7}{8}$ cup of olive oil. He uses $\frac{1}{2}$ cup to make salad dressing and $\frac{1}{4}$ cup to make tomato sauce. How much olive oil does Tom have left?

_____

20. GO DEEPER On Friday, $\frac{1}{6}$ of band practice was spent trying on uniforms. The band spent $\frac{1}{4}$ of practice on marching. The remaining practice time was spent playing music. What fraction of practice time was spent playing music?

_____

21. MATHEMATICAL PRACTICE ❸ **Verify the Reasoning of Others** Jamie had $\frac{4}{5}$ of a spool of twine. He then used $\frac{1}{2}$ of a spool of twine to make friendship knots. He claims to have $\frac{3}{10}$ of the original spool of twine left over. Explain how you know whether Jamie's claim is reasonable.

_____

_____

_____

_____

_____

22. THINK SMARTER Mr. Barber used $\frac{7}{9}$ yard of wire to put up a ceiling fan. He used $\frac{1}{3}$ yard of wire to fix a switch.

Complete the calculations below to write equivalent fractions with a common denominator.

$$\frac{7}{9} = \frac{7 \times }{9 \times } = \frac{}{} \qquad \frac{1}{3} = \frac{1 \times }{3 \times } = \frac{}{}$$

How much wire did Mr. Barber use to put up the ceiling fan and fix the switch combined? Explain how you found your answer.

_____

_____

_____

Name _____

Add and Subtract Fractions

Common Core COMMON CORE STANDARD—5.NF.A.1
Use equivalent fractions as a strategy to add and subtract fractions.

Find the sum or difference. Write your answer in simplest form.

1. $\frac{1}{2} - \frac{1}{7}$

$$\frac{1}{2} \rightarrow \frac{7}{14}$$
$$-\frac{1}{7} \rightarrow -\frac{2}{14}$$
$$\frac{5}{14}$$

2. $\frac{7}{10} - \frac{1}{2}$

_____

3. $\frac{1}{6} + \frac{1}{2}$

_____

4. $\frac{5}{8} + \frac{2}{5}$

_____

5. $\frac{9}{10} - \frac{1}{3}$

_____

6. $\frac{3}{4} - \frac{2}{5}$

_____

7. $\frac{5}{7} - \frac{1}{4}$

_____

8. $\frac{7}{8} + \frac{1}{3}$

_____

9. $\frac{5}{6} + \frac{2}{5}$

_____

Problem Solving · Real World

10. Kaylin mixed two liquids for a science experiment. One container held $\frac{7}{8}$ cup and the other held $\frac{9}{10}$ cup. What is the total amount of the mixture?

_____

11. Henry bought $\frac{1}{4}$ pound of screws and $\frac{2}{5}$ pound of nails to build a skateboard ramp. What is the total weight of the screws and nails?

_____

12. **WRITE** ▸ *Math* How is $\frac{1}{2} + \frac{1}{4}$ solved differently than $\frac{1}{2} + \frac{1}{3}$?

_____

_____

Lesson Check (5.NF.A.1)

1. Lyle bought $\frac{3}{8}$ pound of red grapes and $\frac{5}{12}$ pound of green grapes. How many pounds of grapes did he buy?

2. Jennifer had a $\frac{7}{8}$-foot board. She cut off a $\frac{1}{4}$-foot piece that was for a project. In feet, how much of the board was left?

Spiral Review (5.NBT.B.6, 5.NBT.B.7, 5.NF.B.3)

3. Ivan has 15 yards of green felt and 12 yards of blue felt to make 3 quilts. If Ivan uses the same total number of yards for each quilt, how many yards does he use for each quilt?

4. Eight identical shirts cost a total of $152. How much does one shirt cost?

5. Melissa bought a pencil for $0.34, an eraser for $0.22, and a notebook for $0.98. What is a reasonable estimate for the amount Melissa spent?

6. The 12 members in Dante's hiking club shared 176 ounces of trail mix equally. How many ounces of trail mix did each member receive?

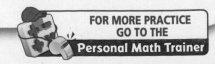

FOR MORE PRACTICE
GO TO THE
Personal Math Trainer

Name _____

Vocabulary

Vocabulary

equivalent fractions

common denominator

common multiple

Choose the best term from the box.

1. A _____ is a number that is a multiple of two or more numbers. (p. 369)

2. A _____ is a common multiple of two or more denominators. (p. 369)

Concepts and Skills

Estimate the sum or difference. (5.NF.A.2)

3. $\frac{8}{9} + \frac{4}{7}$

4. $3\frac{2}{5} - \frac{5}{8}$

5. $1\frac{5}{6} + 2\frac{2}{11}$

Use a common denominator to write an equivalent fraction for each fraction. (5.NF.A.1)

6. $\frac{1}{6}, \frac{1}{9}$ common denominator: _____

_____

7. $\frac{3}{8}, \frac{3}{10}$ common denominator: _____

_____

8. $\frac{1}{9}, \frac{5}{12}$ common denominator: _____

_____

Use the least common denominator to write an equivalent fraction for each fraction. (5.NF.A.1)

9. $\frac{2}{5}, \frac{1}{10}$ least common denominator: _____

_____

10. $\frac{5}{6}, \frac{3}{8}$ least common denominator: _____

_____

11. $\frac{1}{3}, \frac{2}{7}$ common denominator: _____

_____

Find the sum or difference. Write your answer in simplest form. (5.NF.A.1)

12. $\frac{11}{18} - \frac{1}{6}$

13. $\frac{2}{7} + \frac{2}{5}$

14. $\frac{3}{4} - \frac{3}{10}$

15. Mrs. Vargas bakes a pie for her book club meeting. The shaded part of the diagram below shows the amount of pie left after the meeting. That evening, Mr. Vargas eats $\frac{1}{4}$ of the whole pie. What fraction represents the amount of pie remaining? (5.NF.A.2)

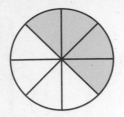

_____

16. [GO DEEPER] Keisha makes a large sandwich for a family picnic. She takes $\frac{1}{2}$ of the sandwich to the picnic. At the picnic, her family eats $\frac{3}{8}$ of the whole sandwich. What fraction of the whole sandwich does Keisha bring back from the picnic? (5.NF.A.2)

_____

17. Mike is mixing paint for his walls. He mixes $\frac{1}{6}$ gallon blue paint and $\frac{5}{8}$ gallon green paint in a large container. What fraction represents the total amount of paint Mike mixes? (5.NF.A.2)

_____

Name _____

Add and Subtract Mixed Numbers

Essential Question How can you add and subtract mixed numbers with unlike denominators?

Common Core **Number and Operations—Fractions—5.NF.A.1** *Also 5.NF.A.2*
MATHEMATICAL PRACTICES
MP1, MP2, MP6

 **Unlock the Problem** Real World

Denise mixed $1\frac{4}{5}$ ounces of blue paint with $2\frac{1}{10}$ ounces of yellow paint. How many ounces of paint did Denise mix?

- What operation should you use to solve the problem?

  _____

- Do the fractions have the same denominator?

  _____

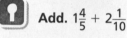 **Add.** $1\frac{4}{5} + 2\frac{1}{10}$

To find the sum of mixed numbers with unlike denominators, you can use a common denominator.

STEP 1 Estimate the sum. _____

STEP 2 Find a common denominator. Use the common denominator to write equivalent fractions with like denominators.

STEP 3 Add the fractions. Then add the whole numbers. Write the answer in simplest form.

$$1\frac{4}{5} = \underline{}$$

$$+2\frac{1}{10} = +\underline{}$$

So, Denise mixed _____ ounces of paint.

Math Talk **MATHEMATICAL PRACTICES ❷**
Connect Symbols and Words Did you use the least common denominator? Explain.

1. **MATHEMATICAL PRACTICE ❶ Evaluate Reasonableness** Explain how you know whether your answer is reasonable.

_____

_____

2. What other common denominator could you have used? _____

_____

🔑 Example

Subtract. $4\frac{5}{6} - 2\frac{3}{4}$

You can also use a common denominator to find the difference of mixed numbers with unlike denominators.

STEP 1   Estimate the difference. _____

STEP 2   Find a common denominator. Use the common denominator to write equivalent fractions with like denominators.

STEP 3   Subtract the fractions. Subtract the whole numbers. Write the answer in simplest form.

$$4\frac{5}{6} = \boxed{}$$

$$-2\frac{3}{4} = -\boxed{}$$

$$\overline{}$$

$$\boxed{}$$

3. **MATHEMATICAL PRACTICE ①** **Evaluate Reasonableness** Explain how you know whether your answer is reasonable.

_____

_____

Share and Show   MATH BOARD

1. Use a common denominator to write equivalent fractions with like denominators and then find the sum. Write your answer in simplest form.

$$7\frac{2}{5} = \boxed{}$$

$$+4\frac{3}{4} = +\boxed{}$$

$$\overline{}$$

$$\boxed{}$$

Find the sum. Write your answer in simplest form.

2. $2\frac{3}{4} + 3\frac{3}{10}$ 3. $5\frac{3}{4} + 1\frac{1}{3}$ ✓4. $3\frac{4}{5} + 2\frac{3}{10}$

Name _____

Find the difference. Write your answer in simplest form.

5. $9\frac{5}{6} - 2\frac{1}{3}$

6. $10\frac{5}{9} - 9\frac{1}{6}$

✓7. $7\frac{2}{3} - 3\frac{1}{6}$

On Your Own

Math Talk MATHEMATICAL PRACTICES ⑥
Explain why you need to write equivalent fractions with common denominators to add $4\frac{5}{6}$ and $1\frac{1}{8}$.

Find the sum or difference. Write your answer in simplest form.

8. $1\frac{3}{10} + 2\frac{2}{5}$

9. $8\frac{1}{6} + 7\frac{3}{8}$

10. $2\frac{1}{2} + 2\frac{1}{3}$

11. $12\frac{3}{4} - 6\frac{1}{6}$

12. $2\frac{5}{8} - 1\frac{1}{4}$

13. $14\frac{7}{12} - 5\frac{1}{4}$

Practice: Copy and Solve Find the sum or difference. Write your answer in simplest form.

14. $1\frac{5}{12} + 4\frac{1}{6}$

15. $8\frac{1}{2} + 6\frac{3}{5}$

16. $2\frac{1}{6} + 4\frac{5}{9}$

17. $3\frac{5}{8} + \frac{5}{12}$

18. $3\frac{2}{3} - 1\frac{1}{6}$

19. $5\frac{6}{7} - 1\frac{2}{3}$

20. $2\frac{7}{8} - \frac{1}{2}$

21. $4\frac{7}{12} - 1\frac{2}{9}$

22. **GO DEEPER** Dakota makes a salad dressing by combining $6\frac{1}{3}$ fluid ounces of oil and $2\frac{3}{8}$ fluid ounces of vinegar in a jar. She then pours $2\frac{1}{4}$ fluid ounces of the dressing onto her salad. How much dressing remains in the jar?

_____

23. **GO DEEPER** This week, Maddie worked $2\frac{1}{2}$ hours on Monday, $2\frac{2}{3}$ hours on Tuesday, and $3\frac{1}{4}$ hours on Wednesday. How many more hours will Maddie need to work this week to make her goal of $10\frac{1}{2}$ hours a week?

_____

Problem Solving • Applications

Use the table to solve 24–25.

24. **MATHEMATICAL PRACTICE 2 Reason Quantitatively** Gavin plans to mix a batch of Tangerine paint. He expects to have a total of $5\frac{3}{10}$ ounces of paint after he mixes the amounts of red and yellow. Explain how you can tell if Gavin's expectation is reasonable.

_____

_____

_____

Paint Gavin Uses (in ounces)		
Red	**Yellow**	**Shade**
$2\frac{5}{8}$	$3\frac{1}{4}$	Sunrise Orange
$3\frac{9}{10}$	$2\frac{3}{8}$	Tangerine
$5\frac{5}{6}$	$5\frac{5}{6}$	Mango

25. **THINK SMARTER** Gavin mixes the amount of red from one shade of paint with the amount of yellow from a different shade of paint. He mixes the batch so he will have the greatest possible amount of paint. What amounts of red and yellow from which shades are used in the mixture? Explain your answer.

_____

_____

_____

26. **THINK SMARTER** Martin won first place in the 100-meter dash with a time of $14\frac{23}{100}$ seconds. Samuel came in second place with a time of $15\frac{7}{10}$ seconds. For 26a–26d, select True or False for each statement.

26a. A common denominator of the mixed numbers is 100.   ○ True   ○ False

26b. To find the difference between the runners' times, Samuel's time needs to be rewritten.   ○ True   ○ False

26c. Samuel's time written with a denominator of 100 is $15\frac{70}{100}$.   ○ True   ○ False

26d. Martin beat Samuel by $\frac{21}{25}$ second.   ○ True   ○ False

Add and Subtract Mixed Numbers

Common Core — **COMMON CORE STANDARD—5.NF.A.1**
Use equivalent fractions as a strategy to add and subtract fractions.

Find the sum or difference. Write your answer in simplest form.

1. $3\frac{1}{2} - 1\frac{1}{5}$

$3\frac{1}{2} \rightarrow 3\frac{5}{10}$

$\underline{-1\frac{1}{5} \rightarrow -1\frac{2}{10}}$

$\quad\quad 2\frac{3}{10}$

2. $2\frac{1}{3} + 1\frac{3}{4}$

3. $4\frac{1}{8} + 2\frac{1}{3}$

4. $5\frac{1}{3} + 6\frac{1}{6}$

5. $2\frac{1}{4} + 1\frac{2}{5}$

6. $5\frac{17}{18} - 2\frac{2}{3}$

7. $6\frac{3}{4} - 1\frac{5}{8}$

8. $5\frac{3}{7} - 2\frac{1}{5}$

Problem Solving · Real World

9. Jacobi bought $7\frac{1}{2}$ pounds of meatballs. He decided to cook $1\frac{1}{4}$ pounds and freeze the rest. How many pounds did he freeze?

10. Jill walked $8\frac{1}{8}$ miles to a park and then $7\frac{2}{5}$ miles home. How many miles did she walk?

11. **WRITE** ▸*Math* Write your own story problem using mixed numbers. Show the solution.

Lesson Check (5.NF.A.1)

1. Ming has a goal to jog $4\frac{1}{2}$ miles each day. On Monday she jogged $5\frac{9}{16}$ miles. By how much did she exceed her goal for that day?

2. At the deli, Ricardo ordered $3\frac{1}{5}$ pounds of cheddar cheese and $2\frac{3}{4}$ pounds of mozzarella cheese. How many pounds of cheese did he order all together?

Spiral Review (5.NBT.A.2, 5.NBT.B.6, 5.NBT.B.7)

3. The theater has 175 seats. There are 7 seats in each row. How many rows are there?

4. During the first 14 days, 2,744 people visited a new store. The same number of people visited the store each day. About how many people visited the store each day?

5. What number is 100 times as great as 0.3?

6. Mark said that the product of 0.02 and 0.7 is 14. Mark is wrong. What is the product?

FOR MORE PRACTICE
GO TO THE
Personal Math Trainer

Subtraction with Renaming

Essential Question How can you use renaming to find the difference of two mixed numbers?

Common Core **Number and Operations—Fractions—5.NF.A.1** *Also 5.NF.A.2*

MATHEMATICAL PRACTICES
MP1, MP5, MP6

Unlock the Problem Real World

To practice for a race, Kara is running $2\frac{1}{2}$ miles. When she reaches the end of her street, she knows that she has already run $1\frac{5}{6}$ miles. How many miles does Kara have left to run?

- Underline the sentence that tells you what you need to find.

- What operation should you use to solve the problem?

  _____

One Way Rename the first mixed number.

Subtract. $2\frac{1}{2} - 1\frac{5}{6}$

STEP 1 Estimate the difference. _____

STEP 2 Find a common denominator. Use the common denominator to write equivalent fractions with like denominators.

STEP 3 Since $\frac{6}{12}$ is less than $\frac{10}{12}$, rename $2\frac{6}{12}$ as a mixed number with a fraction greater than 1.

Think: $2\frac{6}{12} = 1 + 1 + \frac{6}{12} = 1 + \frac{12}{12} + \frac{6}{12} = 1\frac{18}{12}$

$2\frac{6}{12} = $ _____

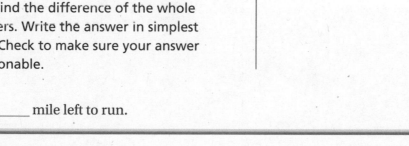

$$2\frac{1}{2} = 2\frac{6}{12} = \boxed{}$$

$$-1\frac{5}{6} = -1\frac{10}{12} = -1\frac{10}{12}$$

$$\boxed{} = \boxed{}$$

STEP 4 Find the difference of the fractions. Then find the difference of the whole numbers. Write the answer in simplest form. Check to make sure your answer is reasonable.

So, Kara has _____ mile left to run.

- **MATHEMATICAL PRACTICE 6** **Explain** why it is important to write equivalent fractions before renaming. _____

_____

🔒 Another Way Rename both mixed numbers as fractions greater than 1.

Subtract. $2\frac{1}{2} - 1\frac{5}{6}$

STEP 1 Write equivalent fractions, using a common denominator.

A common denominator of $\frac{1}{2}$ and $\frac{5}{6}$ is 6.

$2\frac{1}{2} \longrightarrow$

$1\frac{5}{6} \longrightarrow$

STEP 2 Rename both mixed numbers as fractions greater than 1.

$2\frac{3}{6} =$ Think: $\frac{6}{6} + \frac{6}{6} + \frac{3}{6}$

$1\frac{5}{6} =$ Think: $\frac{6}{6} + \frac{5}{6}$

STEP 3 Find the difference of the fractions. Then write the answer in simplest form.

$$\boxed{} - \boxed{} = \boxed{}$$

$$= \boxed{}$$

$2\frac{1}{2} - 1\frac{5}{6} = \underline{\hspace{2cm}}$

Share and Show MATH BOARD

Estimate. Then find the difference and write it in simplest form.

☑ **1.** Estimate: _____

$4\frac{1}{2} - 3\frac{4}{5}$

☑ **2.** Estimate: _____

$9\frac{1}{6} - 2\frac{3}{4}$

Math Talk

MATHEMATICAL PRACTICES ⑤

Communicate Explain the strategy you could use to solve $3\frac{1}{9} - 2\frac{1}{3}$.

Name _____

Estimate. Then find the difference and write it in simplest form.

3. Estimate: _____

$3\frac{2}{3} - 1\frac{11}{12}$

4. Estimate: _____

$4\frac{1}{4} - 2\frac{1}{3}$

5. Estimate: _____

$5\frac{2}{5} - 1\frac{1}{2}$

Practice: Copy and Solve Find the difference and write it in simplest form.

6. $11\frac{1}{9} - 3\frac{2}{3}$

7. $6 - 3\frac{1}{2}$

8. $4\frac{3}{8} - 3\frac{1}{2}$

9. $9\frac{1}{6} - 3\frac{5}{8}$

10. $1\frac{1}{5} - \frac{1}{2}$

11. $13\frac{1}{6} - 3\frac{4}{5}$

12. $12\frac{2}{5} - 5\frac{3}{4}$

13. $7\frac{3}{8} - 2\frac{7}{9}$

14. **GO DEEPER** Three commercials are played in a row between songs on the radio. The three commercials fill exactly 3 minutes of time. If the first commercial uses $1\frac{1}{6}$ minutes, and the second uses $\frac{3}{5}$ minute, how long is the third commercial?

_____

15. **THINK SMARTER** Four students made videos for an art project. The table shows the length of each video.

Match each pair of videos with the correct difference between their times.

Art in Nature	
Video	**Time (in hours)**
1	$4\frac{3}{4}$
2	$4\frac{2}{5}$
3	$2\frac{5}{6}$
4	$2\frac{1}{2}$

Video 1 and Video 3 •   • $1\frac{17}{30}$ hours

Video 2 and Video 3 •   • $1\frac{9}{10}$ hours

Video 2 and Video 4 •   • $1\frac{11}{12}$ hours

Connect to Reading

Summarize

An amusement park in Sandusky, Ohio, offers 17 amazing roller coasters for visitors to ride. One of the roller coasters runs at 60 miles per hour and has 3,900 feet of twisting track. This coaster also has 3 trains with 8 rows per train. Riders stand in rows of 4, for a total of 32 riders per train.

The operators of the coaster recorded the number of riders on each train during a run. On the first train, the operators reported that $7\frac{1}{4}$ rows were filled. On the second train, all 8 rows were filled, and on the third train, $5\frac{1}{2}$ rows were filled. How many more rows were filled on the first train than on the third train?

When you *summarize*, you restate the most important information in a shortened form to more easily understand what you have read.

16. **MATHEMATICAL PRACTICE ①** **Analyze** Identify and summarize the important information given in the problem.

_____

_____

_____

_____

Use the summary from item 16 to solve.

17. Solve the problem above.

_____

_____

18. **THINK SMARTER** How many rows were empty on the first train? How many additional riders would it take to fill the empty rows? Explain your answer.

_____

_____

_____

Name _____

Subtraction with Renaming

Common Core

COMMON CORE STANDARD—5.NF.A.1
Use equivalent fractions as a strategy to add
and subtract fractions.

Estimate. Then find the difference and write it in simplest form.

1. Estimate: _____

$6\frac{1}{3} - 1\frac{2}{5}$

$$6\frac{1}{3} \rightarrow 6\frac{5}{6}\frac{20}{15}$$

$$-1\frac{2}{5} \rightarrow -1\frac{6}{15}$$

$$\overline{4\frac{14}{15}}$$

2. Estimate: _____

$4\frac{1}{2} - 3\frac{5}{6}$

3. Estimate: _____

$9 - 3\frac{7}{8}$

4. Estimate: _____

$2\frac{1}{6} - 1\frac{2}{7}$

5. Estimate: _____

$8 - 6\frac{1}{9}$

6. Estimate: _____

$9\frac{1}{4} - 3\frac{2}{3}$

Problem Solving Real World

7. Carlene bought $8\frac{1}{16}$ yards of ribbon to decorate a shirt. She only used $5\frac{1}{2}$ yards. How much ribbon does she have left over?

_____

8. During his first vet visit, Pedro's puppy weighed $6\frac{1}{8}$ pounds. On his second visit, he weighed $9\frac{1}{16}$ pounds. How much weight did he gain between visits?

_____

9. **WRITE** *Math* Write a subtraction problem that has mixed numbers and requires renaming. Draw a model illustrating the steps you take to solve the problem.

_____

_____

Lesson Check (5.NF.A.1)

1. Natalia picked $7\frac{1}{6}$ bushels of apples today and $4\frac{5}{8}$ bushels yesterday. How many more bushels did she pick today?

2. Max needs $10\frac{1}{4}$ cups of flour to make a batch of pizza dough for the pizzeria. He only has $4\frac{1}{2}$ cups of flour. How much more flour does he need to make the dough?

Spiral Review (5.NBT.A.1, 5.NBT.A.2, 5.NBT.B.6, 5.NBT.B.7)

3. The accountant charged $35 for the first hour of work and $23 for each hour after that. He earned a total of $127. How many hours did he work?

4. The soccer league needs to transport all 133 players to the tournament. If 4 players can ride in one car, how many cars are needed?

5. What is five hundred million, one hundred fifteen written in standard form?

6. Find the quotient.

$$6.39 \div 0.3$$

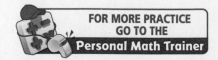

FOR MORE PRACTICE
GO TO THE
Personal Math Trainer

Name _____

Patterns with Fractions

Essential Question How can you use addition or subtraction to describe a pattern or create a sequence with fractions?

Common Core **Number and Operations—Fractions—5.NF.A.1**
MATHEMATICAL PRACTICES
MP1, MP7, MP8

Unlock the Problem Real World

Mr. Patrick wants to develop a new chili recipe for his restaurant. Each batch he makes uses a different amount of chili powder. The first batch uses $3\frac{1}{2}$ ounces, the second batch uses $4\frac{5}{6}$ ounces, the third uses $6\frac{1}{6}$ ounces, and the fourth uses $7\frac{1}{2}$ ounces. If this pattern continues, how much chili powder will he use in the sixth batch?

You can find the pattern in a sequence by comparing one term with the next term.

STEP 1 Write the terms in the sequence as equivalent fractions with a common denominator. Then examine the sequence and compare the consecutive terms to find the rule used to make the sequence of fractions.

$$+1\frac{2}{6}$$

difference between terms

$$3\frac{1}{2}, 4\frac{5}{6}, 6\frac{1}{6}, 7\frac{1}{2}, \cdots \rightarrow \quad \text{oz,} \quad \text{oz,} \quad \text{oz,} \quad \text{oz}$$

terms with common denominator

batch 1   batch 2   batch 3   batch 4

STEP 2 Write a rule that describes the pattern in the sequence.

- Is the sequence increasing or decreasing from one term to the next? **Explain**.

_____

_____

Rule: _____

STEP 3 Extend the sequence to solve the problem.

$$3\frac{1}{2}, 4\frac{5}{6}, 6\frac{1}{6}, 7\frac{1}{2}, \underline{\quad\quad}, \underline{\quad\quad}$$

So, Mr. Patrick will use _____ ounces of chili powder in the sixth batch.

🔑 Example Find the unknown terms in the sequence.

$1\frac{3}{4}$, $1\frac{9}{16}$, $1\frac{3}{8}$, $1\frac{3}{16}$, _____ , _____ , _____ , $\frac{7}{16}$ $\frac{1}{4}$

STEP 1 Write the terms in the sequence as equivalent fractions with a common denominator.

_____ , _____ , _____ , _____ , $\underset{?}{\_\_\_\_\_}$, $\underset{?}{\_\_\_\_\_}$, $\underset{?}{\_\_\_\_\_}$, _____ , _____

_____

STEP 2 Write a rule describing the pattern in the sequence.

• What operation can be used to describe a sequence that increases?

_____

• What operation can be used to describe a sequence that decreases?

_____

Rule: _____

STEP 3 Use your rule to find the unknown terms. Then complete the sequence above.

> **Math Talk**
>
> **MATHEMATICAL PRACTICES ①**
>
> **Analyze** How do you know whether your rule for a sequence would involve addition or subtraction?

Try This!

Ⓐ Write a rule for the sequence. Then find the unknown term.

$1\frac{1}{12}$, $\frac{5}{6}$, _____ , $\frac{1}{3}$, $\frac{1}{12}$

Rule: _____

Ⓑ Write the first four terms of the sequence.

Rule: start at $\frac{1}{4}$, add $\frac{3}{8}$

_____ , _____ , _____ , _____

Name _____

Write a rule for the sequence.

1. $\frac{1}{4}, \frac{1}{2}, \frac{3}{4}, \dots$

   Think: Is the sequence increasing or decreasing?

   Rule: _____

2. $\frac{1}{9}, \frac{1}{3}, \frac{5}{9}, \dots$

   Rule: _____

Write a rule for the sequence. Then, find the unknown term.

3. $\frac{3}{10}, \frac{2}{5}, \underline{\hspace{2cm}}, \frac{3}{5}, \frac{7}{10}$

   Rule: _____

4. $10\frac{2}{3}, 9\frac{11}{18}, 8\frac{5}{9}, \underline{\hspace{2cm}}, 6\frac{4}{9}$

   Rule: _____

On Your Own

Write the first four terms of the sequence.

5. **Rule:** start at $5\frac{3}{4}$, subtract $\frac{5}{8}$

   _____ , _____ , _____ , _____

6. **Rule:** start at $\frac{3}{8}$, add $\frac{3}{16}$

   _____ , _____ , _____ , _____

7. **Rule:** start at $2\frac{1}{3}$, add $2\frac{1}{4}$

   _____ , _____ , _____ , _____

8. **Rule:** start at $\frac{8}{9}$, subtract $\frac{1}{18}$

   _____ , _____ , _____ , _____

9. **MATHEMATICAL PRACTICE 7 Look for a Pattern** Vicki started jogging. The first time she ran, she ran $\frac{3}{16}$ mile. The second time, she ran $\frac{3}{8}$ mile, and the third time, she ran $\frac{9}{16}$ mile. If she continued this pattern, when was the first time she ran more than 1 mile? Explain.

_____

_____

_____

10. **GO DEEPER** Mr. Conners drove $78\frac{1}{3}$ miles on Monday, $77\frac{1}{12}$ miles on Tuesday, and $75\frac{5}{6}$ miles on Wednesday. If he continues this pattern on Thursday and Friday, how many fewer miles will he drive on Friday than on Tuesday?

_____

Problem Solving • Applications

11. When Bill bought a marigold plant, it was $\frac{1}{4}$ inch tall. After the first week, it measured $1\frac{1}{12}$ inches tall. After the second week, it was $1\frac{11}{12}$ inches. After week 3, it was $2\frac{3}{4}$ inches tall. Assuming the growth of the plant was constant, what was the height of the plant at the end of week 4?

_____

12. **THINK SMARTER** What if Bill's plant grew at the same rate but was $1\frac{1}{2}$ inches when he bought it? How tall would the plant be after 3 weeks?

_____

13. **THINK SMARTER** Kendra hiked each day for a week. The first day she hiked $\frac{1}{8}$ mile, the second day she hiked $\frac{3}{8}$ mile, and the third day she hiked $\frac{5}{8}$ mile.

What is the rule for the distance Kendra hikes each day? Show how you can check your answer.

_____

_____

_____

If the pattern continues, how many miles will Kendra hike on day 7? Explain how you found your answer.

_____

_____

Patterns with Fractions

Common Core
COMMON CORE STANDARD—5.NF.A.1
Use equivalent fractions as a strategy to add and subtract fractions.

Write a rule for the sequence. Then, find the unknown term.

1. $\frac{1}{2}, \frac{2}{3}, \underline{\quad\frac{5}{6}\quad}, 1, 1\frac{1}{6}$

Think: The pattern is increasing. Add $\frac{1}{6}$ to find the next term.

Rule: _____

2. $1\frac{3}{8}, 1\frac{3}{4}, 2\frac{1}{8}, \underline{\qquad}, 2\frac{7}{8}$

Rule: _____

3. $1\frac{9}{10}, 1\frac{7}{10}, \underline{\qquad}, 1\frac{3}{10}, 1\frac{1}{10}$

Rule: _____

4. $2\frac{5}{12}, 2\frac{1}{6}, 1\frac{11}{12}, \underline{\qquad}, 1\frac{5}{12}$

Rule: _____

Write the first four terms of the sequence.

5. Rule: start at $\frac{1}{2}$, add $\frac{1}{3}$

_____

6. Rule: start at $3\frac{1}{8}$, subtract $\frac{3}{4}$

_____

Problem Solving · Real World

7. Jarett's puppy weighed $3\frac{3}{4}$ ounces at birth. At one week old, the puppy weighed $5\frac{1}{8}$ ounces. At two weeks old, the puppy weighed $6\frac{1}{2}$ ounces. If the weight gain continues in this pattern, how much will the puppy weigh at three weeks old?

_____

8. A baker started out with 12 cups of flour. She had $9\frac{1}{4}$ cups of flour left after the first batch of batter she made. She had $6\frac{1}{2}$ cups of flour left after the second batch of batter she made. If she makes two more batches of batter, how many cups of flour will be left?

_____

9. **WRITE** ▸ *Math* Make up your own sequence of 5 fractions or mixed numbers. Offer the sequence to another student to try and find the next fraction in the sequence.

_____

Lesson Check (5.NF.A.1)

1. What is a rule for the sequence?

$$\frac{5}{6},\ 1\frac{1}{2},\ 2\frac{1}{6},\ 2\frac{5}{6},\ \dots$$

2. Jaime biked $5\frac{1}{4}$ miles on Monday, $6\frac{7}{8}$ miles on Tuesday, and $8\frac{1}{2}$ miles on Wednesday. If he continues the pattern, how many miles will he bike on Friday?

Spiral Review (5.OA.A.2, 5.NBT.B.5, 5.NBT.B.7)

3. Jaylyn rode her bicycle in a bike-a-thon. She rode 33.48 miles in 2.7 hours. If she rode at the same speed, what was her speed in miles per hour?

4. One week a company filled 546 boxes with widgets. Each box held 38 widgets. How many widgets did the company pack in boxes that week?

5. Write an expression that represents the statement "Add 9 and 3, then multiply by 6."

6. Mason took 9.4 minutes to complete the first challenge in the Champs Challenge. He completed the second challenge 2.65 minutes faster than the first challenge. How long did it take Mason to complete the second challenge?

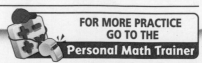

FOR MORE PRACTICE
GO TO THE
Personal Math Trainer

Problem Solving •
Practice Addition and Subtraction

Essential Question How can the strategy *work backward* help you solve
a problem with fractions that involves addition and subtraction?

Common Core **Number and Operations—**
Fractions—5.NF.A.2 *Also 5.NF.A.1*
MATHEMATICAL PRACTICES
MP1, MP2, MP4, MP6

Unlock the Problem Real World

The Diaz family is cross-country skiing the Big Tree trails,
which have a total length of 4 miles. Yesterday, they skied the $\frac{7}{10}$
mile Oak Trail. Today, they skied the $\frac{3}{5}$ mile Pine Trail. If they
plan to ski all of the Big Tree trails, how many more miles do
they have left to ski?

Use the graphic organizer to help you solve the problem.

Read the Problem

What do I need to find?	**What information do I need to use?**	**How will I use the information?**
I need to find the distance _____.	I need to use the distance _____ and the total distance _____.	I can work backward by starting with the _____ and _____ each distance they have already skied to find the distance they have left.

Solve the Problem

Addition and subtraction are inverse operations. By working backward and
using the same numbers, one operation undoes the other.

- Write an equation.

miles skied yesterday	+	miles skied today	+	miles they need to ski	=	total distance
↓		↓		↓		↓
_____	+	_____	+	m	=	4

- Then work backward to find *m*.

_____ − _____ − _____ = m

_____ = m

So, the family has _____ miles left to ski.

- **MATHEMATICAL PRACTICE ①** **Evaluate Reasonableness** Explain how you know your answer is reasonable. _____

_____

🔓 Try Another Problem

As part of their study of Native American basket weaving, Lia's class is making wicker baskets. Lia starts with a strip of wicker 36 inches long. From the strip, she first cuts one piece but does not know its length, and then cuts a piece that is $6\frac{1}{2}$ inches long. The piece left is $7\frac{3}{4}$ inches long. What is the length of the first piece she cut from the strip?

Read the Problem

What do I need to find?	What information do I need to use?	How will I use the information?

Solve the Problem

So, the length of the first piece cut was _____ inches.

Math Talk

MATHEMATICAL PRACTICES ❶

Make Sense of Problems What other strategy could you use to solve the problem?

Name _____

Share and Show

Unlock the Problem
- ✓ Plan your solution by deciding on the steps you will use.
- ✓ Check your exact answer by comparing it with your estimate.
- ✓ Check your answer for reasonableness.

✓**1.** Caitlin has $4\frac{3}{4}$ pounds of clay. She uses $1\frac{1}{10}$ pounds to make a cup, and another 2 pounds to make a jar. How many pounds are left?

First, write an equation to model the problem.

_____

Next, work backwards and rewrite the equation to find x.

_____

Solve.

_____

So, _____ pounds of clay remain.

2. **THINK SMARTER** **What if** Caitlin had used more than 2 pounds of clay to make a jar? Would the amount remaining have been more or less than your answer to Exercise 1?

_____

✓**3.** A pet store donated 50 pounds of food for adult dogs, puppies, and cats to an animal shelter. $19\frac{3}{4}$ pounds was adult dog food and $18\frac{7}{8}$ pounds was puppy food. How many pounds of cat food did the pet store donate?

_____

4. Thelma spent $\frac{1}{6}$ of her weekly allowance on dog toys, $\frac{1}{4}$ on a dog collar, and $\frac{1}{3}$ on dog food. What fraction of her weekly allowance is left?

_____

WRITE ▸ Math • **Show Your Work**

© Houghton Mifflin Harcourt Publishing Company

On Your Own

5. **GO DEEPER** Martin is making a model of a Native American canoe. He has $5\frac{1}{2}$ feet of wood. He uses $2\frac{3}{4}$ feet for the hull and $1\frac{1}{4}$ feet for a paddle. How much wood does he have left?

_____

6. **THINK SMARTER** Beth's summer vacation lasted 87 days. At the beginning of her vacation, she spent some time at soccer camp, 5 days at her grandmother's house, and 13 days visiting Glacier National Park with her parents. She then had 48 vacation days remaining. How many weeks did Beth spend at soccer camp?

_____

7. **MATHEMATICAL PRACTICE 2** **Reason Quantitatively** You can buy 2 DVDs for the same price you would pay for 3 CDs selling for $13.20 apiece. Explain how you could find the price of 1 DVD.

_____

_____

_____

8. **THINK SMARTER** Julio caught 3 fish weighing a total of $23\frac{1}{2}$ pounds. One fish weighed $9\frac{5}{8}$ pounds and another weighed $6\frac{1}{4}$ pounds. How much did the third fish weigh? Use the numbers and symbols to write an equation that represents the problem. Then solve the equation. Symbols may be used more than once or not at all.

$23\frac{1}{2}$	$9\frac{5}{8}$	$6\frac{1}{4}$	x	$=$	$+$

_____

weight of third fish: _____ pounds

Problem Solving • Practice Addition and Subtraction

COMMON CORE STANDARD—5.NF.A.2
Use equivalent fractions as a strategy to add and subtract fractions.

Read each problem and solve.

1. From a board 8 feet in length, Emmet cut two $2\frac{1}{3}$-foot bookshelves. How much of the board remained?

   Write an equation: $8 = 2\frac{1}{3} + 2\frac{1}{3} + x$

   Rewrite the equation to work backward:

   $$8 - 2\frac{1}{3} - 2\frac{1}{3} = x$$

   Subtract twice to find the length remaining: $3\frac{1}{3}$ **feet**

2. Lynne bought a bag of grapefruit, $1\frac{5}{8}$ pounds of apples, and $2\frac{3}{16}$ pounds of bananas. The total weight of her purchases was $7\frac{1}{2}$ pounds. How much did the bag of grapefruit weigh? _____

3. Mattie's house consists of two stories and an attic. The first floor is $8\frac{5}{6}$ feet tall, the second floor is $8\frac{1}{2}$ feet tall, and the entire house is $24\frac{1}{3}$ feet tall. How tall is the attic? _____

4. It is $10\frac{3}{5}$ miles from Alston to Barton and $12\frac{1}{2}$ miles from Barton to Chester. The distance from Alston to Durbin, via Barton and Chester, is 35 miles. How far is it from Chester to Durbin? _____

5. Marcie bought a 50-foot roll of packing tape. She used two $8\frac{5}{6}$-foot lengths. How much tape is left on the roll? _____

6. **WRITE** ▸ *Math* Write a word problem involving fractions for which you would use the *work backward* strategy and addition to solve. Include your solution.

_____

_____

Lesson Check (5.NF.A.2)

1. Paula spent $\frac{3}{8}$ of her allowance on clothes and $\frac{1}{6}$ on entertainment. What fraction of her allowance did she spend on other items?

_____

2. Della bought a tree seedling that was $2\frac{1}{4}$ feet tall. During the first year, it grew $1\frac{1}{6}$ feet. After two years, it was 5 feet tall. How much did the seedling grow during the second year?

_____

Spiral Review (5.OA.A.1, 5.NBT.A.2, 5.NBT.B.6, 5.NF.B.7)

3. What is a way to write 100,000 using exponents?

_____

4. What expression can be used for estimating 868 ÷ 28?

_____

5. Justin gave the clerk $20 to pay a bill of $6.57. How much change should Justin get?

_____

6. What is the value of the following expression?

$$7 + 18 \div (6 - 3)$$

_____

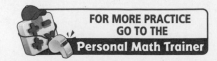

FOR MORE PRACTICE GO TO THE Personal Math Trainer

Name _____

Use Properties of Addition

Essential Question How can properties help you add fractions with unlike denominators?

Common Core Number and Operations—
Fractions—5.NF.A.1
MATHEMATICAL PRACTICES
MP4, MP7, MP8

CONNECT You can use properties of addition to help you add fractions with unlike denominators.

> Commutative Property: $\frac{1}{2} + \frac{3}{5} = \frac{3}{5} + \frac{1}{2}$
>
> Associative Property: $\left(\frac{2}{9} + \frac{1}{8}\right) + \frac{3}{8} = \frac{2}{9} + \left(\frac{1}{8} + \frac{3}{8}\right)$

Remember
Parentheses ( ) tell which operation to do first.

Unlock the Problem Real World

Jane and her family are driving to Big Lagoon State Park. On the first day, they travel $\frac{1}{3}$ of the total distance. On the second day, they travel $\frac{1}{3}$ of the total distance in the morning and then $\frac{1}{6}$ of the total distance in the afternoon. How much of the total distance has Jane's family driven by the end of the second day?

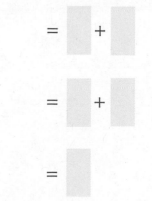 **Use the Associative Property.**

Day 1 + Day 2

$$\frac{1}{3} + \left(\frac{1}{3} + \frac{1}{6}\right) = \left(\boxed{} + \boxed{}\right) + \boxed{}$$

$$= \boxed{} + \boxed{}$$

$$= \boxed{} + \boxed{}$$

$$= \boxed{}$$

Write the number sentence to represent the problem. Use the Associative Property to group fractions with like denominators together.

Use mental math to add the fractions with like denominators.

Write equivalent fractions with like denominators. Then add.

So, Jane's family has driven _____ of the total distance by the end of the second day.

Math Talk

MATHEMATICAL PRACTICES ❽

Generalize Explain why grouping the fractions differently makes it easier to find the sum.

🔐 Example Add. $\left(2\frac{5}{8} + 1\frac{2}{3}\right) + 1\frac{1}{8}$

Use the Commutative Property and the Associative Property.

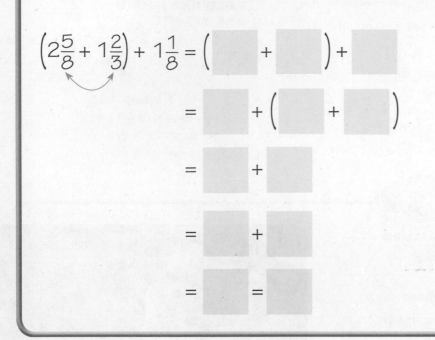

Use the Commutative Property to put fractions with like denominators next to each other.

Use the Associative Property to group fractions with like denominators together.

Use mental math to add the fractions with like denominators.

Write equivalent fractions with like denominators.
Then add.

Rename and simplify.

Try This! Use properties to solve. Show each step and name the property used.

A $5\frac{1}{4} + \left(\frac{3}{4} + 1\frac{5}{12}\right)$

B $\left(\frac{1}{5} + \frac{3}{10}\right) + \frac{2}{5}$

Name _____

Use the properties and mental math to solve. Write your answer in simplest form.

1. $\left(2\frac{5}{8} + \frac{5}{6}\right) + 1\frac{1}{8}$

✓ 2. $\frac{5}{12} + \left(\frac{5}{12} + \frac{3}{4}\right)$

✓ 3. $\left(3\frac{1}{4} + 2\frac{5}{6}\right) + 1\frac{3}{4}$

Math Talk   MATHEMATICAL PRACTICES ❼

Identify Relationships
How is solving Exercise 3 different from solving Exercise 1?

On Your Own

Use the properties and mental math to solve. Write your answer in simplest form.

4. $\left(\frac{2}{7} + \frac{1}{3}\right) + \frac{2}{3}$

5. $\left(\frac{1}{5} + \frac{1}{2}\right) + \frac{2}{5}$

6. $\left(\frac{1}{6} + \frac{3}{7}\right) + \frac{2}{7}$

7. $\left(2\frac{5}{12} + 4\frac{1}{4}\right) + \frac{1}{4}$

8. $1\frac{1}{8} + \left(5\frac{1}{2} + 2\frac{3}{8}\right)$

9. $\frac{5}{9} + \left(\frac{1}{9} + \frac{4}{5}\right)$

10. **GO DEEPER**   Tina used $10\frac{1}{2}$ yards of yarn to make three yarn dolls. She used $4\frac{1}{2}$ yards of yarn for the first doll and $2\frac{1}{5}$ yards for the second doll. How much yarn did Tina use for the third doll?

Problem Solving • Applications Real World

Use the map to solve 11–12.

11. **GO DEEPER** Julie rides her bike from the sports complex to the school. Then she rides from the school to the mall, and then on to the library. Kyle rides his bike from his house to the mall, and then to the library. Who rides farther? How many miles farther?

_____

12. **THINK SMARTER** On one afternoon, Mario walks from his house to the library. That evening, Mario walks from the library to the mall, and then to Kyle's house. Describe how you can use the properties to find how far Mario walks

_____

_____

_____

_____

13. **MATHEMATICAL PRACTICE ④ Write an Expression** Kyle is adding the distances between the school and the mall, the mall and the park, and the mall and his house. He writes $\frac{2}{5} + \frac{2}{3} + \frac{4}{5}$. Rewrite Kyle's expression using properties so the fractions are easier to add.

_____

14. **THINK SMARTER** For 14a–14c, tell whether the Commutative Property or the Associative Property can be used to show each equation is true without calculating. Choose the correct property of addition.

14a. $\frac{9}{10} + \left(\frac{3}{10} + \frac{5}{6}\right) = \left(\frac{9}{10} + \frac{3}{10}\right) + \frac{5}{6}$

Associative Property

Commutative Property

14b. $\left(\frac{3}{4} + \frac{1}{5}\right) + \frac{1}{4} = \left(\frac{1}{5} + \frac{3}{4}\right) + \frac{1}{4}$

Associative Property

Commutative Property

14c. $\left(3\frac{1}{2} + 2\frac{1}{8}\right) + 1\frac{5}{8} = 3\frac{1}{2} + \left(2\frac{1}{8} + 1\frac{5}{8}\right)$

Associative Property

Commutative Property

Map:

Sports Complex — School: $\frac{2}{3}$ mile

Mall — Kyle's House: $\frac{2}{5}$ mile

Park — Mall: $\frac{2}{3}$ mile

Mall — Kyle's House (lower): $\frac{4}{5}$ mile

Library: $1\frac{1}{3}$ miles

$1\frac{3}{5}$ miles — Mario's House

Use Properties of Addition

COMMON CORE STANDARD—5.NF.A.1
Use equivalent fractions as a strategy to add and subtract fractions.

Use the properties and mental math to solve. Write your answer in simplest form.

1. $\left(2\frac{1}{3} + 1\frac{2}{5}\right) + 3\frac{2}{3}$

$= \left(1\frac{2}{5} + 2\frac{1}{3}\right) + 3\frac{2}{3}$

$= 1\frac{2}{5} + \left(2\frac{1}{3} + 3\frac{2}{3}\right)$

$= 1\frac{2}{5} + 6$

$= 7\frac{2}{5}$

2. $8\frac{1}{5} + \left(4\frac{2}{5} + 3\frac{3}{10}\right)$

3. $\left(2\frac{3}{8} + 1\frac{3}{4}\right) + 5\frac{7}{8}$

4. $2\frac{1}{10} + \left(1\frac{2}{7} + 4\frac{9}{10}\right)$

5. $3\frac{1}{4} + \left(3\frac{1}{4} + 5\frac{1}{5}\right)$

6. $1\frac{1}{4} + \left(3\frac{2}{3} + 5\frac{3}{4}\right)$

Problem Solving *Real World*

7. Elizabeth rode her bike $6\frac{1}{2}$ miles from her house to the library and then another $2\frac{2}{5}$ miles to her friend Milo's house. If Carson's house is $2\frac{1}{2}$ miles beyond Milo's house, how far would she travel from her house to Carson's house?

8. Hassan made a vegetable salad with $2\frac{3}{8}$ pounds of tomatoes, $1\frac{1}{4}$ pounds of asparagus, and $2\frac{7}{8}$ pounds of potatoes. How many pounds of vegetables did he use altogether?

9. **WRITE** ▸*Math* Write Commutative Property and Associative Property at the top of the page. Underneath the name of each property, write its definition and three examples of its use.

_____

_____

Lesson Check (5.NF.A.1)

1. What is the sum of $2\frac{1}{3}$, $3\frac{5}{6}$, and $6\frac{2}{3}$?

2. Letitia has $7\frac{1}{6}$ yards of yellow ribbon, $5\frac{1}{4}$ yards of orange ribbon, and $5\frac{1}{6}$ yards of brown ribbon. How much ribbon does she have altogether?

Spiral Review (5.OA.A.1, 5.NBT.B.6, 5.NBT.B.7, 5.NF.A.1)

3. Juanita wrote 3×47 as $3 \times 40 + 3 \times 7$. What property did she use to rewrite the expression?

4. What is the value of the expression?

$$18 - 2 \times (4 + 3)$$

5. Evan spent $15.89 on 7 pounds of birdseed. How much did the birdseed cost per pound?

6. Cade rode $1\frac{3}{5}$ miles on Saturday and $1\frac{3}{4}$ miles on Sunday. How far did he ride on the two days?

 © Houghton Mifflin Harcourt Publishing Company

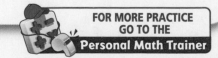
FOR MORE PRACTICE
GO TO THE
Personal Math Trainer

Name _____

1. Sophia babysat for $3\frac{7}{12}$ hours on Friday. She babysat for $2\frac{5}{6}$ hours on Saturday. For 1a–1c, estimate how long Sophia babysat on Friday and Saturday combined. Choose the correct benchmarks and sum.

1a. Sophia babysat for about

2
3
$3\frac{1}{2}$
4

hours on Friday.

1b. Sophia babysat for about

1
2
$2\frac{1}{2}$
3

hours on Saturday.

1c. Sophia babysat for about

5
$5\frac{1}{2}$
6
$6\frac{1}{2}$

hours on Friday and Saturday combined.

2. Rodrigo practiced playing the guitar $15\frac{1}{3}$ hours over the past 3 weeks. He practiced for $6\frac{1}{4}$ hours during the first week and $4\frac{2}{3}$ hours during the second week. How much time did Rodrigo spend practicing during the third week? Use the numbers and symbols to write an equation that represents the problem. Then solve the equation. Symbols may be used more than once or not at all.

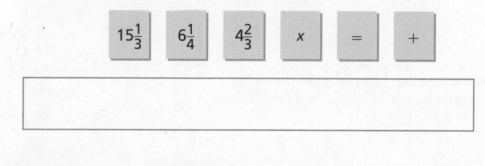

$$\boxed{15\frac{1}{3}} \quad \boxed{6\frac{1}{4}} \quad \boxed{4\frac{2}{3}} \quad \boxed{x} \quad \boxed{=} \quad \boxed{+}$$

Practice time during third week: _____ hours

© Houghton Mifflin Harcourt Publishing Company

3. Liam bought $5\frac{7}{8}$ pounds of steak. He used $2\frac{1}{16}$ pounds of the steak for a cookout. For 3a–3c, fill in each blank.

   3a. Rounded to the closest benchmark, Liam bought about ☐ pounds of steak.

   3b. Rounded to the closest benchmark, Liam used about ☐ pounds of steak for the cookout.

   3c. Liam has about ☐ pounds of steak remaining after the cookout.

4. Jackson picked apples for his family. He picked a total of $6\frac{1}{2}$ pounds. He took $2\frac{3}{4}$ pounds to his aunt and $1\frac{5}{8}$ pounds to his mother. How many pounds of apples were left to give to his grandmother? Use the numbers and symbols to write an equation that represents the problem, then solve the equation. Symbols may be used more than once or not at all.

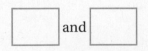

| $6\frac{1}{2}$ | $2\frac{3}{4}$ | $1\frac{5}{8}$ | x | = | + |

Weight of apples Jackson gave to his grandmother: _____ pounds

5. Write $\frac{2}{5}$ and $\frac{1}{3}$ as equivalent fractions using a common denominator.

☐ and ☐

6. Jill brought $2\frac{1}{3}$ boxes of carrot muffins for a bake sale. Mike brought $1\frac{3}{4}$ boxes of apple muffins. What is the total number of boxes of muffins Jill and Mike brought to the bake sale?

_____ boxes of muffins

7. The shaded part of the diagram shows what Genie has left from a meter of string. She will use $\frac{3}{5}$ meter of string to make bracelets. She wants to determine how much of the string she will have remaining after making the bracelets. For 7a–7c, select True or False for each statement.

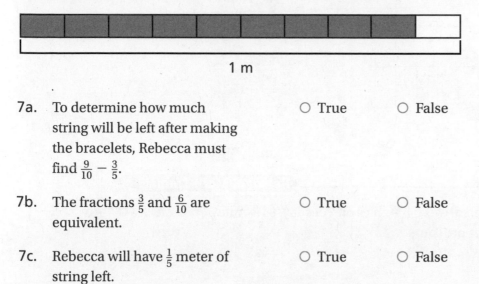

1 m

7a. To determine how much   ○ True   ○ False
     string will be left after making
     the bracelets, Rebecca must
     find $\frac{9}{10} - \frac{3}{5}$.

7b. The fractions $\frac{3}{5}$ and $\frac{6}{10}$ are   ○ True   ○ False
     equivalent.

7c. Rebecca will have $\frac{1}{5}$ meter of   ○ True   ○ False
     string left.

8. For 8a–8c, tell whether the Commutative Property or the Associative Property can be used to show each equation is true without calculating. Choose the correct property of addition.

8a. $\frac{1}{6} + \left(\frac{7}{8} + \frac{5}{6}\right) = \frac{1}{6} + \left(\frac{5}{6} + \frac{7}{8}\right)$

| Associative Property |
| Commutative Property |

8b. $\left(\frac{7}{10} + \frac{1}{3}\right) + \frac{1}{10} = \left(\frac{1}{3} + \frac{7}{10}\right) + \frac{1}{10}$

| Associative Property |
| Commutative Property |

8c. $\left(6\frac{2}{5} + \frac{4}{9}\right) + 3\frac{2}{9} = 6\frac{2}{5} + \left(\frac{4}{9} + 3\frac{2}{9}\right)$

| Associative Property |
| Commutative Property |

9. Joshua uses a rule to write the following sequence of numbers.

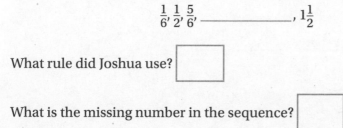

$\frac{1}{6}, \frac{1}{2}, \frac{5}{6}, \underline{\hspace{2cm}}, 1\frac{1}{2}$

What rule did Joshua use? ☐

What is the missing number in the sequence? ☐

10. Jeffrey walked $\frac{1}{3}$ mile on Monday and jogged $\frac{3}{4}$ mile on Tuesday. How far did he walk and jog on Monday and Tuesday combined? Use the tiles to complete the fraction strip model to show how you found your answer. The fractions may be used more than once or not at all.

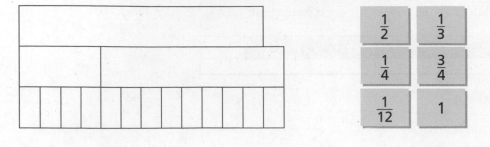

_____ mile(s)

11. **THINK** SMARTER + Mr. Cohen drives $84\frac{2}{10}$ miles on Tuesday, $84\frac{6}{10}$ miles on Wednesday, and 85 miles on Thursday.

Part A

What is the rule for the distance Mr. Cohen drives each day? Show how you can check your answer.

Part B

If the pattern continues, how many miles will Mr. Cohen drive on Sunday? Explain how you found your answer.

12. Alana bought $\frac{3}{8}$ pound of Swiss cheese and $\frac{1}{4}$ pound of American cheese. Which pairs of fractions are equivalent to the amounts Alana bought? Mark all that apply.

(A) $\frac{24}{64}$ and $\frac{8}{64}$

(C) $\frac{12}{32}$ and $\frac{6}{32}$

(B) $\frac{6}{16}$ and $\frac{4}{16}$

(D) $\frac{15}{40}$ and $\frac{10}{40}$

13. **GO DEEPER** Four students spent time volunteering last weekend. The table shows how much time each student spent volunteering.

Volunteering	
Student	Time (in hours)
Amy	$4\frac{5}{6}$
Beth	$6\frac{1}{2}$
Victor	$5\frac{3}{4}$
Cal	$5\frac{2}{3}$

Match each pair of students with the difference between how much time they spent volunteering.

Amy and Victor •   • $\frac{3}{4}$ hour

Cal and Beth •   • $\frac{11}{12}$ hour

Beth and Victor •   • $\frac{5}{6}$ hour

14. For 14a–14d, tell which expressions require you to rename mixed numbers before you can subtract. Find each difference. Write each expression and the difference as an equation in the correct box.

14a. $2\frac{1}{3} - 1\frac{3}{4}$ 14c. $5\frac{2}{3} - 2\frac{5}{8}$

14b. $1\frac{3}{4} - \frac{7}{8}$ 14d. $6\frac{1}{5} - 2\frac{1}{3}$

Requires Renaming	Does Not Require Renaming

15. Mr. Clements painted his barn for $3\frac{3}{5}$ hours in the morning. He painted the barn for $5\frac{3}{4}$ hours in the afternoon. For 15a–15c, select True or False for each statement.

15a. A common denominator of   ○ True   ○ False
      the mixed numbers is 20.

15b. The amount of time spent   ○ True   ○ False
      painting in the morning can be
      rewritten as $3\frac{15}{20}$ hours.

15c. Mr. Clements spent $2\frac{3}{20}$ hours   ○ True   ○ False
      longer painting in the afternoon
      than the morning.

16. Tom exercised $\frac{4}{5}$ hour on Monday and $\frac{5}{6}$ hour on Tuesday.

Part A

Complete the calculations below to write equivalent fractions with a common denominator.

Part B

How much time did Tom spend exercising on Monday and Tuesday combined? Explain how you found your answer.

Part C

How much longer did Tom spend exercising on Tuesday than he spent on Monday? Explain how you found your answer.

© Houghton Mifflin Harcourt Publishing Company

Multiply Fractions

✔ Show What You Know

Personal Math Trainer
Online Assessment and Intervention

Check your understanding of important skills.

Name _____

▶ **Part of a Group** **Write a fraction that names the shaded part.** (3.NF.A.1)

1. shaded parts _____

total parts _____

fraction _____

2. shaded parts _____

total parts _____

fraction _____

▶ **Area** **Write the area of each shape.** (3.MD.C.5)

3. _____ square units

4. _____ square units

5. _____ square units

▶ **Equivalent Fractions** **Write an equivalent fraction.** (4.NF.A.1)

6. $\frac{3}{4}$ _____

7. $\frac{9}{15}$ _____

8. $\frac{24}{40}$ _____

9. $\frac{5}{7}$ _____

Math in the Real World

Carmen recovered 2 gold bars that were stolen from a safe. The first bar weighed $2\frac{2}{5}$ pounds. The second bar weighed $1\frac{2}{3}$ times as much as the first bar. Find out how much gold was recovered.

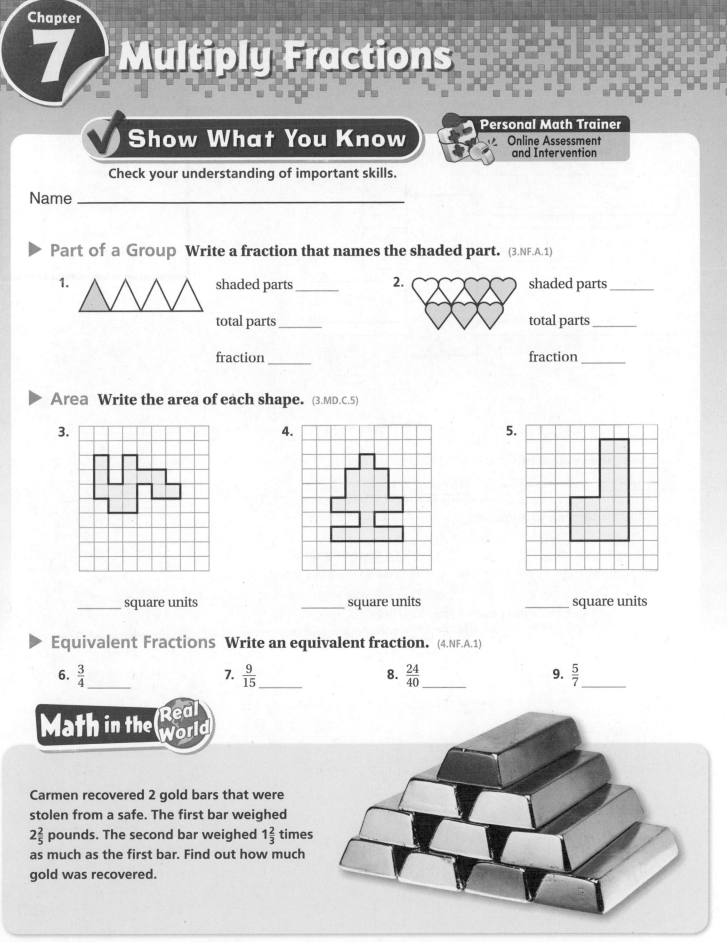

Vocabulary Builder

▶ **Visualize It** •

Match the review words with their examples.

What is it?   **What are some examples?**

_____

→ $\frac{5}{10}$

_____

→ $\frac{5}{10}$

_____

→ $4\frac{1}{5}, 1\frac{3}{8}, 6\frac{3}{6}$

_____

→ $\frac{2}{3}, \frac{4}{6}, \frac{10}{15}$

▶ **Understand Vocabulary** •

Complete the sentences by using the review words.

1. A _____ is a number that is made up of a whole number and a fraction.

2. A fraction is in _____ when the numerator and the denominator have only the number 1 as a common factor.

3. The number below the bar in a fraction that tells how many equal parts are in the whole or in the group is the

   _____.

4. The _____ is the answer to a multiplication problem.

5. Fractions that name the same amount or part are called

   _____.

6. The _____ is the number above the bar in a fraction that tells how many equal parts of the whole are being considered.

GO DIGITAL
• **Interactive Student Edition**
• **Multimedia eGlossary**

common factor factor común 5	**denominator** denominador 15
equivalent fractions fracciones equivalentes 22	**factor** factor 27
mixed number número mixto 40	**numerator** numerador 42
product producto 54	**simplest form** mínima expresión 64

The number below the bar in a fraction that tells how many equal parts are in the whole or in the group.

Example: $\frac{3}{4}$ ← denominator

A number that is a factor of two or more numbers

$$8$$
$$2 \times 2 \times \boxed{2} \leftarrow \text{common factor} \rightarrow \boxed{2} \times 3$$
$$6$$

A number multiplied by another number to find a product.

Example: $46 \times 3 = 138$
$\uparrow \qquad \uparrow$
factor

Fractions that name the same amount or part

Example: $\frac{1}{2}$ and $\frac{4}{8}$ are equivalent.

The number above the bar in a fraction that tells how many equal parts of the whole or group are being considered

Example: $\frac{3}{4}$ ← numerator

A number that is made up of a whole number and a fraction

Example:

whole number part ⟶ $4\frac{1}{2}$ ← fraction part

A fraction is in simplest form when the numerator and denominator have only 1 as a common factor

Examples: $\frac{1}{2}, \frac{2}{3}, \frac{8}{15}$

The answer to a multiplication problem

Example: $3 \times 15 = 45$
$\uparrow$
product

Guess the Word

Word Box

common factor
denominator
equivalent fractions
factor
mixed number
numerators
product
simplest form

For 3 to 4 players

Materials

- timer

How to Play

1. Take turns to play.
2. Choose a math term, but do not say it aloud.
3. Set the timer for 1 minute.
4. Give a one-word clue about your term. Give each player one chance to guess the term.
5. If nobody guesses correctly, repeat Step 4 with a different clue. Repeat until a player guesses the term or time runs out.
6. The player who guesses the term gets 1 point. If he or she can use the term in a sentence, they get 1 more point. Then that player gets a turn.
7. The first player to score 10 points wins.

The Write Way

Reflect

Choose one idea. Write about it.

- Which of the following are equivalent fractions? Tell how you know.

$\frac{3}{6}$ $\frac{3}{15}$ $\frac{9}{15}$ $\frac{9}{18}$

- Write a definition for *common factor* in your own words.

- Explain how to find the product: $\frac{3}{8} \times 24 =$ _____.

- Write a word problem that includes multiplying a fraction by a mixed number.

Find Part of a Group

Essential Question How can you find a fractional part of a group?

Common Core **Number and Operations—Fractions—5.NF.B.4a**

MATHEMATICAL PRACTICES
MP4, MP5, MP6

Unlock the Problem Real World Hands On

▲ The post office cancels stamps to keep them from being reused.

Maya collects stamps. She has 20 stamps in her collection. Four-fifths of her stamps have been canceled. How many of the stamps in Maya's collection have been canceled?

 Find $\frac{4}{5}$ of 20.

- Put 20 counters on your MathBoard.

  Since you want to find $\frac{4}{5}$ of the stamps, you should arrange the 20 counters in _____ equal groups.

- Draw the counters in equal groups below. How many counters are in each group? _____

- Each group represents _____ of the stamps. Circle $\frac{4}{5}$ of the counters.

  How many groups did you circle? _____

  How many counters did you circle? _____

  $\frac{4}{5}$ of 20 = _____, or $\frac{4}{5} \times 20 =$ _____

So, _____ of the stamps have been canceled.

Math Talk

MATHEMATICAL PRACTICES ⑥

Make Connections How many groups would you circle if $\frac{3}{5}$ of the stamps were canceled? Explain.

🔑 Example

Max's stamp collection has stamps from different countries. He has 12 stamps from Canada. Of those twelve, $\frac{2}{3}$ of them have pictures of Queen Elizabeth II. How many stamps have the queen on them?

- Draw an array to represent the 12 stamps by drawing an ✗ for each stamp. Since you want to find $\frac{2}{3}$ of the stamps, your array should

  show _____ rows with an equal number of ✗s.

- Circle _____ of the 3 rows to show $\frac{2}{3}$ of 12.
  Then count the number of ✗s in the circle.

  There are _____ ✗s circled.

- Complete the number sentences.

  $\frac{2}{3}$ of 12 = _____, or $\frac{2}{3} \times 12$ = _____

So, there are _____ stamps with a picture of Queen Elizabeth II.

- **MATHEMATICAL PRACTICE ⑤** **Use Appropriate Tools** On your MathBoard, use counters to find $\frac{4}{6}$ of 12. Explain why the answer is the same as the answer when you found $\frac{2}{3}$ of 12.

_____

_____

Try This! **Draw an array.**

Susana has 16 stamps. In her collection, $\frac{3}{4}$ of the stamps are from the United States. How many of her stamps are from the United States and how many are not?

So, _____ of Susana's stamps are from the United States, and _____ stamps are not.

422

Name _____

1. Complete the model to solve.

$\frac{7}{8}$ of 16, or $\frac{7}{8} \times 16$

• How many rows of counters are there? _____

• How many counters are in each row? _____

• Circle _____ rows to solve the problem.

• How many counters are circled? _____

$\frac{7}{8}$ of 16 = _____, or $\frac{7}{8} \times 16$ = _____

Use a model to solve.

2. $\frac{2}{3} \times 18$ = _____

☑ **3.** $\frac{2}{5} \times 15$ = _____

☑ **4.** $\frac{2}{3} \times 6$ = _____

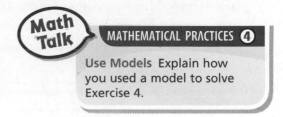

Math Talk MATHEMATICAL PRACTICES ④

Use Models Explain how you used a model to solve Exercise 4.

On Your Own

Use a model to solve.

5. $\frac{5}{8} \times 24$ = _____

6. $\frac{3}{4} \times 24$ = _____

7. $\frac{4}{7} \times 21$ = _____

Solve.

8. MATHEMATICAL PRACTICE ④ Use Diagrams What multiplication problem does the model represent?

_____

Problem Solving • Applications

Use the table for 9–10.

Stamps Collected	
Name	**Number of Stamps**
Zack	30
Teri	18
Paco	24

9. **MATHEMATICAL PRACTICE 4 Use Models** Four-fifths of Zack's stamps have pictures of animals. How many stamps with pictures of animals does Zack have? Use a model to solve.

_____

10. **THINK SMARTER** Zack, Teri, and Paco combined the foreign stamps from their collections for a stamp show. Out of their collections, $\frac{3}{10}$ of Zack's stamps, $\frac{5}{6}$ of Teri's stamps, and $\frac{3}{8}$ of Paco's stamps were from foreign countries. How many stamps were in their display? Explain how you solved the problem.

_____

_____

_____

_____

WRITE ▸ *Math* • **Show Your Work**

11. **GO DEEPER** Paula has 24 stamps in her collection. Among her stamps, $\frac{1}{3}$ have pictures of animals. Out of her stamps with pictures of animals, $\frac{3}{4}$ of those stamps have pictures of birds. How many stamps have pictures of birds on them?

_____

12. **THINK SMARTER** Charlotte bought 16 songs for her MP3 player. Three-fourths of the songs are classical songs. How many of the songs are classical songs? Draw a model to show how you found your answer.

_____

Name _____

Find Part of a Group

COMMON CORE STANDARD—5.NF.B.4a
*Apply and extend previous understandings
of multiplication and division to multiply and
divide fractions.*

Use a model to solve.

1. $\frac{3}{4} \times 12 =$ ___9___

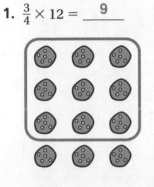

2. $\frac{7}{8} \times 16 =$ _____

3. $\frac{6}{10} \times 10 =$ _____

4. $\frac{2}{3} \times 9 =$ _____

5. $\frac{1}{6} \times 18 =$ _____

6. $\frac{4}{5} \times 10 =$ _____

Problem Solving (Real World)

7. Marco drew 20 pictures. He drew $\frac{3}{4}$ of them in art class. How many pictures did Marco draw in art class?

_____

8. Caroline has 10 marbles. One half of them are blue. How many of Caroline's marbles are blue?

_____

9. **WRITE** ▸*Math* Explain how to find $\frac{3}{4}$ of 20 using a model. Include a drawing.

_____

Chapter 7   425

Lesson Check (5.NF.B.4a)

1. Use the model to find $\frac{1}{3} \times 15$.

○ ○ ○
○ ○ ○
○ ○ ○
○ ○ ○
○ ○ ○

_____

2. Use the model to find $\frac{2}{4} \times 16$.

○ ○ ○ ○
○ ○ ○ ○
○ ○ ○ ○
○ ○ ○ ○

_____

Spiral Review (5.NBT.A.1, 5.NBT.B.6, 5.NF.A.1, 5.NF.A.2)

3. What is the value of the underlined digit?

6,560

_____

4. Nigel has 138 fluid ounces of lemonade. How many 6-fluid-ounce servings of lemonade can he make?

_____

5. Rafi had a board that was $15\frac{1}{2}$ feet long. He cut three pieces off the board that are each $3\frac{7}{8}$ feet long. How much of the board is left?

_____

6. Susie spent $4\frac{1}{4}$ hours on Monday and $3\frac{5}{8}$ hours on Tuesday working on a history project. About how long did she spend working on the project?

_____

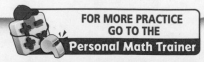
FOR MORE PRACTICE
GO TO THE
Personal Math Trainer

Name _____

Multiply Fractions and Whole Numbers

Essential Question How can you use a model to show the product of a fraction and a whole number?

Common Core
Number and Operations—
Fractions—5.NF.B.4a
MATHEMATICAL PRACTICES
MP4, MP5, MP6

Investigate

Martin is planting a vegetable garden. Each row is 2 meters long. He wants to plant carrots along $\frac{3}{4}$ of each row. How many meters of each row will he plant with carrots?

🔓 **Multiply.** $\frac{3}{4} \times 2$

Materials ■ fraction strips ■ MathBoard

A. Place two 1-whole fraction strips side-by-side to represent the length of each row.

B. To represent the denominator of the factor $\frac{3}{4}$, find 4 fraction strips, all with the same denominator, that fit exactly under the two wholes.

C. Draw a picture of your model.

1	1

D. Circle $\frac{3}{4}$ of 2 on the model you drew.

E. Complete the number sentence. $\frac{3}{4} \times 2 =$ _____

So, Martin will plant carrots along _____ meters of each row.

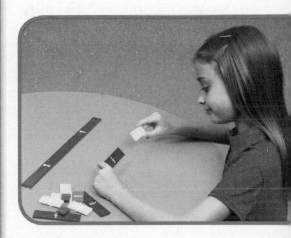

Draw Conclusions

1. **MATHEMATICAL PRACTICE ⑤ Use a Concrete Model** Explain why you placed four fraction strips with the same denominator under the two 1-whole strips.

_____

_____

2. **MATHEMATICAL PRACTICE ⑤ Use a Concrete Model** Explain how you would model $\frac{3}{10}$ of 2.

_____

_____

Make Connections

In the Investigate activity, you multiplied a whole number by a fraction. You can also use a model to multiply a fraction by a whole number.

Margo was helping clean up after a class party. There were 3 boxes remaining with pizza in them. Each box had $\frac{3}{8}$ of a pizza left. How much pizza was left in all?

Materials ■ fraction circles

STEP 1 Find $3 \times \frac{3}{8}$. Model three 1-whole fraction circles to represent the number of boxes containing pizza.

STEP 2 Place $\frac{1}{8}$ fraction circle pieces on each circle to represent the amount of pizza that was left in each box.

- Shade the fraction circles below to show your model.

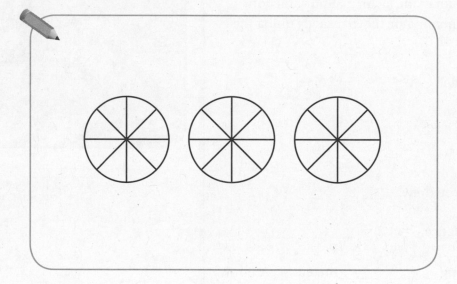

Each circle shows _____ eighths of a whole.

The 3 circles show _____ eighths.

STEP 3 Complete the number sentences.

$$\frac{3}{8} + \frac{3}{8} + \frac{3}{8} = \underline{\hspace{3cm}}$$

$$3 \times \frac{3}{8} = \underline{\hspace{3cm}}$$

So, Margo had _____ pizzas left.

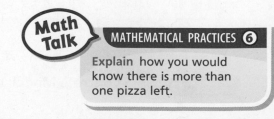

Math Talk

MATHEMATICAL PRACTICES ⑥

Explain how you would know there is more than one pizza left.

Name _____

Use the model to find the product.

1. $\frac{5}{6} \times 3 =$ _____

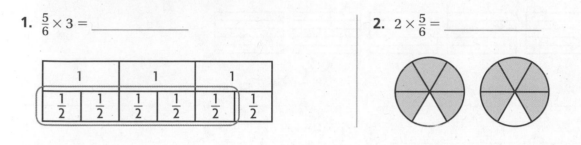

2. $2 \times \frac{5}{6} =$ _____

Find the product.

3. $\frac{5}{12} \times 3 =$ _____

✓ 4. $9 \times \frac{1}{3} =$ _____

✓ 5. $\frac{7}{8} \times 4 =$ _____

Problem Solving • Applications

6. **GO DEEPER** Eliza brought 3 pans of homemade fruit bars to school. Her classmates ate $\frac{7}{12}$ of each pan. Eliza gave 1 whole pan of the leftover fruit bars to the school's secretaries and took the rest home. Explain how to find how much of a pan of fruit bars Eliza took home.

_____

_____

_____

7. **THINK SMARTER** Tracy is cleaning up after tiling a bathroom. There are 4 open boxes of tile. Each box has $\frac{5}{8}$ of the tiles remaining. How many boxes of tile are left? Shade the model and complete the calculations below to show how you found your answer.

$4 \times \frac{5}{8} = \dfrac{\boxed{}}{8} =$ _____ boxes of tile

8. **MATHEMATICAL PRACTICE 4** **Use Models** Tarique drew the model below for a problem. Write 2 problems that can be solved using this model. One of your problems should involve multiplying a whole number by a fraction, and the other problem should involve multiplying a fraction by a whole number.

Pose problems.

Solve your problems.

9. **THINK SMARTER** How could you change the model to give you an answer of $4\frac{4}{5}$? Explain and write a new equation.

Multiply Fractions and Whole Numbers

COMMON CORE STANDARD—5.NF.B.4a
*Apply and extend previous understandings
of multiplication and division to multiply
and divide fractions.*

Use the model to find the product.

1. $\frac{5}{12} \times 3 =$ ___$\frac{5}{4}$, or $1\frac{1}{4}$___

1	1	1
$\frac{1}{4}$ $\frac{1}{4}$ $\frac{1}{4}$ $\frac{1}{4}$	$\frac{1}{4}$ $\frac{1}{4}$ $\frac{1}{4}$ $\frac{1}{4}$	$\frac{1}{4}$ $\frac{1}{4}$ $\frac{1}{4}$ $\frac{1}{4}$

2. $3 \times \frac{3}{4} =$ _____

Find the product.

3. $\frac{2}{5} \times 5 =$ _____

4. $7 \times \frac{2}{3} =$ _____

5. $\frac{3}{8} \times 4 =$ _____

6. $7 \times \frac{5}{6} =$ _____

7. $\frac{5}{12} \times 6 =$ _____

8. $9 \times \frac{2}{3} =$ _____

Problem Solving (Real World)

9. Jody has a 5-pound bag of potatoes. She uses $\frac{4}{5}$ of
the bag to make potato salad. How many pounds
of potatoes does Jody use for the potato salad?

10. Lucas lives $\frac{5}{8}$ mile from school. Kenny lives twice
as far as Lucas from school. How many miles
does Kenny live from school?

11. **WRITE** ▸*Math* Explain how to use models to find $3 \times \frac{3}{4}$ and $\frac{3}{4} \times 3$.
Include a picture of each model.

_____

Lesson Check (5.NF.B.4a)

1. In gym class, Ted runs $\frac{4}{5}$ mile. His teacher runs 6 times that distance each day. How many miles does Ted's teacher run each day?

_____

2. Jon is decorating a banner for a parade. Jon uses a piece of red ribbon, which is $\frac{3}{4}$ yard long. Jon also needs blue ribbon that is 5 times as long as the red ribbon. How much blue ribbon does Jon need?

_____

Spiral Review (5.OA.A.1, 5.NBT.A.3b, 5.NF.A.2, 5.NF.B.3)

3. Mirror Lake Elementary School has 168 students and chaperones going on the fifth grade class trip. Each bus can hold 54 people. What is the least number of buses needed for the trip?

_____

4. From an 8-foot board, a carpenter sawed off one piece that was $2\frac{3}{4}$ feet long and another piece that was $3\frac{1}{2}$ feet long. How much of the board was left?

_____

5. What is the value of the expression?

$$30 - 5 \times 4 + 2$$

_____

6. Which of the following decimals has the least value? 0.3; 0.029; 0.003; 0.01

_____

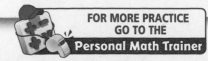

FOR MORE PRACTICE
GO TO THE
Personal Math Trainer

Fraction and Whole Number Multiplication

Common Core **Number and Operations— Fractions—5.NF.B.4a**
MATHEMATICAL PRACTICES
MP2, MP5, MP6

Essential Question How can you find the product of a fraction and a whole number without using a model?

Unlock the Problem Real World

Charlene has five 1-pound bags of sand, each a different color. For an art project, she will use $\frac{3}{8}$ pound of each bag of sand to create a colorful sand-art jar. How much sand will be in Charlene's sand-art jar?

- How much sand is in each bag?

  _____

- Will Charlene use all of the sand in each bag? Explain.

  _____

Multiply a fraction by a whole number.

MODEL	RECORD

- Shade the model to show 5 groups of $\frac{3}{8}$.

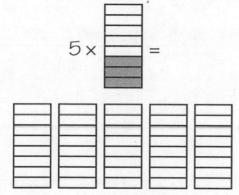

$5 \times$ ▭ $=$

- Rearrange the shaded pieces to fill as many wholes as possible.

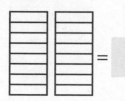

- Write an expression to represent the problem.

  $5 \times \dfrac{3}{8}$ **Think:** I need to find 5 groups of 3 eighth-size pieces.

- Multiply the number of eighth-size pieces in each whole by 5. Then write the answer as the total number of eighth-size pieces.

  $$\frac{ \times }{8} = \frac{}{}$$

- Write the answer as a mixed number in simplest form.

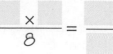

So, there are _____ pounds of sand in Charlene's sand-art jar.

Math Talk MATHEMATICAL PRACTICES ⑤
Communicate Explain how you can find how much sand Charlene has left.

🔓 Example Multiply a whole number by a fraction.

Kirsten brought in 4 loaves of sliced bread to make sandwiches for the class picnic. Her classmates used $\frac{2}{3}$ of the bread. How many loaves of bread were used?

MODEL

- Shade the model to show $\frac{2}{3}$ of 4.

Think: I can cut the loaves into thirds and show $\frac{2}{3}$ of them being used.

- Rearrange the shaded pieces to fill as many wholes as possible.

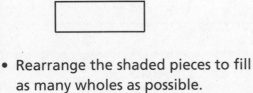

RECORD

- Write an expression to represent the problem.

$$\frac{2}{3} \times 4$$

Think: I need to find $\frac{2}{3}$ of 4 wholes.

- Multiply 4 by the number of third-size pieces in each whole. Then, write the answer as the total number of third-size pieces.

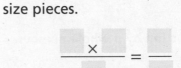

- Write the answer as a mixed number.

So, _____ loaves of bread were used.

- **MATHEMATICAL PRACTICE ⑥** Would we have the same amount of bread if we had 4 groups of $\frac{2}{3}$ of a loaf? **Explain.**

Try This! Find the product. Write the product in simplest form.

Ⓐ $4 \times \frac{7}{8}$

Ⓑ $\frac{5}{9} \times 12$

Name _____

Find the product. Write the product in simplest form.

1. $3 \times \frac{2}{5} =$ _____

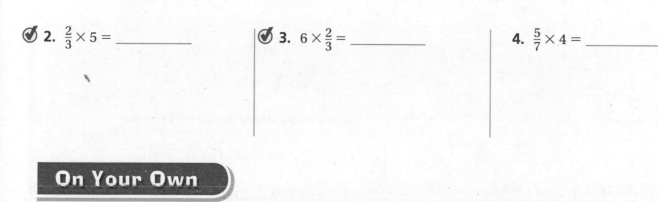

   - Multiply the numerator by the whole number. Write the product over the denominator.

   - Write the answer as a mixed number in simplest form.

☑ 2. $\frac{2}{3} \times 5 =$ _____   ☑ 3. $6 \times \frac{2}{3} =$ _____   4. $\frac{5}{7} \times 4 =$ _____

On Your Own

Practice: Copy and Solve Find the product. Write the product in simplest form.

5. $\frac{3}{5} \times 11$ 6. $3 \times \frac{3}{4}$ 7. $\frac{5}{8} \times 3$

MATHEMATICAL PRACTICE ② Use Reasoning **Algebra** Find the unknown digit.

8. $\frac{\blacksquare}{2} \times 8 = 4$ 9. $\blacksquare \times \frac{5}{6} = \frac{20}{6}$, or $3\frac{1}{3}$ 10. $\frac{1}{\blacksquare} \times 18 = 3$

   $\blacksquare =$ _____ $\blacksquare =$ _____ $\blacksquare =$ _____

11. **THINK SMARTER** Patty wants to run $\frac{5}{6}$ of a mile every day for 5 days. Keisha wants to run $\frac{3}{4}$ of a mile every day for 6 days. Who will run the greater distance?

   _____

12. **GO DEEPER** A baker made 5 pounds of dough. He used $\frac{4}{9}$ of the dough to make sandwich rolls. How much of the dough is left over?

   _____

Unlock the Problem (Real World)

13. A caterer wants to have enough turkey to feed 24 people. If he wants to provide $\frac{3}{4}$ of a pound of turkey for each person, how much turkey does he need?

a. What do you need to find? _____

_____

b. What operation will you use? _____

c. What information are you given? _____

_____

d. Solve the problem.

e. Complete the sentences.

The caterer wants to serve 24 people

_____ of a pound of turkey each.

He will need _____ × _____, or

_____ pounds of turkey.

Personal Math Trainer

14. **THINK SMARTER +** Julie is using this recipe to make salad dressing. The recipe makes 1 batch of dressing. She plans to make 5 batches of the dressing. She has 4 cups of vegetable oil.

Write a multiplication expression to show how much vegetable oil is needed for 5 batches.

_____

Does Julie have enough vegetable oil for 5 batches of the salad dressing? Explain your reasoning.

_____

_____

Salad Dressing
$1\frac{1}{2}$ teaspoons paprika
1 teaspoon dry mustard
$1\frac{1}{2}$ teaspoons salt
$\frac{1}{8}$ teaspoon onion powder
$\frac{3}{4}$ cup vegetable oil
$\frac{1}{4}$ cup vinegar

Fraction and Whole Number Multiplication

Common Core | **COMMON CORE STANDARD—5.NF.B.4a**
Apply and extend previous understandings of multiplication and division to multiply and divide fractions.

Find the product. Write the product in simplest form.

1. $4 \times \frac{5}{8} =$ _____ $2\frac{1}{2}$ _____

   $4 \times \frac{5}{8} = \frac{20}{8}$

   $\frac{20}{8} = 2\frac{4}{8}$, or $2\frac{1}{2}$

2. $\frac{2}{9} \times 3 =$ _____

3. $\frac{4}{5} \times 10 =$ _____

4. $\frac{3}{4} \times 9 =$ _____

5. $8 \times \frac{5}{6} =$ _____

6. $7 \times \frac{1}{2} =$ _____

7. $\frac{2}{5} \times 6 =$ _____

8. $9 \times \frac{2}{3} =$ _____

9. $\frac{3}{10} \times 9 =$ _____

Problem Solving Real World

10. Leah makes aprons to sell at a craft fair. She needs $\frac{3}{4}$ yard of material to make each apron. How much material does Leah need to make 6 aprons?

    _____

11. The gas tank of Mr. Tanaka's car holds 15 gallons of gas. He used $\frac{2}{3}$ of a tank of gas last week. How many gallons of gas did Mr. Tanaka use?

    _____

12. **WRITE** ▸*Math* Write a word problem that can be solved by multiplying a whole number and a fraction. Include the solution.

    _____

Lesson Check (5.NF.B.4a)

1. At the movies, Liz eats $\frac{1}{4}$ of a box of popcorn. Her friend Kyra eats two times as much popcorn as Liz eats. How much of a box of popcorn does Kyra eat?

2. It takes Ed 45 minutes to complete his science homework. It takes him $\frac{2}{3}$ as long to complete his math homework. How long does it take Ed to complete his math homework?

Spiral Review (5.NBT.A.2, 5.NBT.B.7, 5.NF.A.1, 5.NF.A.2)

3. What is the best estimate for the quotient?

$$591.3 \div 29$$

4. Sandy bought $\frac{3}{4}$ yard of red ribbon and $\frac{2}{3}$ yard of white ribbon to make some hair bows. Altogether, how many yards of ribbon did she buy?

5. Eric jogged $3\frac{1}{4}$ miles on Monday, $5\frac{5}{8}$ miles on Tuesday, and 8 miles on Wednesday. Suppose he continues the pattern for the remainder of the week. How far will Eric jog on Friday?

6. Sharon bought 25 pounds of ground beef and made 100 hamburger patties of equal weight. What is the weight of each hamburger patty?

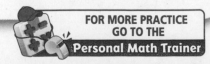

FOR MORE PRACTICE
GO TO THE
Personal Math Trainer

Multiply Fractions

Essential Question How can you use an area model to show the product of two fractions?

Number and Operations—Fractions—5.NF.B.4a, 5.NF.B.4b

MATHEMATICAL PRACTICES
MP1, MP3, MP5

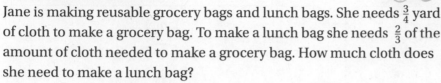

Investigate

Jane is making reusable grocery bags and lunch bags. She needs $\frac{3}{4}$ yard of cloth to make a grocery bag. To make a lunch bag she needs $\frac{2}{3}$ of the amount of cloth needed to make a grocery bag. How much cloth does she need to make a lunch bag?

Find $\frac{2}{3}$ of $\frac{3}{4}$. **Materials** ■ color pencils

A. Fold a sheet of paper vertically into 4 equal parts. Using the vertical folds as a guide, shade $\frac{3}{4}$ yellow.

B. Fold the paper horizontally into 3 equal parts. Using the horizontal folds as a guide, shade $\frac{2}{3}$ of the yellow sections blue.

C. Count the number of sections into which the whole sheet of paper is folded.

  • How many rectangles are formed by all

    the folds in the paper? _____

  • What fraction of the whole sheet of paper

    does one rectangle represent? _____

D. Count the sections that are shaded twice and record

  the answer. $\frac{2}{3} \times \frac{3}{4} =$ _____

So, Jane needs _____ yard of cloth to make a lunch bag.

Draw Conclusions

1. Explain why you shaded $\frac{2}{3}$ of the yellow sections blue rather than shading $\frac{2}{3}$ of the whole.

_____

_____

2. **MATHEMATICAL PRACTICE ①** **Analyze** what you are finding if a model shows $\frac{1}{2}$ of a sheet of paper shaded yellow and $\frac{1}{3}$ of the yellow section shaded blue.

_____

Make Connections

You can find a part of a part in different ways. Marguerite and James both correctly solved the problem $\frac{1}{3} \times \frac{3}{4}$ using the steps shown.

Use the steps to show how each person found $\frac{1}{3} \times \frac{3}{4}$.

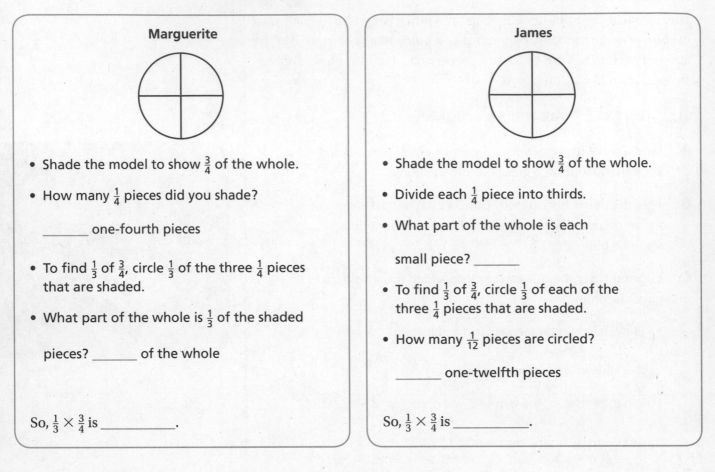

Marguerite

- Shade the model to show $\frac{3}{4}$ of the whole.

- How many $\frac{1}{4}$ pieces did you shade?

  _____ one-fourth pieces

- To find $\frac{1}{3}$ of $\frac{3}{4}$, circle $\frac{1}{3}$ of the three $\frac{1}{4}$ pieces that are shaded.

- What part of the whole is $\frac{1}{3}$ of the shaded

  pieces? _____ of the whole

So, $\frac{1}{3} \times \frac{3}{4}$ is _____.

James

- Shade the model to show $\frac{3}{4}$ of the whole.

- Divide each $\frac{1}{4}$ piece into thirds.

- What part of the whole is each

  small piece? _____

- To find $\frac{1}{3}$ of $\frac{3}{4}$, circle $\frac{1}{3}$ of each of the three $\frac{1}{4}$ pieces that are shaded.

- How many $\frac{1}{12}$ pieces are circled?

  _____ one-twelfth pieces

So, $\frac{1}{3} \times \frac{3}{4}$ is _____.

- **Pose a Problem** that can be solved using the equation above.

_____

_____

Share and Show

Use the model or *i*Tools to find the product.

1.

$\frac{3}{5} \times \frac{1}{3} =$ _____

2.

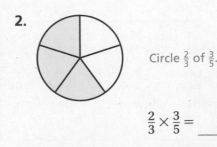

Circle $\frac{2}{3}$ of $\frac{3}{5}$.

$\frac{2}{3} \times \frac{3}{5} =$ _____

440

Name _____

Find the product. Draw a model.

✓ **3.** $\frac{2}{3} \times \frac{1}{5} =$ _____

✓ **4.** $\frac{1}{2} \times \frac{5}{6} =$ _____

5. $\frac{3}{5} \times \frac{1}{3} =$ _____

6. $\frac{3}{4} \times \frac{1}{6} =$ _____

Problem Solving • Applications

7. 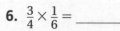 **Evaluate Reasonableness** Ricardo's recipe for 4 loaves of bread requires $\frac{2}{3}$ cup of olive oil. He only wants to make 1 loaf. Ricardo makes a model to find out how much oil he needs to use. He folds a piece of paper into three parts and shades two parts. Then he folds the paper into four parts and shades $\frac{1}{4}$ of the shaded part. Ricardo decides he needs $\frac{1}{4}$ cup of olive oil. Is he right? Explain.

_____

_____

_____

8. **GO DEEPER** Three-fourths of a spinach casserole is leftover after Sam has lunch. Jackie and Alicia each take $\frac{1}{2}$ of the leftover casserole. Jackie eats only $\frac{2}{3}$ of her portion. What fraction of a whole casserole did Jackie eat? Draw a model.

_____

THINK SMARTER **What's the Error?**

9. Cheryl and Marcus are going to make 2 batches of muffins. The smaller batch is $\frac{2}{3}$ the size of the larger batch. The recipe for the larger batch requires $\frac{3}{5}$ cup of water. How much water will they need to make the smaller batch?

They made a model to represent the problem. Cheryl says they need $\frac{6}{9}$ cup of water. Marcus says they need $\frac{2}{5}$ cup of water. Who is correct? Explain.

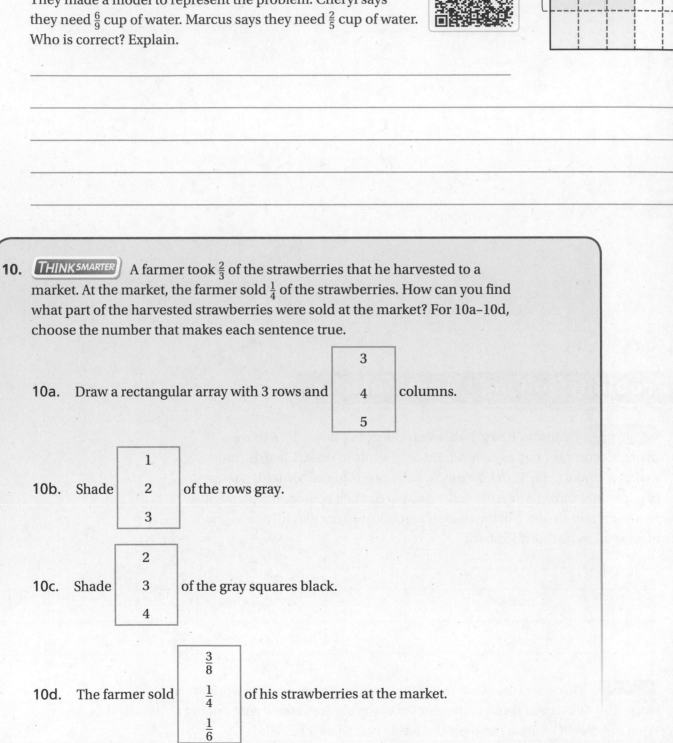

_____

_____

_____

_____

_____

10. **THINK SMARTER** A farmer took $\frac{2}{3}$ of the strawberries that he harvested to a market. At the market, the farmer sold $\frac{1}{4}$ of the strawberries. How can you find what part of the harvested strawberries were sold at the market? For 10a–10d, choose the number that makes each sentence true.

10a.   Draw a rectangular array with 3 rows and [3 / 4 / 5] columns.

10b.   Shade [1 / 2 / 3] of the rows gray.

10c.   Shade [2 / 3 / 4] of the gray squares black.

10d.   The farmer sold [$\frac{3}{8}$ / $\frac{1}{4}$ / $\frac{1}{6}$] of his strawberries at the market.

Multiply Fractions

Common Core
COMMON CORE STANDARD—5.NF.B.4b
Apply and extend previous understandings of multiplication and division to multiply and divide fractions.

Find the product.

1.

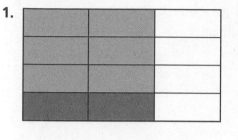

$\frac{1}{4} \times \frac{2}{3} =$ _____ $\frac{2}{12}$, or $\frac{1}{6}$

2.

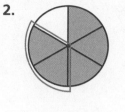

$\frac{2}{5} \times \frac{5}{6} =$ _____

Find the product. Draw a model.

3. $\frac{4}{5} \times \frac{1}{2} =$ _____

4. $\frac{3}{4} \times \frac{1}{3} =$ _____

5. $\frac{3}{8} \times \frac{2}{3} =$ _____

6. $\frac{3}{5} \times \frac{3}{5} =$ _____

Problem Solving Real World

7. Nora has a piece of ribbon that is $\frac{3}{4}$ yard long. She will use $\frac{1}{2}$ of it to make a bow. What length of the ribbon will she use for the bow?

8. Marlon bought $\frac{7}{8}$ pound of turkey at the deli. He used $\frac{2}{3}$ of it to make sandwiches for lunch. How much of the turkey did Marlon use for sandwiches?

Lesson Check (5.NF.B.4b)

1. Tina has $\frac{3}{5}$ pound of rice. She will use $\frac{2}{3}$ of it to make fried rice for her family. How much rice will Tina use to make fried rice?

2. The Waterfall Trail is $\frac{3}{4}$ mile long. At $\frac{1}{6}$ of the distance from the trailhead, there is a lookout. In miles, how far is the lookout from the trailhead?

Spiral Review (5.OA.A.1, 5.NF.A.1, 5.NF.A.2, 5.NF.B.4a)

3. Hayden bought 48 new trading cards. Three-fourths of the new cards are baseball cards. How many baseball cards did Hayden buy?

4. Yesterday, Annie walked $\frac{9}{10}$ mile to her friend's house. Together, they walked $\frac{1}{3}$ mile to the library. Which is the best estimate for how far Annie walked yesterday?

5. Erin is going to sew a jacket and a skirt. She needs $2\frac{3}{4}$ yards of material for the jacket and $1\frac{1}{2}$ yards of material for the skirt. Altogether, how many yards of material does Erin need?

6. Simplify the following expression.

$$[(3 \times 6) + (5 \times 2)] \div 7$$

© Houghton Mifflin Harcourt Publishing Company

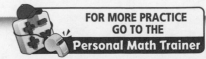

FOR MORE PRACTICE
GO TO THE
Personal Math Trainer

Name _____

Compare Fraction Factors and Products

Essential Question How does the size of the product compare to the size of one factor when multiplying fractions?

Common Core

Number and Operations— Fractions—5.NF.B.5a, 5.NF.B.5b

MATHEMATICAL PRACTICES
MP2, MP3, MP6

Unlock the Problem

Multiplication can be thought of as resizing one number by another number. For example, 2×3 will result in a product that is 2 times as great as 3.

What happens to the size of a product when a number is multiplied by a fraction rather than a whole number?

One Way Use a model.

A During the week, the Delgado family ate $\frac{3}{4}$ of a box of cereal.

- Shade the model to show $\frac{3}{4}$ of a box of cereal.

- Write an expression for $\frac{3}{4}$ of 1 box of cereal. $\frac{3}{4} \times$ _____

- Will the product be *equal to, greater than,* or *less than* 1?

_____

B The Ling family has 4 boxes of cereal. They ate $\frac{3}{4}$ of all the cereal during the week.

- Shade the model to show $\frac{3}{4}$ of 4 boxes of cereal.

- Write an expression for $\frac{3}{4}$ of 4 boxes of cereal. $\frac{3}{4} \times$ _____

- Will the product be *equal to, greater than,* or *less than* 4?

_____

C The Carter family has only $\frac{1}{2}$ of a box of cereal at the beginning of the week. They ate $\frac{3}{4}$ of the $\frac{1}{2}$ box of cereal.

- Shade the model to show $\frac{3}{4}$ of $\frac{1}{2}$ box of cereal.

- Write an expression to show $\frac{3}{4}$ of $\frac{1}{2}$ box of cereal. $\frac{3}{4} \times$ _____

- Will the product be *equal to, greater than,* or *less than* $\frac{1}{2}$? *than* $\frac{3}{4}$?

_____

🔑 Another Way Use a diagram.

You can use a diagram to show the relationship between the products when a fraction is multiplied or scaled (resized) by a number.

Graph a point to show $\frac{3}{4}$ scaled by 1, $\frac{1}{2}$, and 4.

Ⓐ $1 \times \frac{3}{4}$

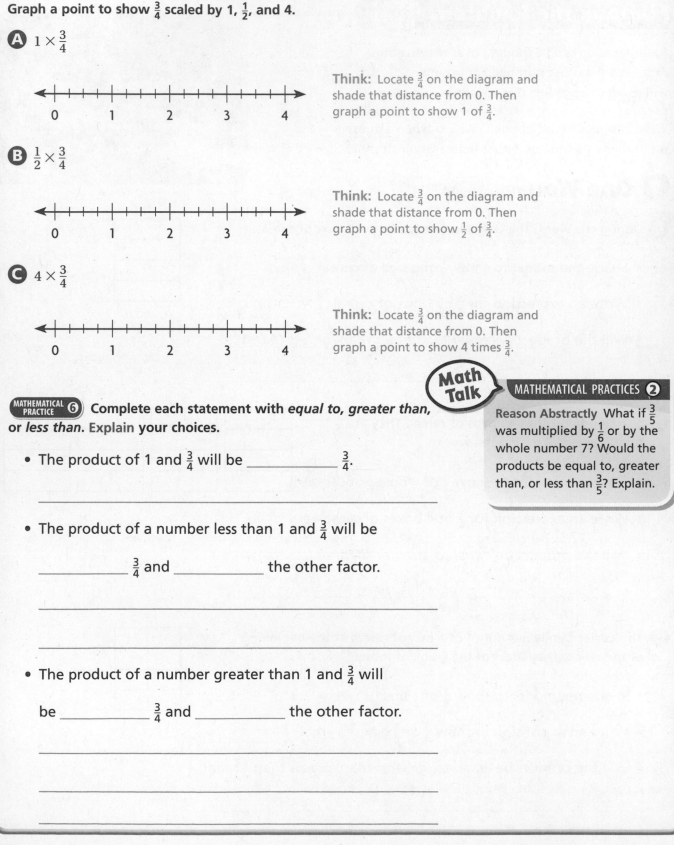

Think: Locate $\frac{3}{4}$ on the diagram and shade that distance from 0. Then graph a point to show 1 of $\frac{3}{4}$.

Ⓑ $\frac{1}{2} \times \frac{3}{4}$

Think: Locate $\frac{3}{4}$ on the diagram and shade that distance from 0. Then graph a point to show $\frac{1}{2}$ of $\frac{3}{4}$.

Ⓒ $4 \times \frac{3}{4}$

Think: Locate $\frac{3}{4}$ on the diagram and shade that distance from 0. Then graph a point to show 4 times $\frac{3}{4}$.

MATHEMATICAL PRACTICE ⑥ Complete each statement with *equal to*, *greater than*, or *less than*. **Explain** your choices.

- The product of 1 and $\frac{3}{4}$ will be _____ $\frac{3}{4}$.

  _____

- The product of a number less than 1 and $\frac{3}{4}$ will be

  _____ $\frac{3}{4}$ and _____ the other factor.

  _____

  _____

- The product of a number greater than 1 and $\frac{3}{4}$ will

  be _____ $\frac{3}{4}$ and _____ the other factor.

  _____

  _____

Math Talk

MATHEMATICAL PRACTICES ②

Reason Abstractly What if $\frac{3}{5}$ was multiplied by $\frac{1}{6}$ or by the whole number 7? Would the products be equal to, greater than, or less than $\frac{3}{5}$? Explain.

Name _____

Share and Show MATH BOARD

Complete the statement with *equal to, greater than,* or *less than.*

1. $4 \times \frac{7}{8}$ will be _____ $\frac{7}{8}$.

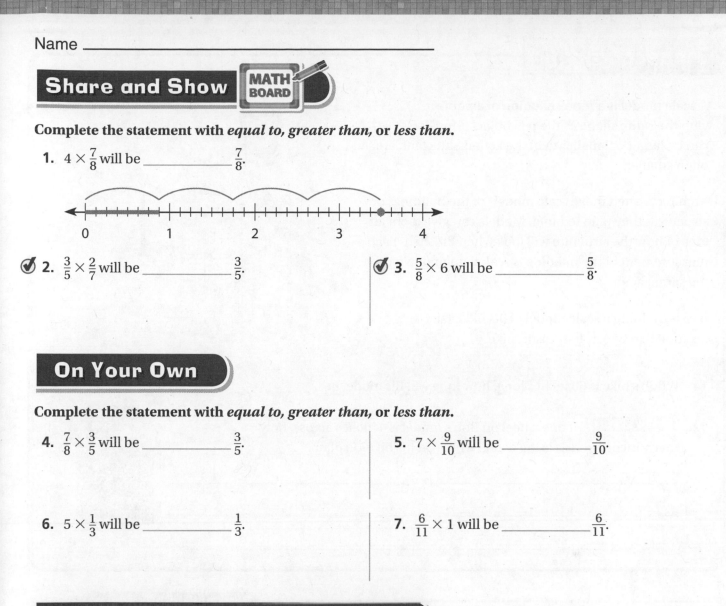

2. $\frac{3}{5} \times \frac{2}{7}$ will be _____ $\frac{3}{5}$.

3. $\frac{5}{8} \times 6$ will be _____ $\frac{5}{8}$.

On Your Own

Complete the statement with *equal to, greater than,* or *less than.*

4. $\frac{7}{8} \times \frac{3}{5}$ will be _____ $\frac{3}{5}$.

5. $7 \times \frac{9}{10}$ will be _____ $\frac{9}{10}$.

6. $5 \times \frac{1}{3}$ will be _____ $\frac{1}{3}$.

7. $\frac{6}{11} \times 1$ will be _____ $\frac{6}{11}$.

Problem Solving • Applications

8. Peter is planning on spending $\frac{2}{3}$ as many hours watching television this week as he did last week. Is Peter going to spend more hours or fewer hours watching television this week?

_____

9. **GO DEEPER** Mrs. Rodriguez has 18 packages of pens in stock at her store on Monday. On Tuesday, she has $\frac{5}{6}$ the number of pens she had on Monday. On Wednesday, she has $\frac{2}{5}$ of the number of pens she had on Tuesday. How many packages of pens does she have on Wednesday?

_____

10. **MATHEMATICAL PRACTICE ②** **Represent a Problem** Ariel goes running for $\frac{5}{6}$ of an hour. The next day, she runs for $\frac{3}{4}$ as much time. Does she spend more or less time running the second day? Draw a diagram or make a model to represent the problem.

_____

Connect to Art

A scale model is a representation of an object with the same shape as the real object. Models can be larger or smaller than the actual object but are often smaller.

Architects often make scale models of the buildings or structures they plan to build. Models can give them an idea of how the structure will look when finished. Each measurement of the building is scaled up or down by the same factor.

Bob is building a scale model of his bike. He wants his model to be $\frac{1}{5}$ as long as his bike.

11. If Bob's bike is 60 inches long, how long will his model be? _____

12. **THINK SMARTER** If one wheel on Bob's model is 4 inches across, how many inches across is the actual wheel on his bike? Explain.

_____

_____

_____

Personal Math Trainer

13. **THINK SMARTER +** Write each multiplication expression in the correct box.

$\frac{5}{6} \times \frac{2}{3}$ $2 \times \frac{5}{6}$ $\frac{5}{6} \times \frac{4}{4}$ $\frac{5}{6} \times \frac{7}{3}$ $\frac{10}{10} \times \frac{5}{6}$ $\frac{5}{6} \times \frac{5}{6}$

Product is equal to $\frac{5}{6}$.	Product is greater than $\frac{5}{6}$.	Product is less than $\frac{5}{6}$.

Compare Fraction Factors and Products

COMMON CORE STANDARD—5.NF.B.5a,
5.NF.B.5b Apply and extend previous understandings of multiplication and division to multiply and divide fractions.

Complete the statement with *equal to*, *greater than*, **or** *less than*.

1. $\frac{3}{5} \times \frac{4}{7}$ will be ___**less than**___ $\frac{4}{7}$.

Think: $\frac{4}{7}$ is multiplied by a number less than 1;

so, $\frac{3}{5} \times \frac{4}{7}$ will be less than $\frac{4}{7}$.

2. $5 \times \frac{7}{8}$ will be _____ $\frac{7}{8}$.

3. $6 \times \frac{2}{5}$ will be _____ $\frac{2}{5}$.

4. $\frac{1}{9} \times 1$ will be _____ $\frac{1}{9}$.

5. $\frac{4}{9} \times \frac{3}{8}$ will be _____ $\frac{3}{8}$.

6. $\frac{4}{5} \times \frac{7}{7}$ will be _____ $\frac{4}{5}$.

Problem Solving · Real World

7. Starla is making hot cocoa. She plans to multiply the recipe by 4 to make enough hot cocoa for the whole class. If the recipe calls for $\frac{1}{2}$ teaspoon vanilla extract, will she need more than $\frac{1}{2}$ teaspoon or less than $\frac{1}{2}$ teaspoon of vanilla extract to make all the hot cocoa?

_____

8. Miles is planning to spend $\frac{2}{3}$ as many hours bicycling this week as he did last week. Is Miles going to spend more hours or fewer hours bicycling this week than last week?

_____

9. **WRITE** *Math* Explain how you can compare the size of a product to the size of a factor when multiplying fractions without actually doing the multiplication. Include a model.

_____

Lesson Check (5.NF.B.5a, 5.NF.B.5b)

1. Trevor saves $\frac{2}{3}$ of the money he earns at his after-school job. Suppose Trevor starts saving $\frac{1}{4}$ as much as he is saving now. Will he be saving less, more, or the same amount?

_____

_____

2. Suppose you multiply a whole number greater than 1 by the fraction $\frac{3}{5}$. Will the product be greater than, less than, or equal to $\frac{3}{5}$?

_____

_____

Spiral Review (5.NBT.B.6, 5.NBT.B.7, 5.NF.A.1)

3. In the next 10 months, Colin wants to save $900 for his vacation. He plans to save $75 each of the first 8 months. How much must he save each of the last 2 months in order to meet his goal if he saves the same amount each month?

_____

4. What is the total cost of 0.5 pound of peaches selling for $0.80 per pound and 0.7 pound of oranges selling for $0.90 per pound?

_____

5. Megan hiked 15.12 miles in 6.3 hours. If Megan hiked the same number of miles each hour, how many miles did she hike each hour?

_____

6. It is $42\frac{1}{2}$ miles from Eaton to Baxter, and $37\frac{4}{5}$ miles from Baxter to Wellington. How far is it from Eaton to Wellington, if you go by way of Baxter?

_____

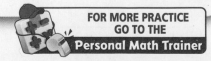

FOR MORE PRACTICE
GO TO THE
Personal Math Trainer

Fraction Multiplication

Essential Question How do you multiply fractions?

 Common Core Number and Operations—
Fractions—5.NF.B.4a, 5.NF.B.5b
Also 5.NF.B.5a
MATHEMATICAL PRACTICES
MP1, MP2, MP3, MP6

Unlock the Problem Real World

Sasha has $\frac{3}{5}$ of a scarf left to knit. If she finishes $\frac{1}{2}$ of that today, how much of the scarf will Sasha knit today?

Multiply. $\frac{1}{2} \times \frac{3}{5}$

One Way Use a model.

- Shade $\frac{3}{5}$ of the model yellow.

- Draw a horizontal line across the rectangle to show 2 equal parts.

- Shade $\frac{1}{2}$ of the yellow sections blue.

- Count the sections that are shaded twice and write a fraction for the parts of the whole that are shaded twice.

$$\frac{1}{2} \times \frac{3}{5} = _____$$

- Compare the numerator and denominator of the product with the numerators and denominators of the factors. **Describe** what you notice.

_____

_____

_____

- How much of the scarf does Sasha have left to knit?

_____

- Of the fraction that is left, how much will she finish today?

_____

Another Way Use paper and pencil.

You can multiply fractions without using a model.

- Multiply the numerators.

- Multiply the denominators.

$$\frac{1}{2} \times \frac{3}{5} = \frac{1 \times \boxed{}}{2 \times \boxed{}}$$

$$= \frac{\boxed{}}{\boxed{}}$$

So, Sasha will knit _____ of the scarf today.

CONNECT Remember you can write a whole number as a fraction with a denominator of 1.

🔒 Example

Find $4 \times \frac{5}{12}$. Write the product in simplest form.

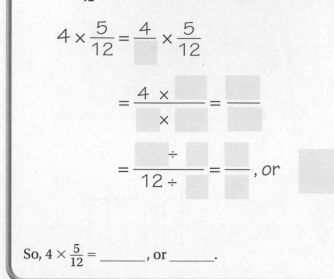

$$4 \times \frac{5}{12} = \frac{4}{\square} \times \frac{5}{12}$$
Write the whole number as a fraction.

$$= \frac{4 \times \square}{\square \times \square} = \frac{\square}{\square}$$
Multiply the numerators.
Multiply the denominators.

$$= \frac{\square \div \square}{12 \div \square} = \frac{\square}{\square}, \text{ or } \square$$
Write the product as a fraction or a mixed number in simplest form.

So, $4 \times \frac{5}{12} = $ _____, or _____.

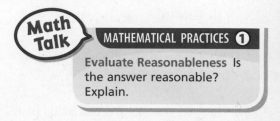

Math Talk

MATHEMATICAL PRACTICES ❶

Evaluate Reasonableness Is the answer reasonable? Explain.

Try This! Evaluate $c \times \frac{4}{5}$ for $c = \frac{2}{2}$.

- What is another way to write the value of c? _____

- What happens when you multiply a whole number by 1?

  _____

- Replace c in the expression with _____.

- Multiply the numerators.

- Multiply the denominators.

- What do you notice about the product?

  _____

So, multiplying $c \times \frac{4}{5}$ is equal to _____ when $c = \frac{2}{2}$.

$$\frac{\square}{\square} \times \frac{4}{5}$$

$$\frac{\square \times \square}{\square \times \square} = \frac{\square}{\square}$$

$$\frac{\square}{\square} = \frac{\square}{\square}$$

- **MATHEMATICAL PRACTICE ❸ Use Reasoning** Will you get the same result if you multiply $\frac{4}{5}$ by any fraction with a numerator and denominator that are the same digit? Explain.

  _____

  _____

Name _____

Find the product. Write the product in simplest form.

1. $6 \times \frac{3}{8}$

$$\frac{6}{1} \times \frac{3}{8} = \frac{18}{8}$$

2. $\frac{3}{8} \times \frac{8}{9}$

$$\frac{1}{6} \leftarrow \frac{24}{72}$$

3. $\frac{2}{3} \times 27$

$$\begin{array}{r} 2 \\ 27 \\ 27 \\ +27 \\ \hline 81 \end{array}$$

$$26 \frac{54}{81}$$

4. $\frac{5}{12} \times \frac{3}{5}$

$$\frac{1}{4} = \frac{15}{60}$$

$$\begin{array}{r} 2 \\ 15 \\ 15 \\ 15 \\ +15 \\ \hline 60 \end{array}$$

5. $\frac{1}{2} \times \frac{3}{5}$

$$\frac{3}{10}$$

6. $\frac{2}{3} \times \frac{4}{5}$

$$\frac{8}{15}$$

7. $\frac{1}{3} \times \frac{5}{8}$

$$\frac{5}{24}$$

8. $4 \times \frac{1}{5}$

$$3\frac{1}{4} = 3\frac{4}{20}$$

Math Talk — MATHEMATICAL PRACTICES 6

Explain how to find the product $\frac{1}{6} \times \frac{2}{3}$ in simplest form.

On Your Own

Find the product. Write the product in simplest form.

9. $2 \times \frac{1}{8}$

$$\frac{1}{?} = \times \frac{2}{16}$$

10. $\frac{4}{9} \times \frac{4}{5}$

$$\frac{16}{45}$$

11. $\frac{1}{12} \times \frac{2}{3}$

$$\frac{1}{17} \quad \frac{2}{36}$$

12. $\frac{1}{7} \times 30$

$$29\frac{1}{7} = \frac{30}{210}$$

$$\times \frac{30}{7} \over 210$$

13. $\frac{2}{5} \times \frac{4}{7}$

$$= \frac{8}{35}$$

14. $\frac{7}{8} \times \frac{4}{5}$

$$\frac{28}{40}$$

15. $\frac{2}{3} \times \frac{8}{8}$

$$\frac{16}{24}$$

16. $5 \times \frac{4}{5}$

$$4\frac{20}{25}$$

17. Of the pets in the pet show, $\frac{5}{6}$ are cats. $\frac{4}{5}$ of the cats are calico cats. What fraction of the pets are calico cats?

$$\frac{2}{3} = \frac{20}{30}$$

18. GO DEEPER Five cats each ate $\frac{1}{4}$ cup of canned food and $\frac{1}{4}$ cup of dry food. How much food did they eat altogether?

$$\frac{1}{16}$$

Problem Solving • Applications

Speedskating is a popular sport in the Winter Olympics. Many young athletes in the United States participate in speedskating clubs and camps.

19. At a camp in Green Bay, Wisconsin, $\frac{7}{9}$ of the participants were from Wisconsin. Of that group, $\frac{3}{5}$ were 12 years old. What fraction of the group was from Wisconsin and 12 years old?

_____

20. **THINK SMARTER** Maribel wants to skate $1\frac{1}{2}$ miles on Monday. If she skates $\frac{9}{10}$ mile Monday morning and $\frac{2}{3}$ of that distance Monday afternoon, will she reach her goal? Explain.

_____

_____

_____

21. **MATHEMATICAL PRACTICE 2 Reason Quantitatively** On the first day of camp, $\frac{5}{6}$ of the skaters were beginners. Of the beginners, $\frac{1}{3}$ were girls. What fraction of the skaters were girls and beginners? Explain why your answer is reasonable.

_____

_____

22. **THINK SMARTER** A scientist had $\frac{3}{5}$ liter of solution. He used $\frac{1}{6}$ of the solution for an experiment. How much solution did the scientist use for the experiment? Use the numbers on the tiles to complete the calculations. You may use numbers more than once or not at all.

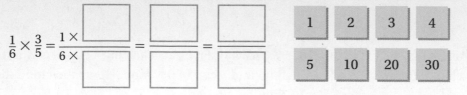

$$\frac{1}{6} \times \frac{3}{5} = \frac{1 \times \boxed{}}{6 \times \boxed{}} = \frac{\boxed{}}{\boxed{}} = \frac{\boxed{}}{\boxed{}}$$

| 1 | 2 | 3 | 4 |
| 5 | 10 | 20 | 30 |

_____ liter

Fraction Multiplication

Common Core **COMMON CORE STANDARD—5.NF.B.4a**
Apply and extend previous understandings of multiplication and division to multiply and divide fractions.

Find the product. Write the product in simplest form.

1. $\frac{4}{5} \times \frac{7}{8} = \frac{4 \times 7}{5 \times 8}$

$= \frac{28}{40}$

$= \frac{7}{10}$

2. $3 \times \frac{1}{6}$

$2\frac{1}{6}$

3. $\frac{5}{9} \times \frac{3}{4}$

$\frac{15}{36}$

4. $\frac{4}{7} \times \frac{1}{2}$

$\frac{4}{14}$

5. $\frac{1}{8} \times 20$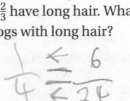

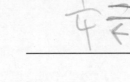

6. Karen raked $\frac{3}{5}$ of the yard. Minni raked $\frac{1}{3}$ of the amount Karen raked. How much of the yard did Minni rake?

$\frac{1}{5} = \frac{3}{15}$

7. In the pet show, $\frac{3}{8}$ of the pets are dogs. Of the dogs, $\frac{2}{3}$ have long hair. What fraction of the pets are dogs with long hair?

$\frac{1}{4} = \frac{6}{24}$

Algebra **Evaluate for the given value of the variable.**

8. $\frac{7}{8} \times c$ for $c = 8$

9. $t \times \frac{3}{4}$ for $t = \frac{8}{9}$

10. $\frac{1}{2} \times s$ for $s = \frac{3}{10}$

$\frac{3}{5}$

11. $y \times 6$ for $y = \frac{2}{3}$

Problem Solving · Real World

12. Jason ran $\frac{5}{7}$ of the distance around the school track. Sara ran $\frac{4}{5}$ of Jason's distance. What fraction of the total distance around the track did Sara run?

13. A group of students attend a math club. Half of the students are boys and $\frac{4}{9}$ of the boys have brown eyes. What fraction of the group are boys with brown eyes?

14. **WRITE** *Math* Explain how multiplying fractions is similar to multiplying whole numbers and how it is different.

_____

Lesson Check (5.NF.B.4a)

1. Fritz attended band practice for $\frac{5}{6}$ hour. Then he went home and practiced for $\frac{2}{5}$ as long as band practice. How many minutes did he practice at home?

2. Darlene read $\frac{5}{8}$ of a 56-page book. How many pages did Darlene read?

_____

_____

Spiral Review (5.NBT.A.2, 5.NF.A.1, 5.NF.B.3, 5.NF.B.4a)

3. What is the quotient of $\frac{18}{1,000}$?

4. A machine produces 1,000 bowling pins per hour, each valued at $8.37. What is the total value of the pins produced in 1 hour?

_____

_____

5. Keith had $8\frac{1}{2}$ cups of flour. He used $5\frac{2}{3}$ cups to make bread. How many cups of flour does Keith have left?

6. The Blue Lake Trail is $11\frac{3}{8}$ miles long. Gemma has hiked $2\frac{1}{2}$ miles each hour for 3 hours. How far is she from the end of the trail?

_____

_____

© Houghton Mifflin Harcourt Publishing Company

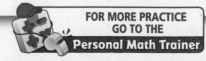

FOR MORE PRACTICE
GO TO THE
Personal Math Trainer

Name _____

✓ Mid-Chapter Checkpoint

Concepts and Skills

1. **Explain** how you would model $5 \times \frac{2}{3}$. (5.NF.B.4a)

   _____

   _____

2. When you multiply $\frac{2}{3}$ by a fraction less than one, how does the product compare to the factors? **Explain.** (5.NF.B.5a)

   _____

   _____

Find the product. Write the product in simplest form. (5.NF.B.4a, 5.NF.B.4b)

3. $\frac{2}{3} \times 6$

4. $\frac{4}{5} \times 7$

5. $8 \times \frac{5}{7}$

6. $\frac{7}{8} \times \frac{3}{8}$

7. $\frac{1}{2} \times \frac{3}{4}$

8. $\frac{7}{8} \times \frac{4}{7}$

9. $2 \times \frac{3}{11}$

10. $\frac{5}{8} \times \frac{2}{3}$

11. $\frac{7}{12} \times 8$

Complete the statement with *equal to, greater than,* or *less than*. (5.NF.B.5a)

12. $3 \times \frac{2}{3}$ will be _____ 3.

13. $\frac{5}{7} \times 3$ will be _____ $\frac{5}{7}$.

14. **GO DEEPER** There is $\frac{5}{6}$ of an apple pie left from dinner. Tomorrow, Victor plans to eat $\frac{1}{6}$ of the pie that was left. How much of the whole pie will be left after he eats tomorrow? (5.NF.B.4a)

_____

15. Everett and Marie are going to make fruit bars for their family reunion. They want to make 4 times the amount the recipe makes. If the recipe calls for $\frac{2}{3}$ cup of oil, how much oil will they need? (5.NF.B.5a)

_____

16. Matt made the model below to help him solve his math problem. Write an expression that matches Matt's model. (5.NF.B.4b)

_____

Name _____

Area and Mixed Numbers

Essential Question How can you use a unit tile to find the area of a rectangle with fractional side lengths?

Common Core **Number and Operations—Fractions—5.NF.B.4b**
MATHEMATICAL PRACTICES
MP2, MP4, MP5

Investigate

You can use square tiles with side lengths that are unit fractions to find the area of a rectangle.

Li wants to cover the rectangular floor of her closet with tile. The floor is $2\frac{1}{2}$ feet by $3\frac{1}{2}$ feet. She wants to use the fewest tiles possible and doesn't want to cut any tiles. The tiles come in three sizes: 1 foot by 1 foot, $\frac{1}{2}$ foot by $\frac{1}{2}$ foot, and $\frac{1}{4}$ foot by $\frac{1}{4}$ foot. Choose the tile that Li should use. What is the area of the closet floor?

A. Choose the largest tile Li can use to tile the floor of the closet and avoid gaps or overlaps.

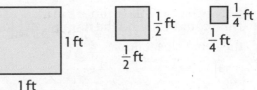

- Which square tile should Li choose? **Explain.** _____

_____

_____

B. On the grid, let each square represent the dimensions of the tile you chose. Then draw a diagram of the floor.

C. Count the squares in your diagram.

- How many squares cover the diagram?

  _____ × _____ , or _____ squares

- What is the area of the tile you chose? _____

- Since 1 square on your diagram represents an area of _____ square foot,

  the area represented by _____ squares is _____ × _____ ,

  or _____ square feet.

So, the area of the floor written as a mixed number

is _____ square feet.

Math Talk MATHEMATICAL PRACTICES ❺

Communicate Explain how you found the area of the tile you chose.

Draw Conclusions

1. Using the formula for area, write a multiplication expression that could be used to find the area of the floor.

_____

2. **MATHEMATICAL PRACTICE ④** **Write an Expression** Rewrite the expression with fractions greater than 1 and calculate the area. Is it the same as what you found using the model?

_____

3. How many $\frac{1}{4}$ foot by $\frac{1}{4}$ foot tiles would Sonja need to cover one

$\frac{1}{2}$ foot by $\frac{1}{2}$ foot tile? _____

4. How could you find the number of $\frac{1}{4}$ foot by $\frac{1}{4}$ foot tiles needed to cover the same closet floor?

_____

_____

$\frac{1}{2}$ foot

$\frac{1}{2}$ foot

Make Connections

Sometimes it is easier to multiply mixed numbers if you break them apart into whole numbers and fractions.

Use an area model to solve. $1\frac{3}{5} \times 2\frac{3}{4}$

STEP 1 Rewrite each mixed number as the sum of a whole number and a fraction.

$1\frac{3}{5} =$ _____ $2\frac{3}{4} =$ _____

STEP 2 Draw an area model to show the original multiplication problem.

STEP 3 Draw dashed lines and label each section to show how you broke apart the mixed numbers in Step 1.

STEP 4 Find the area of each section.

STEP 5 Add the area of each section to find the total area of the rectangle.

_____

So, the product of $1\frac{3}{5} \times 2\frac{3}{4}$ is _____.

Name _____

 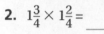
Use the grid to find the area. Let each square represent
$\frac{1}{3}$ **meter by** $\frac{1}{3}$ **meter.**

1. $1\frac{2}{3} \times 1\frac{1}{3}$

   • Draw a diagram to represent the dimensions.

   • How many squares cover the diagram? _____

   • What is the area of each square? _____

   • What is the area of the diagram? _____

Use the grid to find the area. Let each square represent
$\frac{1}{4}$ **foot by** $\frac{1}{4}$ **foot.**

2. $1\frac{3}{4} \times 1\frac{2}{4} =$ _____

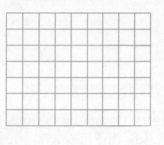

The area is _____ square feet.

☑ 3. $1\frac{1}{4} \times 1\frac{1}{2} =$ _____

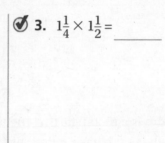

The area is _____ square feet.

Use an area model to solve.

4. $1\frac{1}{3} \times 2\frac{1}{2}$

   _____

5. $1\frac{3}{8} \times 2\frac{1}{2}$

   _____

☑ 6. $1\frac{1}{9} \times 1\frac{2}{3}$

   _____

7. **MATHEMATICAL PRACTICE ② Use Reasoning** Explain how finding the area of a
rectangle with whole-number side lengths compares to finding the area
of a rectangle with fractional side lengths.

_____

_____

Problem Solving • Applications

THINK SMARTER **Pose a Problem**

8. Terrance is designing a garden. He drew this diagram of his garden. Pose a problem using mixed numbers that can be solved using his diagram.

Pose a Problem.

_____
_____
_____
_____
_____

Solve your problem.

9. **GO DEEPER** Tucker's bedroom is a rectangle that measures $3\frac{1}{3}$ yards by $4\frac{1}{2}$ yards. His dad buys two area rugs that each has a length of 4 yards. One rug has an area of 16 square yards. The other is 12 square yards. Which rug will fit Tucker's room? Explain.

_____

_____

10. **THINK SMARTER** Nancy's garden has the dimensions shown. She needs to find the area of the garden so she knows how much topsoil to buy. Complete the area model below to find the area.

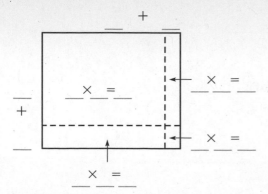

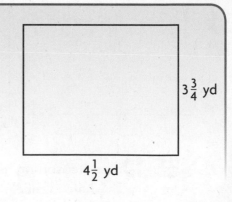

$3\frac{3}{4}$ yd

$4\frac{1}{2}$ yd

The area of the garden is _____ square yards.

Name _____

Area and Mixed Numbers

 COMMON CORE STANDARD—5.NF.B.4b
*Apply and extend previous understandings
of multiplication and division to multiply
and divide fractions.*

Use the grid to find the area.

1. Let each square represent $\frac{1}{4}$ unit by $\frac{1}{4}$ unit.

   $2\frac{1}{4} \times 1\frac{1}{2} = \underline{\quad 3\frac{3}{8} \quad}$

   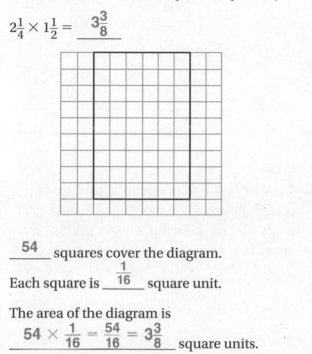

   $\underline{\quad 54 \quad}$ squares cover the diagram.

   Each square is $\underline{\quad \frac{1}{16} \quad}$ square unit.

   The area of the diagram is

   $\underline{54 \times \frac{1}{16} = \frac{54}{16} = 3\frac{3}{8}}$ square units.

2. Let each square represent $\frac{1}{3}$ unit by $\frac{1}{3}$ unit.

   $1\frac{2}{3} \times 2\frac{1}{3} = \underline{\qquad}$

   The area is $\underline{\qquad}$ square units.

Use an area model to solve.

3. $1\frac{3}{4} \times 2\frac{1}{2}$

4. $2\frac{2}{3} \times 1\frac{1}{3}$

5. $3\frac{3}{4} \times 2\frac{1}{2}$

_____   _____   _____

Problem Solving ·Real World

6. Ava's bedroom rug is $2\frac{3}{4}$ feet long and $2\frac{1}{2}$ feet wide. What is the area of the rug?

7. A painting is $2\frac{2}{3}$ feet long and $1\frac{1}{2}$ feet high. What is the area of the painting?

_____   _____

8. **WRITE** ▸*Math* Draw a shape with fractional side lengths. Describe how you will find its area.

_____

_____

Lesson Check (5.NF.B.4b)

1. The base of a fountain is rectangular. Its dimensions are $1\frac{2}{3}$ feet by $2\frac{2}{3}$ feet. What is the area of the base of the fountain?

_____

2. Bill's living room floor is covered with carpet tiles. Each tile is $1\frac{1}{2}$ feet long by $2\frac{3}{5}$ feet wide. What is the area of one tile?

_____

Spiral Review (5.OA.A.2, 5.NBT.B.5, 5.NBT.B.6, 5.NF.B.4a)

3. Lucy earned $18 babysitting on Friday and $20 babysitting on Saturday. On Sunday, she spent half of the money. Write an expression to match the words.

_____

4. A grocery store clerk is putting cans of soup on the shelves. She has 12 boxes, which each contain 24 cans of soup. Altogether, how many cans of soup will the clerk put on the shelves?

_____

5. What is the best estimate for the quotient $5,397 \div 62$?

6. There are 45 vehicles in a parking lot. Three fifths of the vehicles are minivans. How many of the vehicles in the parking lot are minivans?

_____

**FOR MORE PRACTICE
GO TO THE
Personal Math Trainer**

Name _____

Compare Mixed Number Factors and Products

Essential Question How does the size of the product compare to the size of one factor when multiplying fractions greater than one?

Common Core   Number and Operations—
Fractions—5.NF.B.5a, 5.NF.B.5b
MATHEMATICAL PRACTICES
MP2, MP3, MP5, MP6

🔑Unlock the Problem

You can make general statements about the relative size of a product when one factor is equal to 1, less than 1, or greater than 1.

🔑 One Way Use a model.

Sherise has a recipe that requires $1\frac{1}{4}$ cups of flour. She wants to know how much flour she would need if she made the recipe as written, if she made half the recipe, and if she made $1\frac{1}{2}$ times the recipe.

Shade the models to show $1\frac{1}{4}$ scaled by 1, by $\frac{1}{2}$, and by $1\frac{1}{2}$.

Ⓐ $1 \times 1\frac{1}{4}$

Think: I can use what I know about the Identity Property.

- What can you say about the product when $1\frac{1}{4}$ is multiplied by 1?

_____

Ⓑ $\frac{1}{2} \times 1\frac{1}{4}$

Think: The product will be half of what I started with.

- What can you say about the product when $1\frac{1}{4}$ is multiplied by a

fraction less than 1? _____

Ⓒ $1\frac{1}{2} \times 1\frac{1}{4} = \left(1 \times 1\frac{1}{4}\right) + \left(\frac{1}{2} \times 1\frac{1}{4}\right)$

+

Think: The product will be what I started with and $\frac{1}{2}$ more.

- What can you say about the product when $1\frac{1}{4}$ is multiplied by a number greater than 1?

_____

Math Talk

MATHEMATICAL PRACTICES ②

Reason Quantitatively
Explain your answer to part C.

CONNECT You can also use a diagram to show the relationship between the products when a fraction greater than one is multiplied or scaled (resized) by a number.

🔑 Another Way Use a diagram.

Jake wants to train for a road race. He plans to run $2\frac{1}{2}$ miles on the first day. On the second day, he plans to run $\frac{3}{5}$ of the distance he runs on the first day. On the third day, he plans to run $1\frac{2}{5}$ of the distance he runs on the first day. Which distance is greater: the distance on day 2 when he runs $\frac{3}{5}$ of $2\frac{1}{2}$ miles, or the distance on day 3 when he runs $1\frac{2}{5}$ of $2\frac{1}{2}$ miles?

Graph a point on the diagram to show the size of the product. Then complete the statement with *equal to, greater than,* or *less than*.

Ⓐ $1 \times 2\frac{1}{2}$

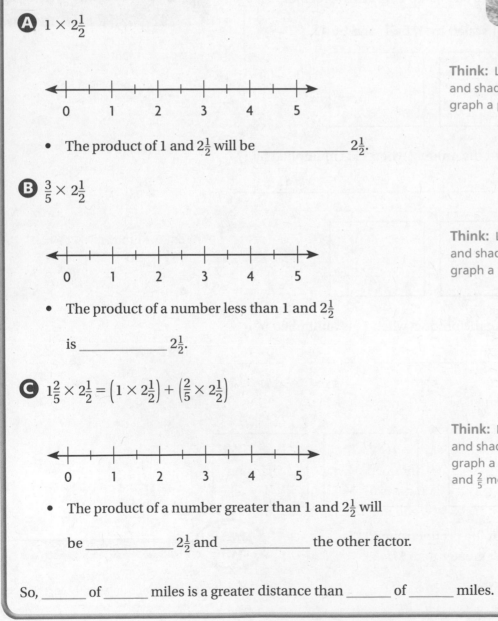

Think: Locate $2\frac{1}{2}$ on the diagram and shade that distance. Then graph a point to show 1 of $2\frac{1}{2}$.

- The product of 1 and $2\frac{1}{2}$ will be _____ $2\frac{1}{2}$.

Ⓑ $\frac{3}{5} \times 2\frac{1}{2}$

Think: Locate $2\frac{1}{2}$ on the diagram and shade that distance. Then graph a point to show $\frac{3}{5}$ of $2\frac{1}{2}$.

- The product of a number less than 1 and $2\frac{1}{2}$

  is _____ $2\frac{1}{2}$.

Ⓒ $1\frac{2}{5} \times 2\frac{1}{2} = \left(1 \times 2\frac{1}{2}\right) + \left(\frac{2}{5} \times 2\frac{1}{2}\right)$

Think: Locate $2\frac{1}{2}$ on the diagram and shade that distance. Then graph a point to show 1 of $2\frac{1}{2}$ and $\frac{2}{5}$ more of $2\frac{1}{2}$.

- The product of a number greater than 1 and $2\frac{1}{2}$ will

  be _____ $2\frac{1}{2}$ and _____ the other factor.

So, _____ of _____ miles is a greater distance than _____ of _____ miles.

Name _____

Complete the statement with *equal to*, *greater than*, or *less than*.

1. $\frac{5}{6} \times 2\frac{1}{5}$ will be _____ $2\frac{1}{5}$.

Shade the model to show $\frac{5}{6} \times 2\frac{1}{5}$.

2. $1\frac{1}{5} \times 2\frac{2}{3}$ will be _____ $2\frac{2}{3}$.

3. $\frac{4}{5} \times 2\frac{2}{5}$ will be _____ $2\frac{2}{5}$.

On Your Own

Complete the statement with *equal to*, *greater than*, or *less than*.

4. $\frac{2}{2} \times 1\frac{1}{2}$ will be _____ $1\frac{1}{2}$.

5. $\frac{2}{3} \times 3\frac{1}{6}$ will be _____ $3\frac{1}{6}$.

MATHEMATICAL PRACTICE 2 Use Reasoning **Algebra** Tell whether the unknown factor is *less than 1* or *greater than 1*.

6. $\blacksquare \times 1\frac{2}{3} = \frac{5}{6}$

7. $\blacksquare \times 1\frac{1}{4} = 2\frac{1}{2}$

The unknown factor is _____ 1.

The unknown factor is _____ 1.

8. **GO DEEPER** Kadeem is making two drawings of an oak leaf. The dimensions of the first drawing will be $\frac{1}{3}$ the dimensions of the leaf. The dimensions of the second drawing will be $2\frac{1}{2}$ the dimensions of the leaf. If the length of the oak leaf is $5\frac{1}{2}$ inches, will the length of each drawing be equal to, greater than, or less than $5\frac{1}{2}$ inches?

_____

_____

Problem Solving • Applications (Real World)

9. **MATHEMATICAL PRACTICE 3** **Verify the Reasoning of Others** Penny wants to make a model of a beetle that is larger than life-size. Penny says she is going to use a scaling factor of $\frac{7}{12}$. Does this make sense? Explain.

_____

_____

_____

10. **THINK SMARTER** Shannon, Mary, and John earn a weekly allowance. Shannon earns an amount that is $\frac{2}{3}$ of what John earns. Mary earns an amount that is $1\frac{2}{3}$ of what John earns. John earns $20 a week. Who earns the greatest allowance? Who earns the least?

_____

11. **THINK SMARTER** Stuart rode his bicycle $6\frac{3}{5}$ miles on Friday. On Saturday he rode $1\frac{1}{3}$ times as far as he rode on Friday. On Sunday he rode $\frac{5}{6}$ times as far as he rode on Friday. For 11a–11d, select True or False for each statement.

11a. Stuart rode more miles on Saturday than he rode on Friday.

⃝ True   ⃝ False

11b. Stuart rode more miles on Friday than he rode on Saturday and Sunday combined.

⃝ True   ⃝ False

11c. Stuart rode fewer miles on Sunday than he rode on Friday.

⃝ True   ⃝ False

11d. Stuart rode more miles on Sunday than he rode on Saturday.

⃝ True   ⃝ False

Compare Mixed Number Factors and Products

Common Core

COMMON CORE STANDARDS—5.NF.B.5a, 5.NF.B.5b *Apply and extend previous understandings of multiplication and division to multiply and divide fractions.*

Complete the statement with *equal to*, *greater than*, **or** *less than*.

1. $\frac{2}{3} \times 1\frac{5}{8}$ will be _____ less than _____ $1\frac{5}{8}$.

   Think: $1 \times 1\frac{5}{8}$ is $1\frac{5}{8}$.

   Since $\frac{2}{3}$ is less than 1,

   $\frac{2}{3} \times 1\frac{5}{8}$ will be less than $1\frac{5}{8}$.

2. $\frac{5}{5} \times 2\frac{3}{4}$ will be _____ $2\frac{3}{4}$.

3. $3 \times 3\frac{2}{7}$ will be _____ $3\frac{2}{7}$.

4. $9 \times 1\frac{4}{5}$ will be _____ $1\frac{4}{5}$.

5. $1\frac{7}{8} \times 2\frac{3}{8}$ will be _____ $2\frac{3}{8}$.

6. $3\frac{4}{9} \times \frac{5}{9}$ will be _____ $3\frac{4}{9}$.

Problem Solving Real World

7. Fraser is making a scale drawing of a dog house. The dimensions of the drawing will be $\frac{1}{8}$ of the dimensions of the actual doghouse. The height of the actual doghouse is $36\frac{3}{4}$ inches. Will the dimensions of Fraser's drawing be equal to, greater than, or less than the dimensions of the actual dog house?

_____

8. Jorge has a recipe that calls for $2\frac{1}{3}$ cups of flour. He plans to make $1\frac{1}{2}$ times the recipe. Will the amount of flour Jorge needs be equal to, greater than, or less than the amount of flour his recipe calls for?

_____

9. **WRITE** *Math* Explain how scaling a mixed number by $\frac{1}{2}$ will affect the size of the number.

_____

_____

_____

Lesson Check (5.NF.B.5a, 5.NF.B.5b)

1. Jenna skis $2\frac{1}{3}$ miles down the mountain. Her instructor skis $1\frac{1}{2}$ times as far. Does Jenna ski a shorter, greater, or the same distance as her instructor?

_____

_____

_____

2. Suppose you multiply a fraction less than 1 by the mixed number $2\frac{3}{4}$. Will the product be less than, greater than, or equal to $2\frac{3}{4}$?

_____

_____

_____

Spiral Review (5.NBT.A.2, 5.NBT.B.7, 5.NF.A.1)

3. Washington County is shaped like a rectangle. It measures 15.9 miles by 9.1 miles. What is the county's area?

_____

4. Marsha jogged 7.8 miles. Erica jogged 0.5 times as far. How far did Erica jog?

_____

5. One bread recipe calls for $2\frac{1}{3}$ cups of flour. Another bread recipe calls for $2\frac{1}{2}$ cups of flour. Tim has 5 cups of flour. If he makes both recipes, how much flour will he have left over?

_____

6. On Monday, it rained $1\frac{1}{4}$ inches. On Tuesday, it rained $\frac{3}{5}$ inch. How much more did it rain on Monday than on Tuesday?

_____

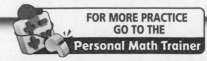

FOR MORE PRACTICE
GO TO THE
Personal Math Trainer

Name _____

Multiply Mixed Numbers

Essential Question How do you multiply mixed numbers?

Common Core Number and Operations—
Fractions—5.NF.B.6
MATHEMATICAL PRACTICES
MP1, MP2, MP6

⚷ Unlock the Problem Real World

One-third of a $1\frac{1}{4}$ acre park has been reserved as a dog park. Find the number of acres that are used as a dog park.

Multiply. $\frac{1}{3} \times 1\frac{1}{4}$

• Is the area of the dog park less than or greater than the area of the $1\frac{1}{4}$ acre park?

_____

🔓 One Way Use a model.

STEP 1 Shade the model to represent the whole park.

Think: The whole park is _____ acres.

_____

STEP 2 Shade the model again to represent the part of the park that is a dog park.

Think: The dog park is _____ of the park.

Draw horizontal lines across each rectangle to show _____.

• How many parts does each rectangle show? _____

• What fraction of each rectangle is shaded twice?

  _____ and _____

• What fraction represents all the parts which are shaded twice?

  _____ + _____ = _____

So, _____ acre has been set aside.

🔓 Another Way Rename the mixed number as a fraction.

STEP 1 Write the mixed number as a fraction greater than 1.

_____

STEP 2 Multiply the fractions.

$$\frac{1}{3} \times 1\frac{1}{4} = \frac{1}{3} \times \frac{\boxed{}}{4}$$

$$= \frac{1 \times \boxed{}}{3 \times 4} = \frac{}{}$$

So, $\frac{1}{3} \times 1\frac{1}{4} =$ _____.

Math Talk MATHEMATICAL PRACTICES ①

Evaluate Reasonableness Explain why your answer is reasonable.

🔑 Example 1 Rename the whole number.

Multiply. $12 \times 2\frac{1}{6}$ **Write the product in simplest form.**

STEP 1 Determine how the product will compare to the greater factor.

$12 \times 2\frac{1}{6}$ will be _____ 12.

STEP 2 Write the whole number and mixed number as fractions.

STEP 3 Multiply the fractions.

STEP 4 Write the product in simplest form.

So, $12 \times 2\frac{1}{6} =$ _____.

$$12 \times 2\frac{1}{6} = \frac{}{1} \times \frac{}{6}$$

$$= \frac{}{} = \frac{}{}, \text{ or } \boxed{}$$

🔑 Example 2 Use the Distributive Property.

Multiply. $16 \times 4\frac{1}{8}$ **Write the product in simplest form.**

STEP 1 Rewrite the expression by using the Distributive Property.

STEP 2 Multiply 16 by each number.

STEP 3 Add.

$$16 \times 4\frac{1}{8} = 16 \times \left(\underline{} + \frac{1}{8}\right)$$

$$= (16 \times 4) + \left(16 \times \frac{}{}\right)$$

$$= \underline{} + 2 = \underline{}$$

So, $16 \times 4\frac{1}{8} =$ _____.

Math Talk

MATHEMATICAL PRACTICES ②

Use Reasoning Explain how you know that your answers to both examples are reasonable.

1. **MATHEMATICAL PRACTICE ②** **Use Reasoning** Explain why you might choose to use the Distributive Property to solve Example 2.

_____

2. When you multiply two factors greater than 1, is the product less than, between, or greater than the two factors? Explain.

_____

_____

Name _____

Find the product. Write the product in simplest form.

1. $1\frac{2}{3} \times 3\frac{4}{5} = \frac{\boxed{}}{3} \times \frac{\boxed{}}{5}$

   $= \frac{\boxed{}}{\boxed{}}$

   $= \underline{}$

☑ 2. $1\frac{1}{8} \times 2\frac{1}{3}$

☑ 3. $\frac{3}{4} \times 6\frac{5}{6}$

Use the Distributive Property to find the product.

4. $16 \times 2\frac{1}{2}$

5. $1\frac{4}{5} \times 15$

On Your Own

Find the product. Write the product in simplest form.

6. $\frac{3}{4} \times 1\frac{1}{2}$

7. $4\frac{2}{5} \times 1\frac{1}{2}$

8. $5\frac{1}{3} \times \frac{3}{4}$

9. $2\frac{1}{2} \times 1\frac{1}{5}$

10. **THINK SMARTER** The table shows how many hours some students worked on their math project.

April worked $1\frac{1}{2}$ times as long on her math project as did Carl. Debbie worked $1\frac{1}{4}$ times as long as Sonia. Richard worked $1\frac{3}{8}$ times as long as Tony. Match each student's name to the number of hours he or she worked on the math project.

Math Project	
Name	**Hours Worked**
Carl	$5\frac{1}{4}$
Sonia	$6\frac{1}{2}$
Tony	$5\frac{2}{3}$

Student	Hours Worked
April •	• $7\frac{19}{24}$
Debbie •	• $7\frac{7}{8}$
Richard •	• $8\frac{1}{8}$

Connect to Health

CHANGING RECIPES

You can make a lot of recipes more healthful by reducing the amounts of fat, sugar, and salt.

Kelly has a muffin recipe that calls for $1\frac{1}{2}$ cups of sugar. She wants to use $\frac{1}{2}$ that amount of sugar. How much sugar will she use?

Multiply $1\frac{1}{2}$ by $\frac{1}{2}$ to find what part of the original amount of sugar to use.

Write the mixed number as a fraction greater than 1.

$$\frac{1}{2} \times 1\frac{1}{2} = \frac{1}{2} \times \frac{}{2}$$

Multiply.

$$= \underline{}$$

So, Kelly will use _____ cup of sugar.

11. **MATHEMATICAL PRACTICE ⑥ Describe a Method** Tony's recipe for soup calls for $1\frac{1}{4}$ teaspoons of salt. He wants to use $\frac{1}{2}$ that amount. How much salt will he use? Describe how you found your answer.

_____

_____

_____

12. **GO DEEPER** Jeffrey's recipe for oatmeal muffins calls for $2\frac{1}{4}$ cups of oatmeal and makes one dozen muffins. If he makes $1\frac{1}{2}$ dozen muffins for a club meeting and 2 dozen muffins for a family reunion, how much oatmeal will he use?

_____

13. **THINK SMARTER** Cara's muffin recipe calls for $1\frac{1}{2}$ cups of flour for the muffins and $\frac{1}{4}$ cup of flour for the topping. If she makes $\frac{1}{2}$ of the original recipe, how much flour will she use?

_____

Multiply Mixed Numbers

Common Core

COMMON CORE STANDARD—5.NF.B.6
Apply and extend previous understandings of multiplication and division to multiply and divide fractions.

Find the product. Write the product in simplest form.

1. $1\frac{2}{3} \times 4\frac{2}{5}$

$1\frac{2}{3} \times 4\frac{2}{5} = \frac{5}{3} \times \frac{22}{5}$

$= \frac{110}{15} = \frac{22}{3}$

$= 7\frac{1}{3}$

2. $1\frac{1}{7} \times 1\frac{3}{4}$

3. $8\frac{1}{3} \times \frac{3}{5}$

4. $2\frac{5}{8} \times 1\frac{2}{3}$

5. $5\frac{1}{2} \times 3\frac{1}{3}$

6. $7\frac{1}{5} \times 2\frac{1}{6}$

7. $\frac{2}{3} \times 4\frac{1}{5}$

8. $2\frac{2}{5} \times 1\frac{1}{4}$

Use the Distributive Property to find the product.

9. $4\frac{2}{5} \times 10$

10. $26 \times 2\frac{1}{2}$

11. $6 \times 3\frac{2}{3}$

Problem Solving (Real World)

12. Jake can carry $6\frac{1}{4}$ pounds of wood in from the barn. His father can carry $1\frac{5}{7}$ times as much as Jake. How many pounds can Jake's father carry?

13. A glass can hold $3\frac{1}{3}$ cups of water. A bowl can hold $2\frac{3}{5}$ times the amount in the glass. How many cups can a bowl hold?

14. **WRITE** ▸*Math* Write and solve a word problem that involves multiplying by a mixed number.

_____

Lesson Check (5.NF.B.6)

1. A vet weighs two puppies. The small puppy weighs $4\frac{1}{2}$ pounds. The large puppy weighs $4\frac{2}{3}$ times as much as the small puppy. How much does the large puppy weigh?

2. Becky lives $5\frac{5}{8}$ miles from school. Steve lives $1\frac{5}{9}$ times as far from school as Becky. How far does Steve live from school?

Spiral Review (5.OA.A.2, 5.NBT.B.7, 5.NF.A.1, 5.NF.A.2)

3. Craig scored 12 points in a game. Marla scored twice as many points as Craig but 5 fewer points than Nelson scored. Write an expression to represent how many points Nelson scored.

4. Yvette earned $66.00 for 8 hours of work. Lizbeth earned $68.80 working the same amount of time. How much more per hour did Lizbeth earn than Yvette?

5. What is the least common denominator of the four fractions listed below?

$$20\frac{7}{10} \qquad 20\frac{3}{4} \qquad 18\frac{9}{10} \qquad 20\frac{18}{25}$$

6. Three girls collected geodes in the desert. Corinne collected $11\frac{1}{8}$ pounds, Ellen collected $4\frac{5}{8}$ pounds, and Leonda collected $3\frac{3}{4}$ pounds. How much more did Corinne collect than the other two girls combined?

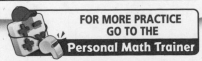

FOR MORE PRACTICE
GO TO THE
Personal Math Trainer

Problem Solving • Find Unknown Lengths

Essential Question How can you use the strategy *guess, check, and revise* to solve problems with fractions?

Common Core Number and Operations—
Fractions—5.NF.B.4b, 5.NF.B.6
MATHEMATICAL PRACTICES
MP1, MP3, MP6

🔑 Unlock the Problem (Real World)

Sara wants to design a rectangular garden with a section for flowers that attract butterflies. She wants the area of this section to be $\frac{3}{4}$ square yard. If she wants the width to be $\frac{1}{3}$ the length, what will the dimensions of the butterfly section be?

Read the Problem

What do I need to find?	What information do I need to use?	How will I use the information?
I need to find _____ _____ _____ _____.	The part of the garden for butterflies has an area of _____ square yard and the width is _____ the length.	I will _____ the sides of the butterfly area. Then I will _____ my guess and _____ it if it is not correct.

Solve the Problem

I can try different lengths and calculate the widths by finding $\frac{1}{3}$ the length. For each length and width, I find the area and then compare. If the product is less than or greater than $\frac{3}{4}$ square yard, I need to revise the length.

Guess		Check	Revise
Length (in yards)	Width (in yards) ($\frac{1}{3}$ of the length)	Area of Butterfly Garden (in square yards)	
$\frac{3}{4}$	$\frac{1}{3} \times \frac{3}{4} = \frac{1}{4}$	$\frac{3}{4} \times \frac{1}{4} = \frac{3}{16}$ too low	Try a longer length.
$2\frac{1}{4}$, or $\frac{9}{4}$			

So, the dimensions of Sara's butterfly garden will be _____ yard by _____ yards.

🔑 Try Another Problem

Marcus is building a rectangular box for his kitten to sleep in. He wants the area of the bottom of the box to be 360 square inches and the length of one side to be $1\frac{3}{5}$ the length of the other side. What should the dimensions of the bottom of the bed be?

Read the Problem

What do I need to find?	What information do I need to use?	How will I use the information?

Solve the Problem

So, the dimensions of the bottom of the kitten's bed will be _____ by _____.

- **MATHEMATICAL PRACTICE ❸** **Apply** What if the longer side was still $1\frac{3}{5}$ the length of the shorter side and the shorter side was 20 inches long? What would the area of the bottom of the bed be then? _____

_____

478

Name _____

1. When Pascal built a dog house, he knew he wanted the floor of the house to have an area of 24 square feet. He also wanted the width to be $\frac{2}{3}$ the length. What are the dimensions of the dog house?

   First, choose two numbers that have a product of 24.

   Guess: _____ feet and _____ feet

   Then, check those numbers. Is the greater number $\frac{2}{3}$ of the other number?

   Check: $\frac{2}{3} \times$ _____ = _____

   My guess is _____.

   Finally, if the guess is not correct, revise it and check again. Continue until you find the correct answer.

   So, the dimensions of the dog house are _____.

2. **What if** Pascal wanted the area of the floor to be 54 square feet and the width still to be $\frac{2}{3}$ the length? What would the dimensions of the floor be?

3. Leo wants to paint a mural that covers a wall with an area of 1,440 square feet. The height of the wall is $\frac{2}{5}$ of its length. What is the length and the height of the wall?

On Your Own

4. **GO DEEPER** Barry wants to make a drawing that is $\frac{1}{4}$ the size of the original. If a tree in the original drawing is 14 inches tall and 5 inches wide, what will be the length and width of the tree in Barry's drawing?

_____

5. **THINK SMARTER** A blueprint is a scale drawing of a building. The dimensions of the blueprint for Patricia's doll house are $\frac{1}{4}$ of the measurements of the actual doll house. The floor of the doll house has an area of 864 square inches. If the width of the doll house is $\frac{2}{3}$ the length, what are the dimensions of the floor on the blueprint of the doll house?

_____

· · · · **WRITE** ▸*Math* · **Show Your Work** · · · ·

6. **MATHEMATICAL PRACTICE ③** **Verify the Reasoning of Others** Beth wants the floor of her tree house to be 48 square feet. She wants the length to be $\frac{3}{4}$ the width. Using the strategy *guess, check, and revise,* Beth guesses the dimensions will be 4 feet by 12 feet. Is Beth's guess the correct dimensions? Explain.

_____

_____

_____

7. **THINK SMARTER** Sally has a photograph that has an area of 35 square inches. She creates two enlargements of the photograph. The enlargements have areas of 140 square inches and 560 square inches. In each photograph, the length is $1\frac{2}{5}$ times the width. Select which of the following could be the dimensions of the original photograph or one of the enlargements. Mark all that apply.

(A) 5 inches by 7 inches

(B) 20 inches by 28 inches

(C) 7 inches by 20 inches

(D) 21 inches by 15 inches

(E) 10 inches by 14 inches

480

Problem Solving • Find Unknown Lengths

COMMON CORE STANDARD—5.NF.B.5b
Apply and extend previous understandings of multiplication and division to multiply and divide fractions.

---

1. Kamal's bedroom has an area of 120 square feet. The width of the room is $\frac{5}{6}$ the length of the room. What are the dimensions of Kamal's bedroom?

Guess: $6 \times 20 = 120$
Check: $\frac{5}{6} \times 20 = 16\frac{2}{3}$; try a longer width.
Guess: $10 \times 12 = 120$
Check: $\frac{5}{6} \times 12 = 10$. Correct!

_____ **10 feet by 12 feet** _____

---

2. Marisol is painting on a piece of canvas that has an area of 180 square inches. The length of the painting is $1\frac{1}{4}$ times the width. What are the dimensions of the painting?

_____

---

3. A small plane is flying a banner in the shape of a rectangle. The area of the banner is 144 square feet. The width of the banner is $\frac{1}{4}$ the length of the banner. What are the dimensions of the banner?

_____

---

4. **⎪WRITE⎪** ▸*Math* Explain how you can use the strategy *guess, check, and revise* to solve problems that involve a given area when the relationship between the side lengths is given too.

_____

Lesson Check (5.NF.B.5b)

1. Consuelo's living room is in the shape of a rectangle and has an area of 360 square feet. The width of the living room is $\frac{5}{8}$ its length. What is the length of the living room?

2. A rectangular park has an area of $\frac{2}{3}$ square mile. The length of the park is $2\frac{2}{3}$ the width of the park. What is the width of the park?

Spiral Review (5.NBT.B.4, 5.NF.A.1, 5.NF.B.4a, 5.NF.B.5a, 5.NF.B.5b)

3. Debra babysits for $3\frac{1}{2}$ hours on Friday and $1\frac{1}{2}$ times as long on Saturday. Did Debra babysit more, fewer, or the same number of hours on Saturday than she did on Friday?

4. Tory practiced her basketball shots for $\frac{2}{3}$ hour. Tim practiced his basketball shots for $\frac{3}{4}$ as much time as Tory did. How long did Tim practice his basketball shots?

5. Leah bought $4\frac{1}{2}$ pounds of grapes. Of the grapes she bought, $1\frac{7}{8}$ pounds were red grapes. The rest were green grapes. How many pounds of green grapes did Leah buy?

6. To which place value is the following number rounded?

5.927 to 5.93

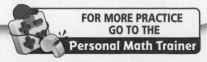

**FOR MORE PRACTICE
GO TO THE
Personal Math Trainer**

Name _____

 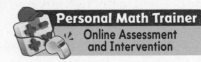

1. Mrs. Williams is organizing her office supplies. There are 3 open boxes of paper clips in her desk drawer. Each box has $\frac{7}{8}$ of the paper clips remaining. How many boxes of paper clips are left? Shade the model and complete the calculations below to show how you found your answer.

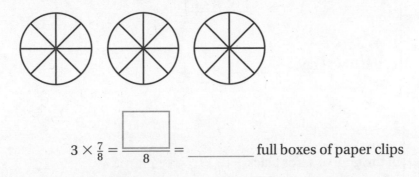

$3 \times \frac{7}{8} = \dfrac{\boxed{}}{8} = $ _____ full boxes of paper clips

2. Diana worked on her science project for $5\frac{1}{3}$ hours. Gabe worked on his science project $1\frac{1}{4}$ times as long as Diana. Paula worked on her science project $\frac{3}{4}$ times as long as Diana. For 2a–2d, select True or False for each statement.

2a.   Diana worked longer on her science project than Gabe worked on his science project.   ○ True   ○ False

2b.   Paula worked less on her science project than Diana worked on her science project.   ○ True   ○ False

2c.   Gabe worked longer on his science project than Paula worked on her science project.   ○ True   ○ False

2d.   Gabe worked longer on his science project than Diana and Paula combined.   ○ True   ○ False

3. **GO DEEPER**   Louis wants to carpet the rectangular floor of his basement. The basement has an area of 864 square feet. The width of the basement is $\frac{2}{3}$ its length. What is the length of Louis's basement?

_____ feet

4. Frannie put $\frac{2}{3}$ of her music collection on an mp3 player. While on vacation, she listened to $\frac{3}{5}$ of the music on the player. How much of Frannie's music collection did she listen to while on vacation? For 4a–4d, choose the correct values to describe how to solve the problem.

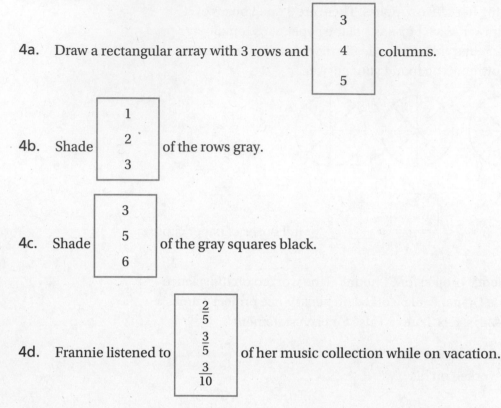

4a. Draw a rectangular array with 3 rows and [3 / 4 / 5] columns.

4b. Shade [1 / 2 / 3] of the rows gray.

4c. Shade [3 / 5 / 6] of the gray squares black.

4d. Frannie listened to [$\frac{2}{5}$ / $\frac{3}{5}$ / $\frac{3}{10}$] of her music collection while on vacation.

5. Logan bought 15 balloons. Four-fifths of the balloons are purple. How many of the balloons are purple? Draw a model to show how you found your answer.

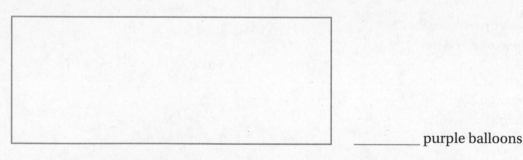

_____ purple balloons

6. Kayla walks $3\frac{2}{5}$ miles each day. Which of the following statements correctly describe how far she walks? Mark all that apply.

(A) Kayla walks $14\frac{2}{5}$ miles in 4 days.

(B) Kayla walks $23\frac{4}{5}$ miles in 7 days.

(C) Kayla walks 34 miles in 10 days.

(D) Kayla walks $102\frac{2}{5}$ miles in 31 days.

7. Write each multiplication expression in the correct box.

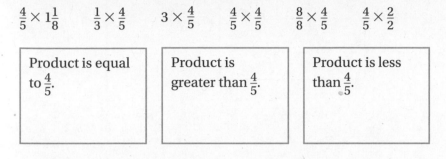

$\frac{4}{5} \times 1\frac{1}{8}$ $\frac{1}{3} \times \frac{4}{5}$ $3 \times \frac{4}{5}$ $\frac{4}{5} \times \frac{4}{5}$ $\frac{8}{8} \times \frac{4}{5}$ $\frac{4}{5} \times \frac{2}{2}$

Product is equal to $\frac{4}{5}$.	Product is greater than $\frac{4}{5}$.	Product is less than $\frac{4}{5}$.

8. A postcard has an area of 24 square inches. Two enlargements of the postcard have areas of 54 square inches and 96 square inches. In each postcard, the length is $1\frac{1}{2}$ times the width. Which of the following could be the dimensions of the postcard or one of the enlargements? Mark all that apply.

(A) 6 inches by 9 inches   (D) 6 inches by 12 inches

(B) 10 inches by 15 inches   (E) 4 inches by 6 inches

(C) 8 inches by 12 inches

9. In a fifth grade class, $\frac{4}{5}$ of the girls have brown hair. Of the brown-haired girls, $\frac{3}{4}$ of them have long hair. Of the girls with long brown hair, $\frac{1}{3}$ of them have green eyes.

Part A

What fraction of the girls in the class have long brown hair?

_____ of the girls

Part B

What fraction of the girls in the class have long brown hair and green eyes? Explain how you found your answer.

_____ of the girls

10. **THINK SMARTER +** Caleb's family room has the dimensions shown. He needs to find the area of the room so that he knows how much carpet to buy. Complete the area model below to find the area of the family room.

$3\frac{7}{8}$ yd

$5\frac{1}{4}$ yd

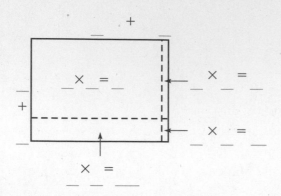

area of the room = _____ square yards

11. Doreen lives $\frac{3}{4}$ mile from the library. Sheila lives $\frac{1}{3}$ as far away from the library as Doreen. For 11a–11c, choose Yes or No to answer each question.

11a. Does Doreen live farther from the library than Sheila?

○ Yes   ○ No

11b. Does Sheila live $\frac{1}{4}$ mile from the library?

○ Yes   ○ No

11c. Does Sheila live twice as far from the library than Doreen?

○ Yes   ○ No

12. Taniqua took a test that had 20 multiple-choice questions and 10 True/False questions. She got $\frac{9}{10}$ of the multiple-choice questions correct, and she got $\frac{4}{5}$ of the True/False questions correct.

12a. How many multiple-choice questions did Taniqua get correct?

_____ multiple-choice questions

12b. How many True/False questions did Taniqua get correct?

_____ True/False questions

© Houghton Mifflin Harcourt Publishing Company

13. The table shows how many hours some of the part-time employees at the toy store worked last week.

Name	Hours Worked
Conrad	$6\frac{2}{3}$
Giovanni	$9\frac{1}{2}$
Sally	$10\frac{3}{4}$

This week, Conrad will work $1\frac{3}{4}$ times as long as last week. Giovanni will work $1\frac{1}{3}$ times as long as last week. Sally will work $\frac{2}{3}$ the number of hours she worked last week. Match each employee's name to the number of hours he or she will work this week.

Employee   **Hours This Week**

Conrad •   • $7\frac{1}{6}$

Giovanni •   • $12\frac{2}{3}$

Sally •   • $11\frac{2}{3}$

14. Peggy is making a quilt using panels that are $\frac{1}{2}$ foot by $\frac{1}{2}$ foot. The quilt is $5\frac{1}{2}$ feet long and 4 feet wide.

Part A

Let each square of the grid below represent $\frac{1}{2}$ foot by $\frac{1}{2}$ foot. Draw a rectangle on the grid to represent the quilt.

Part B

What is the area of the quilt? Explain how you found your answer.

_____ square feet

15. Ruby conducted a survey and found that $\frac{5}{6}$ of her classmates have a pet and $\frac{2}{3}$ of those pets are dogs. What fraction of her classmates has dogs? Write a number from the number tiles in each box to complete the calculations shown below. You may use numbers more than once or not at all.

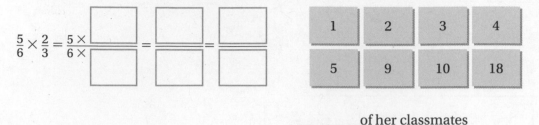

$$\frac{5}{6} \times \frac{2}{3} = \frac{5 \times \boxed{}}{6 \times \boxed{}} = \frac{\boxed{}}{\boxed{}} = \frac{\boxed{}}{\boxed{}}$$

| 1 | 2 | 3 | 4 |
| 5 | 9 | 10 | 18 |

_____ of her classmates

16. Robbie is using the recipe below to make chicken noodle soup. He plans to make 6 batches of the soup. He has $\frac{2}{3}$ teaspoon of black pepper.

> **Chicken Noodle Soup**
>
> 4 cups chicken broth
>
> 1 medium carrot, sliced
>
> 1 stalk celery, sliced
>
> $\frac{1}{2}$ cup uncooked egg noodles
>
> $\frac{1}{8}$ teaspoon ground black pepper
>
> 1 cup shredded cooked chicken

Part A

Write an expression that Robbie can use to determine how much black pepper is needed for 6 batches.

_____

Part B

Draw a model to show how Robbie can find the product from Part A.

Part C

Does Robbie have enough black pepper for 6 batches of the soup? Explain your reasoning.

Chapter 8

Divide Fractions

✓ Show What You Know

Check your understanding of important skills.

Name _____

▶ **Part of a Group** **Write a fraction that names the shaded part.** (3.NF.A.1)

1. total counters _____

   shaded counters _____

   fraction _____

2. total groups _____

   shaded groups _____

   fraction _____

▶ **Relate Multiplication and Division** **Use inverse operations and fact families to solve.** (3.OA.B.6)

3. Since $6 \times 4 = 24$,

   then _____ $\div 4 = 6$.

4. Since _____ $\times 8 = 56$,

   then _____ $\div 7 = 8$.

5. Since $9 \times 3 =$ _____,

   then _____ $\div 3 = 9$.

6. Since _____ $\div 4 = 10$,

   then $4 \times 10 =$ _____,

▶ **Equivalent Fractions** **Write an equivalent fraction.** (4.NF.A.1)

7. $\frac{16}{20}$ _____

8. $\frac{3}{8}$ _____

9. $\frac{5}{12}$ _____

10. $\frac{25}{45}$ _____

Math in the Real World

Emily spent $\frac{1}{2}$ of her money at the grocery store. Then, she spent $\frac{1}{2}$ of what was left at the bakery. Next, at the music store, she spent $\frac{1}{2}$ of what was left on a CD that was on sale. She spent the remaining $6.00 on lunch at the diner. Find how much money Emily started with.

Vocabulary Builder

▶ **Visualize It** ·

Complete the flow map using the review words.

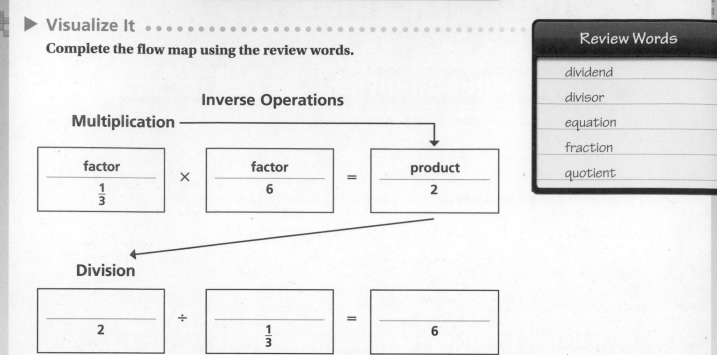

▶ **Understand Vocabulary** ·

Complete the sentences using the review words.

1. The number that divides the dividend is the

   _____.

2. An algebraic or numerical sentence that shows that two

   quantities are equal is an _____.

3. A number that names a part of a whole or a part of a group

   is called a _____.

4. The _____ is the number that is to be divided
   in a division problem.

5. The _____ is the number, not including the
   remainder, that results from dividing.

• **Interactive Student Edition**
• **Multimedia eGlossary**

dividend

dividendo

18

divisor

divisor

19

equation

ecuación

20

fraction

fracción

28

inverse operations

operaciones inversas

32

product

producto

54

quotient

cociente

57

remainder

residuo

59

The number that divides the dividend

Example: $15 \div 3$ or $3\overline{)15}$

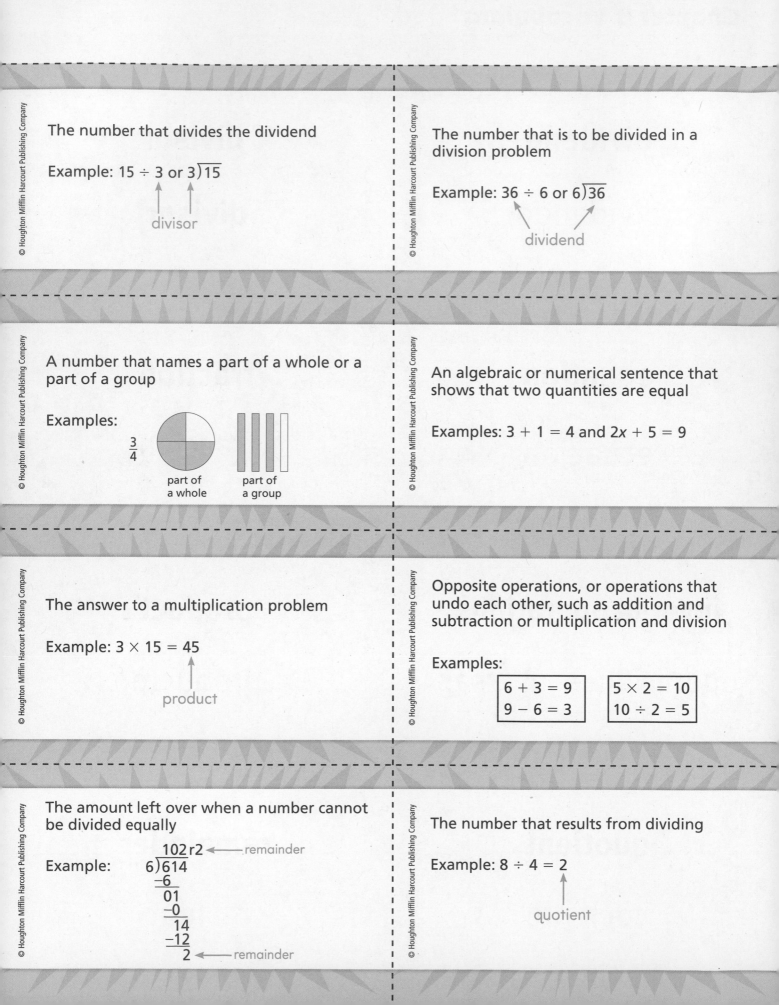

divisor

The number that is to be divided in a division problem

Example: $36 \div 6$ or $6\overline{)36}$

dividend

A number that names a part of a whole or a part of a group

Examples:

$\frac{3}{4}$

part of a whole   part of a group

An algebraic or numerical sentence that shows that two quantities are equal

Examples: $3 + 1 = 4$ and $2x + 5 = 9$

The answer to a multiplication problem

Example: $3 \times 15 = 45$

product

Opposite operations, or operations that undo each other, such as addition and subtraction or multiplication and division

Examples:

| $6 + 3 = 9$ | $5 \times 2 = 10$ |
| $9 - 6 = 3$ | $10 \div 2 = 5$ |

The amount left over when a number cannot be divided equally

Example:
$$
\begin{array}{r}
102\,\text{r}2 \leftarrow \text{remainder} \\
6\overline{)614} \\
\underline{-6} \\
01 \\
\underline{-0} \\
14 \\
\underline{-12} \\
2 \leftarrow \text{remainder}
\end{array}
$$

The number that results from dividing

Example: $8 \div 4 = 2$

quotient

Game

Pick It

For 3 players

Materials

- 4 sets of word cards

How to Play

1. Each player is dealt 5 cards. The remaining cards are a draw pile.

2. To take a turn, ask any player if he or she has a word that matches one of your word cards.

3. If the player has the word, he or she gives the word card to you, and you must define the word.
   - If you are correct, keep the card and put the matching pair in front of you. Take another turn.
   - If your are wrong, return the card. Your turn is over.

4. If the player does not have the word, he or she answers, "Pick it." Then you take a card from the draw pile.

5. If the card you draw matches one of your word cards, follow the directions for Step 3. If it does not, your turn is over.

6. The game is over when one player has no cards left. The player with the most pairs wins.

Word Box

dividend

divisor

equation

fraction

inverse operations

product

quotient

remainder

The Write Way

Reflect

Choose one idea. Write about it.

- Explain how you can use inverse operations to check your answer to a division problem.

- Lena wants to divide 5 sandwiches into fourths. Draw and label a diagram to show how many sandwich pieces she will have.

- Which of the following expressions will have a quotient that is greater than its dividend? Tell how you know.

$$\frac{1}{4} \div 6 \qquad\qquad 6 \div \frac{1}{4}$$

- Write a note to a friend about something you learned in Chapter 8.

Name _____

Divide Fractions and Whole Numbers

Essential Question How do you divide a whole number by a fraction and divide a fraction by a whole number?

Common Core **Number and Operations—Fractions—**
5.NF.B.7a, 5.NF.B.7b *Also 5.NF.B.7c*
MATHEMATICAL PRACTICES
MP2, MP3, MP5

Investigate

Materials ■ fraction strips

A. Mia walks a 2-mile fitness trail. She stops to exercise every $\frac{1}{5}$ mile. How many times does Mia stop to exercise?

- Draw a number line from 0 to 2. Divide the number line into fifths. Label each fifth on your number line.

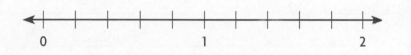

- Skip count by fifths from 0 to 2 to find $2 \div \frac{1}{5}$.

  There are _____ one-fifths in 2 wholes.

You can use the relationship between multiplication and division to explain and check your solution.

- Record and check the quotient.

  $2 \div \frac{1}{5} =$ _____ because _____ $\times \frac{1}{5} = 2$.

So, Mia stops to exercise _____ times.

B. Roger has 2 yards of string. He cuts the string into pieces that are $\frac{1}{3}$ yard long. How many pieces of string does Roger have?

- Model 2 using 2 whole fraction strips.

- Then place enough $\frac{1}{3}$ strips to fit exactly under the

  2 wholes. There are _____ one-third-size pieces in 2 wholes.

- Record and check the quotient.

  $2 \div \frac{1}{3} =$ _____ because _____ $\times \frac{1}{3} = 2$.

So, Roger has _____ pieces of string.

Draw Conclusions

1. When you divide a whole number by a fraction, how does the quotient compare to the dividend? Explain.

_____

_____

2. **Apply** Explain how knowing the number of fifths in 1 could help you find the number of fifths in 2.

_____

_____

3. Describe how you would find $4 \div \frac{1}{5}$.

_____

_____

Make Connections

You can use fraction strips to divide a fraction by a whole number.

Calia shares half of a package of clay equally among herself and each of 2 friends. What fraction of the whole package of clay will each friend get?

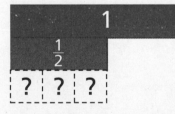

STEP 1 Place a $\frac{1}{2}$ strip under a 1-whole strip to show the $\frac{1}{2}$ package of clay.

_____

STEP 2 Find 3 fraction strips, all with the same denominator, that fit exactly under the $\frac{1}{2}$ strip.

Each piece is _____ of the whole.

_____

STEP 3 Record and check the quotient.

$\frac{1}{2} \div 3 = $ _____ because _____ $\times 3 = \frac{1}{2}$.

So, each friend will get _____ of the whole package of clay.

Think: How much of the whole is each piece when $\frac{1}{2}$ is divided into 3 equal pieces?

Math Talk MATHEMATICAL PRACTICES ②

Reason Quantitatively When you divide a fraction by a whole number, how does the quotient compare to the dividend? Explain.

Name _____

Divide. Check the quotient.

1.

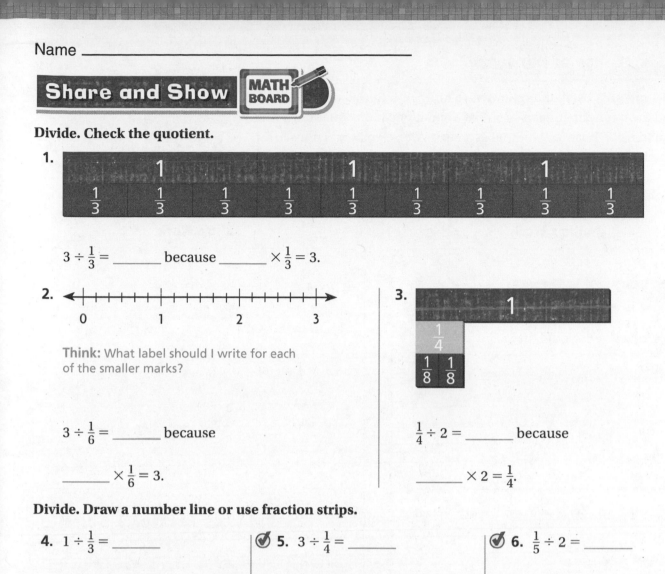

$3 \div \frac{1}{3} =$ _____ because _____ $\times \frac{1}{3} = 3.$

2.

```
←--+++++++--+++++++--+++++++--→
   0        1        2        3
```

Think: What label should I write for each of the smaller marks?

$3 \div \frac{1}{6} =$ _____ because

_____ $\times \frac{1}{6} = 3.$

3.

1
$\frac{1}{4}$
$\frac{1}{8}$ $\frac{1}{8}$

$\frac{1}{4} \div 2 =$ _____ because

_____ $\times 2 = \frac{1}{4}.$

Divide. Draw a number line or use fraction strips.

4. $1 \div \frac{1}{3} =$ _____

5. $3 \div \frac{1}{4} =$ _____

6. $\frac{1}{5} \div 2 =$ _____

7. **GO DEEPER** Luke has $\frac{1}{3}$ of a package of dried apricots. He divides the dried apricots equally into 3 small bags. Luke gives one of the bags to a friend and keeps the other two bags for himself. What fraction of the original package of dried apricots did Luke keep for himself?

_____

8. **THINK SMARTER** For 8a–8e, select True or False for each equation.

8a. $4 \div \frac{1}{3} = \frac{1}{12}$ ○ True   ○ False

8b. $6 \div \frac{1}{2} = 12$ ○ True   ○ False

8c. $\frac{1}{8} \div 2 = 16$ ○ True   ○ False

8d. $\frac{1}{3} \div 4 = \frac{1}{12}$ ○ True   ○ False

8e. $\frac{1}{5} \div 3 = 15$ ○ True   ○ False

THINK SMARTER **Sense or Nonsense?**

9. Emilio and Julia used different ways to find $\frac{1}{2} \div 4$. Emilio used a model to find the quotient. Julia used a related multiplication equation to find the quotient. Whose answer makes sense? Whose answer is nonsense? Explain your reasoning.

Emilio's Work

| 1 |
| $\frac{1}{2}$ |
| $\frac{1}{4}$ | $\frac{1}{4}$ |

$\frac{1}{2} \div 4 = \frac{1}{4}$

_____

_____

_____

_____

Julia's Work

If $\frac{1}{2} \div 4 = $ ▇, then ▇ $\times 4 = \frac{1}{2}$.

I know that $\frac{1}{8} \times 4 = \frac{1}{2}$.

So, $\frac{1}{2} \div 4 = \frac{1}{8}$ because $\frac{1}{8} \times 4 = \frac{1}{2}$.

_____

_____

_____

_____

_____

- For the answer that is nonsense, describe how to find the correct answer.

_____

_____

10. **MATHEMATICAL PRACTICE ⑤** **Use a Concrete Model** If you were going to find $\frac{1}{2} \div 5$, explain how you would find the quotient using fraction strips.

_____

_____

_____

Divide Fractions and Whole Numbers

Common Core **COMMON CORE STANDARDS—**
5.NF.B.7a, 5.NF.B.7b *Apply and extend previous understandings of multiplication and division to multiply and divide fractions.*

Divide and check the quotient.

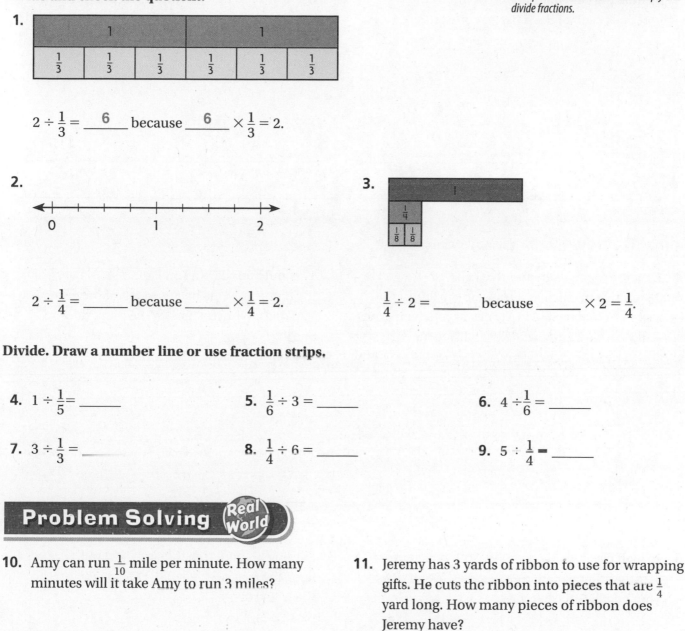

1.

1			1		
$\frac{1}{3}$	$\frac{1}{3}$	$\frac{1}{3}$	$\frac{1}{3}$	$\frac{1}{3}$	$\frac{1}{3}$

$2 \div \frac{1}{3} = $ __6__ because __6__ $\times \frac{1}{3} = 2$.

2.

$2 \div \frac{1}{4} = $ _____ because _____ $\times \frac{1}{4} = 2$.

3.

$\frac{1}{4} \div 2 = $ _____ because _____ $\times 2 = \frac{1}{4}$.

Divide. Draw a number line or use fraction strips.

4. $1 \div \frac{1}{5} = $ _____

5. $\frac{1}{6} \div 3 = $ _____

6. $4 \div \frac{1}{6} = $ _____

7. $3 \div \frac{1}{3} = $ _____

8. $\frac{1}{4} \div 6 = $ _____

9. $5 \div \frac{1}{4} = $ _____

Problem Solving Real World

10. Amy can run $\frac{1}{10}$ mile per minute. How many minutes will it take Amy to run 3 miles?

11. Jeremy has 3 yards of ribbon to use for wrapping gifts. He cuts the ribbon into pieces that are $\frac{1}{4}$ yard long. How many pieces of ribbon does Jeremy have?

_____

_____

12. **WRITE** *Math* Explain how you could use a model to find the quotient $4 \div \frac{1}{3}$.

_____

_____

Lesson Check (5.NF.B.7a, 5.NF.B.7b)

1. Kaley cuts half of a loaf of bread into 4 equal parts. What fraction of the whole loaf does each of the 4 parts represent?

_____

_____

2. When you divide a fraction less than 1 by a whole number greater than 1, is the quotient less than, greater than, or equal to the dividend?

_____

_____

Spiral Review (5.NF.A.1, 5.NF.B.4a, 5.NF.B.6)

3. A recipe for chicken and rice calls for $3\frac{1}{2}$ pounds of chicken. Lisa wants to adjust the recipe so that it yields $1\frac{1}{2}$ times as much chicken and rice. How much chicken will she need?

_____

4. Tim and Sue share a small pizza. Tim eats $\frac{2}{3}$ of the pizza. Sue eats half as much of the pizza as Tim does. What fraction of the pizza does Sue eat?

_____

5. In gym class, you run $\frac{3}{5}$ mile. Your coach runs 10 times that distance each day. How far does your coach run each day?

_____

6. Sterling plants a tree that is $4\frac{3}{4}$ feet tall. One year later, the tree is $5\frac{2}{5}$ feet tall. How many feet did the tree grow?

_____

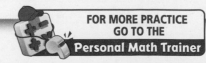

FOR MORE PRACTICE
GO TO THE
Personal Math Trainer

Name _____

Problem Solving • Use Multiplication

Essential Question How can the strategy *draw a diagram* help you solve fraction division problems by writing a multiplication sentence?

Common Core — **Number and Operations—Fractions—5.NF.B.7b**
MATHEMATICAL PRACTICES
MP6, MP8

🔑 Unlock the Problem (Real World)

Erica makes 6 submarine sandwiches and cuts each sandwich into thirds. How many $\frac{1}{3}$-size sandwich pieces does she have?

Read the Problem

What do I need to find?

I need to find _____

_____

_____.

What information do I need to use?

I need to use the size of each _____ of

sandwich and the number of _____ she cuts.

How will I use the information?

I can _____ to organize the information from the problem. Then I can use the organized information to find

_____

_____.

Solve the Problem

Since Erica cuts 6 submarine sandwiches, my diagram needs to show 6 rectangles to represent the sandwiches. I can divide each of the 6 rectangles into thirds.

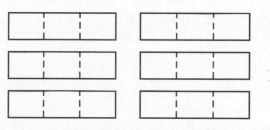

To find the total number of thirds in the 6 rectangles, I can multiply the number of thirds in each rectangle by the number of rectangles.

$6 \div \frac{1}{3} = 6 \times$ _____ = _____

So, Erica has _____ one-third-size sandwich pieces.

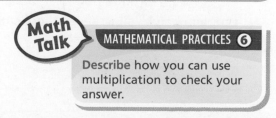

Math Talk

MATHEMATICAL PRACTICES ⑥

Describe how you can use multiplication to check your answer.

🔓 Try Another Problem

Roberto is cutting 3 blueberry pies into halves to give to his neighbors. How many neighbors will get $\frac{1}{2}$ of a pie?

Read the Problem	Solve the Problem
What do I need to find?	
What information do I need to use?	
How will I use the information?	

So, _____ neighbors will get $\frac{1}{2}$ of a pie.

- **MATHEMATICAL PRACTICE 6** **Explain** how the diagram you drew for the division problem helps you write a multiplication sentence.

_____

_____

Name _____

1. A chef has 5 blocks of butter. Each block weighs 1 pound.
   She cuts each block into fourths. How many $\frac{1}{4}$-pound
   pieces of butter does the chef have?

   First, draw rectangles to represent the blocks of butter.

   Then, divide each rectangle into fourths.

   Finally, multiply the number of fourths in each block by the
   number of blocks.

   So, the chef has _____ one-fourth-pound pieces of butter.

   ⊘ 2. **What if** the chef had 3 blocks of butter and cut the blocks into
   thirds? How many $\frac{1}{3}$-pound pieces of butter would the chef have?

   _____

   ⊘ 3. Holly cuts 3 ribbons into eighths for a craft project. How many $\frac{1}{8}$-size
   pieces of ribbon does she have?

   _____

4. Jason has 2 pizzas that he cuts into fourths. How many $\frac{1}{4}$-size pizza
   slices does he have?

   _____

5. Thomas makes 5 sandwiches that he cuts into thirds. How many
   $\frac{1}{3}$-size sandwich pieces does he have?

   _____

WRITE ▸ *Math*
Show Your Work

On Your Own

6. **THINK SMARTER** Julie wants to make a drawing that is $\frac{1}{4}$ the size of the original drawing. Sahil makes a drawing that is $\frac{1}{3}$ the size of the original. A tree in the original drawing is 12 inches tall. What will be the difference between the height of the tree in Julie's and Sahil's drawings?

_____

7. Three friends go to a book fair. Allen spends $2.60. Maria spends 4 times as much as Allen. Akio spends $3.45 less than Maria. How much does Akio spend?

_____

8. **GO DEEPER** Brianna has a sheet of paper that is 6 feet long. She cuts the length of paper into sixths and then cuts the length of each of these $\frac{1}{6}$ pieces into thirds. How many pieces does she have? How many inches long is each piece?

_____

9. **MATHEMATICAL PRACTICE 8** Use Repeated Reasoning Look back at Problem 8. Write a similar problem by changing the length of the paper and the size of the pieces.

_____

_____

_____

_____

_____

_____

Personal Math Trainer

10. **THINK SMARTER +** Adrian made 3 granola bars. He cut each bar into fourths. How many $\frac{1}{4}$-size pieces of granola bar does Adrian have? Draw lines in the model to find the answer.

Adrian has _____ one-quarter-size pieces of granola bar.

Name _____

Problem Solving • Use Multiplication

Common Core

COMMON CORE STANDARD—5.NF.B.7b
Apply and extend previous understandings of multiplication and division to multiply and divide fractions.

1. Sebastian bakes 4 pies and cuts each pie into sixths. How many $\frac{1}{6}$-pie slices does he have?

   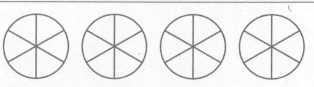

   To find the total number of sixths in the 4 pies, multiply 4 by the number of sixths

   in each pie. $4 \div \frac{1}{6} = 4 \times 6 = 24$ one-sixth-pie slices

2. Ali has 2 vegetable pizzas that she cuts into eighths. How many $\frac{1}{8}$-size pieces does she have?

   _____

3. A baker has 6 loaves of bread. Each loaf weighs 1 pound. He cuts each loaf into thirds. How many $\frac{1}{3}$-pound loaves of bread does the chef now have?

   _____

4. Suppose the baker has 4 loaves of bread and cuts the loaves into halves. How many $\frac{1}{2}$-pound loaves of bread would the baker have?

   _____

5. Madalyn has 3 watermelons that she cuts into halves to give to her neighbors. How many neighbors will get a $\frac{1}{2}$-size piece of watermelon?

   _____

6. **WRITE** ▸*Math* Draw a diagram and explain how you can use it to find $3 \div \frac{1}{5}$.

   _____

   _____

Lesson Check (5.NF.B.7b)

1. Julia has 12 pieces of fabric and cuts each piece into fourths. How many $\frac{1}{4}$ pieces of fabric does she have?

_____

2. Josue has 3 chicken pot pies that he cuts into thirds. How many $\frac{1}{3}$-size chicken pot pies pieces does he have?

_____

Spiral Review (5.NBT.A.2, 5.NF.B.4a, 5.NF.B.7a, 5.NF.B.7b)

3. Write a related multiplication sentence that could help you find the quotient of $6 \div \frac{1}{4}$.

_____

4. Ellie uses 12.5 pounds of potatoes to make mashed potatoes. She uses one-tenth as many pounds of butter as potatoes. How many pounds of butter does Ellie use?

_____

5. Tiffany collects perfume bottles. She has 99 bottles in her collection. Two-thirds of her perfume bottles are made of crystal. How many of the perfume bottles in Tiffany's collection are made of crystal?

_____

6. Stephen buys a melon and divides it into 6 servings. He eats $\frac{1}{3}$ of the melon over the weekend. How many slices of melon does Stephen eat over the weekend?

_____

FOR MORE PRACTICE
GO TO THE
Personal Math Trainer

Name _____

Connect Fractions to Division

Essential Question How does a fraction represent division?

Common Core **Number and Operations—Fractions—5.NF.B.3**
MATHEMATICAL PRACTICES
MP1, MP2, MP6

CONNECT A fraction can be written as a division problem.

$$\frac{3}{4} = 3 \div 4 \qquad\qquad \frac{12}{2} = 12 \div 2$$

Unlock the Problem Real World

There are 3 students in a crafts class and 2 sheets of construction paper for them to share equally. What part of the construction paper will each student get?

- Circle the dividend.
- Underline the divisor.

Use a drawing.

Divide. $2 \div 3$

STEP 1 Draw lines to divide each piece of paper into 3 equal pieces.

Each student's share of one sheet of construction paper is _____.

_____

STEP 2 Count the number of thirds each student will get. Since there are 2 sheets of construction paper, each student will

get 2 of the _____, or 2 × _____.

_____

STEP 3 Complete the number sentence.

$2 \div 3 =$

_____

STEP 4 Check your answer.

Since _____ × _____ = _____, the quotient is correct.
      quotient divisor dividend

So, each student will get _____ of a sheet of construction paper.

Math Talk MATHEMATICAL PRACTICES ⑥

Describe a division problem where each student gets $\frac{3}{4}$ of a sheet of construction paper.

🔑 Example

Four friends share 6 sheets of poster board equally. How many sheets of poster board does each friend get?

Divide. 6 ÷ 4

STEP 1 Draw lines to divide each of the 6 sheets into fourths.

Each friend's share of 1 sheet is _____.

STEP 2 Count the number of fourths each friend gets. Since there are 6 sheets of poster board, each friend will

get _____ of the fourths, or ——.

STEP 3 Complete the number sentence. Write the fraction as a mixed number in simplest form.

6 ÷ 4 = ——, or ▢ ——

STEP 4 Check your answer.

Since _____ × 4 = _____, the quotient is correct.

So, each friend will get _____ sheets of poster board.

Math Talk

MATHEMATICAL PRACTICES ②

Reason Abstractly Describe a different way the sheets of poster board could have been divided into 4 equal shares.

Try This!

Ms. Ruiz has a piece of string that is 125 inches long. For a science experiment, she divides the string equally among 8 groups of students. How much string will each group get?

You can represent this problem as a division equation or a fraction.

- Divide. Write the remainder as a fraction. 125 ÷ 8 = _____

- Write $\frac{125}{8}$ as a mixed number in simplest form. $\frac{125}{8}$ = _____

So, each group will get _____ inches of string.

- **MATHEMATICAL PRACTICE ①** **Evaluate** Explain why 125 ÷ 8 gives the same result as $\frac{125}{8}$.

_____

_____

Name _____

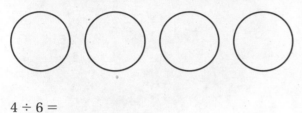 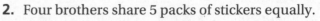
Draw lines on the model to complete the number sentence.

1. Six friends share 4 small pizzas equally.

( ) ( ) ( ) ( )

$4 \div 6 =$ _____

Each friend's share is _____ of a pizza.

2. Four brothers share 5 packs of stickers equally.

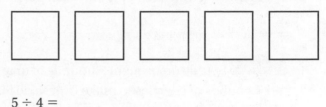

$5 \div 4 =$ _____

Each brother's share is _____ packs of stickers.

Complete the number sentence to solve.

✓ **3.** Twelve friends share 3 melons equally. What fraction of a melon does each friend get?

$3 \div 12 =$ _____

Each friend's share is _____ of a melon.

✓ **4.** Three students share 8 blocks of clay equally. How much clay does each student get?

$8 \div 3 =$ _____

Each student's share is _____ blocks of clay.

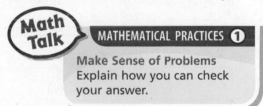

Math Talk MATHEMATICAL PRACTICES ❶

Make Sense of Problems Explain how you can check your answer.

On Your Own

Complete the number sentence to solve.

5. Four students share 7 feet of ribbon equally. How many feet of ribbon does each student get?

$7 \div 4 =$ _____

Each student's share is _____ feet of ribbon.

6. Eight girls share 5 fruit bars equally. What fraction of a fruit bar does each girl get?

$5 \div 8 =$ _____

Each girl's share is _____ of a fruit bar.

7. *THINK SMARTER* Eight students share 12 mini oatmeal muffins equally and 6 students share 15 mini apple muffins equally. Carmine is in both groups of students. What is the total number of mini muffins Carmine gets?

_____

Problem Solving • Applications (Real World)

8. Shawna has 3 adults and 2 children coming over. She is going to serve 2 small apple pies. If she plans to give each person, including herself, an equal amount of pie, how much pie will each person get?

_____

9. GO DEEPER Addison brought 9 pounds of oranges and 7 pounds of cherries to make fruit salad for a fund raiser. She wants to package an equal amount of fruit salad into each of 12 containers. How much fruit salad should Addison put in each container?

_____

10. MATHEMATICAL PRACTICE ② **Use Reasoning** Nine friends order 4 large pizzas. Four of the friends share 2 pizzas equally and the other 5 friends share 2 pizzas equally. In which group does each member get a greater amount of pizza? Explain your reasoning.

_____

_____

_____

_____

_____

11. THINK SMARTER Jason has 5 zucchinis he grew in his garden. He wants to share them equally among 3 of his neighbors. How many zucchinis will each neighbor get? Use the numbers to complete the number sentence. You may use a number more than once or not at all.

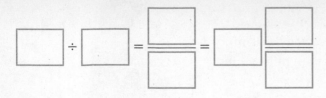

COMMON CORE STANDARD—5.NF.B.3
Apply and extend previous understandings of multiplication and division to multiply and divide fractions.

Complete the number sentence to solve.

1. Six students share 8 apples equally. How many apples does each student get?

$8 \div 6 =$ _____ $\dfrac{8}{6}$, or $1\dfrac{1}{3}$ _____

2. Ten boys share 7 cereal bars equally. What fraction of a cereal bar does each boy get?

$7 \div 10 =$ _____

3. Eight friends share 12 burritos equally. How many burritos does each friend get?

$12 \div 8 =$ _____

4. Three girls share 8 yards of fabric equally. How many yards of fabric does each girl get?

$8 \div 3 =$ _____

5. Five bakers share 2 loaves of bread equally. What fraction of a loaf of bread does each baker get?

$2 \div 5 =$ _____

6. Nine friends share 6 bananas equally. What fraction of a bananas does each friend get?

$6 \div 9 =$ _____

Problem Solving Real World

7. There are 12 students in a jewelry-making class and 8 sets of charms. What fraction of a set of charms will each student get?

_____

_____

8. Five friends share 6 fruit snacks equally. How many fruit snacks will each friend get?

_____

_____

9. **WRITE** *Math* Jason divides 8 pounds of dog food equally among 6 dogs. Draw a diagram and explain how you can use it to find the amount of food each dog receives.

_____

_____

Lesson Check (5.NF.B.3)

1. Eight friends share 4 bunches of grapes equally. What fraction of a bunch of grapes does each friend get?

2. Ten students share 8 pieces of poster board equally. What fraction of a piece of poster board does each student get?

_____

_____

Spiral Review (5.NBT.B.6, 5.NBT.B.7, 5.NF.B.7a, 5.NF.B.7b)

3. Arturo has a log that is 4 yards long. He cuts the log into pieces that are $\frac{1}{3}$-yard long. How many pieces will Arturo have?

4. Vu has 2 pizzas that he cuts into sixths. How many $\frac{1}{6}$-size pieces does he have?

_____

_____

5. Kayaks rent for $35 per day. Write an expression using the Distributive Property that can help you find the cost in dollars of renting 3 kayaks for a day.

6. Louisa is 152.7 centimeters tall. Her younger sister is 8.42 centimeters shorter than she is. How tall is Louisa's younger sister?

_____

_____

_____

_____

FOR MORE PRACTICE
GO TO THE
Personal Math Trainer

Name _____

✓ Mid-Chapter Checkpoint

Personal Math Trainer
Online Assessment
and Intervention

Concepts and Skills

1. **Explain** how you can tell, without computing, whether the quotient $\frac{1}{2} \div 6$ is greater than 1 or less than 1. (5.NF.B.7a, 5.NF.B.7b)

_____

_____

Divide. Draw a number line or use fraction strips. (5.NF.B.7a, 5.NF.B.7b)

2. $3 \div \frac{1}{2} =$ _____

3. $1 \div \frac{1}{4} =$ _____

4. $\frac{1}{2} \div 2 =$ _____

5. $\frac{1}{3} \div 4 =$ _____

6. $2 \div \frac{1}{6} =$ _____

7. $\frac{1}{4} \div 3 =$ _____

Complete the number sentence to solve. (5.NF.B.3)

8. Two students share 3 granola bars equally. How many granola bars does each student get?

    $3 \div 2 =$ _____

    Each student's share is _____ granola bars.

9. Five girls share 4 sandwiches equally. What fraction of a sandwich does each girl get?

    $4 \div 5 =$ _____

    Each girl's share is _____ of a sandwich.

10. Nine boys share 4 pizzas equally. What fraction of a pizza does each boy get?

    $4 \div 9 =$ _____

    Each boy's share is _____ of a pizza.

11. Four friends share 10 fruit bars equally. How many fruit bars does each friend get?

    $10 \div 4 =$ _____

    Each friend's share is _____ fruit bars.

12. Mateo has 8 liters of punch for a party. Each glass holds $\frac{1}{5}$ liter of punch. How many glasses can Mateo fill with punch? (5.NF.B.7b)

_____

13. Four friends share 3 sheets of construction paper equally. What fraction of a sheet of paper does each friend get? (5.NF.B.3)

_____

14. Caleb and 2 friends are sharing $\frac{1}{2}$ quart of milk equally. What fraction of a quart of milk does each of the 3 friends get? (5.NF.B.7a)

_____

15. GO DEEPER Toni and Makayla are working on a craft project. Makayla has 3 yards of ribbon and Toni has 4 yards of ribbon. They cut all the ribbon into pieces that are $\frac{1}{4}$ yard long. How many pieces of ribbon do they have? (5.NF.B.7b)

_____

510

Name _____

Fraction and Whole-Number Division

Essential Question How can you divide fractions by solving a related multiplication sentence?

Common Core — Number and Operations—Fractions—5.NF.B.7c
Also 5.NF.B.7a, 5.NF.B.7b

MATHEMATICAL PRACTICES
MP3, MP5

Unlock the Problem *Real World*

Three friends share a $\frac{1}{4}$-pound package of beads equally. What fraction of a pound of beads does each friend get?

Divide. $\frac{1}{4} \div 3$

- Let the rectangle represent 1 pound of beads. Divide the rectangle into fourths and then divide each fourth into three equal parts.

  The rectangle is now divided into _____ equal parts.

- When you divide one fourth into 3 equal parts, you are finding one of three equal parts or $\frac{1}{3}$ of $\frac{1}{4}$. Shade $\frac{1}{3}$ of $\frac{1}{4}$.

  The shaded part is _____ of the whole rectangle.

- Complete the number sentence.

So, each friend gets _____ of a pound of beads.

$\frac{1}{4}$

$\frac{1}{4} \div 3 - \frac{1}{3} \times \frac{1}{4} = $ _____

Example

Brad has 9 pounds of ground turkey to make turkey burgers for a picnic. How many $\frac{1}{3}$-pound turkey burgers can he make?

Divide. $9 \div \frac{1}{3}$

- Draw 9 rectangles to represent each pound of ground turkey. Divide each rectangle into thirds.

- When you divide the _____ rectangles into thirds, you are finding the number of thirds in 9 rectangles or

  finding 9 groups of _____. There are _____ thirds.

- Complete the number sentence.

So, Brad can make _____ one-third-pound turkey burgers.

- Will the number of turkey burgers be less than or greater than 9?

  _____

$9 \div \frac{1}{3} = $ _____ $\times$ _____ $=$ _____

CONNECT You have learned how to use a model and write a multiplication sentence to solve a division problem.

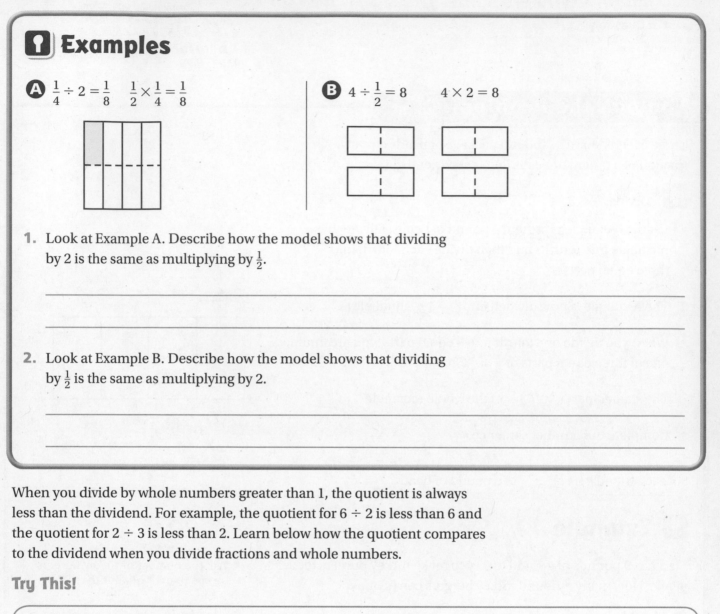

Examples

A $\frac{1}{4} \div 2 = \frac{1}{8}$ $\frac{1}{2} \times \frac{1}{4} = \frac{1}{8}$

B $4 \div \frac{1}{2} = 8$ $4 \times 2 = 8$

1. Look at Example A. Describe how the model shows that dividing by 2 is the same as multiplying by $\frac{1}{2}$.

_____

_____

2. Look at Example B. Describe how the model shows that dividing by $\frac{1}{2}$ is the same as multiplying by 2.

_____

_____

When you divide by whole numbers greater than 1, the quotient is always less than the dividend. For example, the quotient for $6 \div 2$ is less than 6 and the quotient for $2 \div 3$ is less than 2. Learn below how the quotient compares to the dividend when you divide fractions and whole numbers.

Try This!

For the two expressions below, which will have a quotient that is greater than its dividend? Explain.

$\frac{1}{2} \div 3$ $3 \div \frac{1}{2}$

_____

_____

So, when I divide a fraction by a whole number greater than 1, the quotient

is _____ the dividend. When I divide a whole number by a

fraction less than 1, the quotient is _____ the dividend.

Name _____

1. Use the model to complete the number sentence.

$$2 \div \frac{1}{4} = 2 \times \underline{\hspace{1cm}} = \underline{\hspace{1cm}}$$

Write a related multiplication sentence to solve.

✓ **2.** $\frac{1}{9} \div 3$

✓ **3.** $7 \div \frac{1}{2}$

_____   _____

On Your Own

Write a related multiplication sentence to solve.

4. $\frac{1}{3} \div 4$

5. $\frac{1}{4} \div 12$

6. $6 \div \frac{1}{5}$

7. $\frac{2}{3} \div 3$

_____   _____   _____   _____

8. **MATHEMATICAL PRACTICE ③** **Describe Relationships** Describe how the model shows that dividing by 2 is the same as finding $\frac{1}{2}$ of $\frac{1}{4}$.

$$\frac{1}{4} \div 2 = \frac{1}{8}$$

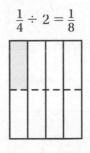

_____

_____

_____

9. **GO DEEPER** Mrs. Lia has 12 pounds of modeling clay. She divides the clay into $\frac{1}{2}$-pound blocks. If Mrs. Lia sets aside 6 of the blocks and gives the rest to the students in her art class, how many $\frac{1}{2}$-pound blocks of clay does Mrs. Lia give to her class?

_____

🔑 Unlock the Problem Real World

10. **THINK SMARTER** The slowest mammal is the three-toed sloth. The top speed of a three-toed sloth on the ground is about $\frac{1}{4}$ foot per second. The top speed of a giant tortoise on the ground is about $\frac{1}{3}$ foot per second. How much longer would it take a three-toed sloth than a giant tortoise to travel 10 feet on the ground?

a. What do you need to find? _____

_____

b. What operations will you use to solve the problem? _____

_____

c. Show the steps you used to solve the problem.

d. Complete the sentences.

A three-toed sloth would travel 10 feet in

_____ seconds.

A giant tortoise would travel 10 feet in

_____ seconds.

Since _____ − _____ = _____,
it would take a three-toed sloth

_____ seconds longer to travel 10 feet.

Personal Math Trainer

11. **THINK SMARTER +** Jamie has a striped fabric that is 5 yards long and a solid fabric that is 4 yards long. She cuts the striped fabric into equal pieces that are $\frac{1}{4}$ yard long and the solid fabric into equal pieces that are $\frac{1}{3}$ yard long. How many more pieces of striped fabric does she have than pieces of solid fabric? Explain how you solved the problem.

_____

_____

_____

_____

Fraction and Whole-Number Division

Common Core

COMMON CORE STANDARD—5.NF.B.7c
Apply and extend previous understandings of multiplication and division to multiply and divide fractions.

Write a related multiplication sentence to solve.

1. $3 \div \frac{1}{2}$

$3 \times 2 = 6$

2. $\frac{1}{5} \div 3$

15

3. $2 \div \frac{1}{8}$

16

4. $\frac{1}{3} \div 4$

12

5. $5 \div \frac{1}{4}$

20

6. $\frac{1}{2} \div 2$

4

7. $\frac{1}{4} \div 6$

24

8. $6 \div \frac{1}{5}$

30

9. $\frac{1}{5} \div 5$

25

10. $4 \div \frac{1}{8}$

32

11. $\frac{1}{3} \div 7$

21

12. $9 \div \frac{1}{2}$

18

Problem Solving Real World

13. Isaac has a piece of rope that is 5 yards long. Into how many $\frac{1}{2}$-yard pieces of rope can Isaac cut the rope?

10

14. Two friends share $\frac{1}{2}$ of a pineapple equally. What fraction of a whole pineapple does each friend get?

1

15. **WRITE** ▸*Math* Tell whether the quotient is greater than or less than the dividend when you divide a whole number by a fraction. Explain your reasoning.

it is greater

Lesson Check (5.NF.B.7c)

1. Sean divides 8 cups of granola into $\frac{1}{4}$-cup servings. How many servings of granola does he have?

32 servings

2. Brandy solved $\frac{1}{6} \div 5$ by using a related multiplication expression. What multiplication expression did she use?

she used $5 \div \frac{1}{6}$

Spiral Review (5.NF.A.2, 5.NF.B.3, 5.NF.B.4a, 5.NF.B.7b)

3. Nine friends share 12 pounds of pecans equally. How many pounds of pecans does each friend get?

1 pound

4. A scientist has $\frac{2}{3}$ liter of solution. He uses $\frac{1}{2}$ of the solution for an experiment. How much solution does the scientist use for the experiment?

$$\frac{5}{6} \quad \frac{3}{4}$$

5. Naomi needs 2 cups of chopped apples for a fruit salad she is making. She only has a $\frac{1}{4}$ cup measuring cup. How many times will Naomi need to fill the measuring cup to get 2 cups of apples?

8 times

6. Michaela catches 3 fish, which weigh a total of $19\frac{1}{2}$ pounds. One fish weighs $7\frac{5}{8}$ pounds and another weighs $5\frac{3}{4}$ pounds. How much does the third fish weigh?

$2\frac{3}{6}$

**FOR MORE PRACTICE
GO TO THE
Personal Math Trainer**

Interpret Division with Fractions

Essential Question How can you use diagrams, equations, and story problems to represent division?

Common Core Number and Operations—
Fractions—5.NF.B.7a, 5.NF.B.7b
Also 5.NF.B.7c
MATHEMATICAL PRACTICES
MP2, MP5

Unlock the Problem Real World

Elisa has 6 cups of raisins. She divides the raisins into $\frac{1}{4}$-cup servings. How many servings does she have?

You can use diagrams, equations, and story problems to represent division.

⬛ Draw a diagram to solve.

- Draw 6 rectangles to represent the cups of raisins. Draw lines to divide each rectangle into fourths.

- To find $6 \div \frac{1}{4}$, count the total number of fourths in the 6 rectangles.

  $6 \div$ _____ = _____

So, Elisa has _____ servings.

- How many $\frac{1}{4}$-cups are in 1 cup?

  _____

- How many cups does Elisa have?

  _____

⬛ Example 1 Write an equation to solve.

Four friends share $\frac{1}{4}$ of a gallon of orange juice. What fraction of a gallon of orange juice does each friend get?

STEP 1

Write an equation.

$\frac{1}{4} \div$ _____ $= n$

STEP 2

Write a related multiplication equation. Then solve.

$\frac{1}{4} \times$ _____ $= n$

_____ $= n$

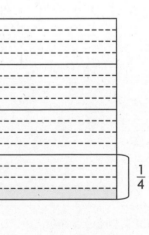

So, each friend will get _____ of a gallon of orange juice.

🔑 Example 2 Write a story problem. Then draw a diagram to solve.

$4 \div \frac{1}{3}$

STEP 1 Choose the item you want to divide.

> **Think:** Your problem should be about how many groups of $\frac{1}{3}$ are in 4 wholes.

Possible items: 4 sandwiches, 4 feet of ribbon, 4 apples

STEP 2 Write a story problem to represent $4 \div \frac{1}{3}$ using the item you chose. Describe how it is divided into thirds. Then ask how many thirds there are.

_____

_____

_____

STEP 3 Draw a diagram to solve.

$4 \div \frac{1}{3} =$ _____

🔑 Example 3 Write a story problem. Then draw a diagram to solve.

$\frac{1}{2} \div 5$

STEP 1 Choose the item you want to divide.

> **Think:** Your problem should describe $\frac{1}{2}$ of an item that can be divided into 5 equal parts.

Possible items: $\frac{1}{2}$ of a pizza, $\frac{1}{2}$ of a yard of rope, $\frac{1}{2}$ of a gallon of milk

STEP 2 Write a story problem to represent $\frac{1}{2} \div 5$ using the item you chose. Describe how it is divided into 5 equal parts. Then ask about the size of each part.

_____

_____

_____

STEP 3 Draw a diagram to solve.

$\frac{1}{2} \div 5 =$ _____

Math Talk

MATHEMATICAL PRACTICES ④

Use Diagrams Explain how you decided what type of diagram to draw for your problem.

© Houghton Mifflin Harcourt Publishing Company • Image Credits: (t) ©Kraig Scarbinsky/Getty Images

Name _____

1. Complete the story problem to represent $3 \div \frac{1}{4}$.

   Carmen has a roll of paper that is _____ feet long. She cuts

   the paper into pieces that are each _____ foot long. How many
   pieces of paper does Carmen have?

2. Draw a diagram to represent the problem.
   Then solve.

   April has 6 fruit bars. She cuts the bars into
   halves. How many $\frac{1}{2}$-size bar pieces does
   she have?

3. Write an equation to represent the problem.
   Then solve.

   Two friends share $\frac{1}{4}$ of a large peach pie. What
   fraction of the whole pie does each friend get?

   _____

   _____

On Your Own

4. *THINK SMARTER* Write an equation to
   represent the problem. Then solve.

   Benito has $\frac{1}{3}$ kilogram of grapes. He
   divides the grapes equally into 3 bags.
   What fraction of a kilogram of grapes is
   in each bag?

   _____

   _____

5. *GO DEEPER* Draw a diagram to represent the
   problem. Then solve.

   Sonya has 5 sandwiches. She cuts each sandwich
   into fourths and gives away 6 pieces. How many
   $\frac{1}{4}$-size sandwich pieces does she have now?

   _____

   _____

6. *MATHEMATICAL PRACTICE ②* **Represent a Problem** Write a story problem to

   represent $2 \div \frac{1}{8}$. Then solve.

   _____

   _____

Problem Solving • Applications Real World

THINK SMARTER Pose a Problem

7. Amy wrote the following problem to represent $4 \div \frac{1}{6}$.

Jacob has a board that is 4 feet long. He cuts the board into pieces that are each $\frac{1}{6}$ foot long. How many pieces does Jacob have now?

Then Amy drew this diagram to solve her problem.

So, Jacob has 24 pieces.

Write a new problem using a different item to be divided and different fractional pieces. Then draw a diagram to solve your problem.

Pose a problem.

_____

_____

_____

_____

_____

_____

_____

Draw a diagram to solve your problem.

8. **THINK SMARTER** Melvin has $\frac{1}{4}$ gallon of fruit punch. He shares the punch equally with each of 2 friends and himself. Which equation represents the fraction of a gallon of punch that each of the 3 friends will get? Mark all that apply.

(A) $\frac{1}{4} \div \frac{1}{3} = n$ (C) $3 \div \frac{1}{4} = n$ (E) $\frac{1}{4} \div 3 = n$

(B) $\frac{1}{4} \times \frac{1}{3} = n$ (D) $3 \div 4 = n$ (F) $3 \times \frac{1}{4} = n$

Interpret Division with Fractions

COMMON CORE STANDARD—5.NF.B.7a,
5.NF.B.7b *Apply and extend previous*
understandings of multiplication and division
to multiply and divide fractions.

Write an equation to represent the problem. Then solve.

1. Daniel has a piece of wire that is $\frac{1}{2}$ yard long. He cuts the wire into 3 equal pieces. What fraction of a yard is each piece?

   $\frac{1}{2} \div 3 = n; \frac{1}{2} \times \frac{1}{3} = n; n = \frac{1}{6}; \frac{1}{6}$ yard

2. Vita has a piece of ribbon that is 5 meters long. She cuts the ribbon into pieces that are each $\frac{1}{3}$ meter long. How many pieces does she cut?

   _____

Draw a diagram to represent the problem. Then solve.

3. Leah has 3 muffins. She cuts each muffin into fourths. How many $\frac{1}{4}$-muffin pieces does she have?

   _____

4. Two friends share $\frac{1}{4}$ gallon of lemonade equally. What fraction of the gallon of lemonade does each friend get?

   _____

5. **WRITE** ▸*Math* Write a story problem to represent $3 \div \frac{1}{2}$.

   _____

   _____

6. **WRITE** ▸*Math* Write a story problem to represent $\frac{1}{4} \div 2$.

   _____

   _____

Problem Solving

7. Spencer has $\frac{1}{3}$ pound of nuts. He divides the nuts equally into 4 bags. What fraction of a pound of nuts is in each bag?

   _____

8. Humma has 3 apples. She slices each apple into eighths. How many $\frac{1}{8}$-apple slices does she have?

   _____

Lesson Check

1. Abigail has $\frac{1}{2}$ gallon of orange juice. She divides the juice equally into 6 glasses. What equation represents the fraction of a gallon of orange juice in each glass?

2. Write an expression to represent the following situation. Riley has a piece of wire that is 4 yards long. He cuts it into pieces that are $\frac{1}{2}$ yard long. How many pieces of wire does Riley have?

Spiral Review (5.NF.A.1, 5.NF.B.3, 5.NF.B.4a, 5.NF.B.6)

3. Hannah buys $\frac{2}{3}$ pound of roast beef. She uses $\frac{1}{4}$ pound to make a sandwich for lunch. How much roast beef does she have left?

4. Alex buys $2\frac{1}{2}$ pounds of grapes. He buys $1\frac{1}{4}$ times as many pounds of apples as grapes. How many pounds of apples does Alex buy?

5. Maritza's car has 16 gallons of gas in the tank. She uses $\frac{3}{4}$ of the gas. How many gallons of gas does Maritza use?

6. Jaime has a board that is 8 feet long. He cuts the board into three equal pieces. How long is each piece?

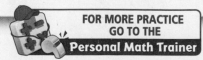

FOR MORE PRACTICE
GO TO THE
Personal Math Trainer

Name _____

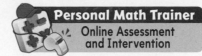
1. A builder has an 8-acre plot divided into $\frac{1}{4}$-acre home sites. How many $\frac{1}{4}$-acre home sites are there?

   There are ☐ home sites.

2. For numbers 2a–2e, select True or False for each equation.

   2a. $3 \div \frac{1}{4} = \frac{1}{12}$ ○ True   ○ False

   2b. $7 \div \frac{1}{2} = 14$ ○ True   ○ False

   2c. $\frac{1}{5} \div 4 = 20$ ○ True   ○ False

   2d. $\frac{1}{2} \div 5 = \frac{1}{10}$ ○ True   ○ False

   2e. $\frac{1}{7} \div 3 = 21$ ○ True   ○ False

3. Twelve pounds of beans are distributed equally into 8 bags to give out at the food bank. How many pounds of beans are in each bag?

   _____ pounds

Personal Math Trainer

4. **THINK SMARTER +** Gabriel made 4 small meatloaves. He cut each meatloaf into fourths. How many $\frac{1}{4}$-size pieces of meatloaf does Gabriel have? Draw lines in the model to find the answer.

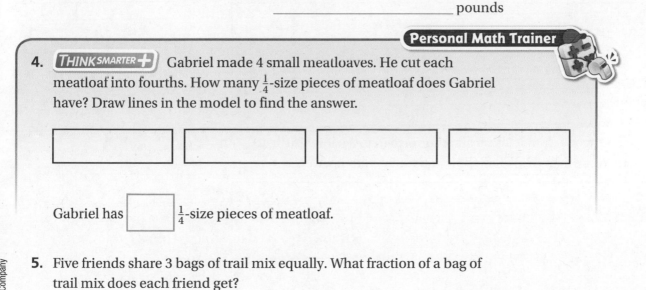

   Gabriel has ☐ $\frac{1}{4}$-size pieces of meatloaf.

5. Five friends share 3 bags of trail mix equally. What fraction of a bag of trail mix does each friend get?

Assessment Options
Chapter Test

6. Landon and Colin bought $\frac{1}{2}$ pound of strawberries. They are sharing the strawberries equally. Each person will receive [ ] pound of strawberries.

7. Choose the numbers to create a story problem that represents $4 \div \frac{1}{3}$.

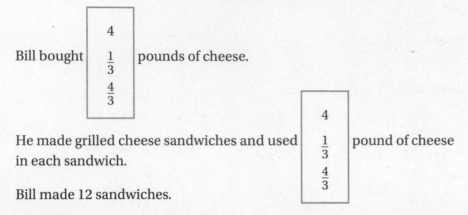

Bill bought | 4 / $\frac{1}{3}$ / $\frac{4}{3}$ | pounds of cheese.

He made grilled cheese sandwiches and used | 4 / $\frac{1}{3}$ / $\frac{4}{3}$ | pound of cheese in each sandwich.

Bill made 12 sandwiches.

8. A giant tortoise can walk about $\frac{1}{10}$ meter per second on land. A cooter turtle can walk about $\frac{1}{2}$ meter per second on land.

Part A

How long would it take a giant tortoise to travel 5 meters?
Show your work.

Part B

How much longer would it take a giant tortoise than a cooter turtle to travel 10 meters on land? Explain how you found your answer.

Name _____

9. Camilla has a $\frac{1}{2}$ pound of raisins that she will divide evenly into 5 bags. Shade the diagram to show the fractional part of a pound that will be in each bag.

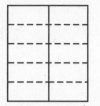

10. Mrs. Green wrote the following problem on the whiteboard:

Lisa and Frank shared $\frac{1}{3}$ pound of cherries equally. What fractional part of a pound did each person receive?

Part A

Molly wrote the following equation to solve the problem: $2 \div \frac{1}{3} = n$. Do you agree with Molly's equation? Support your answer with information from the problem.

Part B

Noah drew this diagram to solve the problem. Can Noah use his diagram to find the fractional part of a pound of cherries that each person received? Support your answer with information from the problem.

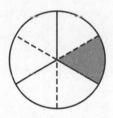

11. Divide. Draw a number line to show your work.

$2 \div \frac{1}{3} =$ ☐

12. Zoe has 5 cucumbers she grew in her garden. She wants to share them equally among 4 of her neighbors. How many cucumbers will each neighbor receive? Use the numbers on the tiles to complete the number sentence. You may use a number more than once or not at all.

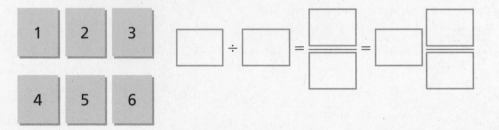

13. Dora buys one package each of 1-pound, 2-pound, and 4-pound packages of ground beef to make hamburgers.

How many $\frac{1}{4}$-pound hamburgers can she make? Show your work using words, pictures, or numbers.

14. Adan has $\frac{1}{2}$ quart of milk. If he pours the same amount of milk into

3 glasses, each glass will contain ☐ quart of milk.

15. Nine friends share 3 pumpkin pies equally. What fraction of a pumpkin pie does each friend get?

Each friend will get ☐ of a pumpkin pie.

16. Jesse is making a pitcher of fruit smoothies that contains 3 cups of orange juice. His measuring cup only holds $\frac{1}{4}$ cup. How many times will Jesse need to fill the measuring cup to get the 3 cups of orange juice?

17. Kayleigh has $\frac{1}{4}$-cup of oil. She pours the same amount into each of 2 oil lamps. Which equation represents the fraction of a cup of oil that is in each oil lamp? Mark all that apply.

(A) $\frac{1}{2} \div \frac{1}{4} = n$

(B) $\frac{1}{4} \times \frac{1}{2} = n$

(C) $2 \div \frac{1}{4} = n$

(D) $4 \div 2 = n$

(E) $\frac{1}{4} \div 2 = n$

(F) $2 \times \frac{1}{4} = n$

18. Brendan made a loaf of bread. He gave equal portions of $\frac{1}{2}$ of the loaf of bread to 6 friends. Which diagram could Brendon use to find the fraction of the loaf of bread that each friend received? Mark all that apply.

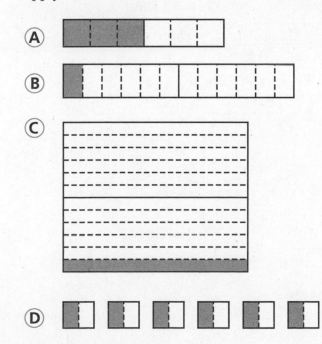

19. Your teacher gives you the problem $6 \div \frac{1}{5}$.

Part A

Draw a diagram to represent $6 \div \frac{1}{5}$.

Part B

Write a story problem to represent $6 \div \frac{1}{5}$.

Part C

Use a related multiplication expression to solve your story problem. Show your work.

20. **GO DEEPER** Seven friends picked 7 quarts of blueberries. Three of the friends will share 4 quarts of blueberries equally and the other 4 friends will share 3 quarts of the blueberries equally. In which group does each friend get a greater amount of blueberries? Explain your reasoning.

Critical Area # Geometry and Measurement

Common Core **CRITICAL AREA** Developing understanding of volume

A lunar rover is a surface exploration vehicle used on the moon. ▶

Space Architecture

NASA's Lunar Architecture Team develops ideas for rovers and space habitats. A space habitat is made up of modules linked by airlocks. Airlocks are double doors that allow people to move between the modules without losing atmosphere.

Get Started

Work with a partner to design a space habitat made up of 3 modules. The Important Facts name some modules that you can choose for your design. Cut out, fold, and tape the patterns for each of the modules that you have selected, and for the measuring cube.

Use a formula to find the volume of the measuring cube in cubic centimeters. Estimate the volume of each module by filling it with rice, then pouring the rice into the measuring cube. Let every cubic centimeter in the measuring cube represent 32 cubic feet. Determine what the volume of your space habitat would be in cubic feet.

Connect the modules to complete your space habitat.

_____

_____

_____

_____

_____

_____

_____

Completed by _____

Algebra: Patterns and Graphing

✔ Show What You Know

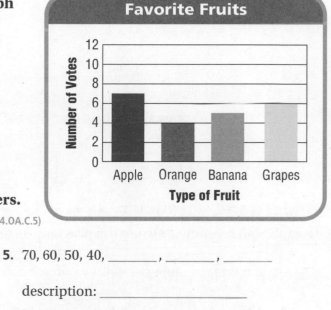

Personal Math Trainer
Online Assessment and Intervention

Check your understanding of important skills.

Name _____

▶ **Read and Use a Bar Graph** Use the graph to answer the questions. (3.MD.B.3)

1. Which fruit received the most votes?

_____

2. Which fruit received 5 votes? _____

3. There were _____ votes in all.

Favorite Fruits

▶ **Extend Patterns** Find the missing numbers. Then write a description for each pattern. (4.OA.C.5)

4. 0, 5, 10, 15, _____ , _____ , _____

   description: _____

5. 70, 60, 50, 40, _____ , _____ , _____

   description: _____

6. 12, 18, 24, 30, _____ , _____ , _____

   description: _____

7. 150, 200, 250, 300, _____ , _____ , _____

   description: _____

8. 200, 180, 160, 140, _____ , _____ , _____

   description: _____

Graph and connect the map coordinates to locate the secret documents in the lost briefcase.

(3, 3), (4, 2), (4, 4), (5, 3)

Vocabulary Builder

▶ **Visualize It** •

Use the checked words to complete the tree map.

data
<
_____
_____

coordinate grid
<
_____
_____
_____
_____

▶ **Understand Vocabulary** •

Complete the sentences using the preview words.

1. A graph that uses line segments to show how data changes over time

   is called a _____.

2. The pair of numbers used to locate points on a grid is

   an _____.

3. The point, (0, 0), also called the _____, is where the
   x-axis and the *y*-axis intersect.

4. On a coordinate grid, the horizontal number line is the _____
   and the vertical number line is the _____.

5. The first number in an ordered pair is the _____ and
   the second number in an ordered pair is the _____.

6. The difference between the values on the scale of a graph

   is an _____.

• **Interactive Student Edition**
• **Multimedia eGlossary**

Chapter 9 Vocabulary

coordinate grid

cuadrícula de coordenadas

9

data

datos

10

interval

intervalo

31

line graph

gráfica lineal

35

line plot

diagrama de puntos

36

ordered pair

par ordenado

45

origin

origen

46

scale

escala

61

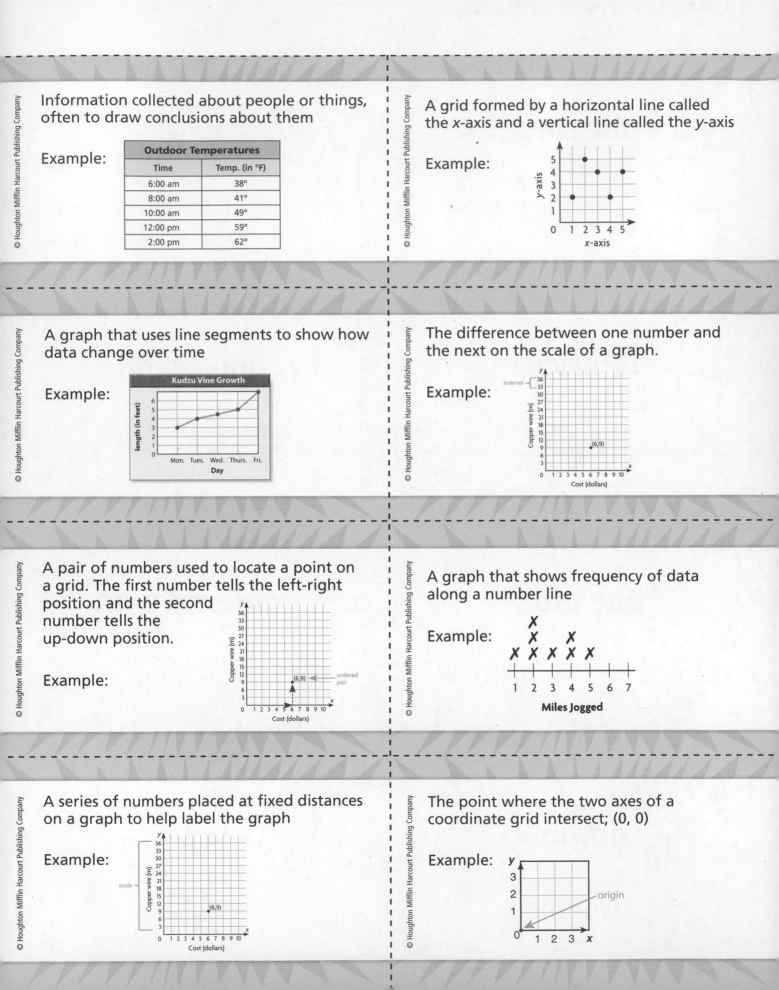

Information collected about people or things, often to draw conclusions about them

Example:

Outdoor Temperatures	
Time	Temp. (in °F)
6:00 am	38°
8:00 am	41°
10:00 am	49°
12:00 pm	59°
2:00 pm	62°

A grid formed by a horizontal line called the *x*-axis and a vertical line called the *y*-axis

Example:

A graph that uses line segments to show how data change over time

Example:

Kudzu Vine Growth

The difference between one number and the next on the scale of a graph.

Example:

A pair of numbers used to locate a point on a grid. The first number tells the left-right position and the second number tells the up-down position.

Example:

A graph that shows frequency of data along a number line

Example:

Miles Jogged

A series of numbers placed at fixed distances on a graph to help label the graph

Example:

The point where the two axes of a coordinate grid intersect; (0, 0)

Example:

x-**axis**

eje de la *x*

72

x-**coordinate**

coordenada *x*

73

y-**axis**

eje de la *y*

74

y-**coordinate**

coordenada *y*

75

The first number in an ordered pair; tells the distance to move right or left from (0, 0)

Example:

The horizontal number line on a coordinate plane

Example:

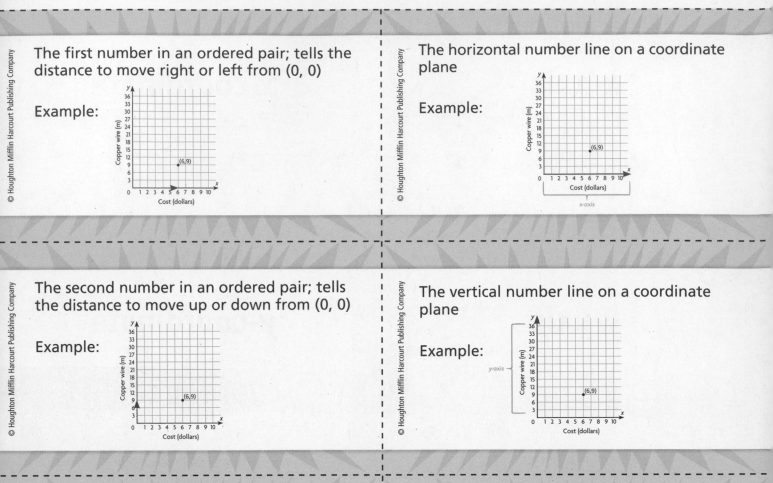

The second number in an ordered pair; tells the distance to move up or down from (0, 0)

Example:

The vertical number line on a coordinate plane

Example:

Going to the Moon

Image Credits: (bg) ©StockTrek/PhotoDisc/Getty Images; (b) ©Brand X Pictures/Getty Images

Word Box

coordinate grid
data
interval
line graph
line plot
ordered pair
origin
scale
x-axis
x-coordinate
y-axis
y-coordinate

For 2 players

Materials

- 1 each: red and blue playing pieces
- 1 number cube

How to Play

1. Each player chooses a playing piece and puts it on START.

2. Toss the number cube to take a turn. Move your playing piece that many spaces.

3. If you land on these spaces:

   Light Green Tell the meaning of the math term or use it in a sentence. If your answer is correct, jump to the next space with the same term.

   Dark Green Follow the directions in the space. If there are no directions, stay where you are.

4. The first player to reach FINISH wins.

© Houghton Mifflin Harcourt Publishing Company

DIRECTIONS Each player puts a playing piece on START. • Toss the number cube to take a turn. Move your playing piece that many spaces. • If you land on these spaces: Light Green: Tell the meaning of the math term or use it in a sentence. If your answer is correct, jump to the next space with the same term. Dark Green: Follow the directions in the space. If there are no directions, stay where you are. The first player to reach FINISH wins.

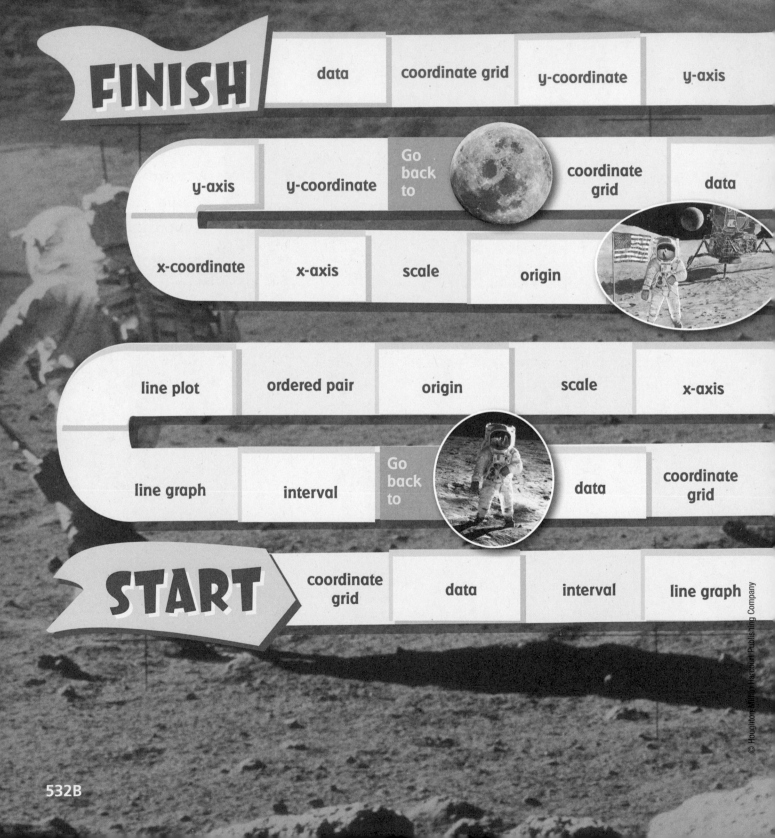

FINISH

| data | coordinate grid | y-coordinate | y-axis |

| y-axis | y-coordinate | Go back to | coordinate grid | data |

| x-coordinate | x-axis | scale | origin |

| line plot | ordered pair | origin | scale | x-axis |

| line graph | interval | Go back to | data | coordinate grid |

START

| coordinate grid | data | interval | line graph |

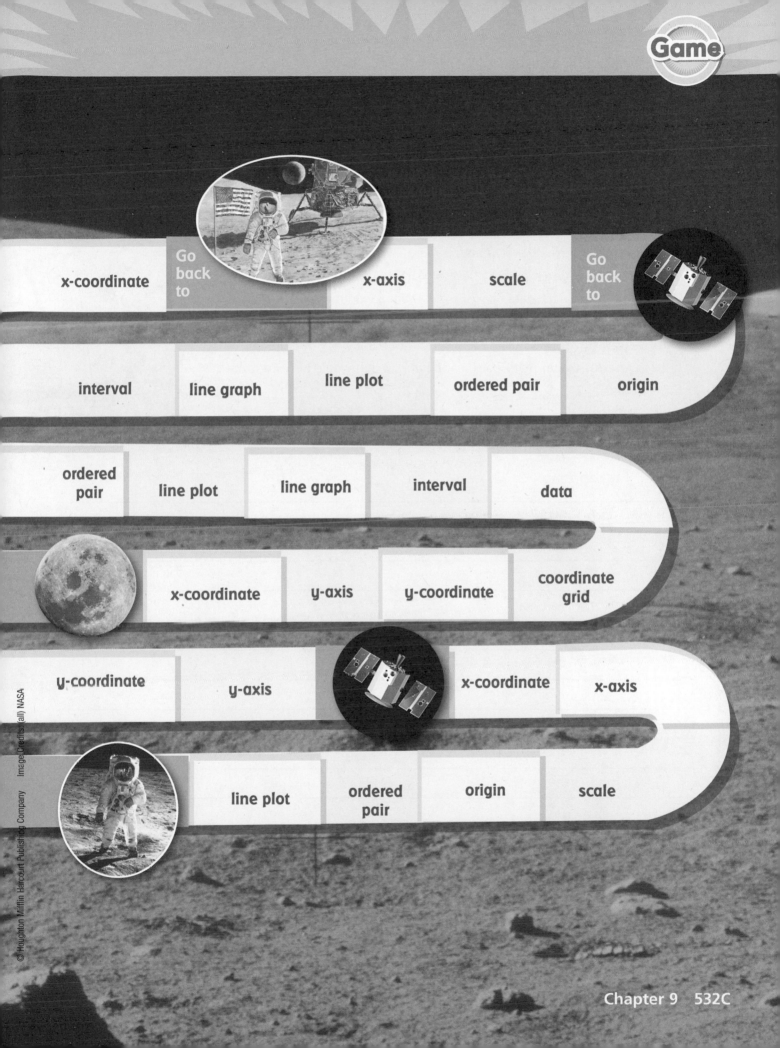

x-coordinate

Go back to

x-axis

scale

Go back to

interval

line graph

line plot

ordered pair

origin

ordered pair

line plot

line graph

interval

data

x-coordinate

y-axis

y-coordinate

coordinate grid

y-coordinate

y-axis

x-coordinate

x-axis

line plot

ordered pair

origin

scale

The Write Way

Reflect

Choose one idea. Write about it.

- Explain how the terms *x-coordinate*, *y-coordinate*, and *ordered pair* relate.
- Tell how far the ordered pair (4, 2) is from the origin.
- When would you place data on a line plot? When would you place it on a line graph? Explain your answer.
- During a rainstorm, you measure the amount of rain every hour for six hours. Describe a chart with a scale and interval that would be appropriate for your data.

Name _____

Line Plots

Essential Question How can a line plot help you find an average with data given in fractions?

Common Core — Measurement and Data—5.MD.B.2
Also 5.OA.A.1
MATHEMATICAL PRACTICES
MP1, MP2, MP4

Unlock the Problem Real World

Students have measured different amounts of water into beakers for an experiment. The amount of water in each beaker is listed below.

$\frac{1}{4}$ cup, $\frac{1}{4}$ cup, $\frac{1}{2}$ cup, $\frac{3}{4}$ cup, $\frac{1}{4}$ cup, $\frac{1}{4}$ cup,

$\frac{1}{4}$ cup, $\frac{1}{2}$ cup, $\frac{1}{4}$ cup, $\frac{3}{4}$ cup, $\frac{1}{4}$ cup, $\frac{3}{4}$ cup

If the total amount of water stayed the same, what would be the average amount of water in a beaker?

Water Used (in cups)

STEP 1 Count the number of cups for each amount. Draw an **✗** for the number of times each amount is recorded to complete the line plot.

$\frac{1}{4}$: _____ $\frac{1}{2}$: _____ $\frac{3}{4}$: _____

STEP 2 Find the total amount of water in all of the beakers that contain $\frac{1}{4}$ cup of water.

There are _____ beakers with $\frac{1}{4}$ cup of water. So, there are _____ fourths, or

□/□, or □ □/□ cups.

STEP 3 Find the total amount of water in all of the beakers that contain $\frac{1}{2}$ cup of water.

There are _____ beakers with $\frac{1}{2}$ cup of water. So, there are _____ halves, or

□/□, or 1 cup.

STEP 4 Find the total amount of water in all of the beakers that contain $\frac{3}{4}$ cup of water.

$3 \times \frac{3}{4} = \dfrac{□}{□}$, or $□\dfrac{□}{□}$

STEP 5 Add to find the total amount of water in all of the beakers.

$1\frac{3}{4} + 1 + 2\frac{1}{4} = \underline{}$

STEP 6 Divide the sum you found in Step 5 by the number of beakers to find the average.

$5 \div 12 = \dfrac{□}{□}$

So, the average amount of water in a beaker is _____ cup.

Try This!

You can use the order of operations to find the average. Solve the problem as a series of expressions that use parentheses and brackets to separate them. Perform operations from inside the parentheses to the outer brackets.

$$\left[\left(7 \times \tfrac{1}{4}\right) + \left(2 \times \tfrac{1}{2}\right) + \left(3 \times \tfrac{3}{4}\right)\right] \div 12$$

Perform the operations inside the parentheses.

$$\left[\,\frac{\ \ }{\ \ } + \boxed{\ \ } + \frac{\ \ }{\ \ }\,\right] \div 12$$

Next, perform the operations in the brackets.

$$\boxed{\ \ } \div 12$$

Divide.

$$\frac{\ \ }{\ \ }$$

Write the expression as a fraction.

🔒 Example

Raine divides three 2-ounce bags of rice into smaller bags. The first bag is divided into bags weighing $\tfrac{1}{6}$-ounce each, the second bag is divided into bags weighing $\tfrac{1}{3}$-ounce each, and the third bag is divided into bags weighing $\tfrac{1}{2}$-ounce each.

Find the number of $\tfrac{1}{6}$-, $\tfrac{1}{3}$-, and $\tfrac{1}{2}$-ounce rice bags. Then graph the results on the line plot.

STEP 1 Write a title for your line plot. It should describe what you are counting.

STEP 2 Label $\tfrac{1}{6}$, $\tfrac{1}{3}$, and $\tfrac{1}{2}$ on the line plot to show the different amounts into which the three 2-ounce bags of rice are divided.

STEP 3 Use division to find the number of $\tfrac{1}{6}$-ounce, $\tfrac{1}{3}$-ounce, and $\tfrac{1}{2}$-ounce bags that were made from the three original 2-ounce bags of rice.

$$2 \div \frac{1}{6} \qquad\qquad 2 \div \frac{1}{3} \qquad\qquad 2 \div \frac{1}{2}$$

$$2 \times \boxed{\ } = \boxed{\ } \qquad 2 \times \boxed{\ } = \boxed{\ } \qquad 2 \times \boxed{\ } = \boxed{\ }$$

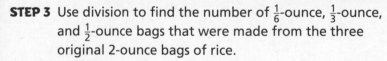

$$\frac{1}{6} \qquad\qquad \frac{1}{3} \qquad\qquad \frac{1}{2}$$

STEP 4 Draw an ✗ above $\tfrac{1}{6}$, $\tfrac{1}{3}$, or $\tfrac{1}{2}$ to show the number of rice bags.

Math Talk

MATHEMATICAL PRACTICES ②

Reason Quantitatively Explain why there are more $\tfrac{1}{6}$-ounce rice bags than $\tfrac{1}{2}$-ounce rice bags.

Name _____

Use the data to complete the line plot. Then answer the questions.

Liliana needs to buy beads for a necklace. The beads are sold by mass. She sketches a design to determine what beads are needed, and then writes down their sizes. The sizes are shown below.

$\frac{2}{5}$ g, $\frac{2}{5}$ g, $\frac{4}{5}$ g, $\frac{2}{5}$ g, $\frac{1}{5}$ g, $\frac{1}{5}$ g, $\frac{3}{5}$ g,

$\frac{4}{5}$ g, $\frac{1}{5}$ g, $\frac{2}{5}$ g, $\frac{3}{5}$ g, $\frac{3}{5}$ g, $\frac{2}{5}$ g

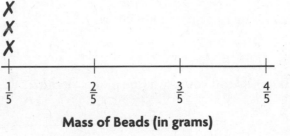

Mass of Beads (in grams)

1. What is the combined mass of the beads with a mass of $\frac{1}{5}$ gram?

    Think: There are _____ Xs above $\frac{1}{5}$ on the line plot, so the combined mass of the beads

    is _____ fifths, or _____ gram.

2. What is the combined mass of all the beads with a mass of $\frac{2}{5}$ gram?

    _____

3. What is the combined mass of all the beads on the necklace?

    _____

4. What is the average mass of the beads on the necklace?

    _____

On Your Own

Use the data to complete the line plot. Then answer the questions.

A breakfast chef used different amounts of milk when making pancakes, depending on the number of pancakes ordered. The results are shown below.

$\frac{1}{2}$ c, $\frac{1}{4}$ c, $\frac{1}{2}$ c, $\frac{3}{4}$ c, $\frac{1}{2}$ c, $\frac{3}{4}$ c, $\frac{1}{2}$ c, $\frac{1}{4}$ c, $\frac{1}{2}$ c, $\frac{1}{2}$ c

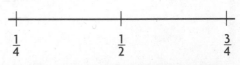

Milk in Pancake Orders (in cups)

5. How much milk combined is used in $\frac{1}{2}$-cup amounts? _____

6. **THINK SMARTER** What is the average amount of milk used for an order of pancakes? _____

7. **GO DEEPER** How many more orders of pancakes used $\frac{1}{2}$ cup of milk than $\frac{1}{4}$ cup and $\frac{3}{4}$ cup of milk combined?

8. **MATHEMATICAL PRACTICE ②** Use Reasoning
Describe an amount you could add to the data that would make the average increase.

_____

Unlock the Problem (Real World)

9. **MATHEMATICAL PRACTICE ①** **Make Sense of Problems** For 10 straight days, Samantha measured the amount of food that her cat Dewey ate, recording the results, which are shown below. Graph the results on the line plot. What is the average amount of cat food that Dewey ate daily?

$\frac{1}{2}$ c, $\frac{3}{8}$ c, $\frac{5}{8}$ c, $\frac{1}{2}$ c, $\frac{5}{8}$ c, $\frac{1}{4}$ c, $\frac{3}{4}$ c, $\frac{1}{4}$ c, $\frac{1}{2}$ c, $\frac{5}{8}$ c

$\frac{1}{4}$ $\frac{3}{8}$ $\frac{1}{2}$ $\frac{5}{8}$ $\frac{3}{4}$

Amount of Cat Food Eaten (in cups)

a. What do you need to know? _____

_____

b. How can you use a line plot to organize the information?

_____

_____

c. What steps could you use to find the average amount of food that Dewey ate daily?

_____

_____

d. Fill in the blanks for the totals of each amount measured.

$\frac{1}{4}$ cup: _____ $\frac{5}{8}$ cup: _____

$\frac{3}{8}$ cup: _____ $\frac{3}{4}$ cup: _____

$\frac{1}{2}$ cup: _____

e. Find the total amount of cat food eaten over 10 days.

_____ + _____ + _____ + _____ +

_____ = _____

So, the average amount was _____.

10. **THINK SMARTER** Maya measured the heights of the seedlings she is growing. The heights were $\frac{3}{4}$ in., $\frac{7}{8}$ in., $\frac{1}{2}$ in., $\frac{3}{4}$ in., $\frac{5}{8}$ in., $\frac{3}{4}$ in., $\frac{7}{8}$ in., $\frac{5}{8}$ in., $\frac{1}{2}$ in., and $\frac{3}{4}$ in. Organize the information in a line plot.

What is the average height of the seedlings? _____ inch

Common Core **COMMON CORE STANDARD—5.MD.B.2**
Represent and interpret data.

Use the data to complete the line plot. Then answer the questions.

A clerk in a health food store makes bags of trail mix. The amount of trail mix in each bag is listed below.

$\frac{1}{4}$ lb, $\frac{1}{4}$ lb, $\frac{3}{4}$ lb, $\frac{1}{2}$ lb, $\frac{1}{4}$ lb, $\frac{3}{4}$ lb,

$\frac{3}{4}$ lb, $\frac{3}{4}$ lb, $\frac{1}{2}$ lb, $\frac{1}{4}$ lb, $\frac{1}{2}$ lb, $\frac{1}{2}$ lb

1. What is the combined weight of the $\frac{1}{4}$-lb bags? ___1 lb___

   Think: There are four $\frac{1}{4}$-pound bags.

2. What is the combined weight of the $\frac{1}{2}$-lb bags? _____

3. What is the combined weight of the $\frac{3}{4}$-lb bags? _____

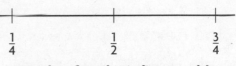

$\frac{1}{4}$ $\frac{1}{2}$ $\frac{3}{4}$

Weight of Trail Mix (in pounds)

4. What is the total weight of the trail mix used in

   all the bags? _____

5. What is the average amount of trail mix in each bag? _____

Julie uses crystals to make a bracelet. The lengths of the crystals are shown below.

$\frac{1}{2}$ in., $\frac{5}{8}$ in., $\frac{3}{4}$ in., $\frac{1}{2}$ in., $\frac{3}{8}$ in., $\frac{1}{2}$ in., $\frac{3}{4}$ in.,

$\frac{3}{8}$ in., $\frac{3}{4}$ in., $\frac{5}{8}$ in., $\frac{1}{2}$ in., $\frac{3}{8}$ in., $\frac{5}{8}$ in., $\frac{3}{4}$ in.

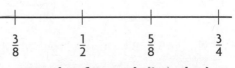

$\frac{3}{8}$ $\frac{1}{2}$ $\frac{5}{8}$ $\frac{3}{4}$

6. What is the combined length of the $\frac{1}{2}$-in. crystals? _____   **Lengths of Crystals (in inches)**

7. What is the combined length of the $\frac{5}{8}$-in. crystals? _____

8. What is the total length of all the crystals in the bracelet? _____

9. What is the average length of each crystal in the bracelet? _____

10. **WRITE** ▸*Math* Describe the steps you can use to find an average of fractional amounts.

_____

Lesson Check (5.MD.B.2)

A baker uses different amounts of salt when she bakes loaves of bread, depending on which recipe she is following. The amount of salt called for in each recipe is shown on the line plot.

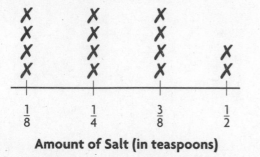

Amount of Salt (in teaspoons)

1. Based on the line plot, how many recipes call for more than $\frac{1}{4}$ tsp of salt?

   _____

2. What is the average amount of salt called for in each recipe?

   _____

Spiral Review (5.NBT.A.4, 5.NF.A.1, 5.NF.B.4a, 5.NF.B.7c)

3. Ramona had $8\frac{3}{8}$ in. of ribbon. She used $2\frac{1}{2}$ in. for an art project. How many inches of ribbon does she have left? Find the difference in simplest form.

4. Ben bought $\frac{1}{2}$ pound of cheese for 3 sandwiches. If he puts the same amount of cheese on each sandwich, how much cheese will each sandwich have?

5. What is 92.583 rounded to the nearest tenth?

6. In Yoshi's garden, $\frac{3}{4}$ of the flowers are tulips. Of the tulips, $\frac{2}{3}$ are yellow. What fraction of the flowers in Yoshi's garden are yellow tulips?

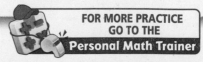

FOR MORE PRACTICE
GO TO THE
Personal Math Trainer

Name _____

Ordered Pairs

Essential Question How can you identify and plot points on a coordinate grid?

Common Core Geometry—5.G.A.1

MATHEMATICAL PRACTICES
MP4, MP6

CONNECT Locating a point on a coordinate grid is similar to describing directions using North-South and West-East. The horizontal number line on the grid is the **x-axis**. The vertical number line on the grid is the **y-axis**.

Each point on the coordinate grid can be described by an **ordered pair** of numbers. The **x-coordinate** is the first number in the ordered pair. It is the horizontal location, or the distance the point is from 0 in the direction of the x-axis. The **y-coordinate** is the second number in the ordered pair. It is the vertical location, or the distance the point is from 0 in the direction of the y-axis.

$$(x, y)$$

x-coordinate ⌐ ⌐ y-coordinate

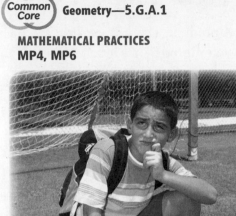

The x-axis and the y-axis intersect at the point (0, 0), called the **origin**.

Unlock the Problem Real World

🔑 **Write the ordered pairs for the locations of the arena and the aquarium.**

Locate the point for which you want to write an ordered pair.

Look below at the x-axis to identify the point's horizontal distance from 0, which is its x-coordinate.

Look to the left at the y-axis to identify the point's vertical distance from 0, which is its y-coordinate.

So, the ordered pair for the arena is (3, 2) and the ordered pair for the aquarium

is (_____ , _____).

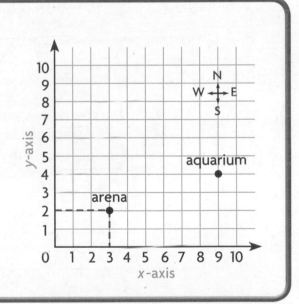

• Describe the path you would take to get from the origin to the aquarium, using horizontal, then vertical movements.

_____

_____

Math Talk MATHEMATICAL PRACTICES ④

Use Graphs Use the x- and y-coordinates to describe the distance of the point (3, 2) from the x- and y-axes.

🔑 Example 1 Use the graph.

A point on a coordinate grid can be labeled with an ordered pair, a letter, or both.

Ⓐ **Plot the point (5, 7) and label it J.**

From the origin, move right 5 units and then up 7 units.

Plot and label the point.

Ⓑ **Plot the point (8, 0) and label it S.**

From the origin, move right _____ units and

then up _____ units.

Plot and label the point.

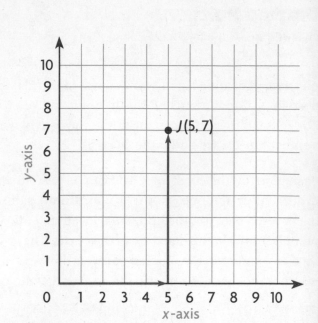

🔑 Example 2 Find the distance between two points.

You can find the distance between two points when the points are along the same horizontal or vertical line.

- Draw a line segment to connect point A and point B.

- Count vertical units between the two points.

There are _____ units between points A and B.

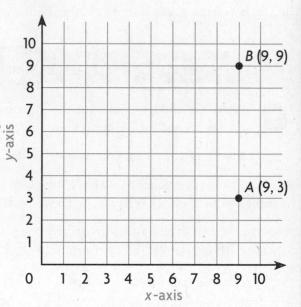

1. Points A and B form a vertical line segment and have the same x-coordinates. How can you use subtraction to find the distance between the points?

_____

_____

_____

_____

2. Graph the points (3, 2) and (5, 2). Explain how you can use subtraction to find the horizontal distance between these two points.

_____

_____

540

Name _____

Use Coordinate Grid A to write an ordered pair for the given point.

1. C _____

2. D _____

3. E _____

✓ **4.** F _____

Plot and label the points on Coordinate Grid A.

5. M(0, 9)

6. H(8, 6)

7. K(10, 4)

8. T(4, 5)

9. W(5, 10)

✓ **10.** R(1, 3)

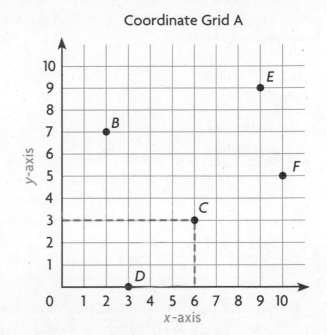

Coordinate Grid A

On Your Own

Use Coordinate Grid B to write an ordered pair for the given point.

11. G _____

12. H _____

13. I _____

14. J _____

15. K _____

16. L _____

Plot and label the points on Coordinate Grid B.

17. W(8, 2)

18. E(0, 4)

19. X(2, 9)

20. B(3, 4)

21. R(4, 0)

22. F(7, 6)

23. T(5, 7)

24. A(7, 1)

25. WRITE ▸ *Math* Explain how to find the distance between point F and point A.

_____

_____

Problem Solving · Applications

Nathan and his friends are planning a trip to New York City. Use the map for 26–30. Each unit represents 1 city block.

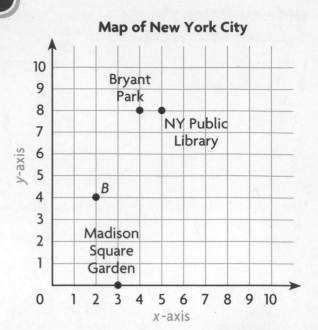

Map of New York City

26. What ordered pair gives the location of Bryant Park?

_____

27. **MATHEMATICAL PRACTICE ④ Use Graphs** The Empire State Building is located 5 blocks right and 1 block up from (0, 0). Write the ordered pair for this location. Plot and label a point for the Empire State Building.

_____

28. **THINK SMARTER** **What's the Error?** Nathan says that Madison Square Garden is located at (0, 3) on the map. Is his ordered pair correct? Explain.

_____

_____

29. **GO DEEPER** Paulo walks from point B to Bryant Park. Raul walks from point B to Madison Square Garden. If they only walk along the grid lines, who walks farther? Explain.

_____

_____

Personal Math Trainer

30. **THINK SMARTER +** Look at the map of New York City above. Suppose a subway station is located at (6, 5). Which of the following accurately describes the location of the subway station? Mark all that apply.

Ⓐ The station is 2 blocks right and 3 blocks down from Bryant Park.

Ⓑ The station is 4 blocks right and 1 block down from point B.

Ⓒ The station is 1 block right and 3 blocks down from the library.

Ⓓ The station is 5 blocks right and 3 blocks up from Madison Square Garden.

Ordered Pairs

Use Coordinate Grid A to write an ordered pair for the given point.

COMMON CORE STANDARD—5.G.A.1
Graph points on the coordinate plane to solve real-world and mathematical problems.

1. *A* (2, 3)

2. *B*

3. *C*

4. *D*

5. *E*

6. *F*

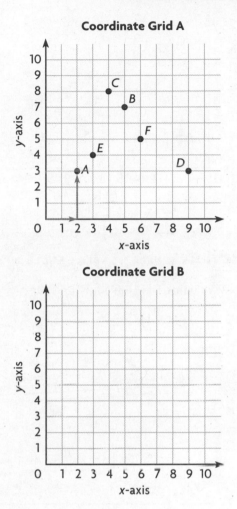

Coordinate Grid A

Plot and label the points on Coordinate Grid B.

7. *N* (7, 3)

8. *R* (0, 4)

9. *O* (8, 7)

10. *M* (2, 1)

11. *P* (5, 6)

12. *Q* (1, 5)

Coordinate Grid B

Problem Solving

Use the map for 13–14.

13. Which building is located at (5, 6)?

_____

14. What is the distance between Kip's Pizza and the bank?

_____

15. **WRITE** ▸*Math* What is a situation in which you might locate points on a coordinate grid?

_____

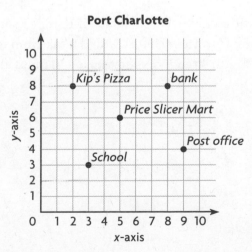

Port Charlotte

Lesson Check (5.G.A.1)

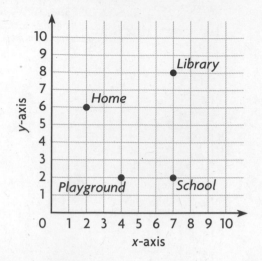

1. What ordered pair describes the location of the playground?

_____

2. What is the distance between the school and the library?

_____

Spiral Review (5.NBT.A.1, 5.NBT.B.5, 5.NBT.B.6)

3. What is the value of the underlined digit?

45,7<u>6</u>9,331

4. Andrew charges $18 for each lawn he mows. Suppose he mows 17 lawns per month. How much money will Andrew make per month?

5. Harlow can bicycle at a rate of 18 miles per hour. How many hours would it take him to bicycle a stretch of road that is 450 miles long?

6. Molly uses 192 beads to make a bracelet and a necklace. It takes 5 times as many beads to make a necklace as it does to make a bracelet. How many beads are used to make the necklace?

FOR MORE PRACTICE
GO TO THE
Personal Math Trainer

Name _____

Graph Data

Essential Question How can you use a coordinate grid to display data collected in an experiment?

Common Core Geometry—
5.G.A.2
MATHEMATICAL PRACTICES
MP3, MP4, MP8

Investigate

Materials ■ paper cup ■ water ■ Fahrenheit thermometer
■ ice cubes ■ stopwatch

When data is collected, it can be organized in a table.

A. Fill the paper cup more than halfway with room-temperature water.

B. Place the Fahrenheit thermometer in the water and find its beginning temperature before adding any ice. Record this temperature in the table at 0 seconds.

C. Place three cubes of ice in the water and start the stopwatch. Find the temperature every 10 seconds for 60 seconds. Record the temperatures in the table.

Water Temperature	
Time (in seconds)	Temperature (in °F)
0	
10	
20	
30	
40	
50	
60	

Draw Conclusions

1. Explain why you would record the beginning temperature at 0 seconds.

_____

_____

2. Describe what happens to the temperature of the water in 60 seconds, during the experiment.

_____

_____

3. **Draw Conclusions** Analyze your observations of the temperature of the water during the 60 seconds, and explain what you think would happen to the temperature if the experiment continued for 60 seconds longer.

_____

_____

_____

Make Connections

You can use a coordinate grid to graph and analyze the data you collected in the experiment.

STEP 1 Write the related pairs of data as ordered pairs.

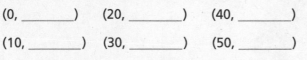

(0, _____)   (20, _____)   (40, _____)

(10, _____)   (30, _____)   (50, _____)

(60, _____)

_____

STEP 2 Construct a coordinate grid and write a title for it. Label each axis.

_____

STEP 3 Plot a point for each ordered pair.

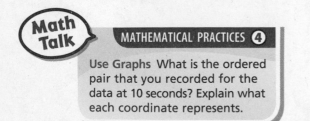

Math Talk

MATHEMATICAL PRACTICES ④

Use Graphs What is the ordered pair that you recorded for the data at 10 seconds? Explain what each coordinate represents.

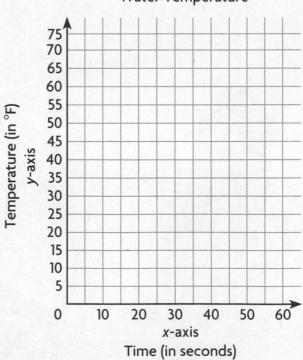

Water Temperature

Name _____

For items 1–3, graph the data on the coordinate grid.

☑ 1. Write the ordered pairs for each point.

_____

2. What does the ordered pair (3, 38) tell you about Ryan's age and height?

_____

_____

☑ 3. Why would the point (6, 42) be nonsense?

_____

_____

_____

_____

Ryan's Height					
Age (in years)	1	2	3	4	5
Height (in inches)	30	35	38	41	44

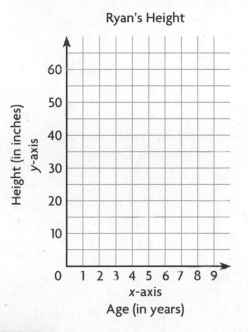

Ryan's Height

Problem Solving • Applications

4. **THINK SMARTER** The table shows the depth of the Dakota River at different times during a rainstorm.

Graph the ordered pairs from the tiles on the coordinate grid.

Dakota River					
Time (hours)	1	2	3	4	5
Depth (feet)	7	8	10	12	15

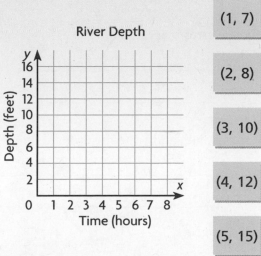

River Depth

(1, 7)

(2, 8)

(3, 10)

(4, 12)

(5, 15)

THINK SMARTER   **What's the Error?**

5. Mary places a miniature car onto a track with launchers. The speed of the car is recorded every foot. Some of the data is shown in the table. Mary graphs the data on the coordinate grid below.

Miniature Car's Speed	
Distance (in feet)	Speed (in miles per hour)
0	0
1	4
2	8
3	6
4	3

Look at Mary's graphed data.
Find her error.

Graph the data and correct the error.

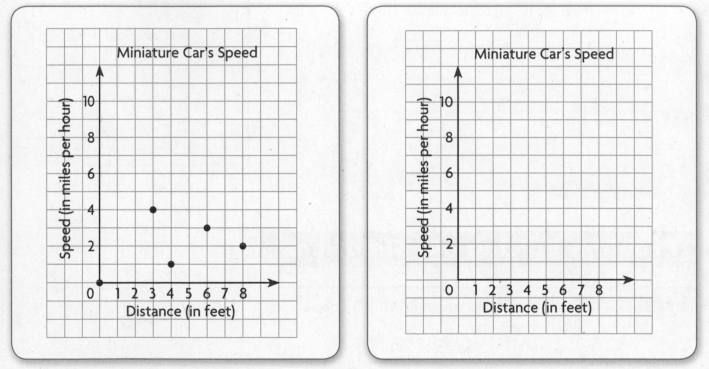

6. **MATHEMATICAL PRACTICE ③ Verify the Reasoning of Others**   Describe the error Mary made.

_____

_____

7. **GO DEEPER**   At what distance do you think the car will stop? Explain and write the ordered pair.

_____

_____

Name _____

Graph Data

COMMON CORE STANDARD—5.G.A.2
Graph points on the coordinate plane to solve real-world and mathematical problems.

Graph the data on the coordinate grid.

1.

Outdoor Temperature					
Hour	1	3	5	7	9
Temperature (°F)	61	65	71	75	77

a. Write the ordered pairs for each point.

_____

_____

b. How would the ordered pairs be different if the outdoor temperature were recorded every hour for 4 consecutive hours?

_____

_____

_____

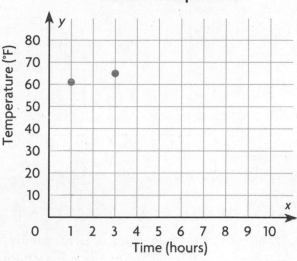

Outdoor Temperature

Problem Solving · Real World

2.

Windows Repaired					
Day	1	2	3	4	5
Total Number Repaired	14	30	45	63	79

a. Write the ordered pairs for each point.

_____

_____

b. What does the ordered pair (2, 30) tell you about the number of windows repaired?

_____

_____

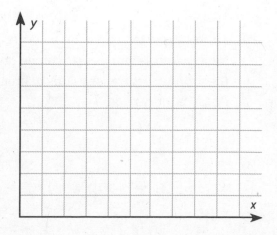

Lesson Check (5.G.A.2)

Amount of Dog Food Consumed

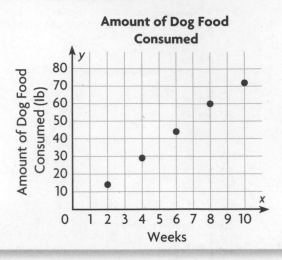

1. About how many weeks did it take for the dog to consume 45 pounds of food?

_____

2. By the end of Week 8, how much food had the dog consumed?

_____

Spiral Review (5.OA.A.2, 5.NBT.B.6, 5.NF.A.2)

3. A restaurant chain ordered 3,940 pounds of rice in 20-pound bags. About how many 20-pound bags of rice did the chain order?

4. The population of Linton is 12 times as great as the population of Ellmore. The combined population of both towns is 9,646 people. What is the population of Linton?

5. Timothy needs $\frac{1}{2}$ cup of bread crumbs for a casserole and $\frac{1}{3}$ cup of bread crumbs for the topping. How many cups of bread crumbs does Timothy need?

6. Jessie bought 3 T-shirts for $6 each and 4 T-shirts for $5 each. What expression can you use to describe what Jessie bought?

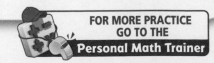

**FOR MORE PRACTICE
GO TO THE
Personal Math Trainer**

Line Graphs

Essential Question How can you use a line graph to display
and analyze real-world data?

Common Core Geometry—
5.G.A.2
MATHEMATICAL PRACTICES
MP4, MP6

🔑 Unlock the Problem Real World

A **line graph** is a graph that uses line segments to show how data changes
over time. The series of numbers placed at fixed distances that label
the graph are the graph's **scale**. The **interval**, or difference between one
number and the next on the scale, should be equal.

🔒 **Graph the data. Use the graph to determine
the times between which the greatest
temperature change occurred.**

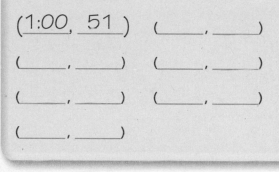

- Write related number pairs of data
  as ordered pairs.

(1:00 , 51) (____ , ____)

(____ , ____) (____ , ____)

(____ , ____) (____ , ____)

(____ , ____)

Recorded Temperatures

Time (A.M.)	1:00	2:00	3:00	4:00	5:00	6:00	7:00
Temperature (in °F)	51	49	47	44	45	44	46

STEP 1 For the vertical axis, choose a scale and
an interval that are appropriate for the
data. You can show a break in the scale
between 0 and 40, since there are no
temperatures between 0°F and 44°F.

STEP 2 For the horizontal axis, write the times
of day. Write a title for the graph and
name each axis. Then graph the ordered
pairs. Complete the graph by connecting
the points with line segments.

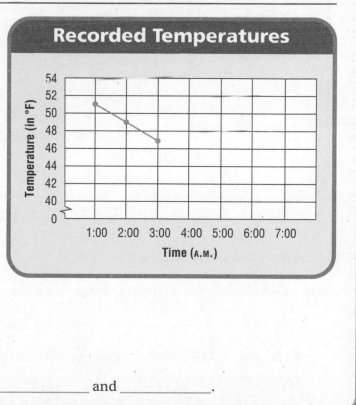

Look at each line segment in the graph. Find the
line segment that shows the greatest change in
temperature between two consecutive points.

The greatest temperature change occurred between _____ and _____.

Try This! Jill used a rain gauge to collect data on the total rainfall during 6 days at her home in Miami. She read the amount of rain collected in the rain gauge each day and did not pour it out. Her data is shown in the table. Make a line graph to display Jill's data.

STEP 1 Write related pairs of data as ordered pairs.

(Mon, 2) (____, ____) (____, ____)

(____, ____) (____, ____) (____, ____)

_____

STEP 2 Choose a scale and an interval for the data.

_____

STEP 3 Label the horizontal and vertical axes. Write a title for the graph. Graph the ordered pairs. Connect the points with line segments.

Rainfall Collected

Day	Rainfall (in inches)
Mon	2
Tue	2
Wed	3
Thu	6
Fri	8
Sat	9

Math Talk

MATHEMATICAL PRACTICES ④

Model Mathematics How could you use the graph to identify the two readings between which it did not rain?

Use the graph to answer the questions.

1. On which day was the total rainfall recorded the greatest?

_____

2. On which day did Jill record the greatest increase in rainfall collected from the previous day?

_____

Name _____

Use the table at the right for 1–3.

1. What scale and interval would be appropriate to make a graph of the data?

   _____

   _____

2. Write the related pairs as ordered pairs.

   _____

   _____

✓3. Make a line graph of the data.

✓4. Use the graph to determine between which two months the least change in average temperature occurs.

   _____

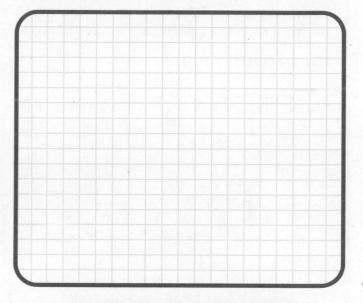

Average Monthly Temperature in Tupelo, Mississippi					
Month	Jan	Feb	Mar	Apr	May
Temperature (in °F)	40	44	54	62	70

On Your Own

Use the table at the right for 5–7.

5. Write the related number pairs for the plant height as ordered pairs.

   _____

6. What scale and interval would be appropriate to make a graph of the data?

   _____

7. Make a line graph of the data.

8. **GO DEEPER** Use the graph to find between which two months the plant grew the most? the least?

   _____

   _____

9. **THINK SMARTER** Use the graph to estimate the height at $1\frac{1}{2}$ months.

   _____

Plant Height				
Month	1	2	3	4
Height (in inches)	20	25	29	32

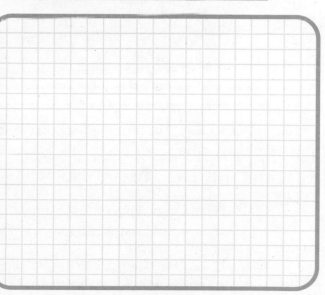

Evaporation changes water on Earth's surface into water vapor. Water vapor condenses in the atmosphere and returns to the surface as precipitation. This process is called the water cycle. The ocean is an important part of this cycle. It influences the average temperature and precipitation of a place.

The overlay graph below uses two vertical scales to show monthly average precipitation and temperatures for Redding, California.

Use the graph for 10–11.

10. **MATHEMATICAL PRACTICE ❹ Use Graphs** Explain how the overlay graph helps you relate precipitation and temperature for each month.

_____

_____

_____

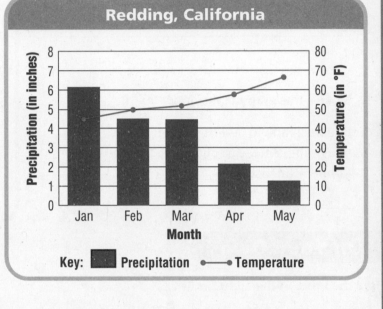

11. **GO DEEPER** Describe how the average temperature changes in the first 5 months of the year. Describe the relationship between the average temperature and the amount of precipitation.

_____

_____

12. **THINK SMARTER** The line graph shows the amount of snowfall over several days.

For 12a–12c, select True or False for each statement.

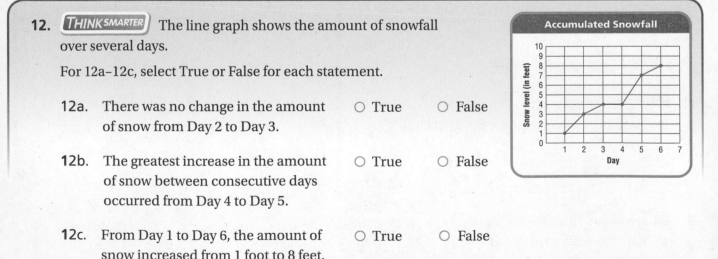

12a. There was no change in the amount of snow from Day 2 to Day 3.　　○ True　　○ False

12b. The greatest increase in the amount of snow between consecutive days occurred from Day 4 to Day 5.　　○ True　　○ False

12c. From Day 1 to Day 6, the amount of snow increased from 1 foot to 8 feet.　　○ True　　○ False

Line Graphs

Common Core

COMMON CORE STANDARD—5.G.A.2
Graph points on the coordinate plane to solve
real-world and mathematical problems.

Use the table for 1–5.

Hourly Temperature							
Time	10 A.M.	11 A.M.	12 noon	1 P.M.	2 P.M.	3 P.M.	4 P.M.
Temperature (°F)	8	11	16	27	31	38	41

1. Write the related number pairs for the hourly temperature
   as ordered pairs.

   (10, 8); _____

   _____

2. What scale would be appropriate to graph
   the data?

   _____

3. What interval would be appropriate to graph
   the data?

   _____

4. Make a line graph of the data.

   _____

5. Use the graph to find the difference in temperature
   between 11 A.M. and 1 P.M.

   _____

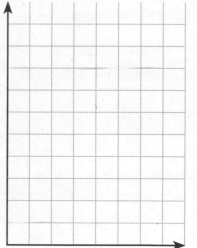

Problem Solving · Real World

6. Between which two hours did the least change in
   temperature occur?

   _____

   _____

7. What was the change in temperature between
   12 noon and 4 P.M.?

Lesson Check (5.G.A.2)

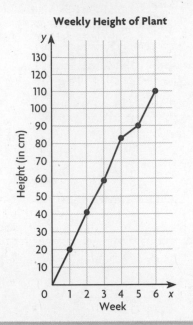

Weekly Height of Plant

1. About how many centimeters did the plant grow in the first three weeks?

_____

2. Between which two weeks did the plant grow the least?

_____

Spiral Review (5.OA.A.2, 5.NBT.B.6, 5.NF.B.6, 5.NF.B.7c)

3. Write an expression using the Distributive Property to find the product of 7 × 63.

_____

_____

4. Lexi needs to buy 105 vases for a party. Each package has 6 vases. How many packages should Lexi buy?

_____

_____

5. A student athlete runs $3\frac{1}{3}$ miles in 30 minutes. A professional runner can run $1\frac{1}{4}$ times as far in 30 minutes. How far can the professional runner run in 30 minutes?

6. A recipe for salad dressing calls for $\frac{1}{4}$ cup of vinegar. You have 4 cups of vinegar. How many batches of salad dressing could you make with the vinegar?

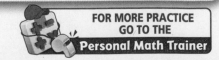

FOR MORE PRACTICE
GO TO THE
Personal Math Trainer

Name _____

✓ Mid-Chapter Checkpoint

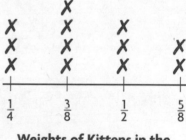

Personal Math Trainer
Online Assessment
and Intervention

Vocabulary

Choose the best term from the box.

1. The _____ is the horizontal number line on the coordinate grid. (p. 539)

2. A _____ is a graph that uses line segments to show how data changes over time. (p. 551)

Concepts and Skills

Use the line plot at the right for 3–5. (5.MD.B.2)

3. How many kittens weigh at least $\frac{3}{8}$ of a pound?

   _____

4. What is the combined weight of all the kittens?

   _____

5. **GO DEEPER** What is the average weight of the kittens in the shelter?

   _____

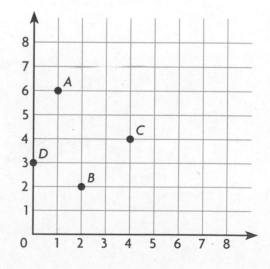

**Weights of Kittens in the
Animal Shelter (lb)**

Use the coordinate grid at the right for 6–13. (5.G.A.1)

Write an ordered pair for the given point.

6. A _____   7. B _____

8. C _____   9. D _____

Plot and label the point on the coordinate grid.

10. E (6, 2)   11. F (5, 0)

12. G (3, 4)   13. H (3, 1)

14. Jane drew a point that was 1 unit to the right of the *y*-axis and 7 units above the *x*-axis. What is the ordered pair for this location? (5.G.A.1)

---

15. The graph below shows the amount of snowfall in a 6-hour period.

Total Amount of Snow

Between which hours did the least amount of snow fall? (5.G.A.2)

---

16. Joy recorded the distances she walked each day for five days. How far did she walk in 5 days? (5.MD.B.2)

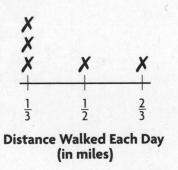

**Distance Walked Each Day
(in miles)**

Numerical Patterns

Essential Question How can you identify a relationship between two numerical patterns?

Common Core Operations and Algebraic Thinking—5.OA.B.3
MATHEMATICAL PRACTICES
MP6, MP7, MP8

Unlock the Problem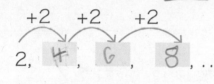

On the first week of school, Joel purchases 2 movies and 6 songs from his favorite media website. If he purchases the same number of movies and songs each week, how does the number of songs purchased compare to the number of movies purchased from one week to the next?

STEP 1 Use the two rules given in the problem to generate the first 4 terms in the sequence for the number of movies and the sequence for number of songs.

• The sequence for the number of <u>movies</u> each week is:

$$\overset{+2}{\frown} \ \overset{+2}{\frown} \ \overset{+2}{\frown}$$
2, 4 , 6 , 8 , ...

• The sequence for the number of <u>songs</u> each week is:

$$\overset{+6}{\frown} \ \overset{+6}{\frown} \ \overset{+6}{\frown}$$
6, 12 , 18 , 24 , ...

STEP 2 Write number pairs that relate the number of movies to the number of songs.

Week 1: ___2, 6___   Week 2: ___4, 12___

Week 3: ___6, 18___   Week 4: ___8, 24___

STEP 3 For each number pair, compare the number of movies to the number of songs. Write a rule to describe this relationship.

Think: For each related number pair, the second number is ___3___ times as great as the first number.

Rule: ___Multiply by 3.___

So, from one week to the next, the number of songs Joel purchased

is ___3___ times as many as the number of movies purchased.

• How many movies does Joel purchase each week?

___2 movies___

• How many songs does Joel purchase each week?

___6 songs___

🔓 Example

When Alice completes each level in her favorite video game, she wins 3 extra lives and 6 gold coins. What rule can you write to relate the number of gold coins to the number of extra lives she has won at any level? How many extra lives will Alice have won after she completes 8 levels?

Add __3__.

Add __6__.

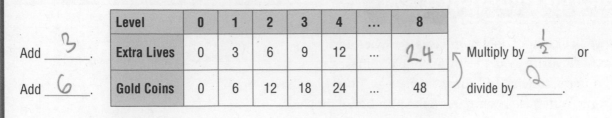

Level	0	1	2	3	4	...	8
Extra Lives	0	3	6	9	12	...	24
Gold Coins	0	6	12	18	24	...	48

Multiply by __$\frac{1}{2}$__ or

divide by __2__.

STEP 1 To the left of the table, complete the rule for how you could find the number of extra lives won from one level to the next.

+3 +3 +3 +3 ← difference between consecutive terms

0,   3,   6,   9,   12

From one level to the next, Alice wins __3__ more extra lives.

STEP 2 To the left of the table, complete the rule for how you could find the number of gold coins won from one level to the next.

+6 +6 +6 +6 ← difference between consecutive terms

0,   6,   12,   18,   24

From one level to the next, Alice wins _____ more gold coins.

STEP 3 Write number pairs that relate the number of gold coins to the number of extra lives won at each level.

Level 1: __6, 3__   Level 2: __6, 12__

Level 3: __9, 18__   Level 4: __12, 24__

STEP 4 Complete the rule to the right of the table that describes how the number pairs are related. Use your rule to find the number of extra lives at level 8.

Think: For each level, the number of extra lives is _____ as great as the number of gold coins.

Rule:_____

So, after 8 levels, Alice will have won _____ extra lives.

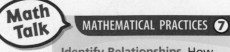

Math Talk

MATHEMATICAL PRACTICES 7

Identify Relationships How would your rule change if you were relating extra lives to gold coins instead of gold coins to extra lives?

Name _____

Use the given rules to complete each sequence. Then, complete the
rule that describes how nickels are related to dimes.

1.

Number of coins	1	2	3	4	5
Add 5. **Nickels (¢)**	5	10	15	20	*25*
Add 10. **Dimes (¢)**	10	20	30	40	*50*

) Multiply by __*2*__.

Complete the rule that describes how one sequence is related to the
other. Use the rule to find the unknown term.

2. Multiply the number of books by __*4*__
to find the amount spent.

Day	1	2	3	4	...	8
Number of Books	3	6	9	12	...	24
Amount Spent ($)	12	24	36	48	...	*96*

3. Divide the weight of the bag by _____
to find the number of marbles.

Bags	1	2	3	4	...	12
Number of Marbles	10	20	30	40	...	*120*
Weight of Bag (grams)	30	60	90	120	...	360

B ÷ M

$$\begin{array}{r} 360 \\ -120 \\ \hline 240 \end{array}$$

Complete the rule that describes how one sequence is related to the
other. Use the rule to find the unknown term.

4. Multiply the number of eggs by __*6*__
to find the number of muffins.

e × 6 = M

$$\begin{array}{r} 18 \\ \times 6 \\ \hline 108 \end{array}$$

Batches	1	2	3	4	...	9
Number of Eggs	2	4	6	8	...	18
Muffins	12	24	36	48	...	*108*

801

5. Divide the number of meters by _____
to find the number of laps.

Runners	1	2	3	4
Number of Laps	4	8	12	
Number of Meters	1,600	3,200	4,800	6,400

6. **MATHEMATICAL PRACTICE 6** **Make Connections** Suppose the number of eggs used in
Exercise 4 is changed to 3 eggs for each batch of 12 muffins, and 48 eggs
are used. How many batches and how many muffins will be made?

_____

Problem Solving • Applications

7. **GO DEEPER** Emily has a road map with a key that shows every inch on the map equals 5 miles of actual distance. She will drive on two roads to get to the beach. One road is 7 inches long on the map. The other road is 5 inches long. What is the actual distance Emily will drive to the beach? Write the rule you used to find the actual distance.

_____

_____

8. **MATHEMATICAL PRACTICE 7** Identify Relationships To make a shade of lavender paint, Jon mixes 4 ounces of red tint and 28 ounces of blue tint into one gallon of white paint. If 20 gallons of white paint and 80 ounces of red tint are used, how much blue tint should be added? Write a rule that you can use to find the amount of blue tint needed.

_____

_____

_____

9. **THINK SMARTER** In the cafeteria, tables are arranged in groups of 4, with each table seating 8 students. How many students can sit at 10 groups of tables? Write the rule you used to find the number of students.

_____

_____

10. **THINK SMARTER** Jessie made a table to show how many miles the runners ran.

Day	1	2	3	4	5
Number of Runners	4	8	12	16	20
Number of Miles	12	24	36	48	?

For 10a–10b, choose the correct values to describe how one sequence is related to the other.

10a. The unknown number in Day 5 is
| 54 |
| 56 |
| 60 |
.

10b. The rule that relates the number of miles to the number of runners is
| multiply by 3 |
| add 10 |
| multiply by 5 |
.

Name _____

Numerical Patterns

 COMMON CORE STANDARD—5.OA.B.3
Analyze patterns and relationships.

Complete the rule that describes how one sequence is related to the other. Use the rule to find the unknown term.

1. Multiply the number of laps by ___50___ to find the number of yards.

   Think: The number of yards is 50 times the number of laps.

Swimmers	1	2	3	4
Number of Laps	4	8	12	16
Number of Yards	200	400	600	800

2. Multiply the number of pounds by _____ to find total cost.

Boxes	1	2	3	4	6
Number of Pounds	3	6	9	12	18
Total Cost ($)	12	24	36	48	

3. Multiply the number of hours by _____ to find the number of miles.

Cars	1	2	3	4
Number of Hours	2	4	6	8
Number of Miles	130	260	390	

4. Multiply the number of hours by _____ to find the amount earned.

Days	1	2	3	4	7
Number of Hours	8	16	24	32	56
Amount Earned ($)	96	192	288	384	

Problem Solving Real World

5. A map's key shows that every of 5 inches on the map represents 200 miles of actual distance. Suppose the distance between two cities on the map is 7 inches. What is the actual distance between the two cities? Write the rule you used to find the actual distance.

   _____

   _____

   _____

   _____

6. To make each costume, Rachel uses 6 yards of material and 3 yards of trim. Suppose she uses a total of 48 yards of material to make several costumes. How many yards of trim does she use? Write the rule you used to find the number of yards of trim.

   _____

   _____

   _____

   _____

7. **WRITE** ▸ *Math* Give an example using the subject of time to describe how two number patterns are related. _____

Lesson Check (5.OA.B.3)

Use the table below to answer questions 1 and 2.

Term Number	1	2	3	4	...	6
Sequence 1	4	8	12	16	...	24
Sequence 2	12	24	36	48	...	?

1. What rule could you write that relates Sequence 2 to Sequence 1?

   _____

2. What is the unknown number in Sequence 2?

   _____

Spiral Review (5.OA.A.1, 5.NBT.A.1, 5.NF.A.2, 5.NF.B.3)

3. What is the value of the following expression?

   $$40 - (3 + 2) \times 6$$

4. What is the value of the digit 9 in the number 597,184?

5. What is the best estimate for the sum of $\frac{3}{8}$ and $\frac{1}{12}$?

6. Terry uses 3 cups of pumpkin seeds to decorate the tops of 12 loaves of bread. She puts an equal amount of seeds on each loaf. How many cups of pumpkin seeds does she put on each loaf of bread?

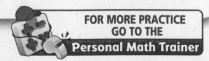

**FOR MORE PRACTICE
GO TO THE
Personal Math Trainer**

Name _____

Problem Solving • Find a Rule

Essential Question How can you use the strategy *solve a simpler problem* to help you solve a problem with patterns?

Common Core · **Operations and Algebraic Thinking—5.OA.B.3**
MATHEMATICAL PRACTICES
MP4, MP6, MP7

🔑 Unlock the Problem *Real World*

On an archaeological dig, Gabriel separates his dig site into sections with areas of 15 square feet each. There are 3 archaeological members digging in every section. What is the area of the dig site if 21 members are digging at one time?

15 sq ft

Read the Problem

What do I need to find?	**What information do I need to use?**	**How will I use the information?**
I need to find the _____ _____ _____ .	I can use the area of each section, which is _____, that there are _____ members in each section, and that there are 21 members digging.	I will use the information to search for patterns to solve a _____ problem.

Solve the Problem

Add 3.

Add 15.

Sections	1	2	3	4	5	6	7
Number of Members	3	6	9	12	15	18	21
Area (in square feet)	15	30	45	60	75	90	

Multiply by _____.

Multiply by _____.

Possible Rules:

• Multiply the number of sections by _____ to find the number of members.

• Multiply the number of members by _____ to find the total area. Complete the table.

So, the area of the dig site if 21 members are digging is _____ square feet.

Math Talk

MATHEMATICAL PRACTICES ❻

Explain how you can use division to find the number of members if you know the dig site area is 135 square feet.

🔒 Try Another Problem

Casey is making a design with triangles and beads for a costume. In his design, each pattern unit adds 3 triangles and 18 beads. Casey uses 72 triangles in his design. How many beads does Casey use?

Use the graphic organizer below to solve the problem.

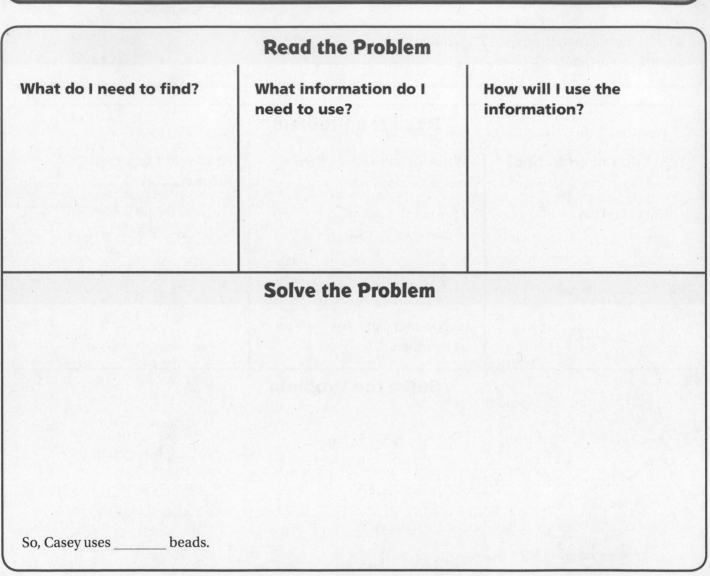

Read the Problem

What do I need to find?	What information do I need to use?	How will I use the information?

Solve the Problem

So, Casey uses _____ beads.

- What rule could you use to find an unknown number of beads if you know the related number of triangles?

_____

_____

Name _____

1 Section

✓ 1. Max builds rail fences. For one style of fence, each section uses 3 vertical fence posts and 6 horizontal rails. How many rails does he need for a fence that has 27 posts?

2 Sections   **3 Sections**

First, think about what the problem is asking and what you know. As each section of fence is added, how does the number of posts and the number of rails change?

Next, make a table and look for a pattern. Use what you know about 1, 2, and 3 sections. Write a rule for the number of posts and rails needed for 9 sections of fence.

Number of Sections	1	2	3	…	9
Number of Posts	3	6	9	…	27
Number of Rails	6	12	18	…	

Possible rule for posts: _____

_____

Possible rule for rails: _____

_____

Finally, use the rule to solve the problem.

✓ 2. **THINK SMARTER** What if another style of rail fencing has 6 rails between each pair of posts? How many rails are needed for 27 posts?

Number of Sections	1	2	3	…	9
Number of Posts	3	6	9	…	27
Number of Rails	12	24	36	…	

Possible rule: _____

On Your Own

3. **MATHEMATICAL PRACTICE ⑦ Look for a Pattern** Jane works as a limousine driver. She earns $50 for every 2-hour shift that she works. How much does Jane earn in one week if she works 40 hours per week? Write a rule and complete the table.

Shift	1	2	3	...	20
Hours Worked	2	4	6	...	40
Jane's Pay ($)	50	100	150	...	

Possible rule: _____

4. **THINK SMARTER** Rosa plays games at a fair. She can buy 8 game tokens for $1. Each game costs 2 tokens. How many games can she play with 120 tokens? Write a rule and complete the table.

Cost ($)	1	2	3	4	...	15
Tokens	8	16	24	32	...	120
Games	4	8	12	16	...	

Possible rule: _____

_____

5. **GO DEEPER** Janelle is making snacks for her classmates. There are two cups of raisins in one batch. For every 2 cups of raisins, Janelle adds 4 cups of oats. How many cups of oats will she need if she has 10 cups of raisins? Draw a table and write a possible rule.

Possible rule: _____

Personal Math Trainer

6. **THINK SMARTER +** Look for a pattern.

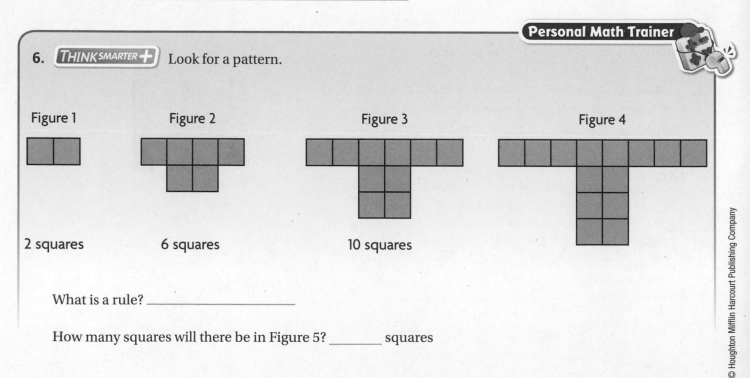

Figure 1   Figure 2   Figure 3   Figure 4

2 squares   6 squares   10 squares

What is a rule? _____

How many squares will there be in Figure 5? _____ squares

Problem Solving • Find a Rule

Common Core

COMMON CORE STANDARD—5.OA.B.3
Analyze patterns and relationships.

Write a rule and complete the table. Then answer the question.

1. Faye buys 15 T-shirts, which are on sale for $3 each. How much money does Faye spend?

Number of T-Shirts	1	2	3	5	10	15
Amount Spent ($)	3	6	9			

Possible rule:

Multiply the number

of T-shirts by 3.

The total amount Faye spends is ____$45____.

2. The Gilman family joins a fitness center. They pay $35 per month. By the 12th month, how much money will the Gilman family have spent?

Number of Months	1	2	3	4	5	12
Total Amount of Money Spent ($)	35	70				

Possible rule:

_____

_____

The Gilman family will have spent _____.

3. Hettie is stacking paper cups. Each stack of 15 cups is 6 inches high. What is the total height of 10 stacks of cups?

Number of stacks	1	2	3	10
Height (in.)	6	12	18	

Possible rule:

_____

_____

The total height of 10 stacks is _____.

4. **WRITE** ▸*Math* You have a table that shows a pattern. Describe two ways that you could find the 15th entry in the table.

_____

Lesson Check (5.OA.B.3)

1. How many squares are needed to make the eighth figure in the pattern?

   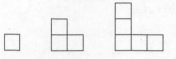

2. What expression could describe the number of squares in the next figure in the pattern, Figure 4?

   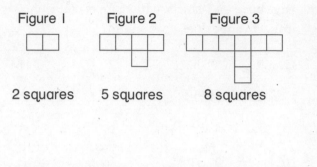

   Figure 1   Figure 2   Figure 3

   2 squares   5 squares   8 squares

Spiral Review (5.NBT.A.2, 5.NBT.B.6, 5.NBT.B.7, 5.NF.A.2)

3. Talia stores her collection of stickers equally in 7 sticker albums. If she has 567 stickers, how many stickers are in each album?

4. Ms. Angelino made 2 pans of lasagna and cut each pan into twelfths. Her family ate $1\frac{1}{12}$ pans of lasagna for dinner. How many pans of lasagna were left?

5. What is the next number in this pattern?

   $0.54, 0.6, 0.66, 0.72,$ ▮, ...

6. How do you write 100 as a power of 10?

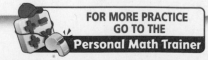

FOR MORE PRACTICE
GO TO THE
Personal Math Trainer

Graph and Analyze Relationships

Essential Question How can you write and graph ordered pairs on a coordinate grid using two numerical patterns?

Common Core Operations and Algebraic Thinking—5.OA.B.3

MATHEMATICAL PRACTICES
MP4, MP7

Unlock the Problem Real World

Sasha is making hot cocoa for a party. For each mug of cocoa, he uses 3 tablespoons of cocoa mix and 6 fluid ounces of hot water. If Sasha uses an entire 18-tablespoon container of cocoa mix, how many fluid ounces of water will he use?

STEP 1 Use the two given rules in the problem to generate the first four terms for the number of tablespoons of cocoa mix and the number of fluid ounces of water.

| Cocoa Mix (tbsp) | 3 | | | | ... | 18 |
| Water (fl oz) | 6 | | | | ... | |

- How many tablespoons of cocoa mix does Sasha add for each mug of cocoa?

  _____

- How many fluid ounces of water does Sasha add for each mug of cocoa?

  _____

STEP 2 Write the number pairs as ordered pairs, relating the number of tablespoons of cocoa mix to the number of fluid ounces of water.

(3, 6)   _____   _____   _____

STEP 3 Graph and label the ordered pairs. Then write a rule to describe how the number pairs are related.

- What rule can you write that relates the amount of cocoa mix to water?

  _____

So, Sasha will use _____ fluid ounces of water if he uses the entire container of cocoa mix.

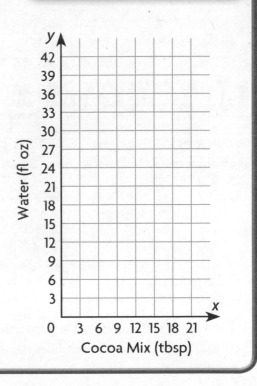

- **MATHEMATICAL PRACTICE 7 Look for Structure** Write the final number pair as an ordered pair. Then graph and label it. Starting at the origin, connect the points with straight line segments. What do the connected points form? Explain why this is formed.

_____

_____

Try This! Find the unknown term in the table.

Each $2-bag of copper wire contains 6 meters of wire.

Write the number pairs as ordered pairs and graph the data. Then write a rule that relates the cost to the number of meters of copper wire.

Think: Multiply the number of dollars by _____ to find the number of meters of copper wire.

Find the unknown term in the table.

Cost (dollars)	2	4	6	8
Copper wire (m)	6	12	18	

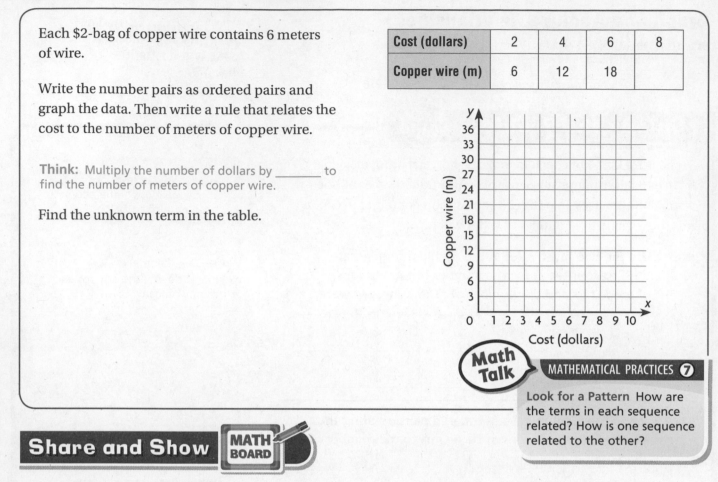

Copper wire (m)

Cost (dollars)

Math Talk MATHEMATICAL PRACTICES ❼

Look for a Pattern How are the terms in each sequence related? How is one sequence related to the other?

Share and Show MATH BOARD

Graph and label the related number pairs as ordered pairs. Complete the rule that describes how one sequence is related to the other. Then use the rule to find the unknown term.

✓ **1.** For every 2 square feet of lawn, Charlie needs 8 ounces of fertilizer.

Lawn (sq ft)	2	4	6	8	10
Weight (oz)	8	16	24	32	

Multiply the number of square feet by _____ to find the ounces of fertilizer needed.

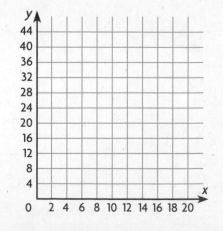

✓ **2.** On Mary's map, every 2 inches represents 10 miles.

Map (in.)	2	4	6	8	10
Miles	10	20	30	40	

Multiply the number of inches by _____ to find the distance in miles.

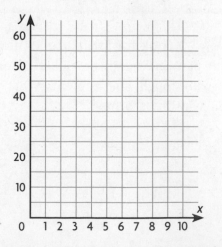

Name _____

On Your Own

3. **GO DEEPER** On Sandy's scale drawing of the school campus, 2 inches equals 4 yards. The distance between the swings and the track is 10 inches on the drawing, and the distance between the track and the basketball court is 4 inches on the drawing. How much farther is the track from the swings than from the basketball court, in actual distance?

Draw your own graph. Write a rule that describes how one sequence of terms is related to the other. Complete the table and solve.

Map (in.)	2	4	6	8	10
Distance (yds)	4	8	12	16	

Rule: _____

_____

_____

_____

4. **THINK SMARTER** Eric recorded the total number of push ups he did each minute for 4 minutes.

Time (minutes)	1	2	3	4
Number of Push Ups	15	30	45	60

Write the number pairs as ordered pairs.

_____

Graph the ordered pairs on a coordinate plane.

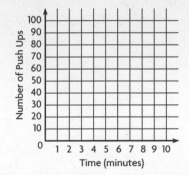

Write a rule to describe how the number pairs are related.

_____

_____

Problem Solving · Applications Real World

THINK SMARTER Sense or Nonsense?

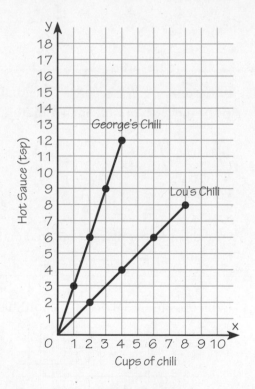

5. Elsa solved the following problem.

Lou and George are making chili for the Annual Firefighter's Ball. Lou uses 2 teaspoons of hot sauce for every 2 cups of chili that he makes, and George uses 3 teaspoons of the same hot sauce for every cup of chili in his recipe. Who has the hotter chili, George or Lou?

Write the related number pairs as ordered pairs and then graph them. Use the graph to compare who has the hotter chili, George or Lou.

Lou's chili (cups)	2	4	6	8
Hot sauce (tsp)	2	4	6	8

George's chili (cups)	1	2	3	4
Hot sauce (tsp)	3	6	9	12

Lou's chili: (2, 2), (4, 4), (6, 6), (8, 8)

George's chili: (1, 3), (2, 6), (3, 9), (4, 12)

Elsa said that George's chili was hotter than Lou's, because the graph showed that the amount of hot sauce in George's chili was always 3 times as great as the amount of hot sauce in Lou's chili. Does Elsa's answer make sense, or is it nonsense? Explain.

_____

_____

_____

_____

_____

_____

Name _____

Graph and Analyze Relationships

Common Core

COMMON CORE STANDARD—5.OA.B.3,
5.G.A.2 *Analyze patterns and relationships.*

**Graph and label the related number pairs as ordered pairs.
Then complete and use the rule to find the unknown term.**

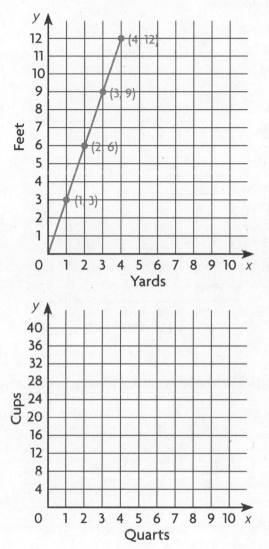

1. Multiply the number of yards by ____3____ to find
   the number of feet.

Yards	1	2	3	4
Feet	3	6	9	12

2. Multiply the number of quarts by _____ to
   find the number of cups that measure the same
   amount.

Quarts	1	2	3	4	5
Cups	4	8	12	16	

3. How can you use the graph for Exercise 2 to find how
   many cups are in 9 quarts?

_____

_____

_____

_____

_____

4. How many cups are equal to 9 quarts? _____

Lesson Check (5.OA.B.3)

Use the data to complete the graph. Then answer the questions.

Paola is making a pitcher of iced tea. For each cup of water, she uses 3 tablespoons of powdered iced tea mix.

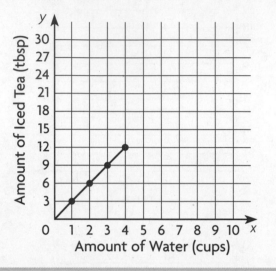

1. Fill in the missing number to complete the following rule.

   Multiply the amount of iced tea mix by _____ to get the amount of water.

2. Suppose Paola uses 18 tablespoons of iced tea mix. How many cups of water does she need to use?

   _____

Spiral Review (5.NBT.A.2, 5.NBT.B.6, 5.NBT.B.7)

3. A biologist counted 10,000 migrating monarch butterflies. How do you express 10,000 as a power of 10?

4. Find the quotient. Write your answer using a decimal and round to the nearest hundredth.

   $$8{,}426 \div 82$$

   _____

5. What is $54.38 + 29.7$?

6. On a certain day, $1 is worth 30.23 Russian rubles. Omar has $75. How many rubles will he get in exchange?

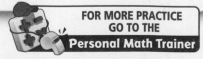

FOR MORE PRACTICE
GO TO THE
Personal Math Trainer

✓ Chapter 9 Review/Test

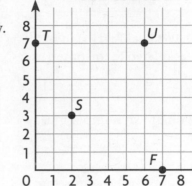

Personal Math Trainer
Online Assessment
and Intervention

1. The letters on the coordinate grid represent the locations of the first four holes on a golf course. Which of the following accurately describes the location of a hole? Mark all that apply.

   Ⓐ Hole *U* is 4 units left and 4 units down from hole *S*.

   Ⓑ Hole *F* is 1 unit right and 7 units down from hole *U*.

   Ⓒ Hole *T* is 2 units left and 4 units up from hole *S*.

   Ⓓ Hole *S* is 3 units left and 5 units up from hole *F*.

Golf Course

2. **GO DEEPER** A builder is buying property to build new houses. The sizes of the lots are $\frac{1}{6}, \frac{1}{2}, \frac{1}{3}, \frac{1}{2}, \frac{1}{6}, \frac{1}{2}, \frac{1}{3}, \frac{1}{6}, \frac{1}{2}, \frac{1}{6}$, $\frac{1}{2}, \frac{1}{6}, \frac{1}{6}$, and $\frac{1}{3}$ acre. Organize the information in a line plot.

   What is the average size of the lots?

   _____ acre

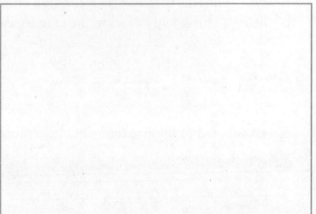

3. For 6 days in a row, Julia measured the depth of the snow in a shaded area of her backyard. The line graph shows her data. Between which two days did the depth of the snow decrease the most?

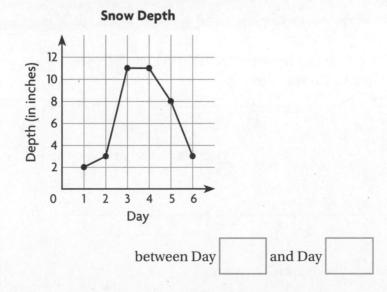

Snow Depth

   between Day ☐ and Day ☐

4. Portia made a table to figure out how much she earned selling T-shirts.

Day	1	2	3	4	5
Number of T-shirts sold	5	10	15	20	25
Amount earned ($)	20	40	60	80	?

For 4a–4b, use the table to choose the correct values to describe how one sequence is related to the other.

4a. The unknown number in Day 5 is .

```
90

100

120
```

4b. The rule that describes how the number of T-shirts sold relates to the amount earned is

```
add 15

multiply by 5

multiply by 4
```

5. Jawan made a table to figure out how much he earns at his job.

Job Earnings					
Week	1	2	3	4	...	6
Hours Worked	6	12	18	24	...	36
Amount Earned ($)	54	108	162	216	...	?

Part A

Write a rule that relates the amount Jawan earns to the number of hours worked. Explain how you can check your rule.

Part B

How much does he earn from his job in Week 6?

$ _____

Name _____

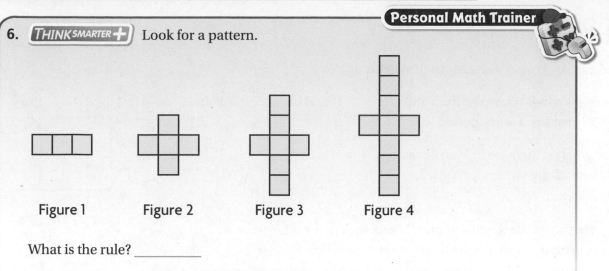

6. **THINK SMARTER +** Look for a pattern.

Figure 1 Figure 2 Figure 3 Figure 4

What is the rule? _____

How many squares will there be in Figure 5? _____ squares

7. Lindsey made a map of her town. Match each location below with the correct ordered pair that marks it on the coordinate grid. Not every ordered pair will be used.

Clock Tower ●   ● (4, 4)

● (4, 1)

Art Museum ●   ● (1, 3)

● (5, 4)

East Park ●   ● (4, 5)

● (3, 1)

Movie Theater ●   ● (2, 4)

● (1, 4)

School ●   ● (4, 2)

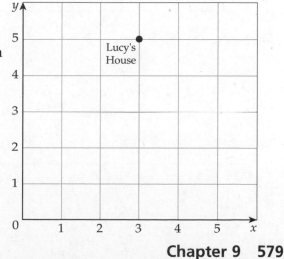

8. Lucy's house is located at the point shown on the coordinate grid. Ainsley's house is located 2 units right and 3 units down from Lucy's house. Plot a point on the coordinate grid to represent the location of Ainsley's house.

What ordered pair represents the location of Lucy's house?

What ordered pair represents the location of Ainsley's house?

© Houghton Mifflin Harcourt Publishing Company

Chapter 9   579

9. Each week, Maria saves some of her allowance. The line graph shows the amount of Maria's savings for the first 5 weeks of the year.

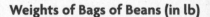

Maria's Savings

For 9a–9b, select True or False for each statement.

9a. Maria's savings increased from $30 to $55 over the 5-week period.　　○ True　　○ False

9b. The greatest increase in Maria's savings occurred from Week 1 to Week 2.　　○ True　　○ False

10. The line plot shows the weights of bags of beans. What is the average weight of the bags? Show your work.


```
                      X
               X      X
   X     X     X      X
   X     X     X      X      X
  -+-----+-----+------+------+-
   1/6   1/3   1/2    2/3    5/6
```

Weights of Bags of Beans (in lb)

11. The table shows how much a puppy weighs from 1 month old to 5 months old.

Puppy's Weight					
Age (in months)	1	2	3	4	5
Weight (in pounds)	12	18	23	31	34

What ordered pairs would you plot to show the puppy's weight on a coordinate grid? How do you think the ordered pairs would be different if the puppy's weight was measured every week instead of every month? Explain your reasoning.

12. Randy is training for a race. She makes a table that shows how long it takes her to run different distances.

Running Time and Distance				
Distance (in miles)	1	2	3	4
Time (in minutes)	10	20	30	40

Part A

Write the number pairs as ordered pairs. Then write the rule to describe how the number pairs are related.

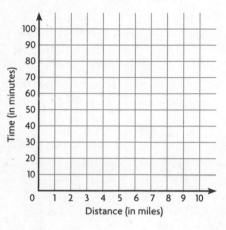

Part B

Graph the ordered pairs on the coordinate plane.

13. A scientist made a line graph that shows how a bear's average heart rate changes over time.

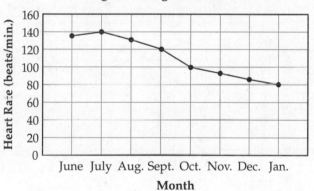

For 13a–13c, select True or False for each statement.

13a. The bear's average heart rate is at its highest in July. ○ True   ○ False

13b. The bear's average heart rate increases by 10 beats per minute from July to August. ○ True   ○ False

13c. The bear's average heart rate is at its lowest in January. ○ True   ○ False

14. The table shows the total number of tickets sold for the school play each day for 5 days.

Ticket Sales					
Day	1	2	3	4	5
Tickets Sold	20	30	45	75	90

Graph the ordered pairs from the tiles on the coordinate grid.

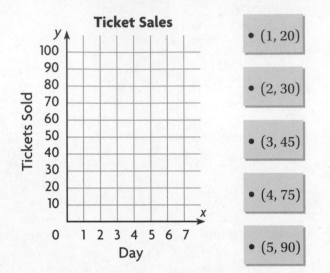

- (1, 20)
- (2, 30)
- (3, 45)
- (4, 75)
- (5, 90)

15. The graph shows the relationship between the amount of milk and water used in a recipe. Determine a rule that relates the amount of milk to the amount of water by writing the correct term or value from the tiles in each blank.

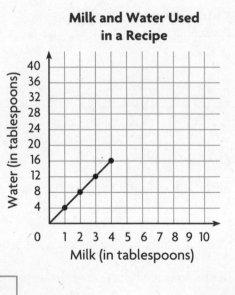

Milk and Water Used in a Recipe

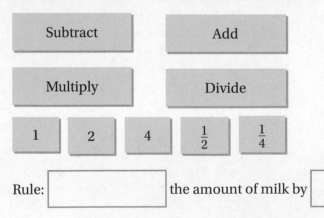

Subtract	Add

Multiply	Divide

| 1 | 2 | 4 | $\frac{1}{2}$ | $\frac{1}{4}$ |

Rule: [   ] the amount of milk by [   ] .

16. Steven is buying a new mountain bike on layaway for $272. If he pays $34 each week, how many weeks will it take Steven to pay for the bike? How can making a table help you solve the problem?

Convert Units of Measure

Show What You Know

Personal Math Trainer
Online Assessment
and Intervention

Check your understanding of important skills.

Name _____

▶ **Measure Length to the Nearest Inch**
Use an inch ruler. Measure the length to the nearest inch. (3.MD.B.4)

1.
about _____ inches

2.
about _____ inches

▶ **Multiply and Divide by 10, 100, and 1,000** **Use mental math.** (4.NBT.B.5)

3. $1 \times 5.98 = 5.98$
$10 \times 5.98 = 59.8$

$100 \times 5.98 =$ _____

$1,000 \times 5.98 =$ _____

4. $235 \div 1 = 235$
$235 \div 10 = 23.5$

$235 \div 100 =$ _____

$235 \div 1,000 =$ _____

▶ **Choose Customary Units** **Write the appropriate unit to measure each.**
Write *inch*, *foot*, *yard*, or *mile*. (4.MD.A.1)

5. length of a pencil _____

6. length of a football field _____

Math in the Real World

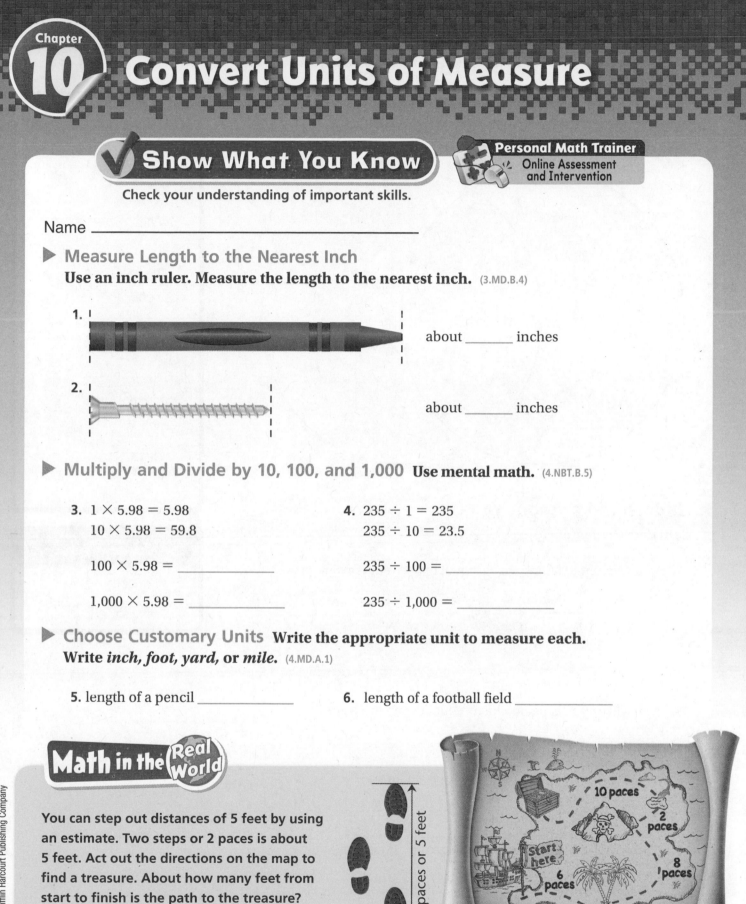

You can step out distances of 5 feet by using an estimate. Two steps or 2 paces is about 5 feet. Act out the directions on the map to find a treasure. About how many feet from start to finish is the path to the treasure?

2 paces or 5 feet

10 paces
2 paces
8 paces
Start here
6 paces

Vocabulary Builder

▶ **Visualize It** •

Sort the review and preview words into the Venn diagram.

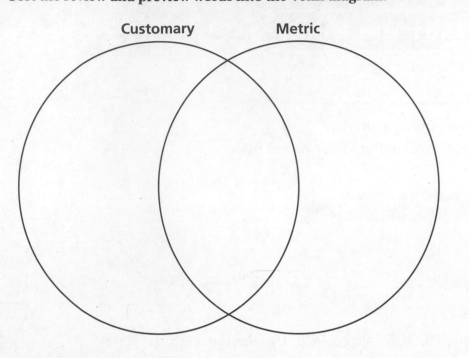

Customary   Metric

▶ **Understand Vocabulary** •

Complete the sentences.

1. A metric unit of length that is equal to one tenth of a meter

   is a _____.

2. A metric unit of length that is equal to one thousandth

   of a meter is a _____.

3. A metric unit of capacity that is equal to one thousandth

   of a liter is a _____.

4. A metric unit of length that is equal to 10 meters

   is a _____.

5. A metric unit of mass that is equal to one thousandth

   of a gram is a _____.

• **Interactive Student Edition**
• **Multimedia eGlossary**

capacity

capacidad

3

decimeter (dm)

decímetro (dm)

13

dekameter (dam)

decámetro

14

mass

masa

37

milligram (mg)

miligramo (mg)

38

milliliter (mL)

mililitro (mL)

39

ton (T)

tonelada (T)

68

weight

peso

71

A metric unit used to measure length or distance; 10 decimeters = 1 meter

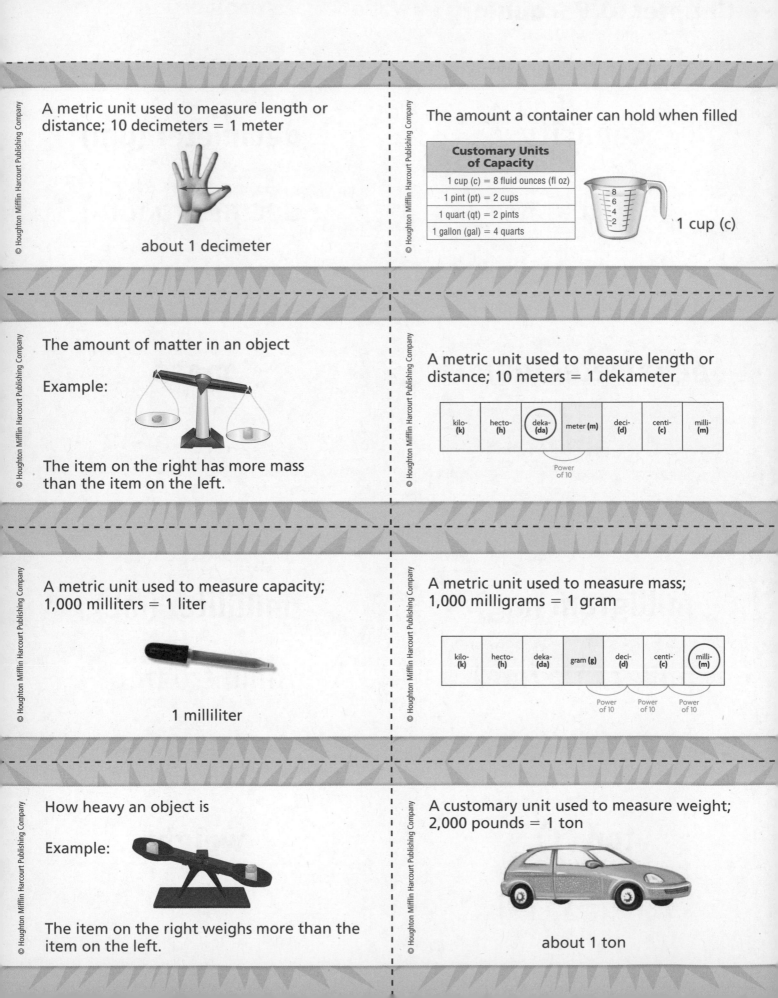

about 1 decimeter

The amount a container can hold when filled

Customary Units of Capacity	
1 cup (c) = 8 fluid ounces (fl oz)	
1 pint (pt) = 2 cups	
1 quart (qt) = 2 pints	
1 gallon (gal) = 4 quarts	

1 cup (c)

The amount of matter in an object

Example:

The item on the right has more mass than the item on the left.

A metric unit used to measure length or distance; 10 meters = 1 dekameter

kilo- (k)	hecto- (h)	deka- (da)	meter (m)	deci- (d)	centi- (c)	milli- (m)

Power of 10

A metric unit used to measure capacity; 1,000 milliters = 1 liter

1 milliliter

A metric unit used to measure mass; 1,000 milligrams = 1 gram

kilo- (k)	hecto- (h)	deka- (da)	gram (g)	deci- (d)	centi- (c)	milli- (m)

Power of 10   Power of 10   Power of 10

How heavy an object is

Example:

The item on the right weighs more than the item on the left.

A customary unit used to measure weight; 2,000 pounds = 1 ton

about 1 ton

Bingo

For 3–6 players

Materials

- 1 set of word cards
- 1 Bingo board for each player
- game markers

How to Play

1. The caller chooses a card and reads the definition. Then the caller puts the card in a second pile.

2. Players put a marker on the word that matches the definition each time they find it on their Bingo boards.

3. Repeat Steps 1 and 2 until a player marks 5 boxes in a line going down, across, or on a slant and calls "Bingo."

- To check the answers, the player who said "Bingo" reads the words aloud while the caller checks the definitions.

Word Box
capacity
decimeter
dekameter
mass
milligram (mg)
milliliter (mL)
ton (T)
weight

The Write Way

Reflect

Choose one idea. Write about it.

- Explain how the word part *milli-* can help you figure out the meaning of the words *milligram* and *milliliter*.
- Write a story that uses these words.

  milligram   ton   weight

- Tell about a time when you needed to know the capacity of a container.
- Explain the difference between mass and weight.

Name _____

Customary Length

Essential Question How can you compare and convert customary units of length?

Common Core Measurement and Data—
5.MD.A.1
MATHEMATICAL PRACTICES
MP1, MP6, MP7

Unlock the Problem

To build a new swing, Mr. Mattson needs 9 feet of rope for each side of the swing and 6 more feet for the monkey bar. The hardware store sells rope by the yard.

- How many feet of rope does Mr. Mattson

  need for the swing? _____

- How many feet does Mr. Mattson need for

  the swing and the monkey bar combined? _____

Mr. Mattson needs to find how many yards of rope he needs to buy. He will need to convert 24 feet to yards. How many groups of 3 feet are in 24 feet?

A 12-inch ruler is 1 foot.		

A yardstick is 1 yard.

_____ feet = 1 yard

Use a bar model to write an equation.

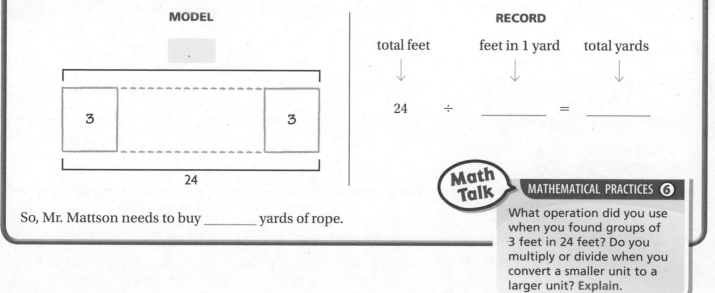

MODEL

```
┌─────┬ ─ ─ ─ ─ ─ ┬─────┐
│  3  │           │  3  │
└─────┴ ─ ─ ─ ─ ─ ┴─────┘
         24
```

RECORD

total feet   feet in 1 yard   total yards

↓   ↓   ↓

$24 \div \underline{\quad} = \underline{\quad}$

So, Mr. Mattson needs to buy _____ yards of rope.

Math Talk MATHEMATICAL PRACTICES ❻

What operation did you use when you found groups of 3 feet in 24 feet? Do you multiply or divide when you convert a smaller unit to a larger unit? Explain.

🔒 Example 1 Use the table to find the relationship between miles and feet.

The distance between the new high school and the football field is 2 miles. How does this distance compare to 10,000 feet?

Customary Units of Length	
1 foot (ft) = 12 inches (in.)	
1 yard (yd) = 3 ft	
1 mile (mi) = 5,280 ft	
1 mile = 1,760 yd	

When you convert larger units to smaller units, you need to multiply.

STEP 1   Convert 2 miles to feet.

Think: 1 mile is equal to 5,280 feet.

I need to _____ the total

number of miles by _____.

total miles	feet in 1 mile	total feet
↓	↓	↓
2 × _____		= _____

2 miles = _____ feet

STEP 2   Compare. Write <, >, or =.

_____ feet ◯ 10,000 feet

Since _____ is _____ than 10,000, the distance between the

new high school and the football field is _____ than 10,000 feet.

🔒 Example 2 Convert to mixed measures.

Mixed measures use more than one unit of measurement. You can convert a single unit of measurement to mixed measures.

Convert 62 inches into feet and inches.

STEP 1   Use the table.

Think: 12 inches is equal to 1 foot

I am changing from a smaller unit to

a larger unit, so I _____.

STEP 2   Convert.

total inches	inches in 1 foot	feet	inches
↓	↓	↓	↓
62 ÷ _____		is _____ r _____	

So, 62 inches is equal to _____ feet _____ inches.

- **MATHEMATICAL PRACTICE ⑥** **Explain** how to convert the mixed measures, 12 yards 2 feet, to a single unit of measurement in feet. How many feet is it?

Name _____

Convert.

1. 2 mi = _____ yd

2. 6 yd = _____ ft

3. 90 in. = _____ ft _____ in.

Math Talk

MATHEMATICAL PRACTICES ①

Make Sense of Problems
How do you know when to multiply to convert a measurement?

On Your Own

Practice: Copy and Solve **Convert.**

4. 125 in. = ■ ft ■ in.

5. 46 ft = ■ yd ■ ft

6. 42 yd 2 ft = ■ ft

Compare. Write <, >, or =.

7. 8 ft ◯ 3 yd

8. 2 mi ◯ 10,500 ft

9. 3 yd 2 ft ◯ 132 in.

10. **GO DEEPER** Terry is making 6 hat and scarf sets. Each scarf requires 2 yards of material and each hat requires 18 inches of material. How many feet of material does he need for all 6 hat and scarf sets?

_____

11. **THINK SMARTER** Choose the correct word and number to complete the sentence.

Katy's driveway is 120 feet long.

To convert feet to yards, I need to

| add |
| subtract | 120 by |
| multiply |
| divide |

| 3 |
| 12 |
| 1,760 |
| 5,280 |

.

Problem Solving · Applications Real World

12. **GO DEEPER** Javon is helping his dad build a tree house. He has a piece of trim that is 13 feet long. How many pieces can Javon cut that are 1 yard long? How much of a yard will he have left over?

_____

13. **THINK SMARTER** Patty is building a rope ladder for a tree house. She needs two 5-foot pieces of rope for the sides of the ladder. She needs 7 pieces of rope, each 18 inches long, for the steps. How many feet of rope does Patty need to make the ladder? Write your answer as a mixed number and as a mixed measure in feet and inches.

_____

Connect to Reading

Compare and Contrast

When you compare and contrast, you tell how two or more things are alike and different. You can compare and contrast information in a table.

Complete the table below. Use the table to answer the questions.

Linear Units				
Yards	1	2	3	4
Feet	3	6	9	
Inches	36	72		

14. **MATHEMATICAL PRACTICE 7** Identify Relationships How are the items in the table alike? How are they different?

_____

_____

15. **MATHEMATICAL PRACTICE 7** Look for a Pattern What do you notice about the relationship between the number of larger units and the number of smaller units as the length increases? Explain.

_____

_____

Customary Length

Common Core **COMMON CORE STANDARD—5.MD.A.1**
Convert like measurement units within a given measurement system.

Convert.

1. 12 yd = ___36___ ft

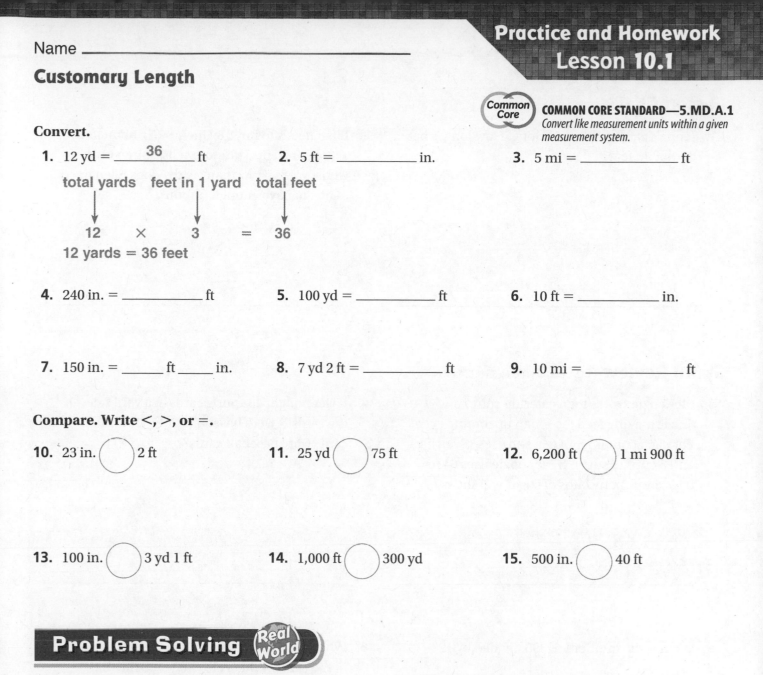

total yards   feet in 1 yard   total feet

12   ×   3   =   36

12 yards = 36 feet

2. 5 ft = _____ in.

3. 5 mi = _____ ft

4. 240 in. = _____ ft

5. 100 yd = _____ ft

6. 10 ft = _____ in.

7. 150 in. = _____ ft _____ in.

8. 7 yd 2 ft = _____ ft

9. 10 mi = _____ ft

Compare. Write <, >, or =.

10. 23 in. ◯ 2 ft

11. 25 yd ◯ 75 ft

12. 6,200 ft ◯ 1 mi 900 ft

13. 100 in. ◯ 3 yd 1 ft

14. 1,000 ft ◯ 300 yd

15. 500 in. ◯ 40 ft

Problem Solving *Real World*

16. Marita orders 12 yards of material to make banners. If she needs 1 foot of fabric for each banner, how many banners can she make?

_____

_____

17. Christy bought an 8-foot piece of lumber to trim a bookshelf. Altogether, she needs 100 inches of lumber for the trim. Did Christy buy enough lumber? Explain.

_____

_____

18. ▮WRITE ▸*Math* Explain how to compare two lengths that are measured in different-sized units.

_____

_____

Lesson Check (5.MD.A.1)

1. Jenna's garden is 5 yards long. How long is her garden in feet?

2. Ellen needs to buy 180 inches of ribbon to wrap a large present. The store sells ribbon only in whole yards. How many yards does Ellen need to buy to have enough ribbon?

Spiral Review (5.OA.B.3, 5.NF.B.6, 5.NF.B.4a)

3. McKenzie works for a catering company. She is making iced tea for an upcoming event. For each container of tea, she uses 16 tea bags and 3 cups of sugar. If McKenzie uses 64 tea bags, how many cups of sugar will she use?

4. Javier bought 48 sports cards at a yard sale. Of the cards, $\frac{3}{8}$ were baseball cards. How many cards were baseball cards?

5. What is the quotient of 396 divided by 12?

6. What is the unknown number in Sequence 2 in the chart? What rule can you write that relates Sequence 2 to Sequence 1?

Sequence Number	1	2	3	8	10
Sequence 1	4	8	12	32	40
Sequence 2	8	16	24	64	?

© Houghton Mifflin Harcourt Publishing Company

FOR MORE PRACTICE GO TO THE Personal Math Trainer

Customary Capacity

Essential Question How can you compare and convert customary units of capacity?

Common Core **Measurement and Data—**
5.MD.A.1
MATHEMATICAL PRACTICES
MP2, MP4, MP6

⚷ Unlock the Problem Real World

Mara has a can of paint with 3 cups of purple paint in it. She also has a bucket with a capacity of 26 fluid ounces. Will the bucket hold all of the paint Mara has?

The **capacity** of a container is the amount the container can hold.

• What capacity does Mara need to convert?

_____

• After Mara converts the units, what does she need to do next?

_____

_____

 1 cup (c) = _____ fluid ounces (fl oz)

🔒 Use a bar model to write an equation.

STEP 1 Convert 3 cups to fluid ounces.

MODEL		RECORD

8	8	8

total cups	fl oz in 1 cup	total fl oz
↓	↓	↓
3 ×	_____ =	_____

STEP 2 Compare. Write <, >, or =. _____ fl oz ◯ 26 fl oz

Since _____ fluid ounces is _____ than 26 fluid ounces,

Mara's bucket _____ hold all of the paint.

• **MATHEMATICAL PRACTICE 6** What if Mara has 7 cups of green paint and a container filled with 64 fluid ounces of yellow paint? Which color paint does Mara have more of? **Explain** your reasoning.

_____

_____

Example

Coral made 32 pints of fruit punch for a party. She needs to carry the punch in 1-gallon containers. How many containers does Coral need?

> To convert a smaller unit to a larger unit, you need to divide. Sometimes you may need to convert more than once.

Customary Units of Capacity	
1 cup (c) = 8 fluid ounces (fl oz)	
1 pint (pt) = 2 cups	
1 quart (qt) = 2 pints	
1 gallon (gal) = 4 quarts	

Convert 32 pints to gallons.

STEP 1 Write an equation to convert pints to quarts.

total pints   pints in 1 qt   total quarts

32 ◯ _____ ◯ _____

STEP 2 Write an equation to convert quarts to gallons.

total quarts   quarts in 1 gal   total gallons

_____ ◯ _____ ◯ _____

So, Coral needs _____ 1-gallon containers to carry the punch.

Share and Show

1. Use the picture to complete the statements and convert 3 quarts to pints.

   a. 1 quart = _____ pints

   b. 1 quart is _____ than 1 pint.

   c. 3 qt ◯ _____ pt in 1 qt = _____ pt

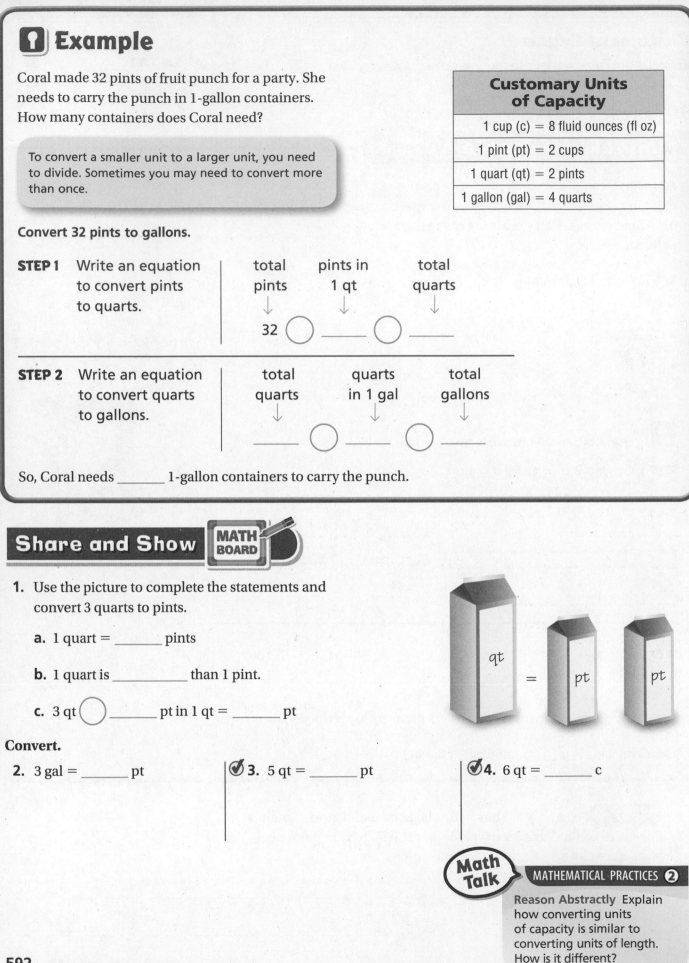

Convert.

2. 3 gal = _____ pt

☑ 3. 5 qt = _____ pt

☑ 4. 6 qt = _____ c

Math Talk

MATHEMATICAL PRACTICES ②

Reason Abstractly Explain how converting units of capacity is similar to converting units of length. How is it different?

Name _____

On Your Own

Convert.

5. 38 c = _____ pt

6. 36 qt = _____ gal

7. 104 fl oz = _____ c

Practice: Copy and Solve Convert.

8. 200 c = ■ qt

9. 22 pt = ■ fl oz

10. 8 gal = ■ qt

11. 72 fl oz = ■ c

12. 2 gal = ■ pt

13. 48 pt = ■ gal

Compare. Write <, >, or =.

14. 28 c ◯ 14 pt

15. 25 pt ◯ 13 qt

16. 20 qt ◯ 80 c

17. 12 gal ◯ 50 qt

18. 320 fl oz ◯ 18 pt

19. 15 qt ◯ 63 c

20. **WRITE** ▸*Math* Which of exercises 14–19 could you solve mentally? Explain your answer for one exercise.

_____

_____

_____

21. **GODEEPER** Larry made 4 batches of punch. Each batch uses 16 fluid ounces of lemon juice and 3 pints of orange juice. If each serving is 1 cup, how many servings did he make all together?

_____

Problem Solving • Applications

Show your work. For 22–24, use the table.

22. **MATHEMATICAL PRACTICE 4** **Use Graphs** Complete the table, and make a graph showing the relationship between quarts and pints.

Quarts	0	1	2	3	4
Pints	0				

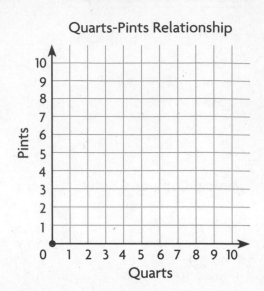

Quarts-Pints Relationship

23. **GO DEEPER** Describe any pattern you notice in the pairs of numbers you graphed. Write a rule to describe the pattern.

_____

_____

_____

_____

24. **THINK SMARTER** What other pair of customary units of capacity have the same relationship as pints and quarts? Explain.

_____

_____

_____

25. **THINK SMARTER** Shelby made 5 quarts of juice for a picnic. She said that she made $1\frac{1}{4}$ cups of juice. Explain Shelby's mistake.

_____

_____

_____

_____

Customary Capacity

Common Core **COMMON CORE STANDARD—5.MD.A.1**
Convert like measurement units within a given measurement system.

Convert.

1. 5 gal = __40__ pt

   Think: 1 gallon = 4 quarts
           1 quart = 2 pints

2. 192 fl oz = _____ pt

3. 15 pt = _____ c

4. 240 fl oz = _____ c

5. 32 qt = _____ gal

6. 10 qt = _____ c

7. 48 c = _____ qt

8. 72 pt = _____ gal

9. 128 fl oz = _____ pt

Compare. Write <, >, or =.

10. 17 qt ◯ 4 gal

11. 96 fl oz ◯ 8 pt

12. 400 pt ◯ 100 gal

13. 100 fl oz ◯ 16 pt

14. 74 fl oz ◯ 8 c

15. 12 c ◯ 3 qt

Problem Solving (Real World)

16. Vickie made a recipe for 144 fluid ounces of scented candle wax. How many 1-cup candle molds can she fill with the recipe?

17. A recipe calls for 32 fluid ounces of heavy cream. How many 1-pint containers of heavy cream are needed to make the recipe?

_____

_____

18. **WRITE** ▸*Math* Give some examples of when you would measure capacity in each of the units of capacity shown in the table on page 592.

_____

_____

Lesson Check (5.MD.A.1)

1. Rosa made 12 gallons of lemonade to sell at a lemonade stand. How many pints of lemonade did she make?

2. Ebonae's fish tank holds 40 gallons. How many quarts does the fish tank hold?

Spiral Review (5.NBT.B.5, 5.NF.A.1, 5.NF.B.3, 5.MD.A.1)

3. A mountain climber climbed 15,840 feet on her way to the summit of a mountain. How many miles did she climb?

4. Jamal is making blueberry muffins. He has $6\frac{3}{4}$ cups of batter, but he needs a total of 12 cups. How much more batter does Jamal need?

5. At a building site, there are 16 pallets with sacks of cement. The total weight of all the pallets and cement is 4,856 pounds. Each pallet with cement weighs the same amount. How much does each pallet with cement weigh?

6. A publisher shipped 15 boxes of books to a bookstore. Each box contained 32 books. How many books did the publisher ship to the bookstore?

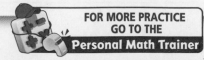

FOR MORE PRACTICE
GO TO THE
Personal Math Trainer

Name _____

Weight

Essential Question How can you compare and convert customary units of weight?

Common Core **Measurement and Data—**
5.MD.A.1
MATHEMATICAL PRACTICES
MP1, MP2

Unlock the Problem Real World

Hector's school is having a model rocket contest. To be in the contest, each rocket must weigh 4 pounds or less. Without any paint, Hector's rocket weighs 62 ounces. If Hector wants to paint his rocket, what is the weight of the most paint he can use?

The **weight** of an object is how heavy the object is.

• What weight does Hector need to convert?

_____

• After Hector converts the weight, what does he need to do next?

_____

1 pound = _____ ounces

🔑 Use a bar model to write an equation.

STEP 1 Convert 4 pounds to ounces.

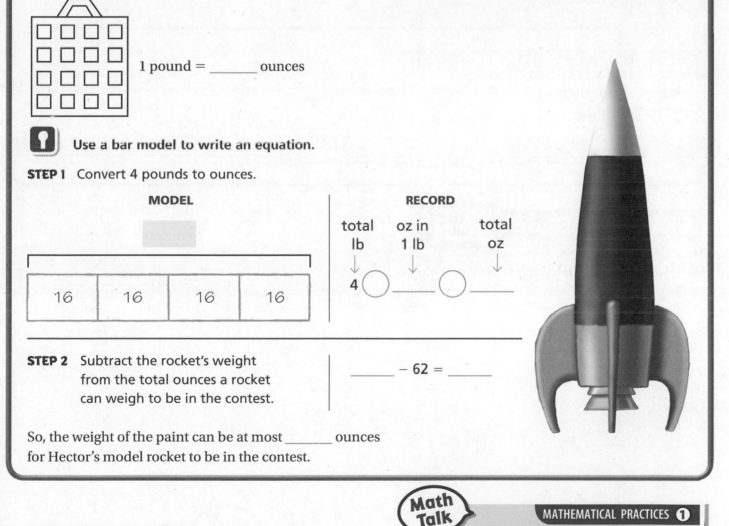

MODEL			
16	16	16	16

RECORD

total
lb   oz in   total
             1 lb   oz
↓   ↓   ↓
4 ◯ _____ ◯ _____

STEP 2 Subtract the rocket's weight from the total ounces a rocket can weigh to be in the contest.

_____ − 62 = _____

So, the weight of the paint can be at most _____ ounces for Hector's model rocket to be in the contest.

Math Talk

MATHEMATICAL PRACTICES ❶

Make Sense of Problems How did you choose which operation to use to change from pounds to ounces? Explain.

Chapter 10 **597**

🔑 Example

The rocket boosters for a U.S. space shuttle weigh 1,292,000 pounds each when the shuttle is launched. How many tons does each rocket booster weigh?

Use mental math to convert pounds to tons.

STEP 1 Decide which operation to use.	Since pounds are smaller than tons, I need to _____ the number of pounds by _____.

Units of Weight

1 pound (lb) = 16 ounces (oz)
1 ton (T) = 2,000 lb

STEP 2 Break 2,000 into two factors that are easy to divide by mentally.	$2,000 = \underline{\hspace{1.5cm}} \times 2$

STEP 3 Divide 1,292,000 by the first factor. Then divide the quotient by the second factor.	$1,292,000 \div \underline{\hspace{1.5cm}} = \underline{\hspace{1.5cm}}$ $\underline{\hspace{1.5cm}} \div 2 = \underline{\hspace{1.5cm}}$

So, each rocket booster weighs _____ tons when launched.

Share and Show 〔MATH BOARD〕

1. Use the picture to complete each equation.

   a. 1 pound = _____ ounces   **b.** 2 pounds = _____ ounces

   c. 3 pounds = _____ ounces   **d.** 4 pounds = _____ ounces

   e. 5 pounds = _____ ounces

Convert.

2. 15 lb = _____ oz

✅ 3. 3 T = _____ lb

✅ 4. 320 oz = _____ lb

Math Talk MATHEMATICAL PRACTICES ②

Reason Quantitatively How can you compare 11 pounds to 175 ounces mentally?

Name _____

On Your Own

Practice: Copy and Solve Convert.

5. 23 lb = ■ oz

6. 6 T = ■ lb

7. 144 oz = ■ lb

8. 15 T = ■ lb

9. 352 oz = ■ lb

10. 18 lb = ■ oz

Compare. Write <, >, or =.

11. 130 oz ◯ 8 lb

12. 34 lb ◯ 544 oz

13. 14 lb ◯ 229 oz

14. 16 T ◯ 32,000 lb

15. 5 lb ◯ 79 oz

16. 85,000 lb ◯ 40 T

17. GO DEEPER Bill has a bike that weighs 56 pounds. Magda has a bike that weighs 52 pounds. She adds a bell and basket to her bike. The bell weighs 12 ounces and the basket weighs 2 pounds 8 ounces. Does Magda's bike with its new bell and basket weigh more than Bill's bike? Explain your reasoning.

_____

_____

Problem Solving • Applications

18. GO DEEPER Rhada has a 5-pound bag of clay. Her craft project requires 5 ounces of clay for each batch of 6 ornaments. If she uses all of the clay, how many ornaments can Rhada make?

19. MATHEMATICAL PRACTICE ② **Represent a Problem** Ellis used 48 ounces of rye flour in a bread recipe. Write an expression you could use to find how many pounds of rye flour Ellis used. Explain how the expression represents the problem.

_____

_____

_____

20. THINK SMARTER Kevin uses 36 ounces of dried apples and 18 ounces of dried cranberries to make a fruit snack. He plans to sell the snack in $\frac{1}{2}$-pound containers. How may containers will he fill? Will any fruit snack be left over?

THINK SMARTER **Pose a Problem**

21. Kia wants to have 4 pounds of munchies for her party. She has 36 ounces of popcorn and wants the rest to be pretzel sticks. How many ounces of pretzel sticks does she need to buy?

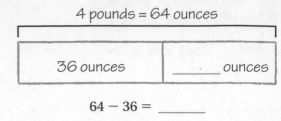

4 pounds = 64 ounces

36 ounces	_____ ounces

$64 - 36 =$ _____

So, Kia needs to buy _____ ounces of pretzel sticks.

Write a new problem using different amounts of snacks. Some weights should be in pounds and others in ounces. Make sure the amount of snacks given is less than the total amount of snacks needed.

Pose a Problem

_____

_____

_____

_____

_____

_____

Draw a bar model for your problem. Then solve.

22. THINK SMARTER For 22a–22c, select True or False for each statement.

22a. $1,500 \text{ lb} > 1 \text{ T}$ ◯ True ◯ False

22b. $32 \text{ oz} < 4 \text{ lb}$ ◯ True ◯ False

22c. $24 \text{ oz} < 1 \text{ lb } 16 \text{ oz}$ ◯ True ◯ False

Weight

Common Core

COMMON CORE STANDARD—5.MD.A.1
Convert like measurement units within a given measurement system.

Convert.

1. 96 oz = ___6___ lb

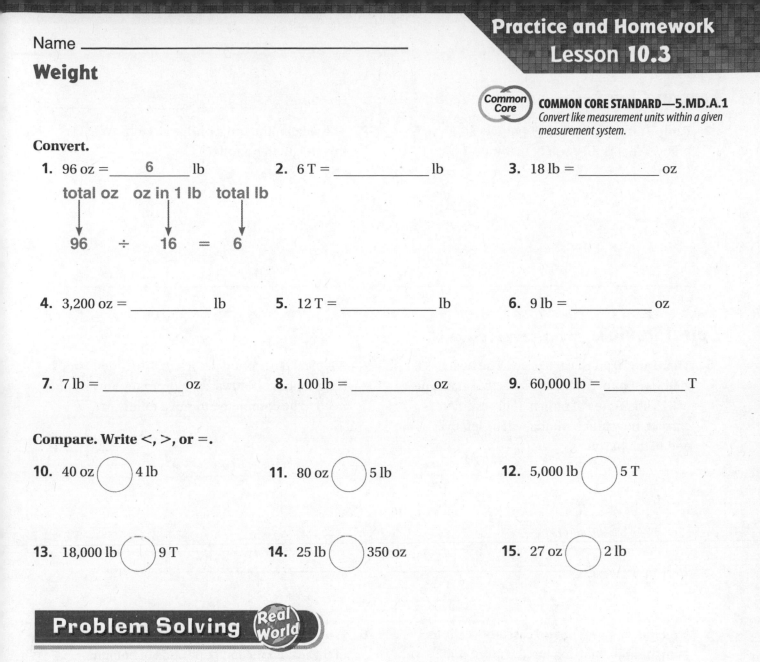

total oz   oz in 1 lb   total lb

96   ÷   16   =   6

2. 6 T = _____ lb

3. 18 lb = _____ oz

4. 3,200 oz = _____ lb

5. 12 T = _____ lb

6. 9 lb = _____ oz

7. 7 lb = _____ oz

8. 100 lb = _____ oz

9. 60,000 lb = _____ T

Compare. Write <, >, or =.

10. 40 oz ◯ 4 lb

11. 80 oz ◯ 5 lb

12. 5,000 lb ◯ 5 T

13. 18,000 lb ◯ 9 T

14. 25 lb ◯ 350 oz

15. 27 oz ◯ 2 lb

Problem Solving Real World

16. Mr. Fields ordered 3 tons of gravel for a driveway at a factory. How many pounds of gravel did he order?

17. Sara can take no more than 22 pounds of luggage on a trip. Her suitcase weighs 112 ounces. How many more pounds can she pack without going over the limit?

_____

_____

18. **WRITE** ▸*Math* Give two examples of items that weigh less than 1 ounce and two examples of items that weigh more than 1 ton.

_____

_____

Lesson Check (5.MD.A.1)

1. Paolo's puppy weighed 11 pounds at the vet's office. What is this weight in ounces?

2. The weight limit on a bridge is 5 tons. What is this weight in pounds?

Spiral Review (5.NF.A.2, 5.NF.B.7c, 5.MD.A.1)

3. There are 20 guests at a party. The host has 8 gallons of punch. He estimates that each guest will drink 2 cups of punch. If his estimate is correct, how much punch will be left over at the end of the party?

4. A typical lap around a track in the United States has a length of 440 yards. How many laps would need to be completed to run a mile?

5. A recipe for sweet potato casserole calls for $\frac{3}{4}$ cup of milk. Martina has 6 cups of milk. How many sweet potato casseroles can she make with that amount of milk?

6. What is the best estimate for the total weight of these cold meats: $1\frac{7}{8}$ pounds of bologna, $1\frac{1}{2}$ pounds of ham, and $\frac{7}{8}$ pound of roast beef?

© Houghton Mifflin Harcourt Publishing Company

FOR MORE PRACTICE
GO TO THE
Personal Math Trainer

Name _____

Multistep Measurement Problems

Essential Question How can you solve multistep problems that include measurement conversions?

Common Core Measurement and Data—
5.MD.A.1
MATHEMATICAL PRACTICES
MP1, MP4, MP6

🔑 Unlock the Problem Real World

A leaky faucet in Jarod's house drips 2 cups of water each day. After 2 weeks of dripping, the faucet is fixed. If it dripped the same amount each day, how many quarts of water dripped from Jarod's leaky faucet in 2 weeks?

 Use the steps to solve the multistep problem.

STEP 1

Record the information you are given.

The faucet drips _____ cups of water each day.

The faucet drips for _____ weeks.

STEP 2

Find the total amount of water dripped in 2 weeks.

Since you are given the amount of water dripped each day, you must convert 2 weeks into days and multiply.

Think: There are 7 days in 1 week.

cups each day	days in 2 weeks	total cups
↓	↓	↓
2	× _____	= _____

The faucet drips _____ cups in 2 weeks.

STEP 3

Convert from cups to quarts.

Think: There are 2 cups in 1 pint.

There are 2 pints in 1 quart.

_____ cups = _____ pints

_____ pints = _____ quarts

So, Jarod's leaky faucet drips _____ quarts of water in 2 weeks.

- **What if** the faucet dripped for 4 weeks before it was fixed? How many quarts of water would have leaked?

_____

Example

A carton of large, Grade A eggs weighs about 1.5 pounds. If a carton holds a dozen eggs, how many ounces does each egg weigh?

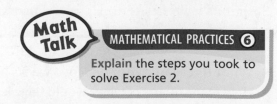

STEP 1

In ounces, find the weight of a carton of eggs.

Think: 1 pound = _____ ounces

Weight of a carton (in ounces):

total lb   oz in 1 lb   total oz
  ↓   ↓   ↓

1.5   ×   _____ = _____

The carton of eggs weighs about _____ ounces.

STEP 2

In ounces, find the weight of each egg in a carton.

Think: 1 carton (dozen eggs) = _____ eggs

Weight of each egg (in ounces):

total oz   eggs in 1 carton   oz of 1 egg
  ↓   ↓   ↓

24   ÷   _____ = _____

So, each egg weighs about _____ ounces.

Share and Show

Solve.

1. After each soccer practice, Scott runs 4 sprints of 20 yards each. If he continues his routine, how many practices will it take for Scott to have sprinted a total of 2 miles combined?

   Scott sprints _____ yards each practice.

   Since there are _____ yards in 2 miles, he will need to continue his routine for

   _____ practices.

2. A worker at a mill is loading 5-lb bags of flour into boxes to deliver to a local warehouse. Each box holds 12 bags of flour. If the warehouse orders 3 Tons of flour, how many boxes are needed to fulfill the order?

3. Cory brings five 1-gallon jugs of juice to serve during parent night at his school. If the paper cups he is using for drinks can hold 8 fluid ounces, how many drinks can Cory serve for parent night?

Math Talk

MATHEMATICAL PRACTICES ❻

Explain the steps you took to solve Exercise 2.

On Your Own

Solve.

4. *GO DEEPER* A science teacher collects 18 pints of lake water for a lab she is teaching. The lab requires each student to use 4 fluid ounces of lake water. If 68 students are participating, how many pints of lake water will the teacher have left over?

5. *MATHEMATICAL PRACTICE 4* **Use Diagrams** A string of decorative lights is 28 feet long. The first light on the string is 16 inches from the plug. If the lights on the string are spaced 4 inches apart, how many lights are there on the string? Draw a picture to help you solve the problem.

6. When Elena's car moves forward such that each tire makes one full rotation, the car has traveled 72 inches. How many full rotations will the tires need to make for Elena's car to travel 10 yards?

7. *GO DEEPER* A male African elephant weighs 7 tons. If a male African lion at the local zoo weighs $\frac{1}{40}$ of the weight of the male African elephant, how many pounds does the lion weigh?

8. Darnell rented a moving truck. The weight of the empty truck was 7,860 pounds. When Darnell filled the truck with his items, it weighed 6 tons. What was the weight in pounds of the items that Darnell placed in the truck?

9. *THINK SMARTER* A gallon of unleaded gasoline weighs about 6 pounds. About how many ounces does 1 quart of unleaded gasoline weigh? HINT: 1 quart = $\frac{1}{4}$ of a gallon

Unlock the Problem Real World

10. **THINK SMARTER** At a local animal shelter there are 12 small-size dogs and 5 medium-size dogs. Every day, the small-size dogs are each given 12.5 ounces of dry food and the medium-size dogs are each given 18 ounces of the same dry food. How many pounds of dry food does the shelter serve in one day?

a. What are you asked to find? _____

_____

b. What information will you use? _____

_____

_____

c. What conversion will you need to do to solve the problem?

_____

_____

d. Show the steps you use to solve the problem.

e. Complete the sentences. The small-size dogs eat a total of _____ ounces of dry food each day.

The medium-size dogs eat a total of

_____ ounces of dry food each day.

The shelter serves _____ ounces,

or _____ pounds, of dry food each day.

Personal Math Trainer

11. **THINK SMARTER +** Gus is painting his house. He uses 2 quarts of paint per hour. Gus paints for 8 hours. How many gallons of paint did he use? Show your work.

_____

_____

Multistep Measurement Problems

COMMON CORE STANDARD—5.MD.A.1
Convert like measurement units within a given measurement system.

Solve.

1. A cable company has 5 miles of cable to install. How many 100-yard lengths of cable can be cut?

   Think: 1,760 yards = 1 mile.
   So the cable company has 5 × 1,760, or 8,800 yards of cable.

   Divide. 8,800 ÷ 100 = 88

   _____**88 lengths**_____

2. Afton made a chicken dish for dinner. She added a 10-ounce package of vegetables and a 14-ounce package of rice to 40 ounces of chicken. What was the total weight of the chicken dish in pounds?

3. A jar contains 26 fluid ounces of spaghetti sauce. How many cups of spaghetti sauce do 4 jars contain?

4. Coach Kent brings 3 quarts of sports drink to soccer practice. He gives the same amount of the drink to each of his 16 players. How many ounces of the drink does each player get?

5. Leslie needs 324 inches of fringe to put around the edge of a tablecloth. The fringe comes in lengths of 10 yards. If Leslie buys 1 package of fringe, how many feet of fringe will she have left over?

6. An office supply company is shipping a case of wooden pencils to a store. There are 64 boxes of pencils in the case. If each box of pencils weighs 2.5 ounces, what is the weight, in pounds, of the case of wooden pencils?

Problem Solving · Real World

7. A pitcher contains 40 fluid ounces of iced tea. Shelby pours 3 cups of iced tea. How many pints of iced tea are left in the pitcher?

8. Olivia ties 2.5 feet of ribbon onto one balloon. How many yards of ribbon does Olivia need for 18 balloons?

9. **WRITE** ▸ *Math* An object moves on a conveyor belt at a speed of 60 inches per second. Explain how you could convert the speed to feet per minute.

Lesson Check (5.MD.A.1)

1. Leah is buying curtains for her bedroom window. She wants the curtains to hang from the top of the window to the floor. The window is 4 feet high. The bottom of the window is $2\frac{1}{2}$ feet above the floor. How many inches long should Leah's curtains be?

_____

2. Brady buys 3 gallons of fertilizer for his lawn. After he finishes spraying the lawn, he has 1 quart of fertilizer left over. How many quarts of fertilizer did Brady spray on the lawn?

_____

Spiral Review (5.OA.B.3, 5.MD.A.1, 5.NF.B.7b)

3. A jump rope is 9 feet long. How long is the jump rope in yards?

_____

4. Fill in the blanks to make the following statement true.

8 cups = _____ quarts = _____ pints.

5. What is the unknown number in Sequence 2 in the chart?

Sequence Number	1	2	3	5	7
Sequence 1	3	6	9	15	21
Sequence 2	6	12	18	30	?

6. A farmer divides 20 acres of land into $\frac{1}{4}$-acre sections. Into how many sections does the farmer divide her land?

608

FOR MORE PRACTICE GO TO THE
Personal Math Trainer

Name _____

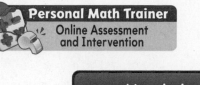

Vocabulary

Choose the best term from the box.

Vocabulary
capacity
length
weight

1. The _____ of an object is how heavy the object is. (p. 597)

2. The _____ of a container is the amount the container can hold. (p. 591)

Concepts and Skills

Convert. (5.MD.A.1)

3. 5 mi = _____ yd

4. 48 qt = _____ gal

5. 9 T = _____ lb

6. 336 oz = _____ lb

7. 14 ft = _____ yd _____ ft

8. 11 pt = _____ fl oz

Compare. Write <, >, or =. (5.MD.A.1)

9. 96 fl oz ◯ 13 c

10. 25 lb ◯ 384 oz

11. 8 yd ◯ 288 in.

Solve. (5.MD.A.1)

12. A standard coffee mug has a capacity of 16 fluid ounces. If Annie needs to fill 26 mugs with coffee, how many total quarts of coffee does she need?

_____

13. The length of a classroom is 34 feet. What is this measurement in yards and feet? (5.MD.A.1)

_____

14. Charlie's puppy, Max, weighs 8 pounds. How many ounces does Max weigh? (5.MD.A.1)

_____

15. Milton purchases a 5-gallon aquarium for his bedroom. To fill the aquarium with water, he uses a container with a capacity of 1 quart. How many times will Milton fill and empty the container before the aquarium is full? (5.MD.A.1)

_____

16. GO DEEPER Sarah uses a recipe to make 2 gallons of her favorite mixed-berry juice. Two of the containers she plans to use to store the juice have a capacity of 1 quart. The rest of the containers have a capacity of 1 pint. How many pint-sized containers will Sarah need? (5.MD.A.1)

_____

17. The average length of a female white-beaked dolphin is about 111 inches. What is this length in feet and inches? (5.MD.A.1)

_____

Name _____

Share and Show MATH BOARD

Complete the equation to show the conversion.

1. 8.47 L ◯ 10 = _____ dL

   8.47 L ◯ 100 = _____ cL

   8.47 L ◯ 1,000 = _____ mL

   Think: Are the units being converted to a larger unit or a smaller unit?

2. 9,824 dg ◯ 10 = _____ g

   9,824 dg ◯ 100 = _____ dag

   9,824 dg ◯ 1,000 = _____ hg

Convert.

3. 4,250 cm = _____ m

4. 6,000 mL = _____ L

5. 4 dg = _____ cg

Math Talk MATHEMATICAL PRACTICES ②

Reason Quantitatively How can you compare the lengths 4.25 dm and 4.25 cm without converting?

On Your Own

Convert.

6. 7 g = _____ mg

7. 5 km = _____ m

8. 1,521 mL = _____ dL

Compare. Write >, <, or =.

9. 32 hg ◯ 3.2 kg

10. 6 km ◯ 660 m

11. 525 mL ◯ 525 cL

12. MATHEMATICAL PRACTICE ② **Use Reasoning** Are there less than 1 million, exactly 1 million, or greater than 1 million milligrams in 1 kilogram? Explain how you know.

_____

_____

_____

13. GO DEEPER Parker ran 100 meters, 1 kilometer, and 5,000 centimeters. How many meters did he run all together ?

_____

Problem Solving • Applications (Real World)

For 14–15, use the table.

Food for Camping	
Item	**Amount**
1 can of juice	150 mL
1 bottle of juice	2 L
1 batch of pancakes	200 g
raisin & pretzel snack mix	1,425 g

14. **GO DEEPER** Kelly made one batch of raisin and pretzel snack mix. How many grams does she need to add to the snack mix to make 2 kilograms?

_____

15. **THINK SMARTER** Kelly plans to take juice on her camping trip. Which will hold more juice, 8 cans or 2 bottles? How much more?

_____

16. Erin's water bottle holds 600 milliliters of water. Dylan's water bottle holds 1 liter of water. Whose water bottle holds more water? How much more water?

_____

WRITE ▸ Math
Show Your Work

17. Liz and Alana each participated in the high jump at the track meet. Liz's high jump was 1 meter. Alana's high jump was 132 centimeters. Who jumped higher? How much higher?

_____

18. **THINK SMARTER** Monica has 426 millimeters of fabric. How many centimeters of fabric does Monica have? Use the numbers and symbols on the tiles to write an equation to show the conversion.

426	4.26	42.6	0.426

×	÷	=

10	100	1,000

Metric Measures

COMMON CORE STANDARD—5.MD.A.1
Convert like measurement units within a given measurement system.

Convert.

1. 16 m = __16,000__ mm
number of   millimeters
meters   in 1 meter

16   × 1,000   = 16,000
16 m = 16,000 mm

2. 6,500 cL = __65__ L
number of
millimeters

3. 15 cm = __0.15__ mm

4. 3,200 g = __3.2__ kg

5. 12 L = _____ mL

6. 200 cm = __0.2__ m

7. 70,000 g = _____ kg

8. 100 dL = __0.1__ L

9. 60 m = _____ mm

Compare. Write <, >, or =.

10. 900 cm (<) 9,000 mm

11. 600 km ( ) 5 m

12. 5,000 cm (>) 5 m

13. 18,000 g ( ) 10 kg

14. 8,456 mL (>) 9 L

15. 2 m ( ) 275 cm

Problem Solving · Real World

16. Bria ordered 145 centimeters of fabric. Jayleen ordered 1.5 meters of fabric. Who ordered more fabric?

_____

17. Ed fills his sports bottle with 1.2 liters of water. After his bike ride, he drinks 200 milliliters of the water. How much water is left in Ed's sports bottle?

_____

18. **WRITE** *Math* Explain the relationship between multiplying and dividing by 10, 100, and 1,000 and moving the decimal point to the right or to the left.

_____

Lesson Check (5.MD.A.1)

1. Quan bought 8.6 meters of fabric. How many centimeters of fabric did he buy?

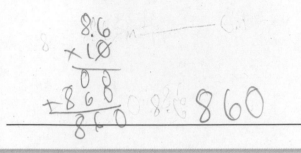

860

2. Jason takes 2 centiliters of medicine. How many milliliters is this?

20

Spiral Review (5.NF.A.1, 5.MD.A.1, 5.G.A.1)

3. Yolanda needs 5 pounds of ground beef to make lasagna for a family reunion. One package of ground beef weighs $2\frac{1}{2}$ pounds. Another package weighs $2\frac{3}{5}$ pounds. How much ground beef will Yolanda have left over after making the lasagna?

4. A soup recipe calls for $2\frac{3}{4}$ quarts of vegetable broth. An open can of broth contains $\frac{1}{2}$ quart of broth. How much more broth do you need to make the soup?

5. Which point on the graph is located at (4, 2)?

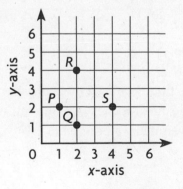

6. A bakery supplier receives an order for 2 tons of flour from a bakery chain. The flour is shipped in crates. Each crate holds eight 10-pound bags of flour. How many crates does the supplier need to ship to fulfill the order?

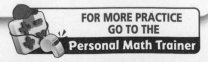

FOR MORE PRACTICE
GO TO THE
Personal Math Trainer

Problem Solving • Customary and Metric Conversions

Essential Question How can you use the strategy *make a table* to help you solve problems about customary and metric conversions?

Common Core **Measurement and Data—5.MD.A.1**
MATHEMATICAL PRACTICES
MP2, MP4, MP7

Unlock the Problem (Real World)

Aaron is making fruit punch for a family reunion. He needs to make 120 cups of punch. If he wants to store the fruit punch in gallon containers, how many gallon containers will Aaron need?

Use the graphic organizer below to help you solve the problem.

Conversion Table

	gal	qt	pt	c
1 gal	1	4	8	16
1 qt	$\frac{1}{4}$	1	2	4
1 pt	$\frac{1}{8}$	$\frac{1}{2}$	1	2
1 c	$\frac{1}{16}$	$\frac{1}{4}$	$\frac{1}{2}$	1

Read the Problem

What do I need to find?

I need to find _____

_____

_____

_____.

What information do I need to use?

I need to use _____

_____

_____.

How will I use the information?

I will make a table to show the relationship between the

number of _____ and

the number of _____.

Solve the Problem

There are _____ cups in 1 gallon. So, each cup is _____ of a gallon. Complete the table below.

c	1	2	3	4	120
gal	$\frac{1}{16}$	$\frac{1}{8}$	$\frac{3}{16}$	$\frac{1}{4}$	

⟩ Multiply by _____.

So, Aaron needs _____ gallon containers to store the punch.

- **MATHEMATICAL PRACTICE ②** **Use Reasoning** Will all of the gallon containers Aaron uses be filled to capacity? Explain. _____

Try Another Problem

Sharon is working on a project for art class. She needs to cut strips of wood that are each 1 decimeter long to complete the project. If Sharon has 7 strips of wood that are each 1 meter long, how many 1-decimeter strips can she cut?

Conversion Table

	m	dm	cm	mm
1 m	1	10	100	1,000
1 dm	$\frac{1}{10}$	1	10	100
1 cm	$\frac{1}{100}$	$\frac{1}{10}$	1	10
1 mm	$\frac{1}{1,000}$	$\frac{1}{100}$	$\frac{1}{10}$	1

Read the Problem

What do I need to find?	What information do I need to use?	How will I use the information?

Solve the Problem

So, Sharon can cut _____ 1-decimeter lengths to complete her project.

- **MATHEMATICAL PRACTICE 7** **Look for a Pattern** What relationship did the table you made show? _____

Math Talk

MATHEMATICAL PRACTICES 4

Use Diagrams How could you use a diagram to solve this problem?

Name _____

1. Edgardo has a drink cooler that holds 10 gallons of water. He is filling the cooler with a 1-quart container. How many times will he have to fill the quart container to fill the cooler?

First, make a table to show the relationship between gallons and quarts. You can use a conversion table to find how many quarts are in a gallon.

gal	1	2	3	4	10
qt	4				

Then, look for a rule to help you complete your table.

number of gallons × _____ = number of quarts

Finally, use the table to solve the problem.

Edgardo will need to fill the quart container _____ times.

WRITE *Math* • **Show Your Work**

2. **THINK SMARTER** What if Edgardo fills the cooler with only 32 quarts of water. How can you use your table to find how many gallons that is?

_____

_____

_____

_____

3. How would the number of times Edgardo uses a container to fill the 10-gallon cooler change if he uses a 1-cup container? Explain.

_____

_____

_____

_____

On Your Own

4. **THINK SMARTER** Maria put trim around a banner that is the shape of a triangle. Each side is 22 inches long. Maria has $\frac{1}{2}$ foot of trim left. What was the length of the trim when she started? Write your answer in yards.

_____

5. Dan owns 9 DVDs. His brother Mark has 3 more DVDs than Dan has. Their sister, Marsha, has more DVDs than either of her brothers. Together, the three have 35 DVDs. How many DVDs does Marsha have?

_____

6. **GO DEEPER** Kevin is making a picture frame. He has a piece of trim that is 4 feet long. How many 14-inch-long pieces can Kevin cut from the trim? How much of a foot will he have left over?

_____

_____

7. **MATHEMATICAL PRACTICE ②** Reason Quantitatively Explain how you could find the number of cups in five gallons of water.

_____

_____

_____

_____

8. Carla uses $2\frac{3}{4}$ cups of whole wheat flour and $1\frac{3}{8}$ cups of rye flour in her bread recipe. How many cups does she use in all?

_____

9. **THINK SMARTER +** A large pot holds 12 gallons of soup. Jared has 1-pint containers of chicken broth. Complete the table to help you find the number of 1-pint containers of chicken broth Jared will need to fill the pot.

gallon	2	4	6	8	10	12
pint						

Jared will need _____ 1-pint containers to fill the pot.

Name _____

Problem Solving • Customary and Metric Conversions

COMMON CORE STANDARD—5.MD.A.1
Convert like measurement units within a given measurement system.

Solve each problem by making a table.

1. Thomas is making soup. His soup pot holds
   8 quarts of soup. How many 1-cup servings of
   soup will Thomas make?

Number of Quarts	1	2	3	4	8
Number of Cups	4	8	12	16	32

   _____ **32 1-cup servings** _____

2. Paulina works out with a 2.5-kilogram mass. What is
   the mass of the 2.5-kilogram mass in grams?

   _____

3. Alex lives 500 yards from the park. How many inches
   does Alex live from the park?

   _____

4. A flatbed truck is loaded with 7,000 pounds of bricks.
   How many tons of brick are on the truck?

   _____

5. **WRITE** ▸*Math* Explain how you could use
   the conversion table on page 618 to convert
   700 centimeters to meters.

   _____

   _____

Lesson Check (5.MD.A.1)

1. At the hairdresser, Jenny had 27 centimeters cut off her hair. How many decimeters of hair did Jenny have cut off?

2. Marcus needs 108 inches of wood to make a frame. How many feet of wood does Marcus need for the frame?

Spiral Review (5.NF.B.7c, 5.MD.A.1, 5.G.A.1)

3. Tara lives 35,000 meters from her grandparents. How many kilometers does Tara live from her grandparents?

4. Dane's puppy weighed 8 ounces when it was born. Now the puppy weighs 18 times as much as it did when it was born. How many pounds does Dane's puppy weigh now?

5. A carpenter is cutting dowels from a piece of wood that is 10 inches long. How many $\frac{1}{2}$-inch dowels can the carpenter cut?

6. What ordered pair describes the location of point *X*?

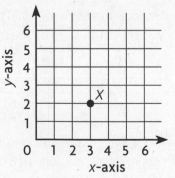

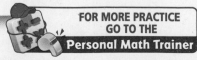

FOR MORE PRACTICE
GO TO THE
Personal Math Trainer

Name _____

Elapsed Time

Essential Question How can you solve elapsed time problems by converting units of time?

Common Core Measurement and Data—
5.MD.A.1
MATHEMATICAL PRACTICES
MP6, MP7

Unlock the Problem Real World

A computer company claims its laptop has a battery that lasts 4 hours. The laptop actually ran for 200 minutes before the battery ran out. Did the battery last 4 hours?

1 hour = _____ minutes

Think: The minute hand moves from one number to the next in 5 minutes.

🔒 **Convert 200 minutes to hours and minutes.**

STEP 1 Convert minutes into hours and minutes.	total min ↓	min in 1 hr ↓	hr ↓	min ↓
200 min − ___ hr ___ min	_____ ◯ _____ is _____ r _____			

STEP 2 Compare. Write <, >, or =.

_____ hr _____ min ◯ 4 hr

Since _____ hours _____ minutes is _____ 4 hours, the

battery _____ last as long as the computer company claims.

Try This! **Convert to mixed measures.**

Jill spent much of her summer away from home. She spent 10 days with her grandparents, 9 days with her cousins, and 22 days at camp. How many weeks and days was she away from home?

STEP 1 Find the total number of days away.

10 days + 9 days + 22 days = _____ days

STEP 2 Convert the days into weeks and days.

_____ ÷ 7 is _____ r _____

So, Jill was away from home _____ weeks and _____ days.

Units of Time
60 seconds (s) = 1 minute (min)
60 minutes = 1 hour (hr)
24 hours = 1 day (d)
7 days = 1 week (wk)
52 weeks = 1 year (yr)
12 months (mo) = 1 year
365 days = 1 year

🔒 One Way Use a number line to find elapsed time.

Monica spent $2\frac{1}{2}$ hours working on her computer. If she started working at 10:30 A.M., what time did Monica stop working?

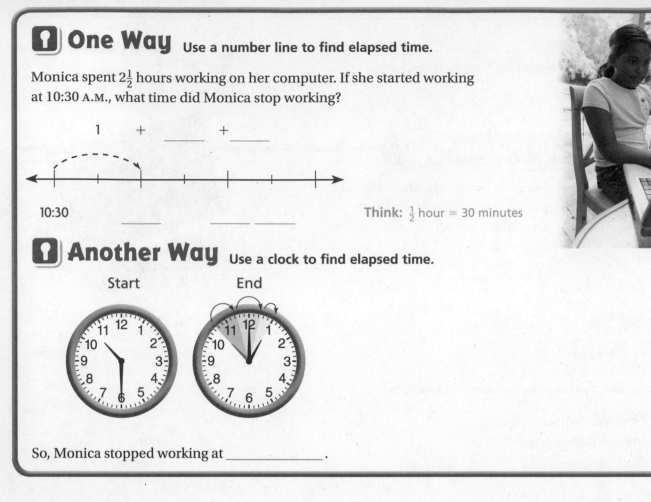

1 + _____ + _____

10:30 _____ _____

Think: $\frac{1}{2}$ hour = 30 minutes

🔒 Another Way Use a clock to find elapsed time.

Start   End

So, Monica stopped working at _____ .

Try This! Find a start time.

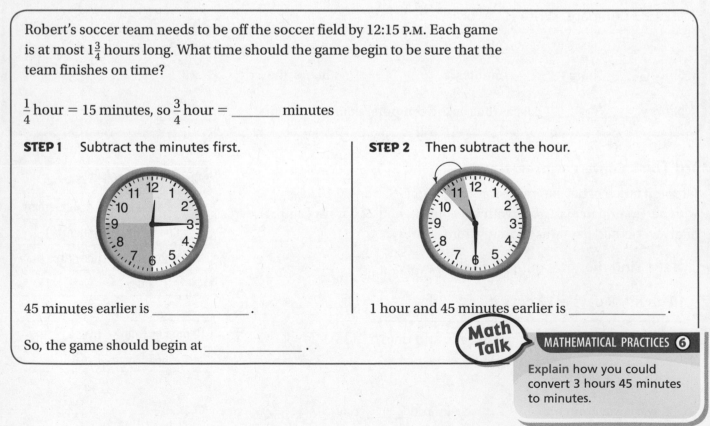

Robert's soccer team needs to be off the soccer field by 12:15 P.M. Each game is at most $1\frac{3}{4}$ hours long. What time should the game begin to be sure that the team finishes on time?

$\frac{1}{4}$ hour = 15 minutes, so $\frac{3}{4}$ hour = _____ minutes

STEP 1 Subtract the minutes first.

STEP 2 Then subtract the hour.

45 minutes earlier is _____ .

1 hour and 45 minutes earlier is _____ .

So, the game should begin at _____ .

Math Talk

MATHEMATICAL PRACTICES ⑥

Explain how you could convert 3 hours 45 minutes to minutes.

Name _____

Convert.

1. 540 min = _____ hr

2. 8 d = _____ hr

✓ **3.** 110 hr = _____ d _____ hr

Find the end time.

✓ **4.** Start time: 9:17 A.M.   Elapsed time: 5 hr 18 min

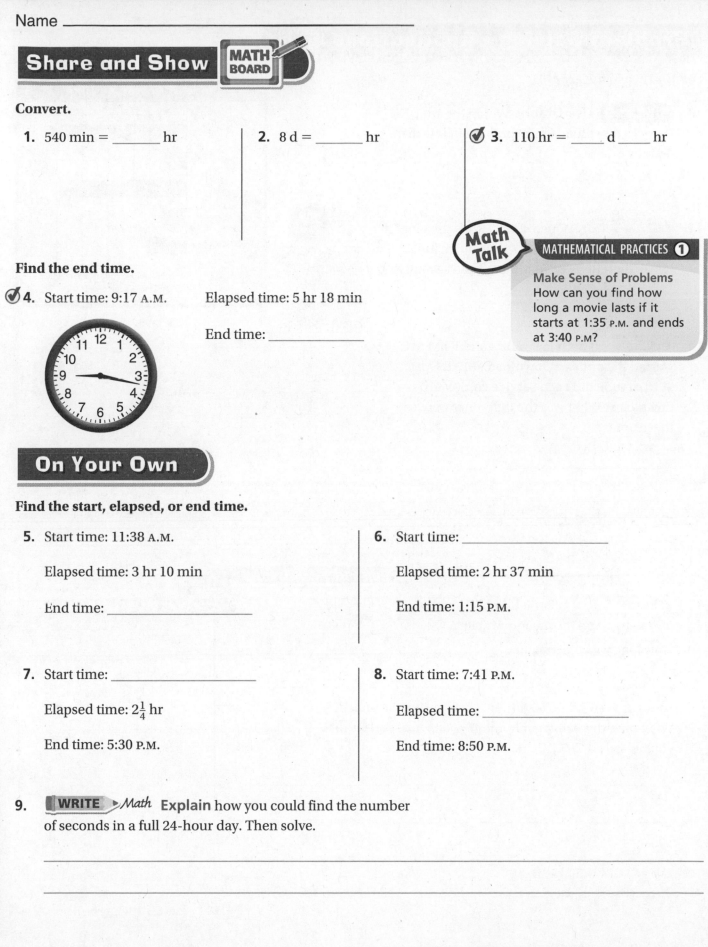

End time: _____

Math Talk

MATHEMATICAL PRACTICES ❶

Make Sense of Problems How can you find how long a movie lasts if it starts at 1:35 P.M. and ends at 3:40 P.M?

On Your Own

Find the start, elapsed, or end time.

5. Start time: 11:38 A.M.

Elapsed time: 3 hr 10 min

End time: _____

6. Start time: _____

Elapsed time: 2 hr 37 min

End time: 1:15 P.M.

7. Start time: _____

Elapsed time: $2\frac{1}{4}$ hr

End time: 5:30 P.M.

8. Start time: 7:41 P.M.

Elapsed time: _____

End time: 8:50 P.M.

9. **WRITE** ▸*Math* **Explain** how you could find the number of seconds in a full 24-hour day. Then solve.

_____

_____

Problem Solving • Applications Real World

For 10–12, use the graph.

Podcast Download Time

10. **MATHEMATICAL PRACTICE ④ Use Graphs** Which Internet services downloaded the podcast in less than 4 minutes?

_____

11. **THINK SMARTER** Which service took the longest to download the podcast? How much longer did it take than Red Fox in minutes and seconds?

_____

12. **GO DEEPER** If both Jackrabbit and Red Fox started the podcast download at 10:05 A.M., at what time did each service complete its download? What was the difference between these times?

_____

_____

Personal Math Trainer

13. **THINK SMARTER ✛** Samit and his friends went to a movie at 7:30 P.M. The movie ended at 9:55 P.M. How long was the movie?

_____

Samit arrived home 35 minutes after the movie ended. What time did Samit get home? Explain how you found your answer.

_____

_____

_____

Elapsed Time

COMMON CORE STANDARD—5.MD.A.1
Convert like measurement units within a given measurement system.

Convert.

1. 5 days = ___120___ hr

2. 8 hr = _____ min

3. 30 min = _____ s

Think: 1 day = 24 hours
$5 \times 24 = 120$

4. 15 hr = _____ min

5. 5 yr = _____ d

6. 7 d = _____ hr

7. 24 hr = _____ min

8. 600 s = _____ min

9. 60,000 min = _____ hr

Find the start, elapsed, or end time.

10. Start time: 11:00 A.M.

    Elapsed time: 4 hours 5 minutes

    End time: _____

11. Start time: 6:30 P.M.

    Elapsed time: 2 hours 18 minutes

    End time: _____

12. Start time: _____

    Elapsed time: $9\frac{3}{4}$ hours

    End time: 6:00 P.M.

13. Start time: 2:00 P.M.

    Elapsed time: _____

    End time: 8:30 P.M.

Problem Solving Real World

14. Kiera's dance class starts at 4:30 P.M. and ends at 6:15 P.M. How long is her dance class?

15. Julio watched a movie that started at 11:30 A.M. and ended at 2:12 P.M. How long was the movie?

_____

_____

16. **WRITE** *Math* Write a real-world word problem that can be solved using elapsed time. Include the solution.

_____

_____

Lesson Check (5.MD.A.1)

1. Michelle went on a hike. She started on the trail at 6:45 A.M. and returned at 3:28 P.M. How long did she hike?

2. Grant started a marathon at 8:00 A.M. He took 4 hours 49 minutes to complete the marathon. When did he cross the finish line?

Spiral Review (5.NBT.A.3b, 5.NF.A.1, 5.NF.B.6, 5.MD.A.1)

3. Molly is filling a pitcher that holds 2 gallons of water. She is filling the pitcher with a 1-cup measuring cup. How many times will she have to fill the 1-cup measuring cup to fill the pitcher?

4. Choose a symbol to make the following statement true. Write >, <, or =.

1.625  1.7

5. Adrian's recipe for raisin muffins calls for $1\frac{3}{4}$ cups raisins for one batch of muffins. Adrian wants to make $2\frac{1}{2}$ batches of the muffins for a bake sale. How many cups of raisins will Adrian use?

6. Kevin is riding his bike on a $10\frac{1}{8}$-mile bike path. He has covered the first $5\frac{3}{4}$ miles already. How many miles does he have left to ride?

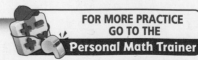
FOR MORE PRACTICE
GO TO THE
Personal Math Trainer

Name _____

✓ Chapter 10 Review/Test

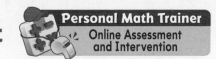

1. The library is 5 miles from the post office. How many yards is the library from the post office?

_____ yards

2. Billy made 3 gallons of juice for a picnic. He said that he made $\frac{3}{4}$ quart of juice. Explain Billy's mistake.

[ ]

3. The Drama Club is showing a video of their recent play. The first showing begins at 2:30 P.M. The second showing is scheduled at 5:25 P.M. with a $\frac{1}{2}$-hour break between the showings.

Part A

How long is the video in hours and minutes?

_____ hours and _____ minutes

Part B

Explain how you can use a number line to find the answer.

[ ]

Part C

The second showing started 20 minutes late. Will the second showing be over by 7:45 P.M.? Explain why your answer is reasonable.

[ ]

 Assessment Options
Chapter Test

4. Fred bought 4 liters of liquid laundry detergent, 3,250 milliliters of fabric softener, and 2.5 liters of bleach. For 4a–4e, select True or False for each statement.

4a. Fred bought 75 milliliters more fabric softener than bleach. ○ True ○ False

4b. Fred bought 1.75 liters more laundry detergent than bleach. ○ True ○ False

4c. Fred bought 750 milliliters more fabric softener than bleach. ○ True ○ False

4d. Fred bought 150 milliliters more laundry detergent than bleach. ○ True ○ False

4e. Fred bought 0.75 liters more laundry detergent than fabric softener. ○ True ○ False

5. A male hippopotamus can weigh up to 10,000 pounds. How many tons is 10,000 pounds?

_____ tons

Personal Math Trainer

6. **THINK SMARTER +** Amar and his friends went to a movie at 4:45 P.M. The movie ended at 6:20 P.M.

Part A

How long was the movie?

_____ hours and _____ minutes

Part B

Amar got home 45 minutes after the movie ended. What time did Amar get home? Explain how you found your answer.

7. Select the objects that hold the same amount of liquid as a 96-fluid-ounce jug. Mark all that apply.

(A) three 1-quart bottles

(B) two 1-quart bottles

(C) two 1-quart bottles and two 1-pint bottles

(D) one 1-quart bottle and eight 8-ounce fluid glasses

(E) two 8-ounce fluid glasses and two 1-pint bottles

8. Lorena's backpack has a mass of 3,000 grams. What is the mass of Lorena's backpack in kilograms?

_____ kilograms

9. GO DEEPER Richard walks every day for exercise at a rate of 1 kilometer every 12 minutes.

Part A

At this rate, how many meters can Richard walk in 1 hour? Explain how you found your answer.

Part B

Suppose Richard walks 1 kilometer every 10 minutes. How many meters further can he walk in 1 hour at this new rate? Explain how you found your answer.

10. Beth filled 32 jars with paint. If each jar holds 1 pint of paint, how many gallons of paint did Beth use?

_____ gallons

11. Griffins's driveway is 36 feet long. Choose the word and number to complete the sentence correctly.

To convert 36 feet to yards,

add
subtract
multiply
divide

36 by

3
12
1,760
5,280

.

12. Carlos bought 5 pounds of carrots. How many ounces of carrots did he buy?

_____ ounces

13. Chandler has 824 millimeters of fabric. How many centimeters of fabric does Chandler have? Use the numbers and symbols on the tiles to write an equation to show the conversion.

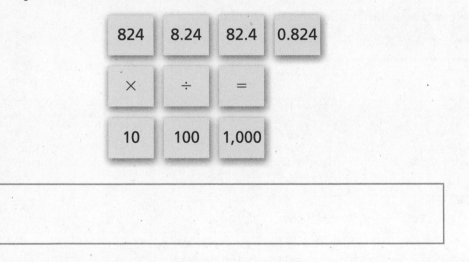

| 824 | 8.24 | 82.4 | 0.824 |

| × | ÷ | = |

| 10 | 100 | 1,000 |

Chandler has _____ centimeters of fabric.

14. Glenn needs to cut pieces of ribbon that are each 1 meter long to make ribbon key chains. If he has 3 pieces of ribbon that are each 1 dekameter long, how many 1-meter pieces of ribbon can he cut?

_____ pieces

15. A large pot holds 8 quarts of spaghetti sauce. Lisa has 1-pint containers of spaghetti sauce. Complete the table to help you find the number of 1-pint containers of spaghetti sauce Lisa will need to fill the pot.

quart	2	4	6	8
pint				

Lisa will need [   ] 1-pint containers to fill the pot.

16. Emily bought 48 yards of fabric to make curtains. How many inches of fabric did Emily buy?

_____ inches

17. Kelly is having a party. She wants to make punch. The recipe for punch uses 3 pints of pineapple juice, 5 cups of orange juice, $\frac{1}{4}$ gallon of lemonade, and 1 quart of apricot nectar.

Part A

Kelly says her recipe will make 20 cups of punch. Is Kelly correct? Explain your answer.

[   ]

Part B

Kelly decides to pour her punch into 1-quart containers to fit into her refrigerator until the party starts. She has four 1-quart containers. Will all of her punch fit into the containers? Explain.

[   ]

18. Sam is practicing long track speed skating at an ice skating rink. The distance around the rink is 250 yards. He has skated around the rink 6 times so far. How many more yards does he need to skate around the rink to complete 3 miles?

_____ yards

19. Maria spent 15 days traveling in South America. How many hours did she spend traveling in South America?

_____ hours

20. A concrete truck loaded with concrete weighs about 30 tons. About how many pounds does the loaded truck weigh?

_____ pounds

21. A plumber has a piece of pipe that is 2-meter long. He needs to cut it into sections that are 10 centimeters long. How many sections will he be able to cut? Show your work. Explain how you found your answer.

22. For 22a–22d, select True or False for each statement.

22a.	2,000 lb > 1 T	○ True	○ False
22b.	56 oz < 4 lb	○ True	○ False
22c.	48 oz = 3 lb	○ True	○ False
22d.	40 oz < 2 lb 4 oz	○ True	○ False

Geometry and Volume

Show What You Know

Personal Math Trainer
Online Assessment
and Intervention

Check your understanding of important skills.

Name _____

▶ **Perimeter** **Count the units to find the perimeter.** (3.MD.D.8)

1.

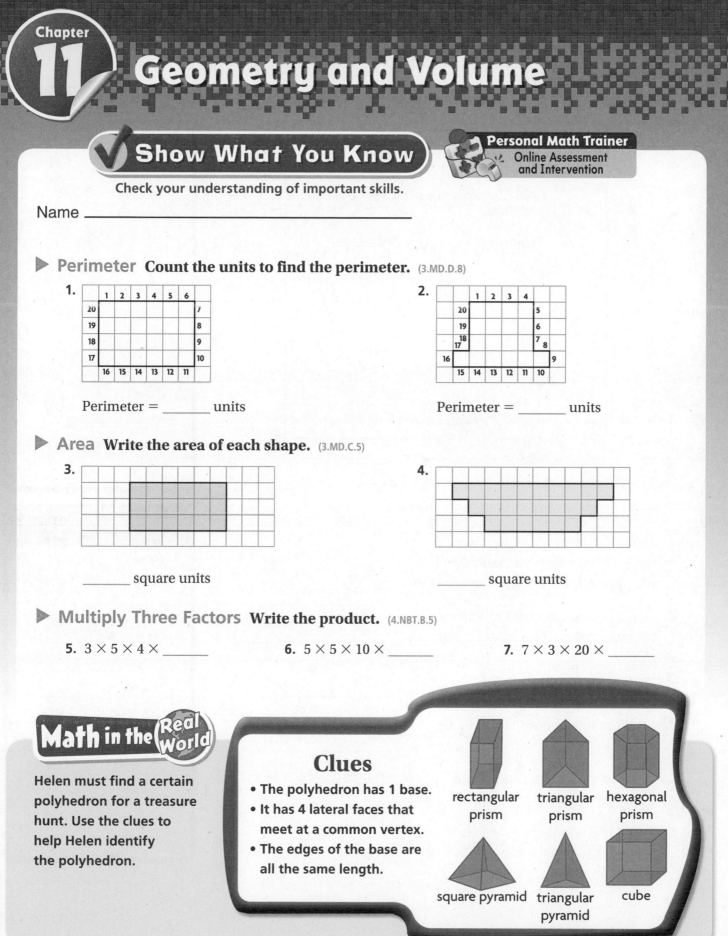

Perimeter = _____ units

2.

Perimeter = _____ units

▶ **Area** **Write the area of each shape.** (3.MD.C.5)

3.

_____ square units

4.

_____ square units

▶ **Multiply Three Factors** **Write the product.** (4.NBT.B.5)

5. $3 \times 5 \times 4 \times$ _____

6. $5 \times 5 \times 10 \times$ _____

7. $7 \times 3 \times 20 \times$ _____

Math in the Real World

Helen must find a certain polyhedron for a treasure hunt. Use the clues to help Helen identify the polyhedron.

Clues
- The polyhedron has 1 base.
- It has 4 lateral faces that meet at a common vertex.
- The edges of the base are all the same length.

rectangular prism   triangular prism   hexagonal prism

square pyramid   triangular pyramid   cube

Vocabulary Builder

▶ Visualize It

Sort the checked words into the circle map.

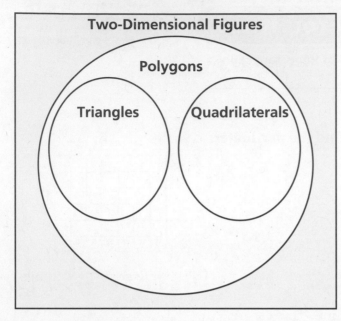

Two-Dimensional Figures

Polygons

Triangles   Quadrilaterals

▶ Understand Vocabulary

Write the preview word that answers the riddle.

1. I am a solid figure with two congruent polygons that are bases, connected with lateral faces that are rectangles. _____

2. I am a polygon in which all sides are congruent and all angles are congruent. _____

3. I am a cube that has a length, width, and height of 1 unit. _____

4. I am a solid figure with faces that are polygons. _____

5. I am the measure of the amount of space a solid figure occupies. _____

6. I am a polygon that connects with the bases of a polyhedron. _____

GO DIGITAL
• Interactive Student Edition
• Multimedia eGlossary

base

base

1

congruent

congruente

8

equilateral triangle

triángulo equilátero

21

heptagon

heptágono

29

isosceles triangle

triángulo isósceles

33

lateral face

cara lateral

34

nonagon

eneágono

41

polygon

polígono

51

Having the same size and the same shape

Examples:

(arithmetic) A number used as a repeated factor

Example: $8^3 = 8 \times 8 \times 8$

base

(geometry) In two dimensions, one side of a triangle or parallelogram that is used to help find the area. In three dimensions, a plane figure, usually a polygon or circle, by which a three-dimensional figure is measured or named

Examples:

height base

base base

base

A polygon with seven sides and seven angles

Example:

A triangle with three congruent sides

Example:

Any surface of a polyhedron other than a base

Example:

← face

A triangle with two congruent sides

Example:

5 cm   5 cm

A closed plane figure formed by three or more line segments

Examples:

Polygons   Not Polygons

A polygon with nine sides and nine angles

Examples:

polyhedron

poliedro

52

prism

prisma

53

pyramid

pirámide

55

quadrilateral

cuadrilátero

56

regular polygon

polígono regular

58

scalene triangle

triángulo escaleno

62

unit cube

cubo unitaria

69

volume

volumen

70

A solid figure that has two congruent, polygon-shaped bases, and other faces that are all rectangles

Examples:

rectangular prism   triangular prism

A solid figure with faces that are polygons

Examples:

A polygon with four sides and four angles

Examples:

A solid figure with a polygon base and all other faces are triangles that meet at a common vertex

Example:

A triangle with no congruent sides

Example:

A polygon in which all sides are congruent and all angles are congruent

Example: a regular pentagon

4 cm 108° 4 cm
108°   108°
4 cm   4 cm
108° 108°
4 cm

The measure of the space that a solid figure occupies

Example:

3 in.   3 in.
4 in.   4 in.
4 in.   4 in.

48 cu in.

A cube that has a length, width, and height of 1 unit

Example:

1 Unit
1 Unit
1 Unit

Picture It

For 3 to 4 players

Materials

- timer
- sketch pad

How to Play

1. Take turns to play.
2. To take a turn, choose a word from the Word Box. Do not say the word.
3. Set the timer for 1 minute.
4. Draw pictures and numbers to give clues about the word.
5. The first player to guess the word before time runs out gets 1 point. If hc or she can use the word in a sentence, they get 1 more point. Then that player gets a turn choosing a word.
6. The first player to score 10 points wins.

Word Box

base (of a power)

congruent figures

equilateral triangle

heptagon

isosceles triangle

lateral face

nonagon

polygon

polyhedron

prism

pyramid

quadrilateral

regular polygon

scalene triangle

unit cube

volume

The Write Way

Reflect

Choose one idea. Write about it.

- Tell how the terms *regular polygon* and *congruent* are related. Draw and label a regular polygon to illustrate your answer.

- Use at least **two** of the following words to describe objects in a familiar place.

  heptagon   **polygon**   **pyramid**   **quadrilateral**

- Compare and contrast an equilateral triangle, an isosceles triangle, and a scalene triangle. How are they alike? How are they different?

- Suppose that you write a math advice column and a reader needs help identifying a type of prism. Write a letter to the reader to explain how to solve this problem.

Polygons

Essential Question How can you identify and classify polygons?

Common Core   Measurement and Data—
5.G.B.3, 5.G.B.4
MATHEMATICAL PRACTICES
MP1, MP2, MP5, MP6

？Unlock the Problem Real World

The Castel del Monte in Apulia, Italy, was built more than 750 years ago. The fortress has one central building with eight surrounding towers. Which polygon do you see repeated in the structure? How many sides, angles, and vertices does this polygon have?

A **polygon** is a closed plane figure formed by three or more line segments that meet at points called vertices. It is named by the number of sides and angles it has. To identify the repeated polygon in the fortress, complete the tables below.

Polygon	Triangle	Quadrilateral	Pentagon	Hexagon
Sides	3	4	5	
Angles				
Vertices				

Polygon	Heptagon	Octagon	Nonagon	Decagon
Sides	7	8		
Angles				
Vertices				

Math Idea
Sometimes the angles inside a polygon are greater than 180°.

275°

So, the _____ is the repeated polygon in the

Castel del Monte because it has _____ sides, _____ angles,

and _____ vertices.

Math Talk   MATHEMATICAL PRACTICES ⑤

Use Patterns What pattern do you see among the number of sides, angles, and vertices a polygon has?

Regular Polygons When line segments have the same length or when angles have the same measure, they are **congruent**. Two polygons are congruent when they have the same size and the same shape. In a **regular polygon**, all sides are congruent and all angles are congruent.

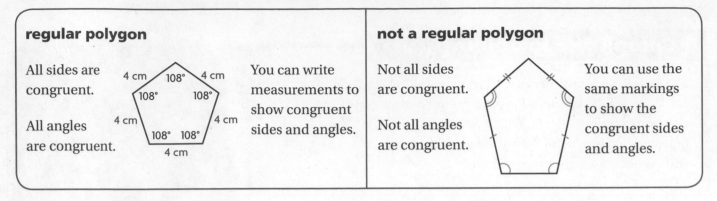

regular polygon	not a regular polygon
All sides are congruent. All angles are congruent.	Not all sides are congruent. Not all angles are congruent.

All sides are congruent.

All angles are congruent.

You can write measurements to show congruent sides and angles.

Not all sides are congruent.

Not all angles are congruent.

You can use the same markings to show the congruent sides and angles.

Try This! Label the Venn diagram to classify the polygons in each group. Then draw a polygon that belongs only to each group.

Congruent _____   Congruent _____

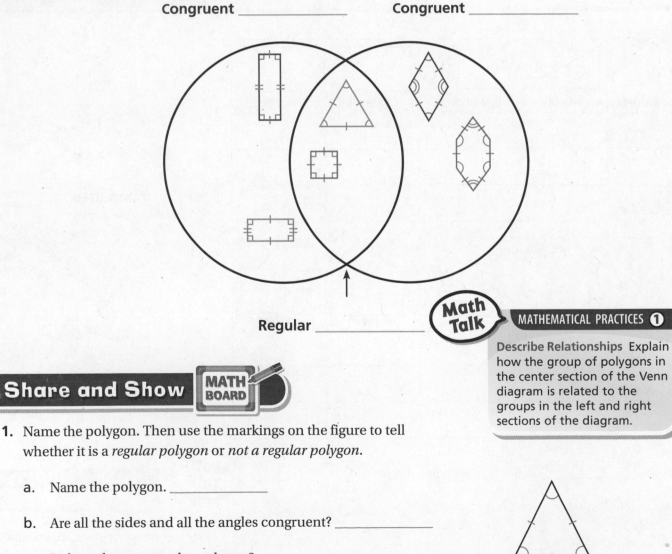

Regular _____

Math Talk

MATHEMATICAL PRACTICES ①

Describe Relationships Explain how the group of polygons in the center section of the Venn diagram is related to the groups in the left and right sections of the diagram.

Share and Show MATH BOARD

1. Name the polygon. Then use the markings on the figure to tell whether it is a *regular polygon* or *not a regular polygon*.

   a. Name the polygon. _____

   b. Are all the sides and all the angles congruent? _____

   c. Is the polygon a regular polygon? _____

Name _____

**Name each polygon. Then tell whether it is a *regular polygon*
or *not a regular polygon*.**

2.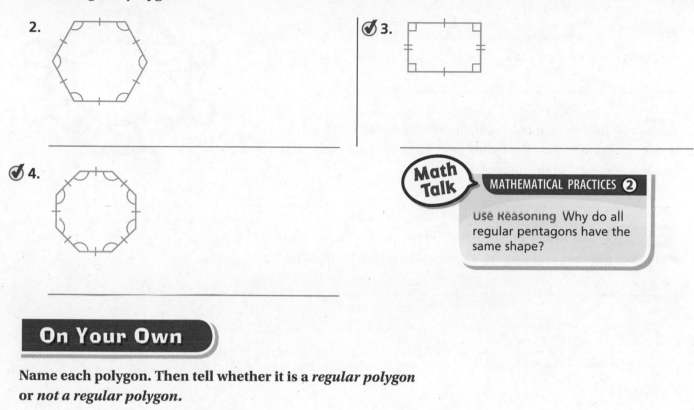

✓3.

✓4.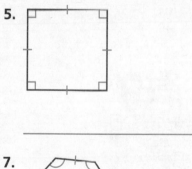

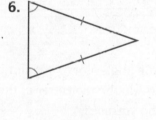

Math Talk

MATHEMATICAL PRACTICES ②

Use Reasoning Why do all
regular pentagons have the
same shape?

On Your Own

**Name each polygon. Then tell whether it is a *regular polygon*
or *not a regular polygon*.**

5.

6.

7.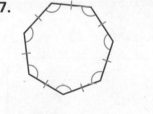

8.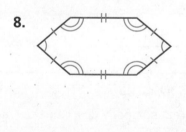

9. **GO DEEPER** Compare the polygons shown in Exercises 2 and 8.
Describe how they are alike and how they are different.

_____

_____

_____

Problem Solving • Applications (Real World)

For 10–11, use the Castel del Monte floor plan at the right.

10. **GO DEEPER** Which polygons in the floor plan have four equal sides and four congruent angles? How many of these polygons are there?

_____

11. **GO DEEPER** Is there a quadrilateral in the floor plan that is not a regular polygon? Name the quadrilateral and tell how many of the quadrilaterals are in the floor plan.

_____

12. **MATHEMATICAL PRACTICE 6** **Use Math Vocabulary** Sketch eight points that are vertices of a closed plane figure. Connect the points to draw the figure.

What kind of polygon did you draw? _____

13. **THINK SMARTER** Look at the angles for all regular polygons. As the number of sides increases, do the measures of the angles increase or decrease? What pattern do you see?

_____

_____

14. **THINK SMARTER** Kayla drew the shape shown. For 14a–14b, choose the values and term that correctly describe the shape Kayla drew.

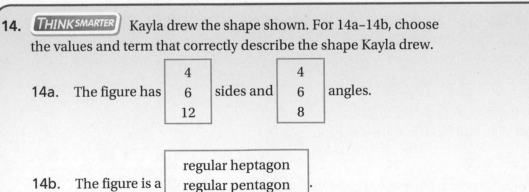

14a. The figure has [4 / 6 / 12] sides and [4 / 6 / 8] angles.

14b. The figure is a [regular heptagon / regular pentagon / regular hexagon] .

Polygons

COMMON CORE STANDARD—5.G.B.3
Classify two-dimensional figures into categories based on their properties.

Name each polygon. Then tell whether it is a *regular polygon* or *not a regular polygon*.

1.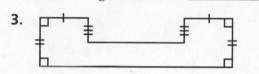

    4 sides, 4 vertices, 4 angles means it is a

    quadrilateral
    _____. The sides are

    not all congruent, so it is _____ not regular _____.

2.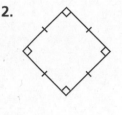

    _____

3.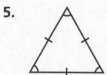

    _____

4.

    _____

5.

    _____

6.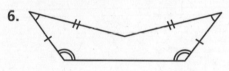

    _____

Problem Solving · Real World

7. Sketch nine points. Then, connect the points to form a closed plane figure. What kind of polygon did you draw?

    _____

8. Sketch seven points. Then, connect the points to form a closed plane figure. What kind of polygon did you draw?

    _____

9. **WRITE** ▸ *Math* Use grid paper to draw one regular hexagon and one hexagon that is not regular. Explain the difference.

    _____

Lesson Check (5.G.B.3)

1. Name the polygon. Write whether it is regular or not regular.

_____

2. Name the polygon. Write whether it is regular or not regular.

_____

Spiral Review (5.OA.A.2, 5.NBT.B.7, 5.MD.A.1)

3. Ann needs 42 feet of fabric to make a small quilt. How many yards of fabric should she buy?

_____

4. Todd begins piano practice at 4:15 P.M. and ends at 5:50 P.M. How long does he practice?

_____

5. Jenna has 30 barrettes. She is organizing her barrettes into 6 boxes. She puts the same number of barrettes in each box. Write an expression that you can use to find the number of barrettes in each box.

_____

6. Melody had $45. She spent $32.75 on a blouse. Then her mother gave her $15.50. How much money does Melody have now?

_____

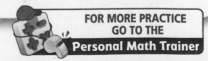

FOR MORE PRACTICE
GO TO THE
Personal Math Trainer

Triangles

Essential Question How can you classify triangles?

Common Core Measurement and Data—
5.G.B.3, 5.G.B.4
MATHEMATICAL PRACTICES
MP2, MP6, MP7, MP8

🔑 Unlock the Problem (Real World)

If you look closely at Epcot Center's Spaceship Earth building in Orlando, Florida, you may see a pattern of triangles. The triangle outlined in the pattern at the right has 3 congruent sides and 3 acute angles. What type of triangle is outlined?

 Complete the sentence that describes each type of triangle.

Classify triangles by the lengths of their sides.	Classify triangles by the measures of their angles.
An **equilateral triangle** has _____ congruent sides. *3 in. 3 in. 3 in.*	A **right triangle** has one 90°, or _____ angle. *60° 30°*
An **isosceles triangle** has _____ congruent sides. *2 in. 3 in. 3 in.*	An **acute triangle** has 3 _____ angles. *75° 30° 75°*
A **scalene triangle** has _____ congruent sides. *5 in. 3 in. 4 in.*	An **obtuse triangle** has 1 _____ angle. *32° 18° 130°*

The type of triangle outlined in the pattern can be classified by the length of its sides as an _____ triangle.

The triangle can also be classified by the measures of its angles as an _____ triangle.

Math Talk

MATHEMATICAL PRACTICES ⑥

Is an equilateral triangle also a regular polygon? Explain.

Activity

Hands On

Classify triangle *ABC* by the lengths of its sides and by the measures of its angles.

Materials ■ centimeter ruler ■ protractor

STEP 1 Measure the sides of the triangle using a centimeter ruler. Label each side with its length. Classify the triangle by the lengths of its sides.

STEP 2 Measure the angles of the triangle using a protractor. Label each angle with its measure. Classify the triangle by the measures of its angles.

- What type of triangle has 3 sides of different lengths?

  _____

- What is an angle called that is greater than 90° and less than 180°?

  _____

Triangle *ABC* is a _____ _____ triangle.

Try This! Draw the type of triangle described by the lengths of its sides and by the measures of its angles.

Triangle by Angle Measure		Triangle by Length of Sides	
		Scalene	**Isosceles**
Acute		**Think:** I need to draw a triangle that is acute and scalene.	
Obtuse			

Math Talk

MATHEMATICAL PRACTICES ②

Reason Abstractly Can you draw a triangle that is right equilateral? Explain.

Name _____

Classify each triangle. Write *isosceles*, *scalene*, or *equilateral*.
Then write *acute*, *obtuse*, or *right*.

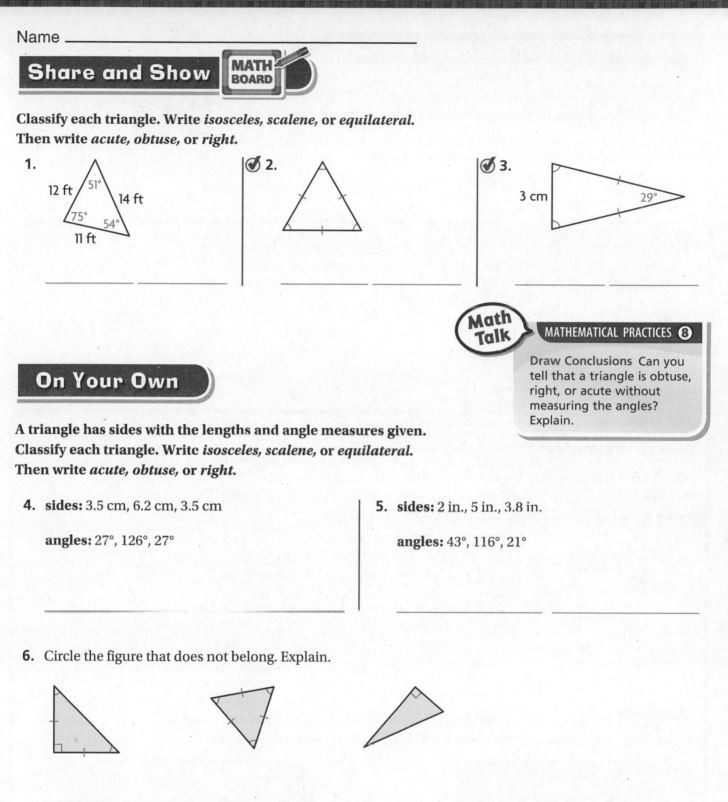

1.

12 ft   51°   14 ft

75°   54°

11 ft

_____

✓ 2.

_____

✓ 3.

3 cm   29°

_____

Math Talk   MATHEMATICAL PRACTICES ❽

Draw Conclusions Can you tell that a triangle is obtuse, right, or acute without measuring the angles? Explain.

On Your Own

A triangle has sides with the lengths and angle measures given.
Classify each triangle. Write *isosceles*, *scalene*, or *equilateral*.
Then write *acute*, *obtuse*, or *right*.

4. **sides:** 3.5 cm, 6.2 cm, 3.5 cm

    angles: 27°, 126°, 27°

5. **sides:** 2 in., 5 in., 3.8 in.

    angles: 43°, 116°, 21°

_____

_____

6. Circle the figure that does not belong. Explain.

_____

_____

7. GO DEEPER Draw 2 equilateral triangles that are congruent and share a side. What polygon is formed? Is it a regular polygon?

_____

_____

Problem Solving • Applications

8. **THINK SMARTER** Shannon said that a triangle with exactly 2 congruent sides and an obtuse angle is an equilateral obtuse triangle. Describe her error.

_____

_____

9. **THINK SMARTER** Kelly drew a triangle with exactly 2 congruent sides and 3 acute angles. Which of the following accurately describes the triangle? Mark all that apply.

Ⓐ isosceles   Ⓒ obtuse

Ⓑ acute   Ⓓ equilateral

Connect to Science

Forces and Balance

What makes triangles good for the construction of buildings or bridges? The 3 fixed lengths of the sides of a triangle, when joined, can form no other shape. So, when pushed, triangles don't bend or break.

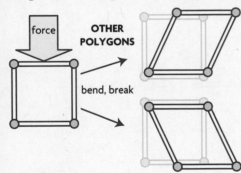

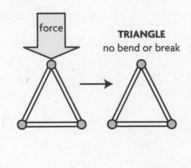

MATHEMATICAL PRACTICE ⑦ **Identify Relationships** Classify the triangles in the structures below. Write *isosceles, scalene,* or *equilateral.* Then write *acute, obtuse,* or *right.*

10.

11.

_____   _____

Triangles

Common Core

COMMON CORE STANDARD—5.G.B.3, 5.G.B.4 *Classify two-dimensional figures into categories based on their properties.*

**Classify each triangle. Write *isosceles, scalene,* or *equilateral.*
Then write *acute, obtuse,* or *right.***

1.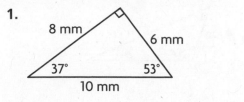

None of the side measures are equal. So, it is

_____scalene_____. There is a right

angle, so it is a _____right_____ triangle.

2.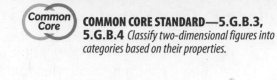

_____   _____

3.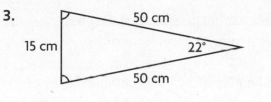

_____   _____

4.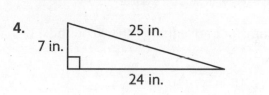

_____   _____

**A triangle has sides with the lengths and angle measures given. Classify
each triangle. Write *scalene, isosceles,* or *equilateral.* Then write *acute,
obtuse,* or *right*.**

5. sides: 44 mm, 28 mm, 24 mm

angles: 110°, 40°, 30°

_____   _____

6. sides: 23 mm, 20 mm, 13 mm

angles: 62°, 72°, 46°

_____   _____

Problem Solving Real World

7. Mary says the pen for her horse is an acute right triangle. Is this possible? **Explain.**

_____

8. Karen says every equilateral triangle is acute. Is this true? **Explain.**

_____

9. **WRITE** *Math* Draw three triangles: one equilateral, one isosceles, and one scalene. Label each and explain how you classified each triangle.

_____

Lesson Check (5.G.B.3, 5.G.B.4)

1. If two of a triangle's angles measure 42° and 48°, how would you classify that triangle? Write *acute, obtuse,* or *right*.

2. What is the classification of the following triangle? Write *scalene, isosceles,* or *right*.

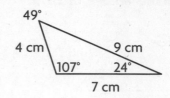

Spiral Review (5.MD.A.1, 5.G.B.3)

3. How many tons are equal to 40,000 pounds?

4. Choose a symbol to make the following statement true. Write >, <, or =.

6 kilometers $\bigcirc$ 600 centimeters

5. What polygon is shown?

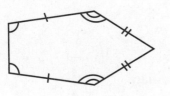

6. Name the polygon. Write whether it is regular or not regular.

FOR MORE PRACTICE
GO TO THE
Personal Math Trainer

Quadrilaterals

Essential Question How can you classify and compare quadrilaterals?

Common Core   Measurement and Data—
5.G.B.3, 5.G.B.4
MATHEMATICAL PRACTICES
MP3, MP7

Unlock the Problem Real World

A seating chart for a baseball field has many four-sided figures, or **quadrilaterals**. What types of quadrilaterals can you find in the seating chart?

There are five special types of quadrilaterals. You can classify quadrilaterals by their properties, such as parallel sides and perpendicular sides. Parallel lines are lines that are always the same distance apart. Perpendicular lines are lines that intersect to form four right angles.

▲ Lower Level

Complete the sentence that describes each type of quadrilateral.

A general quadrilateral has 4 sides and 4 angles.

A **trapezoid** is a quadrilateral with at least 1 pair of _____ sides.

A **parallelogram** is a special trapezoid with opposite _____ that are _____ and parallel.

A **rectangle** is a special parallelogram with _____ right angles and 4 pairs of _____ sides.

A **rhombus** is a special parallelogram with _____ congruent sides.

A **square** is a special parallelogram with _____ congruent sides and _____ right angles.

So, the types of quadrilaterals you can find in the seating chart of the field are

_____ .

Math Talk

MATHEMATICAL PRACTICES ⑦
Identify Relationships How are trapezoids and parallelograms different?

🔒 Activity

Materials ■ quadrilaterals ■ scissors

You can use a Venn diagram to sort quadrilaterals and find out how they are related.

• Draw the diagram below on your MathBoard.

• Cut out the quadrilaterals and sort them into the Venn diagram.

• Record your work by drawing each figure you have placed in the Venn diagram below.

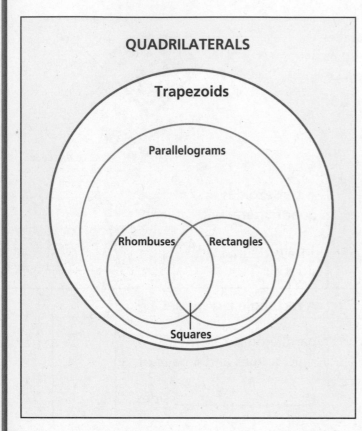

Complete the sentences by writing *always, sometimes,* or *never.*

A rhombus is _____ a square.

A parallelogram is _____ a rectangle.

A rhombus is _____ a parallelogram.

A trapezoid is _____ a parallelogram.

A parellelogram is _____ a trapezoid.

A square is _____ a rhombus.

1. Explain why the circle for parallelograms is inside the circle for trapezoids.

_____

_____

2. Explain why the section of the Venn diagram for squares intersects with both the section for rhombuses and the section for rectangles.

_____

_____

_____

Name _____

1. Use quadrilateral *ABCD* to answer each question. Complete the sentence.

   a. Measure the sides. Are any of the sides congruent? _____
      Mark any congruent sides.

   b. How many right angles, if any, does the quadrilateral have? _____

   c. How many pairs of parallel sides, if any, does the quadrilateral have? _____

   So, quadrilateral *ABCD* is a _____ and a _____.

Classify the quadrilateral in as many ways as possible. Write
quadrilateral, trapezoid, parallelogram, rectangle, rhombus, or *square.*

2. _____

3. _____

Math Talk

MATHEMATICAL PRACTICES ❸

Make Arguments Can a trapezoid have more than one pair of parallel sides that have the same length? Explain your answer.

On Your Own

Classify the quadrilateral in as many ways as possible. Write
quadrilateral, trapezoid, parallelogram, rectangle, rhombus, or *square.*

4. _____

5. _____

6. _____

7. _____

Problem Solving • Applications

8. A quadrilateral has exactly 2 congruent sides. Which quadrilateral types could it be? Which quadrilaterals could it not be?

_____

_____

9. **THINK SMARTER** A quadrilateral has exactly 3 congruent sides. Davis claims that the figure must be a rectangle. Why is his claim incorrect? Use a diagram to explain your answer.

_____

_____

10. **MATHEMATICAL PRACTICE ③** **Make Arguments** The opposite corners of a quadrilateral are right angles. The quadrilateral is not a rhombus. What kind of quadrilateral is this figure? Explain how you know.

_____

_____

11. **GO DEEPER** I am a figure with four sides. I can be placed in the following categories: quadrilateral, trapezoid, parallelogram, rectangle, rhombus, and square. Draw me. Explain why I fit into each category.

_____

_____

_____

_____

12. **THINK SMARTER +** For 12a–12c, write the name of one quadrilateral from the tiles to complete a true statement. Use each quadrilateral only once.

Personal Math Trainer

| square |
| trapezoid |
| rhombus |

12a. A _____ is sometimes a square.

12b. A _____ is always a rectangle.

12c. A parallelogram is always a _____.

Name _____

Quadrilaterals

COMMON CORE STANDARD—5.G.B.4
Classify two-dimensional figures into categories based on their properties.

Classify the quadrilateral in as many ways as possible.
Write *quadrilateral, trapezoid, parallelogram, rectangle, rhombus,* **or** *square.*

1.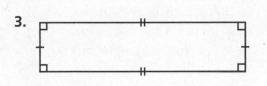

It has 4 sides, so it is a ___quadrilateral___ .
None of the sides are parallel, so there is

___no other classification.___ .

2.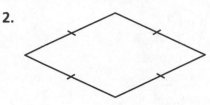

_____

3.

_____

4.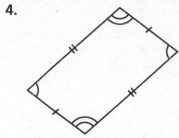

_____

5.

_____

6.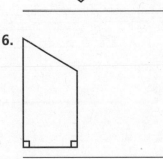

_____

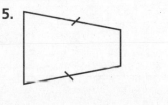

Problem Solving Real World

7. Kevin claims he can draw a trapezoid with three right angles. Is this possible? **Explain.**

_____

_____

_____

8. "If a figure is a square, then it is a regular quadrilateral." Is this true or false? **Explain.**

_____

_____

_____

9. **WRITE** ▶*Math* All rectangles are parallelograms. Are all parallelograms rectangles? Explain.

_____

Lesson Check (5.G.B.4)

1. Complete the following statement. Write *sometimes*, *always*, or *never*.

   A trapezoid _____ has exactly one pair of parallel sides.

2. Complete the following statement. Write *sometimes*, *always*, or *never*.

   A rhombus _____ has four congruent angles.

Spiral Review (5.NF.B.3, 5.MD.A.1, 5.G.B.3, 5.G.B.4)

3. How many kilograms are equal to 5,000 grams?

4. The sides of a triangle measure 6 inches, 8 inches, and 10 inches. The triangle has one 90° angle. What type of triangle is it?

5. A warehouse has 355 books to ship. Each shipping carton holds 14 books. How many cartons does the warehouse need to ship all of the books?

6. How many vertices does a heptagon have?

© Houghton Mifflin Harcourt Publishing Company

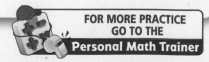

FOR MORE PRACTICE
GO TO THE
Personal Math Trainer

Three-Dimensional Figures

Essential Question How can you identify, describe, and classify three-dimensional figures?

Common Core Measurement and Data—
5.MD.C.3
MATHEMATICAL PRACTICES
MP1, MP6, MP7, MP8

🔑 Unlock the Problem

A solid figure has three dimensions: length, width, and height. **Polyhedrons**, such as prisms and pyramids, are three-dimensional figures with faces that are polygons.

A **prism** is a polyhedron that has two congruent polygons as **bases**.

A polyhedron's **lateral faces** are polygons that connect with the bases. The lateral faces of a prism are rectangles.

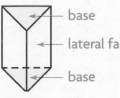
base
lateral face
base

A prism's base shape is used to name the solid figure. The base shape of this prism is a triangle. The prism is a **triangular prism.**

🔒 **Identify the base shape of the prism. Use the terms in the box to correctly name the prism by its base shape.**

> **Math Idea**
>
> A two-dimensional figure has the dimensions length and width, which are used to find the figure's area.
>
> A three-dimensional figure, or solid, has three dimensions: length, width, and height. These dimensions are used to find the figure's volume, or the space it occupies.

> **Types of Prisms**
>
> decagonal prism
> octagonal prism
> hexagonal prism
> pentagonal prism
> rectangular prism
> triangular prism

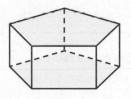

Base shape: _____

Name the solid figure.

_____

Base shape: _____

Name the solid figure.

_____

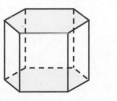

Base shape: _____

Name the solid figure.

_____

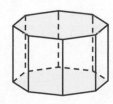

Base shape: _____

Name the solid figure.

_____

Math Talk MATHEMATICAL PRACTICES ⑧

Use Repeated Reasoning What shapes make up a decagonal prism, and how many are there? Explain.

• **MATHEMATICAL PRACTICE** ① **Analyze** What special prism has congruent squares for bases and lateral faces? _____

Pyramid A **pyramid** is a polyhedron with only one base. The lateral faces of a pyramid are triangles that meet at a common vertex.

Like a prism, a pyramid is named for the shape of its base.

 **Identify the base shape of the pyramid. Use the terms in the box to correctly name the pyramid by its base shape.**

Types of Pyramids

pentagonal pyramid

rectangular pyramid

square pyramid

triangular pyramid

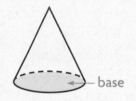

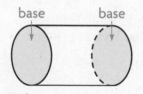

Base shape: _____

Name the solid figure.

_____

Base shape: _____

Name the solid figure.

_____

Base shape: _____

Name the solid figure.

_____

Non-polyhedrons Some three-dimensional figures have curved surfaces. These solid figures are *not* polyhedrons.

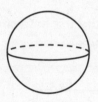

A **cone** has 1 circular base and 1 curved surface.

A **cylinder** has 2 congruent circular bases and 1 curved surface.

A **sphere** has no bases and 1 curved surface.

Share and Show · MATH BOARD

Classify the solid figure. Write *prism, pyramid, cone, cylinder,* or *sphere.*

1.

_____

2.

_____

☑ 3.

_____

Name the solid figure.

4.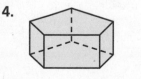

_____

5.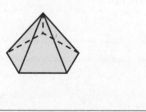

_____

☑ 6.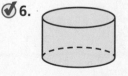

_____

Name _____

Classify the solid figure. Write *prism, pyramid, cone, cylinder,* or *sphere*.

7.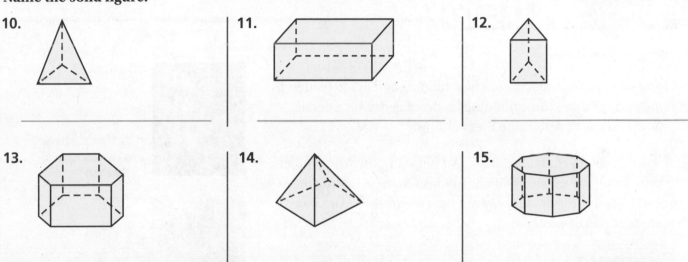

8.

9.

_____ _____ _____

Name the solid figure.

10.

11.

12.

_____ _____ _____

13.

14.

15.

_____ _____ _____

Problem Solving • Applications

16. **MATHEMATICAL PRACTICE 6** **Use Math Vocabulary** Mario is making a sculpture out of stone. He starts by carving a base with five sides. He then carves five triangular lateral faces that all meet at a point at the top. What three-dimensional figure does Mario make?

17. **THINK SMARTER** What is another name for a cube? Explain your reasoning.

_____

_____

_____

18. **GO DEEPER** Compare the characteristics of prisms and pyramids. Tell how they are alike and how they are different.

_____

_____

_____

_____

19. **THINK SMARTER** Write the letter in the box that correctly describes the three-dimensional figure.

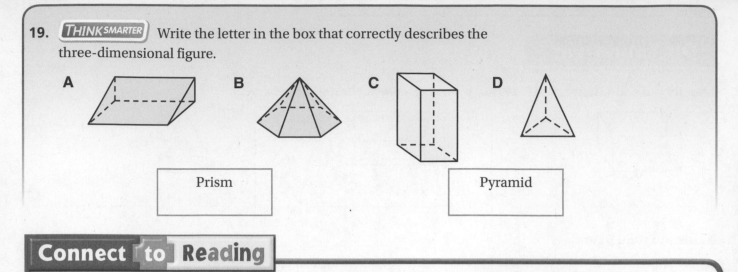

A   B   C   D

Prism		Pyramid

Connect to Reading

Identify the Details

If you were given a description of a building and asked to identify which one of these three buildings is described, which details would you use to determine the building?

A word problem contains details that help you solve the problem. Some details are meaningful and are important to finding the solution and some details may not be. *Identify the details* you need to solve the problem.

Example Read the description. Underline the details you need to identify the solid figure that will name the correct building.

This building is one of the most identifiable structures in its city's skyline. It has a square foundation and 28 floors. The building has four triangular exterior faces that meet at a point at the top of the structure.

◄ **Flatiron Building, New York City, New York**

◄ **Nehru Science Center, Mumbai, India**

◄ **Luxor Hotel, Las Vegas, Nevada**

Identify the solid figure and name the correct building.

20. Solve the problem in the Example.

Solid figure: _____

Building: _____

21. This building was completed in 1902. It has a triangular foundation and a triangular roof that are the same size and shape. The three sides of the building are rectangles.

Solid figure: _____

Building: _____

Three-Dimensional Figures

COMMON CORE STANDARD—5.MD.C.3
Geometric measurements: understand concepts of volume and relate volume to multiplication and to addition.

Classify the solid figure. Write *prism, pyramid, cone, cylinder,* or *sphere.*

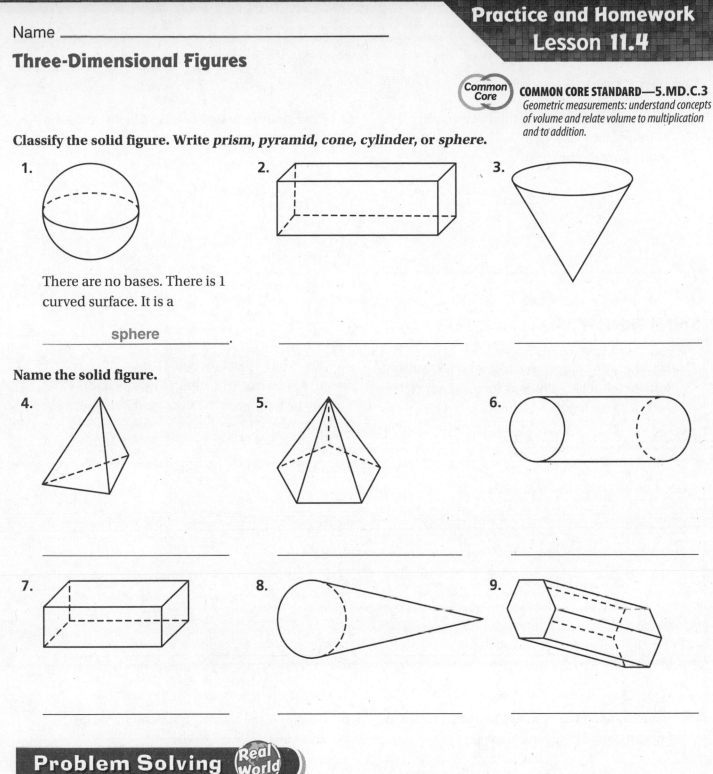

1.

There are no bases. There is 1 curved surface. It is a

_____sphere_____.

2.

_____

3.

_____

Name the solid figure.

4.

_____

5.

_____

6.

_____

7.

_____

8.

_____

9.

_____

Problem Solving · Real World

10. Nanako said she drew a square pyramid and that all of the faces are triangles. Is this possible? **Explain.**

_____

11. **WRITE** ▸*Math* Explain why a three-dimensional figure with a curved surface is not a polyhedron.

_____

Lesson Check (5.MD.C.3)

1. Luke made a model of a solid figure with 1 circular base and 1 curved surface. What solid figure did he make?

_____

2. How many rectangular faces does a hexagonal pyramid have?

_____

Spiral Review (5.NF.A.1, 5.MD.A.1, 5.G.B.3, 5.G.B.4)

3. Laura walks $\frac{3}{5}$ mile to school each day. Isaiah's walk to school is 3 times as long as Laura's. How far does Isaiah walk to school each day?

_____

4. James has $4\frac{3}{4}$ feet of rope. He plans to cut off $1\frac{1}{2}$ feet from the rope. How much rope will be left?

_____

5. Latasha made 128 ounces of punch. How many cups of punch did Latasha make?

_____

6. Complete the following statement. Write *sometimes, always,* or *never.*

Trapezoids are _____ parallelograms.

© Houghton Mifflin Harcourt Publishing Company

**FOR MORE PRACTICE
GO TO THE
Personal Math Trainer**

Name _____

✓ Mid-Chapter Checkpoint

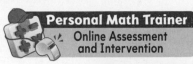
Vocabulary

Choose the best term from the box.

1. A closed plane figure with all sides congruent and all angles

   congruent is called a _____ . (p. 638)

2. Line segments that have the same length, or angles that have

   the same measure, are _____ . (p. 638)

Concepts and Skills

Name each polygon. Then tell whether it is a *regular polygon*
or *not a regular polygon*. (5.G.B.3)

3.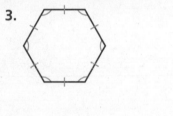

4.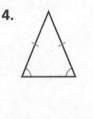

5.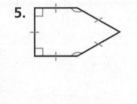

_____   _____   _____

Classify each triangle. Write *isosceles, scalene,* or *equilateral*.
Then write *acute, obtuse,* or *right*. (5.G.B.3, 5.G.B.4)

6.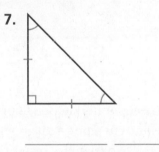

7.

8.

_____   _____   _____

Classify the quadrilateral in as many ways as possible. Write all that apply:
quadrilateral, trapezoid, parallelogram, rectangle, rhombus, or *square.* (5.G.B.4)

9.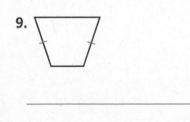

10.

11.

_____   _____   _____

_____   _____   _____

12. What type of triangle is shown below? (5.G.B.3, 5.G.B.4)

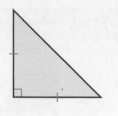

_____

13. Classify the quadrilateral in as many ways as possible. (5.G.B.4)

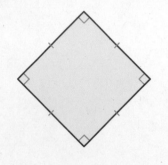

_____

14. Classify the following figure. (5.MD.C.3)

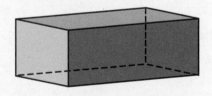

_____

15. **GO DEEPER** Nathan cut a rectangular tile in half for his kitchen floor design. The tile was not a square. He made one cut along a diagonal from one vertex to another vertex. Classify the two triangles resulting from the cut by their angles and their side lengths. (5.G.B.3, 5.G.B.4)

_____

662

Name _____

Unit Cubes and Solid Figures

Essential Question What is a unit cube and how can you use it to build a solid figure?

Common Core **Measurement and Data—**
5.MD.C.3a
MATHEMATICAL PRACTICES
MP2, MP5, MP6

Investigate

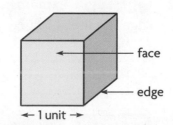

You can build rectangular prisms using unit cubes. How many different rectangular prisms can you build with a given number of unit cubes?

Materials ■ centimeter cubes

A **unit cube** is a cube that has a length, width, and height

of 1 unit. A cube has _____ square faces. All of its faces

are congruent. It has _____ edges. The lengths of all its edges are equal.

face

edge

← 1 unit →

A. Build a rectangular prism with 2 unit cubes.

   Think: When the 2 cubes are pushed together, the faces and edges that are pushed together make 1 face and 1 edge.

   • How many faces does the rectangular prism have? _____

   • How many edges does the rectangular prism have? _____

B. Build as many different rectangular prisms as you can with 8 unit cubes.

C. Record in units the dimensions of each rectangular prism you built with 8 cubes.

Dimensions		

So, with 8 unit cubes, I can build _____ different rectangular prisms.

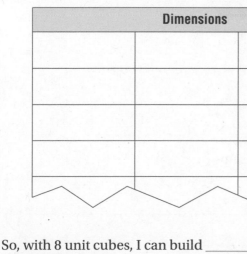

Math Talk   MATHEMATICAL PRACTICES ❺

Communicate Describe the different rectangular prisms that you can make with 4 unit cubes.

Chapter 11 663

Draw Conclusions

1. Explain why a rectangular prism composed of 2 unit cubes has 6 faces. How do its dimensions compare to a unit cube?

_____

_____

_____

2. **MATHEMATICAL PRACTICE** ⑥ **Explain** how the number of edges for the rectangular prism compares to the number of edges for the unit cube.

_____

_____

3. **MATHEMATICAL PRACTICE** ⑥ **Describe** what all of the rectangular prisms you made in Step B have in common.

_____

_____

Make Connections

You can build other solid figures and compare the solid figures by counting the number of unit cubes.

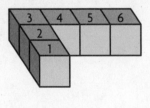

Figure 1

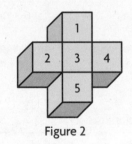

Figure 2

Figure 1 is made up of _____ unit cubes.   Figure 2 is made up of _____ unit cubes.

So, Figure _____ has more unit cubes than Figure _____.

- Use 12 unit cubes to build a solid figure that is not a rectangular prism. Share your model with a partner. Describe how your model is the same and how it is different from your partner's model.

_____

_____

Name _____

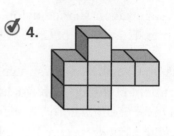

Count the number of cubes used to build each solid figure.

1. The rectangular prism is made up of _____ unit cubes.

2.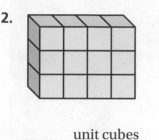

_____ unit cubes

☑3.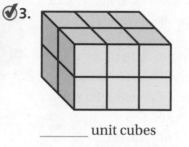

_____ unit cubes

☑4.

_____ unit cubes

5. **WRITE** ▸*Math* How are the rectangular prisms in Exercises 2–3 related? Can you show a different rectangular prism with the same relationship? Explain.

_____

_____

Problem Solving • Applications

Compare the number of unit cubes in each solid figure. Use <, > or =.

6.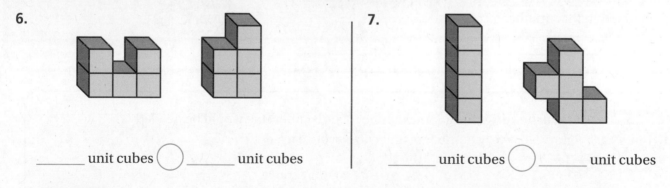

_____ unit cubes ◯ _____ unit cubes

7.

_____ unit cubes ◯ _____ unit cubes

8. **MATHEMATICAL PRACTICE ②** **Use Reasoning** Melissa makes a solid figure by stacking 1 cube on top of a row of 2 cubes on top of a row of 3 cubes. Then she rearranges the cubes to form a rectangular prism. Describe the arrangement of cubes in the rectangular prism.

_____

Connect to Art

Architecture is the art and science of designing buildings and structures.

The Cube Houses of Rotterdam in the Netherlands, shown at the top right, were built in the 1970s. Each cube is a house, tilted and resting on a hexagon-shaped pylon, and is meant to represent an abstract tree. The village of Cube Houses creates a "forest."

The Nakagin Capsule Tower, shown at the right, is an office and apartment building in Tokyo, Japan, made up of modules attached to two central cores. Each module is a rectangular prism connected to a concrete core by four huge bolts. The modules are office and living spaces that can be removed or replaced.

Use the information to answer the questions.

9. **GO DEEPER**   There are 38 Cube Houses. Each house could hold 1,000 unit cubes that are 1 meter by 1 meter by 1 meter. Describe the dimensions of a cube house using unit cubes. Remember that the edges of a cube are all the same length.

_____

_____

10. **THINK SMARTER**   The Nakagin Capsule Tower has 140 modules, and is 14 stories high. If all of the modules were divided evenly among the number of stories, how many modules would be on each floor? How many different rectangular prisms could be made from that number?

_____

11. **THINK SMARTER**   Match the figure with the number of unit cubes that would be needed to build each figure. Not every number of unit cubes will be used.

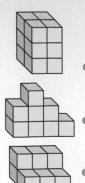

- 6 unit cubes
- 7 unit cubes
- 8 unit cubes
- 9 unit cubes
- 10 unit cubes
- 12 unit cubes

Unit Cubes and Solid Figures

Common Core

COMMON CORE STANDARD—5.MD.C.3a
Geometric measurement: understand concepts of volume and relate volume to multiplication and to addition.

Count the number of cubes used to build each solid figure.

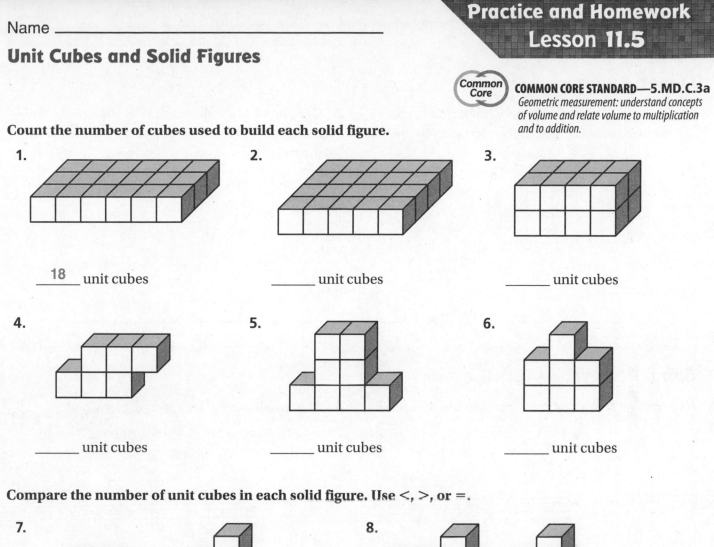

1.

____18____ unit cubes

2.

_____ unit cubes

3.

_____ unit cubes

4.

_____ unit cubes

5.

_____ unit cubes

6.

_____ unit cubes

Compare the number of unit cubes in each solid figure. Use <, >, or =.

7.

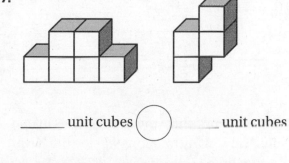

_____ unit cubes $\bigcirc$ _____ unit cubes

8.

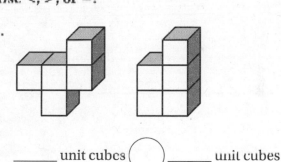

_____ unit cubes $\bigcirc$ _____ unit cubes

Problem Solving *Real World*

9. A carton can hold 1,000 unit cubes that measure 1 inch by 1 inch by 1 inch. Describe the dimensions of the carton using unit cubes.

_____

_____

_____

10. **WRITE** ▸*Math* Draw and label examples of all rectangular prisms built with 16 unit cubes.

Lesson Check (5.MD.C.3a)

1. Cala stacked some blocks to make the figure below. How many blocks are in Cala's figure?

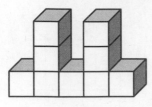

_____

2. Quentin has 18 unit cubes. How many different rectangular prisms can he build if he uses all of the cubes?

_____

Spiral Review (5.MD.A.1, 5.MD.C.3, 5.G.B.4)

3. In what shape are the lateral faces of a pyramid?

_____

4. The Arnold family arrived at the beach at 10:30 A.M. They spent $3\frac{3}{4}$ hours there. What time did they leave the beach?

_____

5. Complete the following statement. Write *sometimes, always,* or *never.*

The opposite sides of a parallelogram

are _____congruent.

6. The tire on Frank's bike moves 75 inches in one rotation. How many rotations will the tire have made after Frank rides 50 feet?

_____

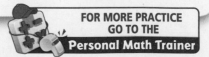

FOR MORE PRACTICE
GO TO THE
Personal Math Trainer

Name _____

Understand Volume

Essential Question How can you use unit cubes to find the volume of a rectangular prism?

Common Core Measurement and Data—
5.MD.C.3b, 5.MD.C.4
MATHEMATICAL PRACTICES
MP3, MP5, MP6

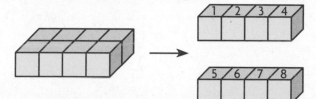

Investigate

Hands On

CONNECT You can find the volume of a rectangular prism by counting unit cubes. **Volume** is the measure of the amount of space a solid figure occupies and is measured in **cubic units**. Each unit cube has a volume of 1 cubic unit.

The rectangular prism above is made up of _____ unit cubes

and has a volume of _____ cubic units.

Materials ■ rectangular prism net A ■ centimeter cubes

A. Cut out, fold, and tape the net to form a rectangular prism.

B. Use centimeter cubes to fill the base of the rectangular prism without gaps or overlaps. Each centimeter cube has a length, width, and height of 1 centimeter and a volume of 1 cubic centimeter.

- How many centimeter cubes make up the length of the first layer? the width? the height?

  length: _____ width: _____ height: _____

- How many centimeter cubes are used to fill the base? _____

C. Continue filling the rectangular prism, layer by layer. Count the number of centimeter cubes used for each layer.

- How many centimeter cubes are in each layer? _____

- How many layers of cubes fill the rectangular prism? _____

- How many centimeter cubes fill the prism? _____

So, the volume of the rectangular prism is _____ cubic centimeters.

Draw Conclusions

1. Describe the relationship among the number of centimeter cubes you used to fill each layer, the number of layers, and the volume of the prism.

_____

_____

_____

2. **MATHEMATICAL PRACTICE 3** **Apply** If you had a rectangular prism that had a length of 3 units, a width of 4 units, and a height of 2 units, how many unit cubes would you need for each layer? How many unit cubes would you need to fill the rectangular prism?

_____

Make Connections

To find the volume of three-dimensional figures, you measure in three directions. For a rectangular prism, you measure its length, width, and height. Volume is measured using cubic units, such as cu cm, cu in., or cu ft.

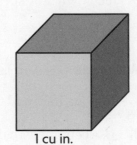

1 cu cm

1 cu in.

- Which has a greater volume, 1 cu cm or 1 cu in.? Explain.

_____

_____

Find the volume of the prism if each cube represents 1 cu cm, 1 cu in., and 1 cu ft.

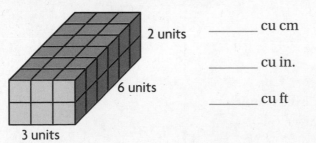

2 units

6 units

3 units

_____ cu cm

_____ cu in.

_____ cu ft

- **MATHEMATICAL PRACTICE 6** Would the prism above be the same size if it were built with centimeter cubes, inch cubes, or foot cubes? **Explain.**

_____

_____

_____

Name _____

Use the unit given. Find the volume.

1.

3 cm

4 cm

4 cm

Each cube = 1 cu cm

Volume = _____ cu _____

2.

4 in.

2 in.

3 in.

Each cube = 1 cu in.

Volume = _____ cu _____

3.

3 ft

2 ft

6 ft

Each cube = 1 cu ft

Volume = _____ cu _____

4.

3 in.

4 in.

5 in.

Each cube = 1 cu in.

Volume = _____ cu _____

Compare the volumes. Write <, >, or =.

5.

2 in.

2 in.

8 in.

Each cube = 1 cu in.

2 in.

4 in.

4 in.

Each cube = 1 cu in.

_____ cu in. ◯ _____ cu in.

6.

3 ft

4 ft

9 ft

Each cube = 1 cu ft

2 ft

5 ft

8 ft

Each cube = 1 cu ft

_____ cu ft ◯ _____ cu ft

Problem Solving • Applications

7. **MATHEMATICAL PRACTICE 3** **Verify the Reasoning of Others** Gerardo says that a cube with edges that measure 10 centimeters has a volume that is twice as much as a cube with sides that measure 5 centimeters. Explain and correct Gerardo's error.

_____

_____

_____

_____

_____

_____

8. **THINK SMARTER** Pia built a rectangular prism with cubes. The base of her prism has 12 centimeter cubes. If the prism was built with 108 centimeter cubes, what is the height of her prism?

_____

9. **GO DEEPER** A packing company makes boxes with edges each measuring 3 feet. What is the volume of the boxes? If 10 boxes are put in a larger, rectangular shipping container and completely fill it with no gaps or overlaps, what is the volume of the shipping container?

_____

10. **THINK SMARTER** Carlton used 1-centimeter cubes to build the rectangular prism shown.

Find the volume of the rectangular prism

Carlton built.

_____ cubic centimeters

5 cm

3 cm

4 cm

Understand Volume

Common Core **COMMON CORE STANDARD—5.MD.C.3b**
5.MD.C.4 *Geometric measurement: understand
concepts of volume and relate volume to
multiplication and to addition.*

Use the unit given. Find the volume.

1.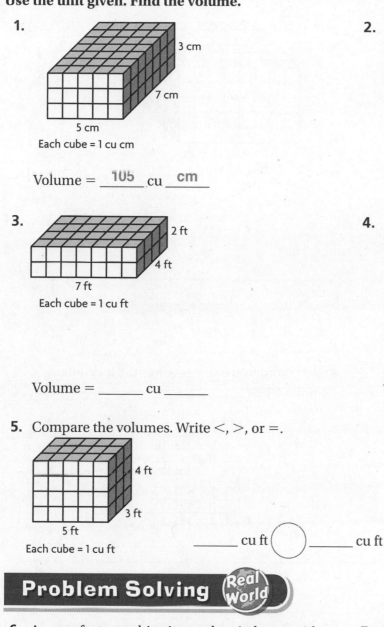

3 cm

7 cm

5 cm

Each cube = 1 cu cm

Volume = ____105____ cu ____cm____

2.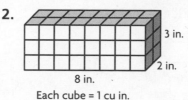

3 in.

2 in.

8 in.

Each cube = 1 cu in.

Volume = _____ cu _____

3.

2 ft

4 ft

7 ft

Each cube = 1 cu ft

Volume = _____ cu _____

4.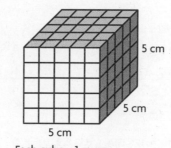

5 cm

5 cm

5 cm

Each cube = 1 cu cm

Volume = _____ cu _____

5. Compare the volumes. Write <, >, or =.

4 ft

3 ft

5 ft

Each cube = 1 cu ft

_____ cu ft 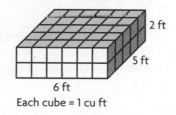 _____ cu ft

2 ft

5 ft

6 ft

Each cube = 1 cu ft

Problem Solving · Real World

6. A manufacturer ships its product in boxes with edges of 4 inches. If 12 boxes are put in a carton and completely fill the carton, what is the volume of the carton?

_____

_____

7. Matt and Mindy each built a rectangular prism that has a length of 5 units, a width of 2 units, and a height of 4 units. Matt used cubes that are 1 cm on each side. Mindy used cubes that are 1 in. on each side. What is the volume of each prism?

_____

_____

Lesson Check (5.MD.C.3b, 5.MD.C.4)

1. Elena packed 48 cubes into this box. Each cube has edges that are 1 centimeter. How many layers of cubes did Elena make?

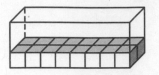

2. What is the volume of the rectangular prism?

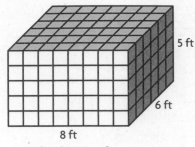

5 ft

6 ft

8 ft

Each cube = 1 cu ft

Spiral Review (5.MD.A.1, 5.G.A.1, 5.G.B.3, 5.G.B.4)

3. Juan made a design with polygons. Which polygon in Juan's design is a pentagon?

4. What ordered pair describes the location of point *P*?

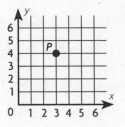

5. What is the least number of acute angles that a triangle can have?

6. Karen bought 3 pounds of cheese to serve at a picnic. How many ounces of cheese did Karen buy?

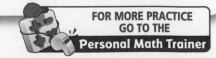

FOR MORE PRACTICE
GO TO THE
Personal Math Trainer

Estimate Volume

Essential Question How can you use an everyday object to estimate the volume of a rectangular prism?

(Common Core) **Measurement and Data—5.MD.C.4**
Also 5.MD.C.3b
MATHEMATICAL PRACTICES
MP1, MP2, MP6

Investigate

Izzy is mailing 20 boxes of crayons to a children's-education organization overseas. She can pack them in one of two different-sized shipping boxes. Using crayon boxes as a cubic unit, about what volume is each shipping box, in crayon boxes? Which shipping box should Izzy use to mail the crayons?

Materials ■ rectangular prism net B ■ 2 boxes, different sizes

A. Cut out, fold, and tape the net to form a rectangular prism. Label the prism "Crayons." You can use this prism to estimate and compare the volume of the two boxes.

B. Using the crayon box that you made, count to find the number of boxes that make up the base of the shipping box. Estimate the length to the nearest whole unit.

Number of crayon boxes that fill the base:

Box 1: _____   Box 2: _____

C. Starting with the crayon box in the same position, count to find the number of crayon boxes that make up the height of the shipping box. Estimate the height to the nearest whole unit.

Number of layers:

Box 1: _____   Box 2: _____

Box 1 has a volume of _____ crayon boxes

and Box 2 has a volume of _____ crayon boxes.

So, Izzy should use Box _____ to ship the crayons.

Draw Conclusions

1. **MATHEMATICAL PRACTICE 6** **Explain** how you estimated the volume of the shipping boxes.

_____

_____

_____

_____

2. **MATHEMATICAL PRACTICE 1** **Analyze** If you had to estimate to the nearest whole unit to find the volume of a shipping box, how might you be able to ship a greater number of crayon boxes in the shipping box than you actually estimated? Explain.

_____

_____

_____

Make Connections

The crayon box has a length of 3 inches, a width of 4 inches, and a height of 1 inch. The volume of the crayon box is _____ cubic inches.

Using the crayon box, estimate the volume of the box at the right in cubic inches.

- The box to the right holds _____ crayon boxes in each of _____ layers, or _____ crayon boxes.

- Multiply the volume of 1 crayon box by the estimated number of crayon boxes that fit in the box at the right.

  _____ × _____ = _____

So, the volume of the shipping box at the right is about _____ cubic inches.

Name _____

Share and Show MATH BOARD

Estimate the volume.

1. Each tissue box has a volume of 125 cubic inches.

   There are _____ tissue boxes in the larger box.

   The estimated volume of the box holding the tissue

   boxes is _____ × 125 = _____ cu in.

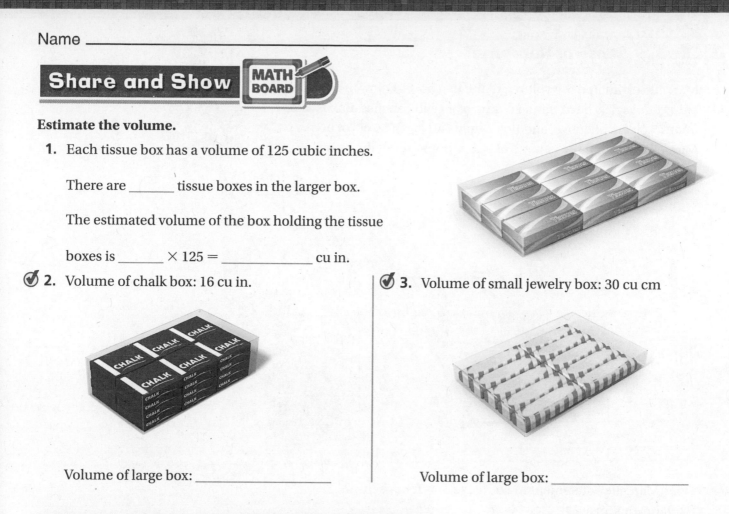

✔ 2. Volume of chalk box: 16 cu in.

   Volume of large box: _____

✔ 3. Volume of small jewelry box: 30 cu cm

   Volume of large box: _____

Problem Solving • Applications

4. **MATHEMATICAL PRACTICE ②** Use Reasoning Jamie is mailing a large box of donated books to a community center. The volume of each book is 80 cubic inches. The picture shows the number of books she put in the box. Jamie can fit one more layer of books in the box. About what is the volume of the box?

   _____

5. **GO DEEPER** Anna is collecting boxes of cereal to deliver to a food bank. The volume of each cereal box is 324 cubic inches. The picture shows the cereal boxes she has collected so far. A large delivery box holds three times as many boxes as Anna collected. About what is the volume of the delivery box?

   _____

THINK SMARTER   **Sense or Nonsense?**

6. Marcelle estimated the volume of the two boxes below, using one of his books. His book has a volume of 48 cubic inches. Box 1 holds about 7 layers of books, and Box 2 holds about 14 layers of books. Marcelle says that the volume of either box is about the same.

Box 1   Box 2

- Does Marcelle's statement make sense or is it nonsense? Explain your answer.

_____

_____

_____

_____

_____

_____

7. THINK SMARTER   A pack of folders has a length of 5 inches, a width of 12 inches, and a height of 1 inch. The pack of folders will be shipped in a box that holds 12 packs of folders. For 7a–7c, select True or False for each statement.

7a.   Each pack of folders has a volume of 60 cubic inches.   ○ True   ○ False

7b.   The box has a volume of about 720 cubic inches.   ○ True   ○ False

7c.   If the box held 15 packs of folders, it would have a volume of about 1,200 cubic inches.   ○ True   ○ False

Estimate Volume

 COMMON CORE STANDARD—5.MD.C.4
Geometric measurement: understand concepts of volume and relate volume to multiplication and to addition.

Estimate the volume.

1. Volume of package of paper: 200 cu in.

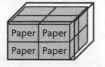

Think: Each package of paper has a volume

of 200 cu in. There are _____8_____ packages of paper in the larger box. So, the volume of the

large box is about _____8_____ × 200, or _____1,600_____ cubic inches.

Volume of large box: _____1,600 cu in._____

2. Volume of rice box: 500 cu cm

Volume of large box: _____

3. Volume of tea box: 40 cu in.

Volume of large box: _____

4. Volume of DVD case: 20 cu in.

Volume of large box: _____

Problem Solving Real World

5. Theo fills a large box with boxes of staples. The volume of each box of staples is 120 cu cm. Estimate the volume of the large box.

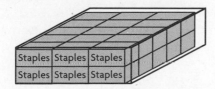

_____

6. **WRITE** *Math* Explain how you can estimate the volume of a large container that holds 5 rows of 4 snack-size boxes of cereal in its bottom layer and is 3 layers high. Each cereal box has a volume of 16 cubic inches.

_____

Lesson Check (5.MD.C.4)

1. Melanie packs boxes of envelopes into a larger box. The volume of each box of envelopes is 1,200 cubic centimeters. What is the approximate volume of the large box?

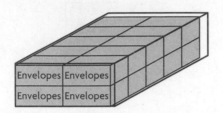

2. Calvin packs boxes of greeting cards into a larger box. The volume of each box of greeting cards is 90 cubic inches. What is the approximate volume of the large box?

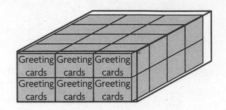

Spiral Review (5.MD.A.1, 5.MD.C.3a, 5.MD.C.3b, 5.MD.C.4)

3. Rosa has 16 unit cubes. How many different rectangular prisms can she build with the cubes?

4. Each cube represents 1 cubic inch. What is the volume of the prism?

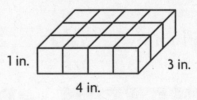

1 in.   3 in.   4 in.

5. A certain aquarium holds 20 gallons of water. How many quarts of water does the aquarium hold?

6. Monique ran in a 5-kilometer race. How many meters did Monique run?

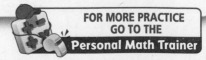

FOR MORE PRACTICE
GO TO THE
Personal Math Trainer

Name _____

Volume of Rectangular Prisms

Essential Question How can you find the volume of a rectangular prism?

(Common Core) **Measurement and Data—5.MD.C.5b, 5.MD.C.5a**
MATHEMATICAL PRACTICES
MP1, MP2, MP6

CONNECT The base of a rectangular prism is a rectangle. You know that area is measured in square units, or units^2, and that the area of a rectangle can be found by multiplying the length and the width.

Volume is measured in cubic units, or units^3. When you build a prism and add each layer of cubes, you are adding a third dimension, height.

The area of the base

is _____ sq units.

Unlock the Problem (Real World)

Yuan built the rectangular prism shown at the right, using 1-inch cubes. The prism has a base that is a rectangle and has a height of 4 cubes. What is the volume of the rectangular prism that Yuan built?

You can find the volume of a prism in cubic units by multiplying the number of square units in the base shape by the number of layers, or its height.

Each layer of Yuan's rectangular prism

is composed of _____ inch cubes.

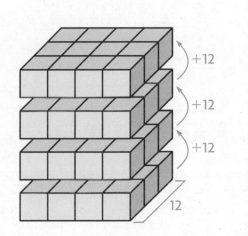

Height (in layers)	1	2	3	4
Volume (in cubic inches)	12	24		

) Multiply the height by _____.

1. How does the volume change as each layer is added?

_____

_____

2. What does the number you multiply the height by represent?

_____

_____

So, the volume of Yuan's rectangular prism is _____ in.^{3}

Relate Height to Volume

Toni stacks cube-shaped beads that measure 1 centimeter on each edge in a storage box. The box can hold 6 layers of 24 beads with no gaps or overlaps. What is the volume of Toni's storage box?

- What are the dimensions of the base of the box?

  _____

- What operation can you use to find the area of the base shape?

  _____

🔑 One Way Use base and height.

The volume of each bead is _____ cm³.

The storage box has a base with an area of _____ cm².

The height of the storage box is _____ centimeters.

The volume of the storage box is

(_____ × _____), or _____ cm³.
   Base
   area

🔑 Another Way Use length, width, and height.

You know that the area of the base of the storage box is 24 cm².

The base has a length of _____ centimeters

and a width of _____ centimeters. The height

is _____ centimeters. The volume of the storage box is

(_____ × _____) × _____ , or _____ × _____ , or _____ cm³.
   Base area

So, the volume of the storage box is _____ cm³.

3. **THINK SMARTER** **What if** each cube-shaped bead measured 2 centimeters on each edge? How would the dimensions of the storage box change? How would the volume change?

_____

_____

_____

Name _____

Share and Show MATH BOARD

Find the volume.

1. The length of the rectangular prism is _____.

   The width is _____. So, the area of the base is _____.

   The height is _____. So, the volume of the prism is _____.

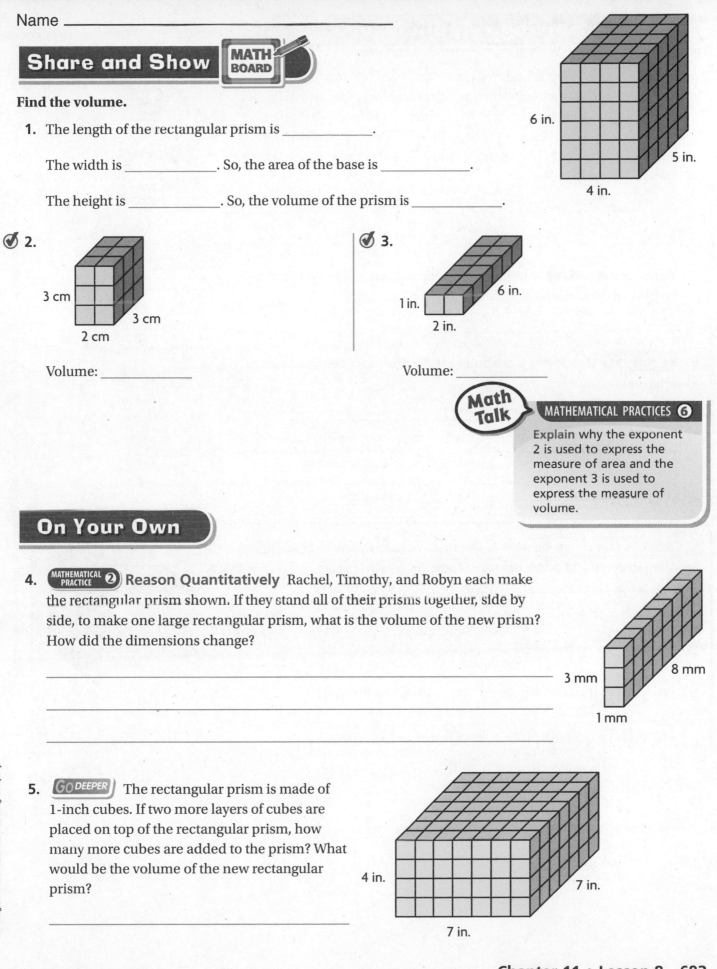

✓ 2.

3 cm
3 cm
2 cm

Volume: _____

✓ 3.

6 in.
1 in.
2 in.

Volume: _____

Math Talk MATHEMATICAL PRACTICES ⑥
Explain why the exponent 2 is used to express the measure of area and the exponent 3 is used to express the measure of volume.

On Your Own

4. **MATHEMATICAL PRACTICE ②** **Reason Quantitatively** Rachel, Timothy, and Robyn each make the rectangular prism shown. If they stand all of their prisms together, side by side, to make one large rectangular prism, what is the volume of the new prism? How did the dimensions change?

   _____

   _____

   _____

   3 mm   8 mm   1 mm

5. **GO DEEPER** The rectangular prism is made of 1-inch cubes. If two more layers of cubes are placed on top of the rectangular prism, how many more cubes are added to the prism? What would be the volume of the new rectangular prism?

   _____

   4 in.   7 in.   7 in.

Problem Solving • Applications Real World

6. **THINK SMARTER** Rich is building a travel crate for his dog, Thomas, a beagle-mix who is about 30 inches long, 12 inches wide, and 24 inches tall. For Thomas to travel safely, his crate needs to be a rectangular prism that is about 12 inches greater than his length and width, and 6 inches greater than his height. What is the volume of the travel crate that Rich should build?

_____

_____

7. What happens to the volume of a rectangular prism if you double the height? Give an example.

_____

8. **MATHEMATICAL PRACTICE 6 Use Math Vocabulary** Describe the difference between area and volume.

_____

_____

_____

9. **THINK SMARTER** John used 1-inch cubes to make the rectangular prism shown. For 9a–9d, write the value from the tiles that makes each statement correct. Each value can be used more than once or not at all.

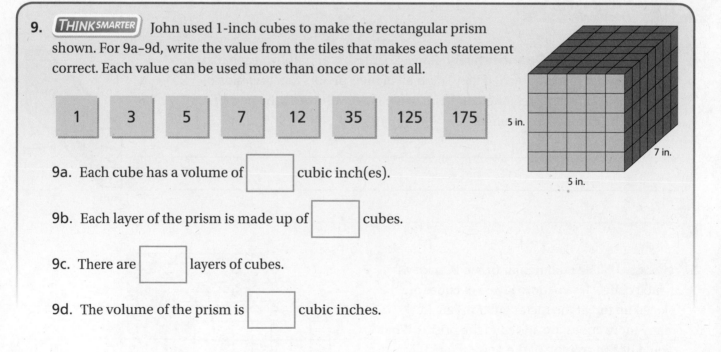

| 1 | 3 | 5 | 7 | 12 | 35 | 125 | 175 |

9a. Each cube has a volume of ☐ cubic inch(es).

9b. Each layer of the prism is made up of ☐ cubes.

9c. There are ☐ layers of cubes.

9d. The volume of the prism is ☐ cubic inches.

Volume of Rectangular Prisms

Common Core   **COMMON CORE STANDARD—5.MD.C.5a**
*Geometric measurement: understand concepts
of volume and relate volume to multiplication
and to addition.*

Find the volume.

1.

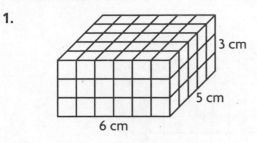

3 cm
5 cm
6 cm

Volume: _____ **90 cm³** _____

2.

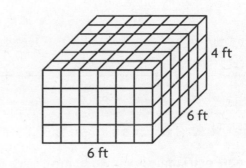

4 in.
2 in.
12 in.

Volume: _____

3.

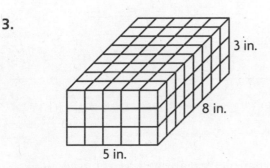

3 in.
8 in.
5 in.

Volume: _____

4.

4 ft
6 ft
6 ft

Volume: _____

Problem Solving Real World

5. Aaron keeps his baseball cards in a cardboard
box that is 12 inches long, 8 inches wide, and
3 inches high. What is the volume of this box?

_____

6. Amanda's jewelry box is in the shape of a cube
that has 6-inch edges. What is the volume of
Amanda's jewelry box?

_____

7. **WRITE** ▸*Math* Write a word problem that involves finding the
volume of a box. Draw the box, solve the problem, and explain how you
found your answer.

_____

_____

_____

Lesson Check (5.MD.C.5a)

1. Laini uses 1-inch cubes to build the box shown below. What is the volume of the box?

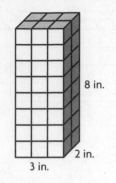

8 in.

2 in.

3 in.

2. Mason stacked 1-foot cube-shaped boxes in a warehouse. What is the volume of the stack of boxes?

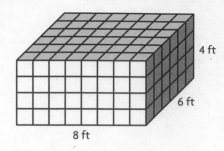

4 ft

6 ft

8 ft

Spiral Review (5.MD.A.1, 5.G.B.3, 5.G.B.4)

3. What type of triangle is shown below?

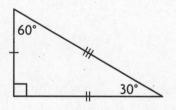

60°

30°

4. What quadrilateral always has 4 congruent angles and opposite sides that are congruent and parallel?

5. Suzanne is 64 inches tall. What is Suzanne's height in feet and inches?

6. Trevor bought 8 gallons of paint to paint his house. He used all but 1 quart. How many quarts of paint did Trevor use?

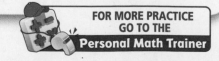

**FOR MORE PRACTICE
GO TO THE**
Personal Math Trainer

Name _____

Apply Volume Formulas

Essential Question How can you use a formula to find the volume of a rectangular prism?

Common Core Measurement and Data—5.MD.C.5a, 5.MD.C.5b
MATHEMATICAL PRACTICES
MP2, MP6

CONNECT Both prisms show the same dimensions and have the same volume.

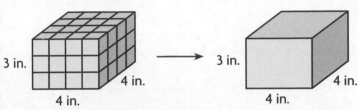

3 in.   4 in.   4 in.

→   3 in.   4 in.   4 in.

Unlock the Problem   Real World

Mike is making a box to hold his favorite DVDs. The length of the box is 7 inches, the width is 5 inches and the height is 3 inches. What is the volume of the box Mike is making?

- Underline what you are asked to find.
- Circle the numbers you need to use to solve the problem.

One Way Use length, width, and height.

You can use a formula to find the volume of a rectangular prism.

> Volume = length × width × height
>
> $V = l \times w \times h$

STEP 1 Identify the length, width, and height of the rectangular prism.

length = _____ in.

width = _____ in.

height = _____ in.

3 in.   5 in.   7 in.

Math Talk   MATHEMATICAL PRACTICES ②

Connect Symbols and Words How can you use the Associative Property to group the part of the formula that represents area.

STEP 2 Multiply the length by the width.

_____ × _____ = _____

STEP 3 Multiply the product of the length and width by the height.

35 × _____ = _____

So, the volume of Mike's DVD box is _____ cubic inches.

You have learned one formula for finding the volume of a rectangular prism. You can also use another formula.

> Volume = Base area × height
> $V = B \times h$
> B = area of the base shape,
> h = height of the solid figure.

🔑 Another Way Use the area of the base shape and height.

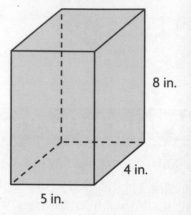

8 in.

4 in.

5 in.

Emilio's family has a sand castle kit. The kit includes molds for several solid figures that can be used to make sand castles. One of the molds is a rectangular prism like the one shown at the right. How much sand will it take to fill the mold?

$V =$ _____ B _____ × h   Replace B with an expression for the area of the base shape. Replace h with the height of the solid figure.

$V = ($_____ × _____$) \times$ _____   Multiply.

$V =$ _____ × _____

$V =$ _____ cu in.

So, it will take _____ cubic inches of sand to fill the rectangular prism mold.

Try This!

A Find the volume.

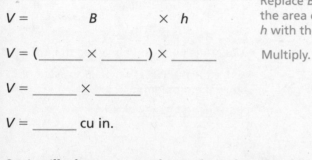

5 ft

4 ft

7 ft

$V = l \times w \times h$

$V =$ _____ × _____ × _____

$V =$ _____ × _____

$V =$ _____ cu ft

B Find the unknown measurement.

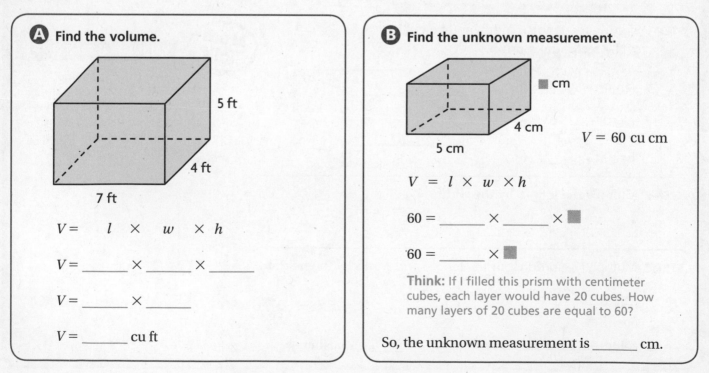

■ cm

4 cm

5 cm

$V = 60$ cu cm

$V = l \times w \times h$

$60 =$ _____ × _____ × ■

$60 =$ _____ × ■

Think: If I filled this prism with centimeter cubes, each layer would have 20 cubes. How many layers of 20 cubes are equal to 60?

So, the unknown measurement is _____ cm.

Name _____

Find the volume.

✓ **1.**

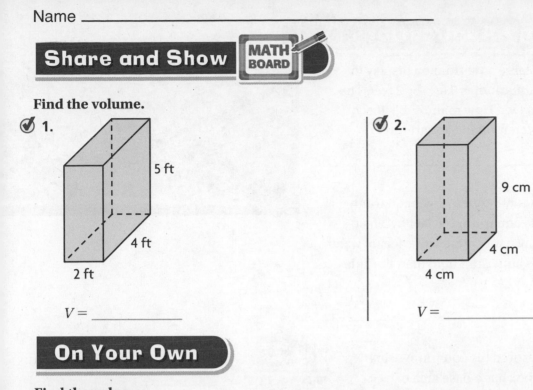

5 ft

4 ft

2 ft

V = _____

✓ **2.**

9 cm

4 cm

4 cm

V = _____

On Your Own

Find the volume.

3.

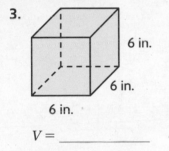

6 in.

6 in.

6 in.

V = _____

4.

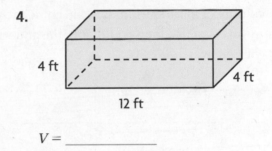

4 ft

4 ft

12 ft

V = _____

5. GO DEEPER Cheryl has a box that is in the shape of a rectangular prism. Its height is twice the length, its length is 3 times its width, and the width measures 6 inches. What is the volume of the box?

_____

MATHEMATICAL PRACTICE ② **Use Reasoning Algebra** Find the unknown measurement.

6.

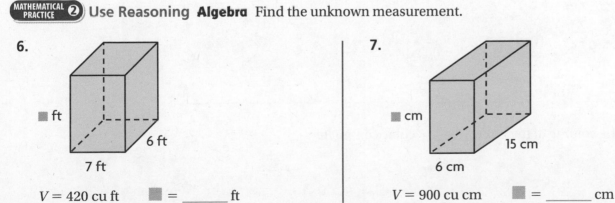

■ ft

6 ft

7 ft

V = 420 cu ft   ■ = _____ ft

7.

■ cm

15 cm

6 cm

V = 900 cu cm   ■ = _____ cm

Problem Solving • Applications Real World

8. The Jade Restaurant has a large aquarium on display in its lobby. The base of the aquarium is 5 feet by 2 feet. The height of the aquarium is 4 feet. How many cubic feet of water are needed to completely fill the aquarium?

_____

9. **GO DEEPER** The Pearl Restaurant put a larger aquarium in its lobby. The base of the aquarium is 6 feet by 3 feet, and the height is 4 feet. How many more cubic feet of water does the Pearl Restaurant's aquarium hold than the Jade Restaurant's aquarium?

_____

10. **THINK SMARTER** Eddie measured his aquarium using a small fish food box. The box has a base area of 6 square inches and a height of 4 inches. Eddie found that the volume of his aquarium is 3,456 cubic inches. How many boxes of fish food could fit in the aquarium? Explain your answer.

_____

_____

_____

_____

11. **THINK SMARTER** Manuel stores his favorite CDs in a box like the one shown.

Use the numbers and symbols on the tiles to write a formula that represents the volume of the box. Symbols may be used more than once or not at all.

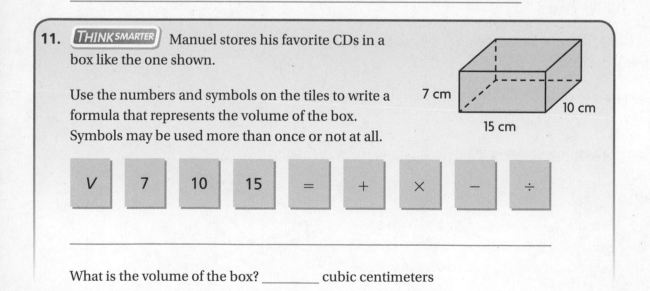

7 cm
10 cm
15 cm

| V | 7 | 10 | 15 | = | + | × | − | ÷ |

_____

What is the volume of the box? _____ cubic centimeters

Apply Volume Formulas

 COMMON CORE STANDARD—5.MD.C.5b
Geometric measurement: understand concepts of volume and relate volume to multiplication and to addition.

Find the volume.

1.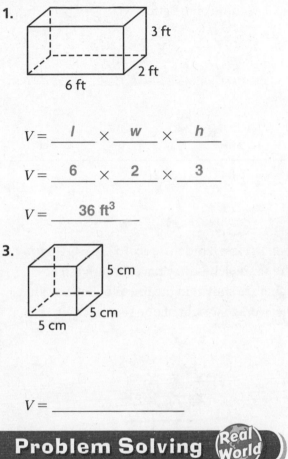

$V = \underline{\quad l \quad} \times \underline{\quad w \quad} \times \underline{\quad h \quad}$

$V = \underline{\quad 6 \quad} \times \underline{\quad 2 \quad} \times \underline{\quad 3 \quad}$

$V = \underline{\quad 36 \text{ ft}^3 \quad}$

2.

5 in.

2 in.

2 in.

$V = \underline{\hspace{3cm}}$

3.

5 cm

5 cm

5 cm

$V = \underline{\hspace{3cm}}$

4.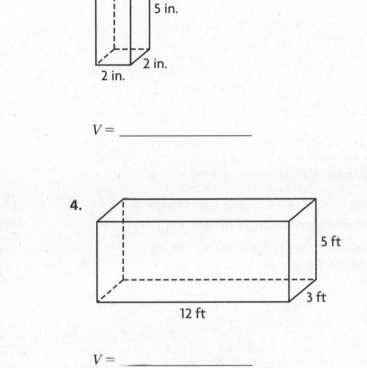

5 ft

3 ft

12 ft

$V = \underline{\hspace{3cm}}$

Problem Solving · Real World

5. A construction company is digging a hole for a swimming pool. The hole will be 12 yards long, 7 yards wide, and 3 yards deep. How many cubic yards of dirt will the company need to remove?

_____

6. Amy rents a storage room that is 15 feet long, 5 feet wide, and 8 feet. What is the volume of the storage room?

_____

7. **WRITE** ▸ *Math* Explain how you would find the height of a rectangular prism if you know that the volume is 60 cubic centimeters and that the area of the base is 10 square centimeters.

_____

_____

Lesson Check (5.MD.C.5b)

1. Sayeed is buying a crate for his puppy. The crate is 20 inches long, 13 inches wide, and 16 inches high. What is the volume of the crate?

_____

2. Brittany has a gift box in the shape of a cube. Each side of the box measures 15 centimeters. What is volume of the gift box?

_____

Spiral Review (5.MD.A.1, 5.MD.B.2, 5.MD.C.3a, 5.MD.C.4)

3. Max packs cereal boxes into a larger box. The volume of each cereal box is 175 cubic inches. What is the approximate volume of the large box?

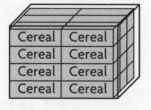

4. In health class, students record the weights of the sandwiches they have for lunch. The weights are shown in the line plot below. What is the average weight of one sandwich?

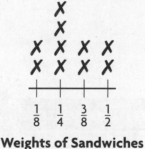

**Weights of Sandwiches
(in pounds)**

_____

5. Chloe has 20 unit cubes. How many different rectangular prisms can she build with the cubes?

_____

6. Darnell went to the movies with his friends. The movie started at 2:35 P.M. and lasted 1 hour 45 minutes. What time did the movie end?

_____

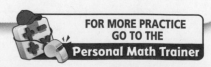

FOR MORE PRACTICE
GO TO THE
Personal Math Trainer

Name _____

Problem Solving • Compare Volumes

Essential Question: How can you use the strategy *make a table* to compare different rectangular prisms with the same volume?

Common Core **Measurement and Data—**
5.MD.C.5b
MATHEMATICAL PRACTICES
MP1, MP6, MP7

?Unlock the Problem Real World

Adam has 50 one-inch cubes. The cubes measure 1 inch on each edge. Adam wonders how many rectangular prisms, each with a different-size base, that he could make with all of the one-inch cubes.

Use the graphic organizer below to help you solve the problem.

Read the Problem

What do I need to find?

I need to find the number of _____,

each with a different-size _____, that have

a volume of _____.

What information do I need to use?

I can use the formula _____

_____ and the factors of _____.

How will I use the information?

I will use the formula and the factors of

50 in a _____ that shows all of the
possible combinations of dimensions with a

volume of _____ without repeating
the dimensions of the bases.

Solve the Problem

Complete the table.

Base (sq in.)	Height (in.)	Volume (cu in.)
(1 × 1)	50	(1 × 1) × 50 = 50
(1 × 2)	25	(1 × 2) × 25 = 50
(1 × 5)	10	(1 × 5) × 10 = 50
(1 × 10)	5	(1 × 10) × 5 = 50
(1 × 25)	?	(1 × 25) × 2 = 50
(1 × 50)	1	(1 × 50) × 1 = 50

1. MATHEMATICAL PRACTICE ① **Evaluate** What else do you need to do to solve the problem? _____

_____

2. How many rectangular prisms with different bases can Adam make

using 50 one-inch cubes? _____

🔑 Try Another Problem

Mrs. Wilton is planning a rectangular flower box for her front window. She wants the flower box to hold exactly 16 cubic feet of soil. How many different flower boxes, all with whole-number dimensions and a different-size base, will hold exactly 16 cubic feet of soil?

Use the graphic organizer below to help you solve the problem.

Read the Problem	Solve the Problem
What do I need to find?	
What information do I need to use?	
How will I use the information?	

> **Math Talk**
>
> **MATHEMATICAL PRACTICES ❶**
>
> **Make Sense of Problems** Explain how a flower box with dimensions of $(1 \times 2) \times 8$ is different from a flower box with dimensions of $(2 \times 8) \times 1$.

3. How many flower boxes with different-size bases will hold exactly 16 cubic feet of soil, using whole-number dimensions?

_____

694

Name _____

Unlock the Problem

✓ Use the Problem Solving MathBoard.
✓ Underline important facts.
✓ Choose a strategy you know.

Share and Show

1. A company makes concrete paving stones in different sizes. Each stone has a volume of 360 cubic inches and a height of 3 inches. The stones have different lengths and widths. No stones have a length or width of 1 or 2 inches. How many different paving stones, each with a different-size base, have a volume of 360 cubic inches?

   First, think about what the problem is asking you to solve, and the information that you are given.

   Next, make a table using the information from the problem.

   Finally, use the table to solve the problem.

   _____

   _____

   _____

✓ 2. What if the 360 cubic-inch paving stones are 4 inches thick and any whole number length and width are possible? How many different paving stones could be made? Suppose that the cost of a paving stone is $2.50, plus $0.18 for every 4 cubic inches of concrete. How much would each paving stone cost?

   _____

   _____

   _____

✓ 3. One company makes inflatable swimming pools that come in four sizes of rectangular prisms. The length of each pool is twice the width and twice the depth. The depth of the pools are each a whole number from 2 to 5 feet. If the pools are filled all the way to the top, what is the volume of each pool?

   _____

   _____

   _____

| WRITE ▶ Math • Show Your Work · · · · · |

© Houghton Mifflin Harcourt Publishing Company

On Your Own

WRITE ▶ Math
Show Your Work

4. **GO DEEPER** Ray wants to buy the larger of two aquariums. One aquarium has a base that is 20 inches by 20 inches and a height that is 18 inches. The other aquarium has a base that is 40 inches by 12 inches and a height that is 12 inches. Which aquarium has a greater volume? By how much?

_____

5. **THINK SMARTER** Mr. Rodriguez works at a store. He wants to arrange 12 toys in a display shaped like a rectangular prism. The toys are in cube-shaped boxes. How many rectangular prisms with a different-size base can he make with the boxes?

_____

6. **MATHEMATICAL PRACTICE 6** Marilyn has 4,000 one-inch cubes. She wants to pack them into a carton. The carton is 1 foot high and its base is 1 foot by 2 feet. Will all the cubes fit into the carton? **Explain** how you know.

_____

_____

_____

_____

7. **THINK SMARTER** Dakota's wading pool has a volume of 8,640 cubic inches. Which could be the dimensions of the wading pool? Mark all that apply.

(A) 24 in. by 30 in. by 12 in.

(B) 27 in. by 32 in. by 10 in.

(C) 28 in. by 31 in. by 13 in.

(D) 30 in. by 37 in. by 18 in.

Problem Solving • Compare Volumes

Common
Core

COMMON CORE STANDARD—5.MD.C.5b
Geometric measurement: understand concepts of volume and relate volume to multiplication and to addition.

Make a table to help you solve each problem.

1. Amita wants to make a mold for a candle. She wants the shape of the candle to be a rectangular prism with a volume of exactly 28 cubic centimeters. She wants the sides to be in whole centimeters. How many different molds can she make?

   _____10 molds_____

2. Amita decides that she wants the molds to have a square base. How many of the possible molds can she use?

   _____

3. Raymond wants to make a box that has a volume of 360 cubic inches. He wants the height to be 10 inches and the other two dimensions to be whole numbers of inches. How many different-sized boxes can he make?

   _____

4. Jeff put a small box that is 12 inches long, 8 inches wide, and 4 inches tall inside a box that is 20 inches long, 15 inches wide, and 9 inches high. How much space is left in the larger box?

   _____

5. Mrs. Nelson has a rectangular flower box that is 5 feet long and 2 feet tall. She wants the width of the box to be no more than 5 feet. If the width is a whole number, what are the possible volumes for the flower box?

   _____

6. **WRITE** ▸*Math* Using drawings of rectangular prisms, define in your own words, perimeter, area, and volume. Use color pencils to highlight what each term refers to.

   _____

Lesson Check (5.MD.C.5b)

1. Corey bought a container shaped like a rectangular prism to hold his photo collection. If the container's dimensions are 6 in. by 8 in. by 10 in., what is its volume?

2. Aleka has a box for keepsakes that has a volume of 576 cubic inches. The length of the box is 12 inches and the width is 8 inches. What is the height of the box?

Spiral Review (5.MD.A.1, 5.MD.C.3, 5.MD.C.5a, 5.MD.C.5b)

3. A movie is 2 hours and 28 minutes long. It starts at 7:50 P.M. At what time will the movie end?

4. How many rectangular faces does a pentagonal pyramid have?

5. An aquarium is in the shape of a rectangular prism. Its length is 24 inches, its width is 12 inches, and its height is 14 inches. How much water can the aquarium hold?

6. What is the volume of the rectangular prism shown?

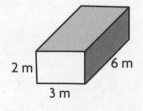

2 m
6 m
3 m

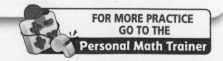

FOR MORE PRACTICE
GO TO THE
Personal Math Trainer

Name _____

Find Volume of Composed Figures

Essential Question How can you find the volume of rectangular prisms that are combined?

Common Core
Measurement and Data—
5.MD.C.5c
Also 5.MD.C.5b
MATHEMATICAL PRACTICES
MP3, MP6

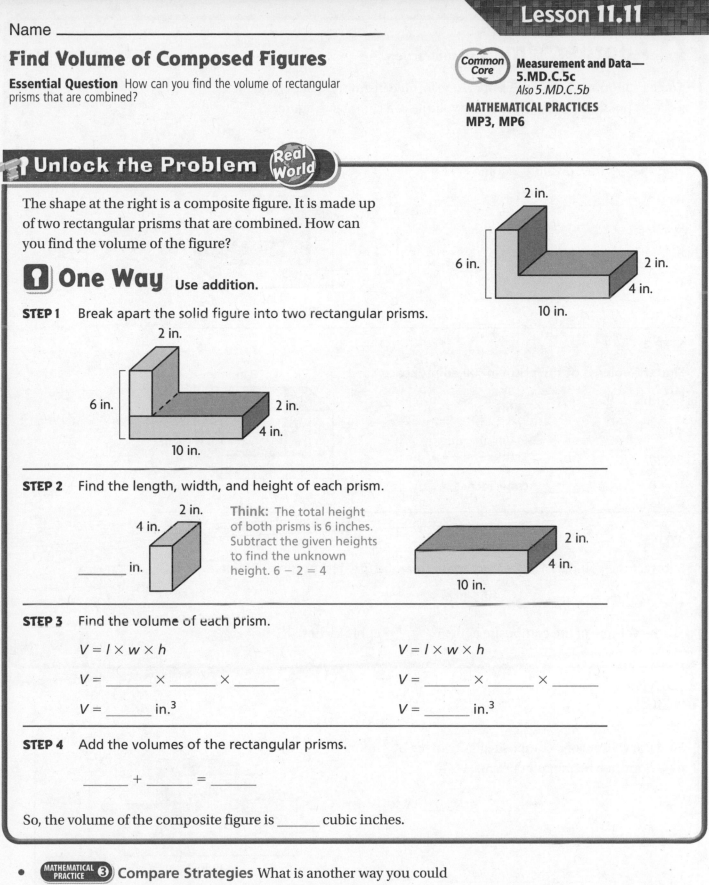

Unlock the Problem Real World

The shape at the right is a composite figure. It is made up of two rectangular prisms that are combined. How can you find the volume of the figure?

One Way Use addition.

STEP 1 Break apart the solid figure into two rectangular prisms.

STEP 2 Find the length, width, and height of each prism.

Think: The total height of both prisms is 6 inches. Subtract the given heights to find the unknown height. $6 - 2 = 4$

STEP 3 Find the volume of each prism.

$V = l \times w \times h$

$V = $ _____ $\times$ _____ $\times$ _____

$V = $ _____ in.³

$V = l \times w \times h$

$V = $ _____ $\times$ _____ $\times$ _____

$V = $ _____ in.³

STEP 4 Add the volumes of the rectangular prisms.

_____ + _____ = _____

So, the volume of the composite figure is _____ cubic inches.

• **MATHEMATICAL PRACTICE ③** **Compare Strategies** What is another way you could divide the composite figure into two rectangular prisms?

_____

_____

🔓 Another Way Use subtraction.

You can subtract the volumes of prisms formed in empty spaces from the greatest possible volume to find the volume of a composite figure.

STEP 1

Find the greatest possible volume.

length = _____ in.

width = _____ in.

height = _____ in.

V = _____ cubic inches

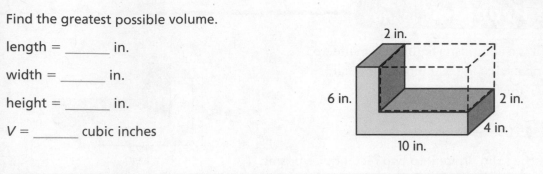

2 in.

6 in.

2 in.

4 in.

10 in.

STEP 2

Find the volume of the prism in the empty space.

length = _____ in. **Think:** 10 − 2 = 8

width = _____ in.

height = _____ in. **Think:** 6 − 2 = 4

V = 8 × 4 × 4 = _____ cubic inches

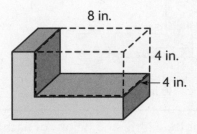

8 in.

4 in.

4 in.

STEP 3

Subtract the volume of the empty space from the greatest possible volume.

_____ − _____ = _____ cubic inches

So, the volume of the composite figure is _____ cubic inches.

Try This!

Find the volume of a composite figure made by putting together three rectangular prisms.

V = _____ × _____ × _____ = _____ cu ft

V = _____ × _____ × _____ = _____ cu ft

V = _____ × _____ × _____ = _____ cu ft

Total volume = _____ + _____ + _____ = _____ cubic feet

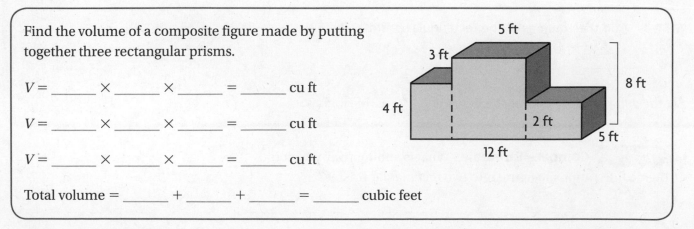

5 ft

3 ft

8 ft

4 ft

2 ft

5 ft

12 ft

700

Name _____

Find the volume of the composite figure.

1.

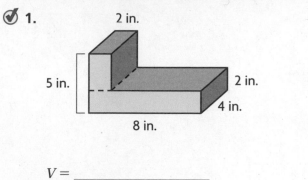

V = _____

2.

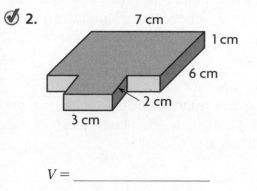

V = _____

On Your Own

Find the volume of the composite figure.

3.

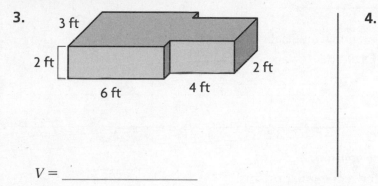

V = _____

4.

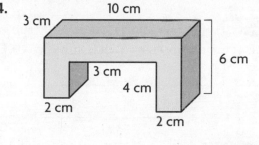

V = _____

5. GO DEEPER Mr. Williams' class built this platform for a school event. They also built a model of the platform in which 1 foot was represented by 2 inches. What is the volume of the platform? What is the volume of the model?

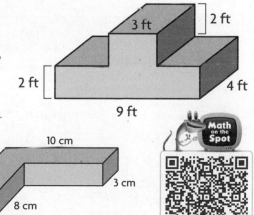

6. THINK SMARTER Patty added the values of the expressions $2 \times 3 \times 11$ and $2 \times 3 \times 10$ to find the volume of the composite figure. Describe her error. What is the correct volume of the composite figure?

_____

_____

_____

Problem Solving · Applications   Real World

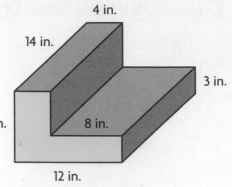

Use the composite figure at the right for 7–9.

7. As part of a wood-working project, Jordan made the figure at the right out of wooden building blocks. How much space does the figure he made take up?

   _____

8. What are the dimensions of the two rectangular prisms you used to find the volume of the figure? What other rectangular prisms could you have used?

   _____

   _____

   _____

   _____

9. **MATHEMATICAL PRACTICE 6** If the volume is found using subtraction, what is the volume of the empty space that is subtracted? **Explain.**

   _____

   _____

10. **WRITE** ▶*Math* Explain how you can find the volume of composite figures that are made by combining rectangular prisms.

    _____

    _____

Personal Math Trainer

11. **THINK SMARTER +** A composite is shown. What is the volume of the composite figure?

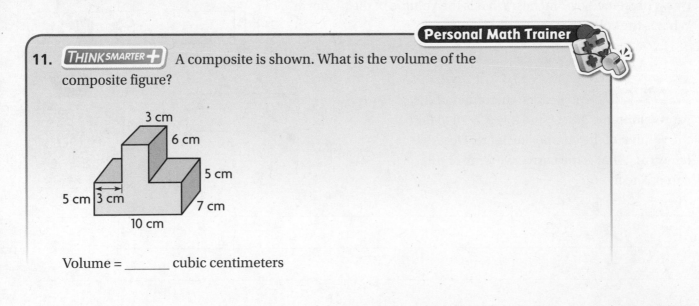

   Volume = _____ cubic centimeters

Find Volume of Composed Figures

Common Core
COMMON CORE STANDARD—5.MD.C.5c
Geometric measurement: understand concepts of volume and relate volume to multiplication and to addition.

Find the volume of the composite figure.

1.

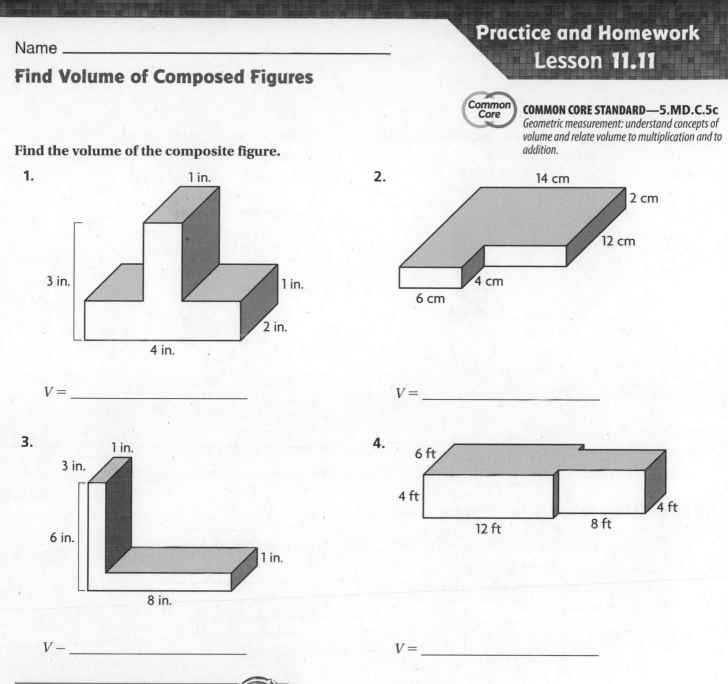

1 in.
3 in.
1 in.
2 in.
4 in.

$V =$ _____

2.

14 cm
2 cm
12 cm
4 cm
6 cm

$V =$ _____

3.

1 in.
3 in.
6 in.
1 in.
8 in.

$V -$ _____

4.

6 ft
4 ft
4 ft
12 ft
8 ft

$V =$ _____

Problem Solving · Real World

5. As part of her shop class, Jules made the figure below out of pieces of wood. How much space does the figure she made take up?

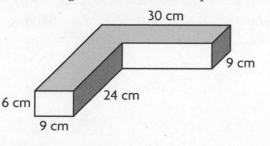

30 cm
9 cm
6 cm
24 cm
9 cm

_____

6. What is the volume of the composite figure below?

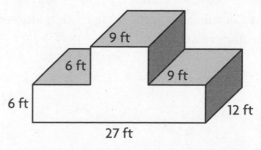

9 ft
6 ft
9 ft
6 ft
12 ft
27 ft

_____

Lesson Check (5.MD.C.5c)

1. Write an expression to represent the volume of the composite figure.

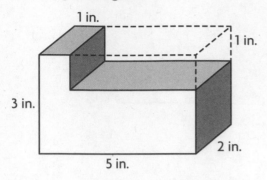

1 in.

1 in.

3 in.

2 in.

5 in.

2. Suppose you take the small prism and stack it on top of the larger prism. What will be the volume of the composite figure?

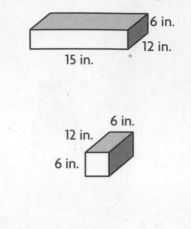

6 in.

12 in.

15 in.

6 in.

12 in.

6 in.

_____

_____

Spiral Review (5.NF.B.6, 5.NF.B.7c, 5.MD.C.5a, 5.MD.C.5b)

3. Jesse wants to build a wooden chest with a volume of 8,100 cubic inches. The length will be 30 inches and the width will be 15 inches. How tall will Jesse's chest be?

4. What is the volume of the rectangular prism?

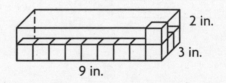

2 in.

3 in.

9 in.

_____

_____

5. Adrian's recipe for cranberry relish calls for $1\frac{3}{4}$ cups of sugar. He wants to use $\frac{1}{2}$ that amount. How much sugar should he use?

6. Joanna has a board that is 6 feet long. She cuts it into pieces that are each $\frac{1}{4}$ foot long. Write an equation to represent the number of pieces she cut.

_____

_____

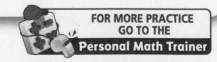

FOR MORE PRACTICE
GO TO THE
Personal Math Trainer

Name _____

Personal Math Trainer
Online Assessment
and Intervention

1. Fran drew a triangle with no congruent sides and 1 right angle. Which term accurately describes the triangle? Mark all that apply.

(A) isosceles   (C) acute

(B) scalene   (D) right

2. Jose stores his baseball cards in a box like the one shown.

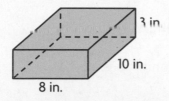

3 in.
10 in.
8 in.

Use the numbers and symbols on the tiles to write a formula that represents the volume of the box. Symbols may be used more than once or not at all.

| V | 3 | 8 | 10 | = | + | × | − | ÷ |

_____

What is the volume of the box? _____ cubic inches

3. Mr. Delgado sees this sign while he is driving. For 3a–3b, choose the values and term that correctly describes the shape Mr. Delgado saw.

YIELD

3a. The figure has [3 / 4 / 5] sides and [0 / 2 / 3] .

3b. All of the sides are congruent, so the figure is [not a polygon / a regular polygon / not a regular polygon] .

GO DIGITAL   Assessment Options
Chapter Test

4. What is the volume of the composite figure?

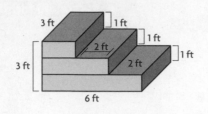

_____ cubic feet

5. Match the figure with the number of unit cubes that would be needed to build each figure. Not every number of unit cubes will be used.

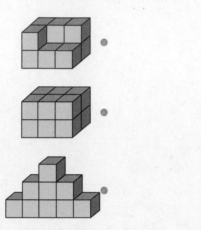

- ● 8 unit cubes

- ● 9 unit cubes

- ●10 unit cubes

- ●11 unit cubes

- ●12 unit cubes

- ●16 unit cubes

6. Chuck is making a poster about polyhedrons for his math class. He will draw figures and organize them in different sections of the poster.

Part A

Chuck wants to draw three-dimensional figures whose lateral faces are rectangles. He says he can draw prisms and pyramids. Do you agree? Explain your answer.

Part B

Chuck says that he can draw a cylinder on his polyhedron poster because it has a pair of bases that are congruent. Is Chuck correct? Explain your reasoning.

7. Javier drew the shape shown. For 7a–7b, choose the values and term that correctly describe the shape Javier drew.

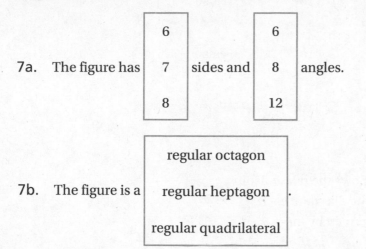

7a.   The figure has

6
7
8

sides and

6
8
12

angles.

7b.   The figure is a

regular octagon
regular heptagon
regular quadrilateral

.

8. Victoria used 1-inch cubes to build the rectangular prism shown. Find the volume of the rectangular prism Victoria built.

_____ cubic inches

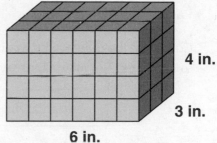

4 in.

3 in.

6 in.

9. Nathan drew a scalene, obtuse triangle. For 9a–9c, choose Yes or No to indicate whether the figure shown could be the triangle that Nathan drew.

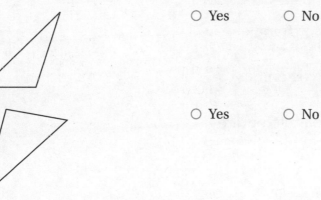

9a.   ○ Yes   ○ No

9b.   ○ Yes   ○ No

9c.   ○ Yes   ○ No

10. A shipping crate holds 20 shoeboxes. The dimensions of a shoebox are 6 inches by 4 inches by 12 inches. For 10a–10b, select True or False for each statement.

10a. Each shoebox has a volume of 22 cubic inches.　　○ True　　○ False

10b. Each crate has a volume of about 440 cubic inches.　　○ True　　○ False

10c. If the crate could hold 27 shoeboxes the volume of the crate would be about 7,776 cubic inches.　　○ True　　○ False

11. GO DEEPER　Mario is making a diagram that shows the relationship between different kinds of quadrilaterals. In the diagram, each quadrilateral on a lower level can also be described by the quadrilateral(s) above it on higher levels.

Part A

Complete the diagram by writing the name of one figure from the tiles in each box. Not every figure will be used.

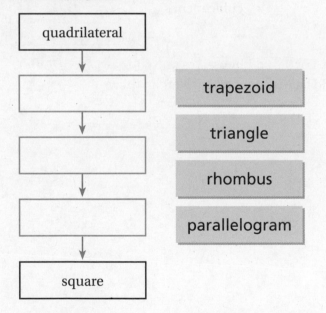

Part B

Mario claims that a rhombus is *sometimes* a square, but a square is *always* a rhombus. Is he correct? Explain your answer.

12. Write the letter in the box that correctly describes the three-dimensional figure.

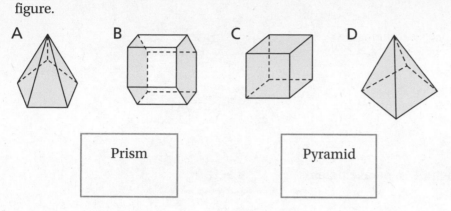

A   B   C   D

Prism		Pyramid

13. Mark packed 1-inch cubes into a box with a volume of 120 cubic inches. How many layers of 1-inch cubes did Mark pack?

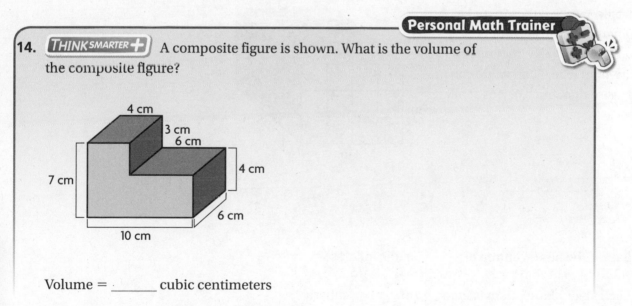

_____ layers

Personal Math Trainer

14. **THINK SMARTER +**   A composite figure is shown. What is the volume of the composite figure?

4 cm

3 cm
6 cm

7 cm

4 cm

6 cm

10 cm

Volume = _____ cubic centimeters

15. For 15a–15c, write the name of one quadrilateral from the tiles to complete a true statement. Use each quadrilateral once only.

15a. A ⬚ is always a parallelogram.

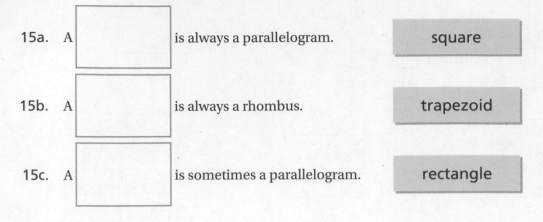

square

15b. A ⬚ is always a rhombus.

trapezoid

15c. A ⬚ is sometimes a parallelogram.

rectangle

16. Megan's aquarium has a volume of 4,320 cubic inches. Which could be the dimensions of the aquarium? Mark all that apply.

(A) 16 in. by 16 in. by 18 in.   (C) 12 in. by 15 in. by 24 in.

(B) 14 in. by 18 in. by 20 in.   (D) 8 in. by 20 in. by 27 in.

17. Ken keeps paper clips in a box that is the shape of a cube. Each side of the cube is 3 inches. What is the volume of the box?

_____ cubic inches

18. Monica used 1-inch cubes to make the rectangular prism shown. For 18a–18d, write the value that makes each statement true. Each value can be used more than once or not at all.

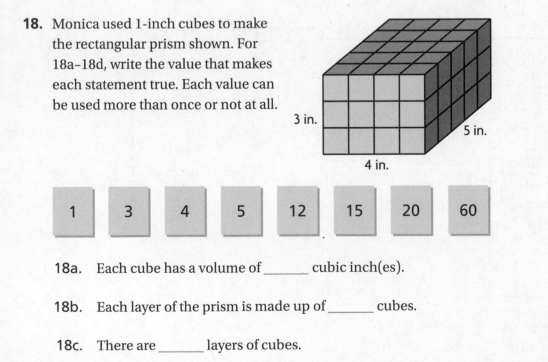

3 in.   4 in.   5 in.

| 1 | 3 | 4 | 5 | 12 | 15 | 20 | 60 |

18a. Each cube has a volume of _____ cubic inch(es).

18b. Each layer of the prism is made up of _____ cubes.

18c. There are _____ layers of cubes.

18d. The volume of the prism is _____ cubic inches.

Glossary

Pronunciation Key

a	add, map	ē	equal, tree	m	move, seem	o͞o	pool, food	u̇	pull, book
ā	ace, rate	f	fit, half	n	nice, tin	p	pit, stop	û(r)	burn, term
â(r)	care, air	g	go, log	ng	ring, song	r	run, poor	yo͞o	fuse, few
ä	palm, father	h	hope, hate	o	odd, hot	s	see, pass	v	vain, eve
b	bat, rub	i	it, give	ō	open, so	sh	sure, rush	w	win, away
ch	check, catch	ī	ice, write	ô	order, jaw	t	talk, sit	y	yet, yearn
d	dog, rod	j	joy, ledge	oi	oil, boy	th	thin, both	z	zest, muse
e	end, pet	k	cool, take	ou	pout, now	th	this, bathe	zh	vision, pleasure
		l	look, rule	o͝o	took, full	u	up, done		

ə the schwa, an unstressed vowel representing the sound spelled a in above, e in sicken, i in possible, o in melon, u in circus

Other symbols:
- · separates words into syllables
- ′ indicates stress on a syllable

A

acute angle [ə•kyo͞ot′ ang′gəl] **ángulo agudo**
An angle that has a measure less than a right angle (less than 90° and greater than 0°)
Example:

Word History

The Latin word for needle is *acus*. This means "pointed" or "sharp." You will recognize the root in the words *acid* (sharp taste), *acumen* (mental sharpness), and *acute*, which describes a sharp or pointed angle.

acute triangle [ə•kyo͞ot′ trī′ang•gəl] **triángulo acutángulo** A triangle that has three acute angles

addend [ad′end] **sumando** A number that is added to another in an addition problem

addition [ə•dish′ən] **suma** The process of finding the total number of items when two or more groups of items are joined; the inverse operation of subtraction

algebraic expression [al•jə•brā′ik ek•spresh′ən] **expresión algebraica** An expression that includes at least one variable
Examples: $x + 5$, $3a - 4$

angle [ang′gəl] **ángulo** A shape formed by two rays that share the same endpoint
Example:

area [âr′ē•ə] **área** The measure of the number of unit squares needed to cover a surface

array [ə•rā′] **matriz** An arrangement of objects in rows and columns
Example:

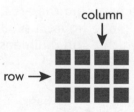

column

row

Associative Property of Addition [ə•sō'shē•āt•iv präp' ər•tē əv ə•dish'ən] **propiedad asociativa de la suma** The property that states that when the grouping of addends is changed, the sum is the same
Example: (5 + 8) + 4 = 5 + (8 + 4)

Associative Property of Multiplication [ə•sō'shē•āt•iv präp'ər•tē əv mul•tə•pli•kā'shən] **propiedad asociativa de la multiplicación** The property that states that factors can be grouped in different ways and still get the same product
Example: (2 × 3) × 4 = 2 × (3 × 4)

balance [bal'əns] **equilibrar** To equalize in weight or number

bar graph [bär graf] **gráfica de barras** A graph that uses horizontal or vertical bars to display countable data
Example:

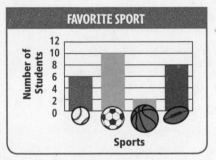

base (arithmetic) [bās] **base** A number used as a repeated factor
Example: $8^3 = 8 \times 8 \times 8$. The base is 8.

base (geometry) [bās] **base** In two dimensions, one side of a triangle or parallelogram that is used to help find the area. In three dimensions, a plane figure, usually a polygon or circle, by which a three-dimensional figure is measured or named
Examples:

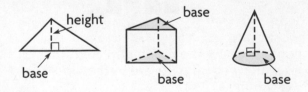

benchmark [bench'märk] **punto de referencia** A familiar number used as a point of reference

capacity [kə•pas'i•tē] **capacidad** The amount a container can hold when filled

Celsius (°C) [sel'sē•əs] **Celsius (°C)** A metric scale for measuring temperature

centimeter (cm) [sen'tə•mēt•ər] **centímetro (cm)** A metric unit used to measure length or distance; 0.01 meter = 1 centimeter

closed figure [klōzd fig'yər] **figura cerrada** A figure that begins and ends at the same point

common denominator [käm'ən dē•näm'ə•nāt•ər] **denominador común** A common multiple of two or more denominators
Example: Some common denominators for $\frac{1}{4}$ and $\frac{5}{6}$ are 12, 24, and 36.

common factor [käm'ən fak'tər] **factor común** A number that is a factor of two or more numbers

common multiple [käm'ən mul'tə•pəl] **múltiplo común** A number that is a multiple of two or more numbers

Commutative Property of Addition [kə•myo͞ot'ə•tiv präp'ər•tē əv ə•dish'ən] **propiedad conmutativa de la suma** The property that states that when the order of two addends is changed, the sum is the same
Example: 4 + 5 = 5 + 4

Commutative Property of Multiplication [kə•myo͞ot'ə•tiv präp'ər•tē əv mul•tə•pli•kā'shən] **propiedad conmutativa de la multiplicación** The property that states that when the order of two factors is changed, the product is the same
Example: 4 × 5 = 5 × 4

compatible numbers [kəm•pat'ə•bəl num'bərz] **números compatibles** Numbers that are easy to compute with mentally

composite number [kəm•päz'it num'bər] **número compuesto** A number having more than two factors
Example: 6 is a composite number, since its factors are 1, 2, 3, and 6.

cone [kōn] **cono** A solid figure that has a flat, circular base and one vertex
Example:

congruent [kən•grōō'ənt] **congruente** Having the same size and shape

coordinate grid [kō•ôrd'n•it grid] **cuadrícula de coordenadas** A grid formed by a horizontal line called the *x*-axis and a vertical line called the *y*-axis
Example:

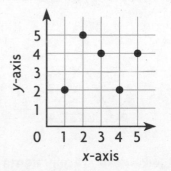

counting number [kount'ing num'bər] **número natural** A whole number that can be used to count a set of objects (1, 2, 3, 4, . . .)

cube [kyōōb] **cubo** A three-dimensional figure with six congruent square faces
Example:

cubic unit [kyōō'bik yōō'nit] **unidad cúbica** A unit used to measure volume such as cubic foot (ft³), cubic meter (m³), and so on

cup (c) [kup] **taza (t)** A customary unit used to measure capacity; 8 ounces = 1 cup

cylinder [sil'ən•dər] **cilindro** A solid figure that has two parallel bases that are congruent circles
Example:

data [dāt'ə] **datos** Information collected about people or things, often to draw conclusions about them

decagon [dek'ə•gän] **decágono** A polygon with ten sides and ten angles
Examples:

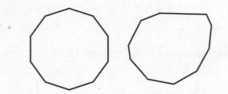

decagonal prism [dek•ag'ə•nəl priz'əm] **prisma decagonal** A three-dimensional figure with two decagonal bases and ten rectangular faces

decimal [des'ə•məl] **decimal** A number with one or more digits to the right of the decimal point

decimal point [des'ə•məl point] **punto decimal** A symbol used to separate dollars from cents in money, and to separate the ones place from the tenths place in a decimal

decimal system [des'ə•məl sis'təm] **sistema decimal** A system of computation based on the number 10

decimeter (dm) [des'i•mēt•ər] **decímetro (dm)** A metric unit used to measure length or distance; 10 decimeters = 1 meter

degree (°) [di•grē'] **grado (°)** A unit used for measuring angles and temperature

degree Celsius (°C) [di•grē' sel'sē•əs] **grado Celsius** A metric unit for measuring temperature

degree Fahrenheit (°F) [di•grē' fâr'ən•hīt] **grado Fahrenheit** A customary unit for measuring temperature

dekameter (dam) [dek'ə•mēt•ər] **decámetro** A metric unit used to measure length or distance; 10 meters = 1 dekameter

denominator [dē•näm'ə•nāt•ər] **denominador** The number below the bar in a fraction that tells how many equal parts are in the whole or in the group
Example: $\frac{3}{4}$ ← denominator

diagonal [dī·ag′ə·nəl] **diagonal** A line segment that connects two non-adjacent vertices of a polygon
Example:

difference [dif′ər·əns] **diferencia** The answer to a subtraction problem

digit [dij′it] **dígito** Any one of the ten symbols 0, 1, 2, 3, 4, 5, 6, 7, 8, 9 used to write numbers

dimension [də·men′shən] **dimensión** A measure in one direction

Distributive Property [di·strib′yoō·tiv präp′ər·tē] **propiedad distributiva** The property that states that multiplying a sum by a number is the same as multiplying each addend in the sum by the number and then adding the products
Example: $3 \times (4 + 2) = (3 \times 4) + (3 \times 2)$
$3 \times 6 = 12 + 6$
$18 = 18$

divide [də·vīd′] **dividir** To separate into equal groups; the inverse operation of multiplication

dividend [div′ə·dend] **dividendo** The number that is to be divided in a division problem
Example: $36 \div 6$; $6\overline{)36}$ The dividend is 36.

division [də·vizh′ən] **división** The process of sharing a number of items to find how many equal groups can be made or how many items will be in each equal group; the inverse operation of multiplication

divisor [də·vī′zər] **divisor** The number that divides the dividend
Example: $15 \div 3$; $3\overline{)15}$ The divisor is 3.

edge [ej] **arista** The line segment made where two faces of a solid figure meet
Example:

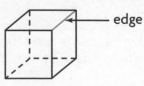
edge

elapsed time [ē·lapst′ tīm] **tiempo transcurrido** The time that passes between the start of an activity and the end of that activity

endpoint [end′ point] **extremo** The point at either end of a line segment or the starting point of a ray

equal to (=) [ē′kwəl toō] **igual a** Having the same value

equation [ē·kwā′zhən] **ecuación** An algebraic or numerical sentence that shows that two quantities are equal

equilateral triangle [ē·kwi·lat′ər·əl trī′ang·gəl] **triángulo equilátero** A triangle with three congruent sides
Example:

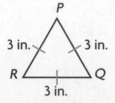

equivalent [ē·kwiv′ə·lənt] **equivalente** Having the same value

equivalent decimals [ē·kwiv′ə·lənt des′ə·məlz] **decimales equivalentes** Decimals that name the same amount
Example: $0.4 = 0.40 = 0.400$

equivalent fractions [ē·kwiv′ə·lənt frak′shənz] **fracciones equivalentes** Fractions that name the same amount or part
Example: $\frac{3}{4} = \frac{6}{8}$

estimate [es′tə·mit] *noun* **estimación (s)** A number close to an exact amount

estimate [es′tə·māt] *verb* **estimar (v)** To find a number that is close to an exact amount

evaluate [ē·val′yoō·āt] **evaluar** To find the value of a numerical or algebraic expression

even [ē′vən] **par** A whole number that has a 0, 2, 4, 6, or 8 in the ones place

expanded form [ek·span′did fôrm] **forma desarrollada** A way to write numbers by showing the value of each digit
Examples: $832 = 8 \times 100 + 3 \times 10 + 2 \times 1$
$3.25 = (3 \times 1) + (2 \times \frac{1}{10}) + (5 \times \frac{1}{100})$

exponent [eks'•pōn•ənt] **exponente** A number that shows how many times the base is used as a factor
Example: $10^3 = 10 \times 10 \times 10$.
3 is the exponent.

expression [ek•spresh'ən] **expresión** A mathematical phrase or the part of a number sentence that combines numbers, operation signs, and sometimes variables, but does not have an equal sign

face [fās] **cara** A polygon that is a flat surface of a solid figure
Example:

— face

fact family [fakt fam'ə•lē] **familia de operaciones** A set of related multiplication and division, or addition and subtraction, equations
Examples: $7 \times 8 = 56; 8 \times 7 = 56;$
$56 \div 7 = 8; 56 \div 8 = 7$

factor [fak'tər] **factor** A number multiplied by another number to find a product

Fahrenheit (°F) [fâr'ən•hīt] **Fahrenheit (°F)** A customary scale for measuring temperature

fluid ounce (fl oz) [flo͞o'id ouns] **onza fluida** A customary unit used to measure liquid capacity; 1 cup = 8 fluid ounces

foot (ft) [fo͝ot] **pie (ft)** A customary unit used to measure length or distance; 1 foot = 12 inches

formula [fôr'myo͞o•lə] **fórmula** A set of symbols that expresses a mathematical rule
Example: $A = b \times h$

fraction [frak'shən] **fracción** A number that names a part of a whole or a part of a group

fraction greater than 1 [frak'shən grāt'ər than wun] **fracción mayor que 1** A number which has a numerator that is greater than its denominator
Example:

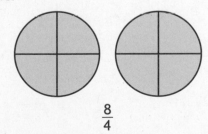

$\frac{8}{4}$

gallon (gal) [gal'ən] **galón (gal)** A customary unit used to measure capacity; 4 quarts = 1 gallon

general quadrilateral [jen'ər•əl kwä•dri•lat'ər•əl] **cuadrilátero en general** See *quadrilateral*.

gram (g) [gram] **gramo (g)** A metric unit used to measure mass; 1,000 grams = 1 kilogram

greater than (>) [grāt'ər than] **mayor que (>)** A symbol used to compare two numbers or two quantities when the greater number or greater quantity is given first
Example: 6 > 4

greater than or equal to (≥) [grāt'ər than ôr ē'kwəl to͞o] **mayor que o igual a** A symbol used to compare two numbers or quantities when the first is greater than or equal to the second

greatest common factor [grāt'əst käm'ən fak'tər] **máximo común divisor** The greatest factor that two or more numbers have in common
Example: 6 is the greatest common factor of 18 and 30.

grid [grid] **cuadrícula** Evenly divided and equally spaced squares on a figure or flat surface

height [hīt] **altura** The length of a perpendicular from the base to the top of a two-dimensional or three-dimensional figure
Example:

height —

heptagon [hep'tə•gän] **heptágono** A polygon with seven sides and seven angles

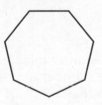

hexagon [hek′sə•gän] **hexágono** A polygon with six sides and six angles
Examples:

hexagonal prism [hek•sag′ə•nəl priz′əm] **prisma hexagonal** A three-dimensional figure with two hexagonal bases and six rectangular faces

horizontal [hôr•i•zänt′l] **horizontal** Extending left and right

hundredth [hun′drədth] **centésimo** One of 100 equal parts
Examples: 0.56, $\frac{56}{100}$, fifty-six hundredths

Identity Property of Addition [ī•den′tə•tē präp′ər•tē əv ə•dish′ən] **propiedad de identidad de la suma** The property that states that when you add zero to a number, the result is that number

Identity Property of Multiplication [ī•den′tə•tē präp′ər•tē əv mul•tə•pli•kā′shən] **propiedad de identidad de la multiplicación** The property that states that the product of any number and 1 is that number

inch (in.) [inch] **pulgada (pulg)** A customary unit used to measure length or distance; 12 inches = 1 foot

inequality [in•ē•kwôl′ə•tē] **desigualdad** A mathematical sentence that contains the symbol <, >, ≤, ≥, or ≠

intersecting lines [in•tər•sekt′ing līnz] **líneas secantes** Lines that cross each other at exactly one point
Example:

interval [in′tər•vəl] **intervalo** The difference between one number and the next on the scale of a graph

inverse operations [in′vûrs äp•ə•rā′shənz] **operaciones inversas** Opposite operations, or operations that undo each other, such as addition and subtraction or multiplication and division

isosceles triangle [ī•säs′ə•lēz trī′ang•gəl] **triángulo isósceles** A triangle with two congruent sides
Example:

10 in.   10 in.

7 in.

key [kē] **clave** The part of a map or graph that explains the symbols

kilogram (kg) [kil′ō•gram] **kilogramo (kg)** A metric unit used to measure mass; 1,000 grams = 1 kilogram

kilometer (km) [kə•läm′ət•ər] **kilómetro (km)** A metric unit used to measure length or distance; 1,000 meters = 1 kilometer

lateral face [lat′ər•əl fās] **cara lateral** Any surface of a polyhedron other than a base

least common denominator [lēst käm′ən dē•näm′ə•nāt•ər] **mínimo común denominador** The least common multiple of two or more denominators
Example: The least common denominator for $\frac{1}{4}$ and $\frac{5}{6}$ is 12.

least common multiple [lēst käm′ən mul′tə•pəl] **mínimo común múltiplo** The least number that is a common multiple of two or more numbers

less than (<) [les <u>th</u>an] **menor que (<)** A symbol used to compare two numbers or two quantities, with the lesser number given first
Example: 4 < 6

less than or equal to (≤) [les <u>th</u>an ôr ē′kwəl too]
menor que o igual a A symbol used to compare two numbers or two quantities, when the first is less than or equal to the second

line [līn] **línea** A straight path in a plane, extending in both directions with no endpoints
Example:

←————————————→

line graph [līn graf] **gráfica lineal** A graph that uses line segments to show how data change over time

line plot [līn plät] **diagrama de puntos** A graph that shows frequency of data along a number line
Example:

```
X
X      X
X  X  X  X  X
+—+—+—+—+—+—+—+
1  2  3  4  5  6  7
```
Miles Jogged

line segment [līn seg′mənt] **segmento** A part of a line that includes two points called endpoints and all the points between them

•————————•

line symmetry [līn sim′ə•trē] **simetría axial** A figure has line symmetry if it can be folded about a line so that its two parts match exactly.

linear unit [lin′ē•ər yoo′nit] **unidad lineal** A measure of length, width, height, or distance

liquid volume [lik′wid väl′yoom] **volumen de un líquido** The amount of liquid in a container

liter (L) [lēt′ər] **litro (L)** A metric unit used to measure capacity; 1 liter = 1,000 milliliters

mass [mas] **masa** The amount of matter in an object

meter (m) [mēt′ər] **metro (m)** A metric unit used to measure length or distance; 1 meter = 100 centimeters

mile (mi) [mīl] **milla (mi)** A customary unit used to measure length or distance; 5,280 feet = 1 mile

milligram (mg) [mil′i•gram] **miligramo** A metric unit used to measure mass; 1,000 milligrams = 1 gram

milliliter (mL) [mil′i•lēt•ər] **mililitro (mL)** A metric unit used to measure capacity; 1,000 milliliters = 1 liter

millimeter (mm) [mil′i•mēt•ər] **milímetro (mm)** A metric unit used to measure length or distance; 1,000 millimeters = 1 meter

million [mil′yən] **millón** 1,000 thousands; written as 1,000,000

mixed number [mikst num′bər] **número mixto** A number that is made up of a whole number and a fraction
Example: $1\frac{5}{8}$

multiple [mul′tə•pəl] **múltiplo** The product of two counting numbers is a multiple of each of those numbers

multiplication [mul•tə•pli•kā′shən] **multiplicación** A process to find the total number of items made up of equal-sized groups, or to find the total number of items in a given number of groups. It is the inverse operation of division.

multiply [mul′tə•plī] **multiplicar** When you combine equal groups, you can multiply to find how many in all; the inverse operation of division

nonagon [nän′ə•gän] **eneágono** A polygon with nine sides and nine angles

not equal to (≠) [not ē′kwəl too] **no igual a** A symbol that indicates one quantity is not equal to another

number line [num′bər līn] **recta numérica** A line on which numbers can be located
Example:

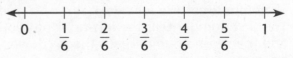

numerator [noo′mər•āt•ər] **numerador** The number above the bar in a fraction that tells how many equal parts of the whole or group are being considered

Example: $\frac{3}{4}$ ← numerator

numerical expression [noo•mer′i•kəl ek•spresh′ən] **expresión numérica** A mathematical phrase that uses only numbers and operation signs

obtuse angle [äb•toos′ ang′gəl] **ángulo obtuso** An angle whose measure is greater than 90° and less than 180°
Example:

obtuse triangle [äb•toos′ trī′ang•gəl] **triángulo obtusángulo** A triangle that has one obtuse angle

octagon [äk′tə•gän] **octágono** A polygon with eight sides and eight angles
Examples:

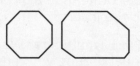

octagonal prism [äk•tag′ə•nəl priz′əm] **prisma octagonal** A three-dimensional figure with two octagonal bases and eight rectangular faces

odd [od] **impar** A whole number that has a 1, 3, 5, 7, or 9 in the ones place

open figure [ō′pən fig′yər] **figura abierta** A figure that does not begin and end at the same point

order of operations [ôr′dər əv äp•ə•rā′shənz] **orden de las operaciones** A special set of rules which gives the order in which calculations are done in an expression

ordered pair [ôr′dərd pâr] **par ordenado** A pair of numbers used to locate a point on a grid. The first number tells the left-right position and the second number tells the up-down position

origin [ôr′ə•jin] **origen** The point where the two axes of a coordinate grid intersect; (0, 0)

ounce (oz) [ouns] **onza (oz)** A customary unit used to measure weight; 16 ounces = 1 pound

overestimate [ō′vər•es•tə•mit] **sobrestimar** An estimate that is greater than the exact answer

pan balance [pan bal′əns] **balanza de platillos** An instrument used to weigh objects and to compare the weights of objects

parallel lines [pâr′ə•lel līnz] **líneas paralelas** Lines in the same plane that never intersect and are always the same distance apart
Example:

parallelogram [pâr•ə•lel′ə•gram] **paralelogramo** A quadrilateral whose opposite sides are parallel and have the same length, or are congruent
Example:

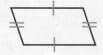

parentheses [pə•ren′thə•sēz] **paréntesis** The symbols used to show which operation or operations in an expression should be done first

partial product [pär′shəl präd′əkt] **producto parcial** A method of multiplying in which the ones, tens, hundreds, and so on are multiplied separately and then the products are added together

partial quotient [pär′shəl kwō′shənt] **cociente parcial** A method of dividing in which multiples of the divisor are subtracted from the dividend and then the quotients are added together

pattern [pat′ərn] **patrón** An ordered set of numbers or objects; the order helps you predict what will come next
Examples: 2, 4, 6, 8, 10

pentagon [pen′tə•gän] **pentágono** A polygon with five sides and five angles
Examples:

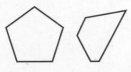

pentagonal prism [pen•tag′ə•nəl priz′əm] **prisma pentagonal** A three-dimensional figure with two pentagonal bases and five rectangular faces

pentagonal pyramid [pen•tag′ə•nəl pir′ə•mid] **pirámide pentagonal** A pyramid with a pentagonal base and five triangular faces

perimeter [pə•rim′ə•tər] **perímetro** The distance around a closed plane figure

period [pir′ē•əd] **período** Each group of three digits separated by commas in a multi-digit number
Example: 85,643,900 has three periods.

perpendicular lines [pər•pən•dik′yōō•lər līnz] **líneas perpendiculares** Two lines that intersect to form four right angles
Example:

picture graph [pik′chər graf] **gráfica con dibujos** A graph that displays countable data with symbols or pictures
Example:

HOW WE GET TO SCHOOL	
Walk	✹ ✹ ✹
Ride a Bike	✹ ✹ ✹ ✹
Ride a Bus	✹ ✹ ✹ ✹ ✹ ◖
Ride in a Car	✹ ✹

Key: Each ✹ = 10 students.

pint (pt) [pīnt] **pinta** A customary unit used to measure capacity; 2 cups = 1 pint

place value [plās val′yōō] **valor posicional** The value of each digit in a number based on the location of the digit

plane [plān] **plano** A flat surface that extends without end in all directions
Example:

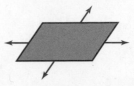

plane figure [plān fig′yər] **figura plana** See *two-dimensional figure*

point [point] **punto** An exact location in space

polygon [päl′i•gän] **polígono** A closed plane figure formed by three or more line segments
Examples:

Polygons   Not Polygons

polyhedron [päl•i•hē′drən] **poliedro** A solid figure with faces that are polygons
Examples:

pound (lb) [pound] **libra (lb)** A customary unit used to measure weight; 1 pound = 16 ounces

prime number [prīm num′bər] **número primo** A number that has exactly two factors: 1 and itself
Examples: 2, 3, 5, 7, 11, 13, 17, and 19 are prime numbers. 1 is not a prime number.

prism [priz′əm] **prisma** A solid figure that has two congruent, polygon-shaped bases, and other faces that are all rectangles
Examples:

rectangular prism   triangular prism

product [präd′əkt] **producto** The answer to a multiplication problem

protractor [prō′trak•tər] **transportador** A tool used for measuring or drawing angles

pyramid [pir′ə•mid] **pirámide** A solid figure with a polygon base and all other faces are triangles that meet at a common vertex
Example:

Word History

A fire is sometimes in the shape of a pyramid, with a point at the top and a wider base. This may be how *pyramid* got its name. The Greek word for fire was *pura*, which may have been combined with the Egyptian word for pyramid, *pimar*.

Q

quadrilateral [kwä•dri•lat′ər•əl] **cuadrilátero** A polygon with four sides and four angles
Example:

quart (qt) [kwôrt] **cuarto (ct)** A customary unit used to measure capacity; 2 pints = 1 quart

quotient [kwō′shənt] **cociente** The number that results from dividing
Example: 8 ÷ 4 = 2. The quotient is 2.

R

range [rānj] **rango** The difference between the greatest and least numbers in a data set

ray [rā] **semirrecta** A part of a line; it has one endpoint and continues without end in one direction
Example:

rectangle [rek′tang•gəl] **rectángulo** A parallelogram with four right angles
Example:

rectangular prism [rek•tang′gyə•lər priz′əm] **prisma rectangular** A three-dimensional figure in which all six faces are rectangles
Example:

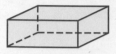

rectangular pyramid [rek•tang′gyə•lər pir′ə•mid] **pirámide rectangular** A pyramid with a rectangular base and four triangular faces

regroup [rē•grōop′] **reagrupar** To exchange amounts of equal value to rename a number
Example: 5 + 8 = 13 ones or 1 ten 3 ones

regular polygon [reg′yə•lər päl′i•gän] **polígono regular** A polygon in which all sides are congruent and all angles are congruent

related facts [ri•lāt′id fakts] **operaciones relacionadas** A set of related addition and subtraction, or multiplication and division, number sentences
Examples: 4 × 7 = 28   28 ÷ 4 = 7
7 × 4 = 28   28 ÷ 7 = 4

remainder [ri•mān′dər] **residuo** The amount left over when a number cannot be divided equally

rhombus [räm′bəs] **rombo** A parallelogram with four equal, or congruent, sides
Example:

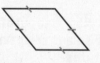

Word History

Rhombus is almost identical to its Greek origin, *rhombos*. The original meaning was "spinning top" or "magic wheel," which is easy to imagine when you look at a rhombus, an equilateral parallelogram.

right angle [rīt ang'gəl] **ángulo recto** An angle that forms a square corner and has a measure of 90°
Example:

right triangle [rīt trī'ang•gəl] **triángulo rectángulo** A triangle that has a right angle
Example:

round [round] **redondear** To replace a number with one that is simpler and is approximately the same size as the original number
Example: 114.6 rounded to the nearest ten is 110 and to the nearest one is 115.

scale [skāl] **escala** A series of numbers placed at fixed distances on a graph to help label the graph

scalene triangle [skā'lēn trī'ang•gəl] **triángulo escaleno** A triangle with no congruent sides
Example:

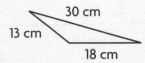

30 cm
13 cm
18 cm

second (sec) [sek'ənd] **segundo (seg)** A small unit of time; 60 seconds = 1 minute

sequence [sē'kwəns] **sucesión** An ordered list of numbers

simplest form [sim'pləst fôrm] **mínima expresión** A fraction is in simplest form when the numerator and denominator have only 1 as a common factor.

skip count [skip kount] **contar salteado** A pattern of counting forward or backward
Example: 5, 10, 15, 20, 25, 30, . . .

solid figure [sä'lid fig'yər] **cuerpo geométrico** See *three-dimensional figure*

solution [sə•lōō'shən] **solución** A value that, when substituted for the variable, makes an equation true

sphere [sfir] **esfera** A solid figure whose curved surface is the same distance from the center to all its points
Example:

square [skwâr] **cuadrado** A polygon with four equal, or congruent, sides and four right angles

square pyramid [skwâr pir'ə•mid] **pirámide cuadrada** A solid figure with a square base and with four triangular faces that have a common vertex
Example:

square unit [skwâr yōō'nit] **unidad cuadrada** A unit used to measure area such as square foot (ft²), square meter (m²), and so on

standard form [stan'dərd fôrm] **forma normal** A way to write numbers by using the digits 0–9, with each digit having a place value
Example: 456 ← standard form

straight angle [strāt ang'gəl] **ángulo llano** An angle whose measure is 180°
Example:

X   Y   Z

subtraction [səb•trak'shən] **resta** The process of finding how many are left when a number of items are taken away from a group of items; the process of finding the difference when two groups are compared; the inverse operation of addition

sum [sum] **suma o total** The answer to an addition problem

tablespoon (tbsp) [tā′bəl•spoon] **cucharada (cda)** A customary unit used to measure capacity; 3 teaspoons = 1 tablespoon

tally table [tal′ē tā′bəl] **tabla de conteo** A table that uses tally marks to record data

teaspoon (tsp) [tē′spoon] **cucharadita (cdta)** A customary unit used to measure capacity; 1 tablespoon = 3 teaspoons

tenth [tenth] **décimo** One of ten equal parts
Example: 0.7 = seven tenths

term [tûrm] **término** A number in a sequence

thousandth [thou′zəndth] **milésimo** One of one thousand equal parts
Example: 0.006 = six thousandths

three-dimensional [thrē də•men′shə•nəl] **tridimensional** Measured in three directions, such as length, width, and height

three-dimensional figure [thrē də•men′shə•nəl fig′yər] **figura tridimensional** A figure having length, width, and height
Example:

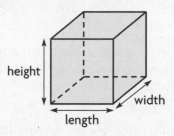

ton (T) [tun] **tonelada** A customary unit used to measure weight; 2,000 pounds = 1 ton

trapezoid [trap′i•zoid] **trapecio** A quadrilateral with at least one pair of parallel sides
Examples:

triangle [trī′ang•gəl] **triángulo** A polygon with three sides and three angles
Examples:

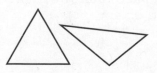

triangular prism [trī•ang′gyə•lər priz′əm] **prisma triangular** A solid figure that has two triangular bases and three rectangular faces

triangular pyramid [trī•ang′gyə•lər pir′ə•mid] **pirámide triangular** A pyramid that has a triangular base and three triangular faces

two-dimensional [too də•men′shə•nəl] **bidimensional** Measured in two directions, such as length and width

two-dimensional figure [too də•men′shə•nəl fig′yər] **figura bidimensional** A figure that lies in a plane; a figure having length and width

underestimate [un•dər•es′tə•mit] **subestimar** An estimate that is less than the exact answer

unit cube [yoo′nit kyoob] **cubo unitaria** A cube that has a length, width, and height of 1 unit

unit fraction [yoo′nit frak′shən] **fracción unitaria** A fraction that has 1 as a numerator

unit square [yoo′nit skwâr] **cuadrado de una unidad** A square with a side length of 1 unit, used to measure area

variable [vâr′ē•ə•bəl] **variable** A letter or symbol that stands for an unknown number or numbers

Venn diagram [ven dī′ə•gram] **diagrama de Venn** A diagram that shows relationships among sets of things
Example:

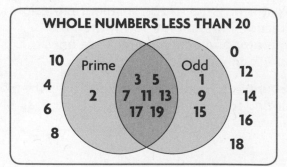

vertex [vûr′teks] **vértice** The point where two or more rays meet; the point of intersection of two sides of a polygon; the point of intersection of three (or more) edges of a solid figure; the top point of a cone; the plural of vertex is vertices
Examples:

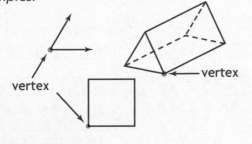

vertex

vertex

Word History

The Latin word *vertere* means "to turn" and also relates to "highest." You can turn a figure around a point, or *vertex*.

vertical [vûr′ti•kəl] **vertical** Extending up and down

volume [väl′yōōm] **volumen** The measure of the space a solid figure occupies

weight [wāt] **peso** How heavy an object is

whole [hōl] **entero** All of the parts of a shape or group

whole number [hōl num′bər] **número entero** One of the numbers 0, 1, 2, 3, 4, . . . ; the set of whole numbers goes on without end

word form [wûrd fôrm] **en palabras** A way to write numbers in standard English
Example: 4,829 = four thousand, eight hundred twenty-nine

X

x-axis [eks ak′sis] **eje de la x** The horizontal number line on a coordinate plane

x-coordinate [eks kō•ôrd′n•it] **coordenada x** The first number in an ordered pair; tells the distance to move right or left from (0, 0)

Y

yard (yd) [yärd] **yarda (yd)** A customary unit used to measure length or distance; 3 feet = 1 yard

y-axis [wī ak′sis] **eje de la y** The vertical number line on a coordinate plane

y-coordinate [wī kō•ôrd′n•it] **coordenada y** The second number in an ordered pair; tells the distance to move up or down from (0, 0)

Z

Zero Property of Multiplication [zē′rō präp′ər•tē əv mul•tə•pli•kā′shən] **propiedad del cero de la multiplicación** The property that states that when you multiply by zero, the product is zero

Correlations

 COMMON CORE STATE STANDARDS

Standards You Will Learn

Mathematical Practices		Some examples are:
MP1	Make sense of problems and persevere in solving them.	Lessons 1.2, 1.3, 1.6, 1.7, 1.9, 2.1, 2.2, 2.3, 2.4, 2.5, 2.6, 2.8, 2.9, 3.8, 3.9, 3.11, 3.12, 4.4, 4.5, 4.7, 4.8, 5.2, 5.3, 5.4, 5.6, 6.5, 6.6, 6.7, 6.8, 6.9, 7.4, 7.6, 7.9, 7.10, 8.3, 9.1, 10.1, 10.3, 10.4, 11.1, 11.4, 11.7, 11.8, 11.10
MP2	Reason abstractly and quantitatively.	Lessons 1.1, 1.2, 1.3, 1.4, 1.5, 1.6, 1.8, 1.9, 1.11, 1.12, 2.2, 2.5, 2.6, 2.7, 3.2, 3.3, 3.6, 3.7, 3.8, 3.9, 3.12, 4.1, 4.2, 4.3, 4.6, 4.8, 5.2, 5.3, 5.4, 5.5, 5.6, 5.7, 5.8, 6.2, 6.3, 6.4, 6.5, 6.6, 6.7, 6.9, 7.3, 7.5, 7.6, 7.7, 7.8, 7.9, 8.1, 8.3, 8.5, 9.1, 10.2, 10.3, 10.5, 10.6, 11.1, 11.2, 11.5, 11.7, 11.8, 11.9
MP3	Construct viable arguments and critique the reasoning of others.	Lessons 1.3, 1.5, 1.6, 1.8, 1.9, 1.10, 1.11, 2.3, 2.4, 2.5, 2.7, 2.9, 3.4, 4.1, 4.3, 4.4, 4.6, 4.7, 5.7, 6.2, 6.3, 6.5, 7.4, 7.5, 7.6, 7.8, 7.10, 8.4, 9.3, 10.6, 11.3, 11.6, 11.11
MP4	Model with mathematics.	Lessons 1.7, 1.10, 1.11, 1.12, 2.1, 2.3, 2.7, 2.9, 3.1, 4.2, 4.5, 5.3, 5.5, 6.1, 6.2, 6.4, 6.9, 6.10, 7.2, 7.7, 9.1, 9.2, 9.3, 9.4, 9.6, 9.7, 10.2, 10.4, 10.6
MP5	Use appropriate tools strategically.	Lessons 1.1, 3.1, 3.5, 3.6, 3.7, 3.9, 3.12, 5.1, 5.2, 5.5, 5.7, 6.1, 6.2, 6.7, 7.1, 7.2, 7.3, 7.4, 7.7, 7.8, 8.1, 8.4, 8.5, 11.1, 11.5, 11.6
MP6	Attend to precision.	Lessons 1.7, 1.8, 1.10, 2.1, 2.3, 2.8, 3.3, 3.4, 3.5, 3.7, 4.1, 4.2, 4.3, 4.4, 4.8, 5.1, 5.2, 5.3, 5.4, 5.5, 5.7, 5.8, 6.1, 6.3, 6.4, 6.6, 6.7, 6.9, 7.1, 7.2, 7.3, 7.5, 7.6, 7.8, 7.9, 7.10, 8.2, 8.3, 9.2, 9.4, 9.5, 9.6, 10.1, 10.2, 10.4, 10.5, 10.7, 11.1, 11.2, 11.4, 11.5, 11.6, 11.7, 11.8, 11.9, 11.10, 11.11
MP7	Look for and make use of structure.	Lessons 1.1, 1.2, 1.4, 1.8, 2.8, 3.1, 3.2, 3.10, 5.1, 5.8, 6.8, 6.10, 9.5, 9.6, 9.7, 10.1, 10.5, 10.6, 10.7, 11.2, 11.3, 11.4, 11.10
MP8	Look for and express regularity in repeated reasoning.	Lessons 1.3, 1.4, 1.5, 2.2, 2.4, 2.6, 3.4, 3.5, 3.6, 3.8, 3.10, 4.6, 4.7, 5.6, 5.7, 6.8, 6.10, 8.2, 9.3, 9.5, 11.2, 11.4

Standards You Will Learn

Domain: Operations and Algebraic Thinking

Write and interpret numerical expressions.

5.OA.A.1	Use parentheses, brackets, or braces in numerical expressions, and evaluate expressions with these symbols.	Lessons 1.3, 1.10, 1.11, 1.12
5.OA.A.2	Write simple expressions that record calculations with numbers, and interpret numerical expressions without evaluating them.	Lesson 1.10, 6.4

Analyze patterns and relationships.

5.OA.B.3	Generate two numerical patterns using two given rules. Identify apparent relationships between corresponding terms. Form ordered pairs consisting of corresponding terms from the two patterns, and graph the ordered pairs on a coordinate plane.	Lessons 9.5, 9.6, 9.7

Domain: Number and Operations in Base Ten

Understand the place value system.

5.NBT.A.1	Recognize that in a multi-digit number, a digit in one place represents 10 times as much as it represents in the place to its right and 1/10 of what it represents in the place to its left.	Lessons 1.1, 1.2, 3.1
5.NBT.A.2	Explain patterns in the number of zeros of the product when multiplying a number by powers of 10, and explain patterns in the placement of the decimal point when a decimal is multiplied or divided by a power of 10. Use whole-number exponents to denote powers of 10.	Lessons 1.4, 1.5, 4.1, 5.1
5.NBT.A.3	Read, write, and compare decimals to thousandths.	
5.NBT.A.3a	Read and write decimals to thousandths using base-ten numerals, number names, and expanded form, e.g., $347.392 = 3 \times 100 + 4 \times 10 + 7 \times 1 + 3 \times (1/10) + 9 \times (1/100) + 2 \times (1/1000)$.	Lesson 3.2
5.NBT.A.3b	Compare two decimals to thousandths based on meanings of the digits in each place, using $>$, $=$, and $<$ symbols to record the results of comparisons.	Lesson 3.3
5.NBT.A.4	Use place value understanding to round decimals to any place.	Lesson 3.4

Standards You Will Learn

Perform operations with multi-digit whole numbers and with decimals to hundredths.

5.NBT.B.5	Fluently multiply multi-digit whole numbers using the standard algorithm.	Lessons 1.6, 1.7
5.NBT.B.6	Find whole-number quotients of whole numbers with up to four-digit dividends and two-digit divisors, using strategies based on place value, the properties of operations, and/or the relationship between multiplication and division. Illustrate and explain the calculation by using equations, rectangular arrays, and/or area models.	Lessons 1.8, 1.9, 2.1, 2.2, 2.3, 2.4, 2.5, 2.6, 2.8, 2.9
5.NBT.B.7	Add, subtract, multiply, and divide decimals to hundredths, using concrete models or drawings and strategies based on place value, properties of operations, and/or the relationship between addition and subtraction; relate the strategy to a written method and explain the reasoning used.	Lessons 3.5, 3.6, 3.7, 3.8, 3.9, 3.10, 3.11, 3.12, 4.2, 4.3, 4.4, 4.5, 4.6, 4.7, 4.8, 5.2, 5.3, 5.4, 5.5, 5.6, 5.7, 5.8

Domain: Number and Operations—Fractions

Use equivalent fractions as a strategy to add and subtract fractions.

5.NF.A.1	Add and subtract fractions with unlike denominators (including mixed numbers) by replacing given fractions with equivalent fractions in such a way as to produce an equivalent sum or difference of fractions with like denominators.	Lessons 6.1, 6.4, 6.5, 6.6, 6.7, 6.8, 6.9, 6.10
5.NF.A.2	Solve word problems involving addition and subtraction of fractions referring to the same whole, including cases of unlike denominators, e.g., by using visual fraction models or equations to represent the problem. Use benchmark fractions and number sense of fractions to estimate mentally and assess the reasonableness of answers.	Lessons 6.1, 6.2, 6.3, 6.5, 6.6, 6.7, 6.9

Apply and extend previous understandings of multiplication and division to multiply and divide fractions.

5.NF.B.3	Interpret a fraction as division of the numerator by the denominator ($a/b = a \div b$). Solve word problems involving division of whole numbers leading to answers in the form of fractions or mixed numbers, e.g., by using visual fraction models or equations to represent the problem.	Lessons 2.7, 8.3
5.NF.B.4	Apply and extend previous understandings of multiplication to multiply a fraction or whole number by a fraction.	
5.NF.B.4a	Interpret the product (a/b) $\times$ q as a parts of a partition of q into b equal parts; equivalently, as the result of a sequence of operations $a \times q \div b$.	Lessons 7.1, 7.2, 7.3, 7.4, 7.6
5.NF.B.4b	Find the area of a rectangle with fractional side lengths by tiling it with unit squares of the appropriate unit fraction side lengths, and show that the area is the same as would be found by multiplying the side lengths. Multiply fractional side lengths to find areas of rectangles, and represent fraction products as rectangular areas.	Lessons 7.7, 7.10

Apply and extend previous understandings of multiplication and division to multiply and divide fractions. *(Continued)*		
5.NF.B.5	Interpret multiplication as scaling (resizing), by:	
5.NF.B.5a	Comparing the size of a product to the size of one factor on the basis of the size of the other factor, without performing the indicated multiplication.	Lessons 7.5, 7.8
5.NF.B.5b	Explaining why multiplying a given number by a fraction greater than 1 results in a product greater than the given number (recognizing multiplication by whole numbers greater than 1 as a familiar case); explaining why multiplying a given number by a fraction less than 1 results in a product smaller than the given number; and relating the principle of fraction equivalence $a/b = (n \times a)/(n \times b)$ to the effect of multiplying a/b by 1.	Lessons 7.5, 7.6, 7.8
5.NF.B.6	Solve real world problems involving multiplication of fractions and mixed numbers, e.g., by using visual fraction models or equations to represent the problem.	Lessons 7.9, 7.10

Apply and extend previous understandings of multiplication and division to multiply and divide fractions. *(Continued)*		
5.NF.B.7	Apply and extend previous understandings of division to divide unit fractions by whole numbers and whole numbers by unit fractions.	
5.NF.B.7a	Interpret division of a unit fraction by a non-zero whole number, and compute such quotients.	Lessons 8.1, 8.5
5.NF.B.7b	Interpret division of a whole number by a unit fraction, and compute such quotients.	Lessons 8.1, 8.2, 8.5
5.NF.B.7c	Solve real world problems involving division of unit fractions by non-zero whole numbers and division of whole numbers by unit fractions, e.g., by using visual fraction models and equations to represent the problem.	Lessons 8.1, 8.4
Domain: Measurement and Data		
Convert like measurement units within a given measurement system.		
5.MD.A.1	Convert among different-sized standard measurement units within a given measurement system (e.g., convert 5 cm to 0.05 m), and use these conversions in solving multi-step, real world problems.	Lessons 10.1, 10.2, 10.3, 10.4, 10.5, 10.6, 10.7

Represent and interpret data.		
5.MD.B.2	Make a line plot to display a data set of measurements in fractions of a unit (1/2, 1/4, 1/8). Use operations on fractions for this grade to solve problems involving information presented in line plots.	Lesson 9.1
Geometric measurement: understand concepts of volume and relate volume to multiplication and to addition.		
5.MD.C.3	Recognize volume as an attribute of solid figures and understand concepts of volume measurement.	Lesson 11.4
5.MD.C.3a	A cube with side length 1 unit, called a "unit cube," is said to have "one cubic unit" of volume, and can be used to measure volume.	Lesson 11.5
5.MD.C.3b	A solid figure which can be packed without gaps or overlaps using n unit cubes is said to have a volume of n cubic units.	Lesson 11.6
5.MD.C.4	Measure volumes by counting unit cubes, using cubic cm, cubic in, cubic ft, and improvised units.	Lessons 11.6, 11.7

Geometric measurement: understand concepts of volume and relate volume to multiplication and to addition. *(Continued)*

5.MD.C.5	Relate volume to the operations of multiplication and addition and solve real world and mathematical problems involving volume.	
5.MD.C.5a	Find the volume of a right rectangular prism with whole-number side lengths by packing it with unit cubes, and show that the volume is the same as would be found by multiplying the edge lengths, equivalently by multiplying the height by the area of the base. Represent threefold whole-number products as volumes, e.g., to represent the associative property of multiplication.	Lessons 11.8, 11.9
5.MD.C.5b	Apply the formulas $V = l \times w \times h$ and $V = b \times h$ for rectangular prisms to find volumes of right rectangular prisms with whole-number edge lengths in the context of solving real world and mathematical problems.	Lessons 11.8, 11.9, 11.10
5.MD.C.5c	Recognize volume as additive. Find volumes of solid figures composed of two non-overlapping right rectangular prisms by adding the volumes of the non-overlapping parts, applying this technique to solve real world problems.	Lesson 11.11

Standards You Will Learn

Domain: Geometry

Graph points on the coordinate plane to solve real-world and mathematical problems.

5.G.A.1	Use a pair of perpendicular number lines, called axes, to define a coordinate system, with the intersection of the lines (the origin) arranged to coincide with the 0 on each line and a given point in the plane located by using an ordered pair of numbers, called its coordinates. Understand that the first number indicates how far to travel from the origin in the direction of one axis, and the second number indicates how far to travel in the direction of the second axis, with the convention that the names of the two axes and the coordinates correspond (e.g., *x*-axis and *x*-coordinate, *y*-axis and *y*-coordinate).	Lesson 9.2
5.G.A.2	Represent real world and mathematical problems by graphing points in the first quadrant of the coordinate plane, and interpret coordinate values of points in the context of the situation.	Lessons 9.3, 9.4

Classify two-dimensional figures into categories based on their properties.

5.G.B.3	Understand that attributes belonging to a category of two-dimensional figures also belong to all subcategories of that category.	Lessons 11.1, 11.2, 11.3
5.G.B.4	Classify two-dimensional figures in a hierarchy based on properties.	Lessons 11.1, 11.2, 11.3

Common Core State Standards © Copyright 2010. National Governors Association Center for Best Practices and Council of Chief State School Officers. All rights reserved. This product is not sponsored or endorsed by the Common Core State Standards Initiative of the National Governors Association Center for Best Practices and the Council of Chief State School Officers.

Index

A

Activities
Activity, 23, 371, 644, 650
Cross-Curricular. *See* Cross-Curricular
Activities and Connections
Investigate, 5, 99, 151, 175, 181, 239,
265, 297, 317, 351, 357, 427, 439, 459,
491, 545, 663, 669, 675
Math in the Real World, 3, 85, 149, 231,
289, 349, 419, 489, 531, 583, 635
Mental Math, 17–20, 29–32, 219, 364,
409, 598

Acute triangles, 643–646

Addition
Associative Property of, 17–20, 219–222,
407–410
Commutative Property of, 17–20,
219–225, 407–410
of decimals, 175–178, 195–198, 289–210,
219–225
estimation and, 189–192, 195–198,
363–366
of fractions with unlike denominators,
351–354, 375–378, 407–410
Identity Property of, 17–20
inverse operations with subtraction,
202, 401–403
of mixed numbers, 381–382, 395–398
of money, 213–216
patterns, 207–210, 395–398
problem solving, 213–216, 401–404
properties of, 17–20, 219–222, 407–410

Algebra
coordinate grid
plot ordered pairs, 539–542, 551–554,
571–574
equations
addition, 17–19, 351–354, 401–404
division, 94, 517–520, 592, 623
multiplication, 17–19, 35, 94, 517,
591, 597
subtraction, 357–360, 401–403, 597
expressions, 17–20, 61–64, 67–70,
73–76
measurement
capacity, 591–594, 611–614

conversions, 585–588, 591–594,
597–600, 603–606, 611–614,
617–620, 623–626
customary units, 585–588, 591–594,
597–600, 617–620
length, 585–588, 611–614
mass, 611–614
metric units, 611–614, 617–620
multistep problems, 603–606
time, 623–626
weight, 597–600
patterns with decimals, 207–210,
233–236, 291–294
volume, 669–672, 675–678, 681–684,
687–690, 693–696, 699–702

Analog clocks, 623–625

Area models, 50, 439, 459–462

Art
Connect to Art, 448, 666

Assessment
Chapter Review/Test, 79–84, 143–148,
225–230, 283–288, 341–346, 413–418,
483–488, 523–528, 577–582, 629–634,
705–710
Constructed Response, 82, 148, 230, 288,
344, 418, 488, 528, 582, 634, 708
Mid-Chapter Checkpoint, 35–36, 111–112,
187–188, 263–264, 315–316, 381–382,
457–458, 509–510, 557–558, 609–610,
661–662
Personal Math Trainer, In every chapter.
Some examples are: 3, 85, 149, 198,
248, 280, 319, 338, 354, 436, 448, 500,
514, 542, 568
Show What You Know, 3, 85, 149, 231,
289, 349, 419, 489, 531, 583, 635

Associative Property of Addition, 17–20,
219–222, 407–410

Associative Property of Multiplication, 17–20

Average (mean), 533–536

B

Bar models, 137–140, 585, 591, 597, 600

Base, 23, 687–690

exponents, 23
prisms, 655–658, 687–690
pyramids, 655–658

Base-ten blocks, 5, 8, 23, 99–102, 175–178, 181–184, 297, 298, 309

Base-ten number system, 5–8, 11–14, 23, 99–102, 175–178, 181–184, 298

Benchmarks
  to estimate decimal sums and
    differences, 189–192
  to estimate fraction sums and
    differences, 363–366

Bubble maps, 290

Calculator, 220

Capacity
  converting customary units, 591–594,
    603–606, 617–620
  converting metric units, 611–614,
    617–620

Centimeters, 611–614

Chapter Openers, 3, 85, 149, 231, 289, 349,
  419, 489, 531, 583, 635

Chapter Review/Test, 79–84, 143–148,
  225–230, 283–288, 341–346, 413–418,
  483–488, 523–528, 577–582, 629–634,
  705–710

Checkpoint, Mid-Chapter. *See* Mid-Chapter
Checkpoint

Choose a method, 219–225

Circle maps, 636

Common Core State Standards,
  H14–H23

Common denominators
  to add and subtract fractions, 369–372,
    375–378, 381–382, 383–386, 389–392,
    395–398
  least, 370–372

Communicate Math Ideas
  Math Talk, In every lesson. Some
    examples are: 5, 30, 365, 604, 700
  Write Math, In some lessons. Some
    examples are: 7, 294, 366, 593,
    625, 702

Commutative Property of Addition, 17–20,
  219–222, 407–410

Commutative Property of Multiplication,
  17–20

Comparing
  decimals, 163–166
  fractions, 445–448
  mixed numbers, 465–468
  quadrilaterals, 649–652
  two-dimensional figures, 649–652

Compatible numbers, estimate division
  with two-digit divisor, 113–116,
  303–306

Cones, 656–658

Connect, 67, 94, 113, 131, 175, 181, 271, 277,
  292, 329, 330, 375, 407, 452, 466, 503,
  512, 681, 687

Connect to Art, 448, 666

Connect to Health, 32, 474

Connect to Reading, 392, 588, 658

Connect to Science, 192, 332, 554, 646

Connect to Social Studies, 102

Conversions
  customary capacity, 591–594, 617–620
  customary length, 585–588, 617–620
  customary weight, 597–600, 617–620
  metric units, 611–614, 617–620
  time, 623–626

Coordinate grid
  distance, 539–542
  plot ordered pairs, 539–542, 545–548,
    551–554, 571–574
  with whole numbers, 539–542, 545–548,
    551–554, 571–574

Correlations
  Common Core State Standards, H14–H23

Critical Area
  Common Core, 1, 347, 529

**Cross-Curricular Activities
and Connections**
  Connect to Art, 448, 666
  Connect to Health, 32, 474
  Connect to Reading, 392, 588, 658
  Connect to Science, 192, 332, 554, 646
  Connect to Social Studies, 102

Cubes, 687–690
  volume of, 669–672, 675–678

Cubic units, 675–678, 687–690, 693–696

Cups, 591–594

Customary units
  capacity, 585–588, 591–594, 617–620

converting, 585–588, 591–594
of length, 585–588
weight, 597–600, 617–620

Cylinders, 656–658

D

Data
collect and analyze, 533–536, 545–548,
551–554
line graphs, 551–554, 571–574
line plots, 533–536
Venn diagram, 4, 584, 638, 650

Days, 623–626

Decagonal prisms, 655

Decagons, 637–640, 655

Decimals
addition
Associative Property, 219–222
choose a method, 219–222
Commutative Property, 219–222
equivalent decimals, 196–198
estimate, 189–192, 195–198, 213–216
through hundredths, 175–178,
195–198
inverse operations, 202
model, 175–178
money, 213–216
place value and, 195–198, 219–222
regrouping, 175–178, 195–198
compare, 163–166
division
estimate, 303–306, 324, 329
model, 297–300, 309, 317–320
patterns, 291–294
place value, 309–312, 323–326
write zeros, 329–332
equivalent, 196–198
money as
addition and subtraction, 213–216
multiplication
expanded form, 251–254
model, 239–242, 245, 251–253,
265–268
money, 257–260, 278
patterns, 233–236
place value, 233–236, 245–248,
251–254, 271–274
zeros in product, 277–280
multistep problems, 335–338
order and compare, 163–166

patterns, 207–210, 233–236, 291–294
place value, 157–160, 195–198, 201–204,
219–222, 233–236, 245–248, 251–254,
271–274
rounding, 169–172, 189–192, 272
subtraction
choose a method, 219–222
equivalent decimals and, 202–204
estimate, 189–192
through hundredths, 181–184,
201–204
inverse operations, 202–204
model, 181–184
money, 213–216
place value, 201–204, 219–222
regrouping, 181–184, 201–204
thousandths
model, 151–154
read and write, 151–154, 157–160

Decimeters, 611–614, 617–620

Dekameters, 611–614

Denominators
addition, with unlike, 351–354, 375–378,
381–382, 407–410
common, 369–372, 375–378
least common denominator, 375–378, 383
subtraction, with unlike, 363–366,
375–378, 381–382

Distributive Property, 18–20, 50–51, 55–58,
252, 472–473

Division
adjusting quotients, 131–134
algorithm for, 93–96, 119–122, 309–312,
323–326, 511–514
bar models, 137–140
by decimals, 291–294, 317–320, 323–326,
329–332
of decimals, 291–294, 297–300,
303–306, 309–312, 317–320, 323–326,
329–332
Distributive Property, 50–51, 55–58
draw a diagram, 213–216, 257–260,
497–500, 517–520, 605
estimate, 87–90, 93–96, 113–116,
119–122,131–134, 303–306, 324, 329
of four-digit numbers, 88–90, 93–112
as a fraction, 125–128, 503–506
interpreting, 517–520
interpret the remainder, 125–128
inverse operation to multiplication,
49–51, 90–95, 491–494

model, 49–51, 99–102, 137–140, 317–320, 491–494, 497–500, 503–506, 511–514, 517–520

by one-digit numbers, 49–51, 55–58, 87–90, 93–96, 137–140

order of operations, 67–70, 73–76

partial quotients, 105–108

patterns, 113–116, 291–294

related to multiplication, 49–51, 94, 491–494, 511–514

remainder, 94, 105–149, 125–128

of three-digit numbers, 55–58, 87–90, 93–96, 99–102, 105–108, 114–116, 119–122

by two-digit numbers, 99–102, 105–108, 113–116, 119–122, 131–134

by unit fractions, 491–494, 497–500, 511–514, 517–520

write zeros, 329–332

Divisor. *See* **Division**

one-digit divisors, 49–51, 55–58, 87–90, 93–112, 137–140

two-digit divisors, 99–102, 105–108, 113–116, 119–122, 131–134

Draw a Diagram, 213–216, 257–260, 497–500, 517–520, 605

Draw Conclusions, 6, 99, 152, 175, 181, 240, 266, 297, 317, 351, 357, 427, 439, 460, 492, 546, 670, 676

Drawing

Draw a Diagram, 213–216, 257–260, 497–500, 517–520, 605

Draw Conclusions, 6, 99, 152, 175, 181, 240, 266, 297, 317, 351, 357, 427, 439, 460, 492, 546, 670, 676

E

Edges

of three-dimensional figures, 663–666

Elapsed time, 623–626

Equilateral triangles, 643–646

Equivalent fractions, 369–372

Errors

What's the Error?, 14, 172, 192, 236, 300, 326, 442, 548

Essential Question, In every lesson. Some examples are: 5, 37, 351, 383, 533, 637

Estimation

decimal sums and differences, 189–192

division, two-digit divisor, 113–116

fraction sums and differences with unlike denominators, 363–366

quotients, 113–116, 303–306

volume, 681–684

Evaluate expressions, 17–20, 67–70, 73–76

with grouping symbols, 73–76

Expanded form, 11–14, 157–160, 251–254

Exponents

exponent form, 23–26

powers of 10, 23–26

word form, 23–26

Expressions

numerical, 17–20, 61–64, 67–70, 73–76

order of operations, 67–70, 73–76

F

Faces, 655–658, 663–666

Fahrenheit thermometer, 545–548

Feet, 585–588

Flow map, 86, 232, 490

Fluid ounces, 591–594

Formulas

for volume, 693–696, 699–702, 687–690

Fractions

addition,

Associative Property, 407–410

common denominator, 375–378, 381–382

Commutative Property, 407–410

equivalent fractions, 351–354, 375–378, 381–382, 407–410

estimate, 363–366, 381–382

mixed numbers, 381–382

models, 351–354

patterns, 395–398

properties of, 407–410

rounding, 363–366

common denominator, 369–372

as division, 503–506

draw a diagram, 497–500, 517–520

interpreting, 517–520

by unit fraction, 491–494, 497–500, 511–514, 517–520
by whole-number, 491–494, 497–500, 511–514, 517–520
write an equation, 517–520
write a story problem, 518–520
equivalent, 369–372
find a fractional part of a group, 421–424
find common denominators, 369–372
least common denominator, 370–372, 375–378
line plots, 533–536
multiplication,
 area, 459–462
 Distributive Property, 472–473
 by a fraction, 421–424, 427–430, 433–436, 439–442, 451–454
 with mixed numbers, 459–462, 465–468, 471–474
 models, 421–424, 427–430, 433–436, 439–442, 445–448, 451, 459–462, 465–468, 471–474
 scaling, 445–448, 465–468
 by whole numbers, 421–424, 427–430, 433–436
operations with line plots, 533–536
rounding, 363–366
subtraction,
 common denominator, 375–378, 386–390, 389–392
 equivalent fractions, 357–360, 375–378, 381–382, 389–392
 estimate, 363–366
 mixed numbers, 381–382, 389–392
 models, 357–360
 patterns, 395–398
 renaming and, 389–392
 rounding, 364–366
with unlike denominators, 351–354
Fraction Strips, 351–354, 357–360, 427–430, 491–494

Gallons, 591–594, 617–620
Geometry. *See also* Polygons; Three-dimensional figures; Two-dimensional figures
classification of figures, 649–652, 655–658
compare two-dimensional figures, 649–652
cones, 655–658
cubes, 635, 663–666, 675–678, 687–690
cylinders, 656–658
decagons, 637, 655
heptagons, 637–640
hexagons, 637–640, 655
model three-dimensional figures, 655–658, 663–666
nonagons, 637
octagons, 637–640, 655
parallelograms, 649–652
pentagons, 637–640, 655–658
polygons, 637–640, 655
polyhedrons, 655–658
prisms, 655–658, 661–664, 687–690, 693–696, 699–702
pyramids, 655–658
quadrilaterals, 637–640, 649–652
rectangles, 649–652
rhombuses, 649–652
spheres, 656–657
squares, 649–652
trapezoids, 649–652
triangles, classify, 643–646
two-dimensional figures, 637–640, 643–646, 649–652
Venn diagrams, 638, 650, 662
volume, 663–666, 669–672, 675–678, 681–684, 687–690, 693–696, 699–702
Glossary, H1–H13
Go Deeper problems, In most lessons. Some examples are: 46, 172, 320, 447, 494, 683
Grams, 611–614
Graphic Organizers. *See* Tables and Charts
Bubble Maps, 290
Circle Map, 636
Flow Map, 86, 232, 490
H-diagram, 350
problem solving, 55–56, 137–138, 213–214, 257–258, 335–336, 401–402, 477–478, 497–498, 565–566, 617–618, 693–694
Tree Map, 150, 532
Venn diagram, 4, 584, 650
Graphs,
intervals, 551–554
line graphs, 551–554, 571–574, 594
line plots, 533–536

plot ordered pairs, 539–542, 551–554, 571–574
  relationships and, 571–574
  Venn diagrams, 4, 584, 638, 650, 662

Grouping symbols, 73–76

Guess, check, and revise, 477–480

H-diagram, 350

Health
  Connect to Health, 32, 474

Heptagons, 637–640

Hexagonal prisms, 635, 655, 657

Hexagons, 637–640, 655

Hours, 623–626

Identity Property of Addition, 17–20

Identity Property of Multiplication, 17–20, 465

Inches, 572–573, 585–588

Interpret the Remainder, 125–128

Intervals, 551–554

Inverse operations
  addition and subtraction, 202, 401–402
  multiplication and division, 49–51, 94–95, 491–494

Investigate, 5, 99, 151, 175, 181, 239, 265, 297, 317, 351, 357, 427, 439, 459, 491, 545, 663, 669, 675

Isosceles triangles, 643–646

*i***Tools,** 352, 359, 440

Kilograms, 611–614

Kilometers, 611–614

Lateral faces, 655–658

Least common denominator
  add and subtract fractions, 375–376
  finding, 370–372

Length
  converting customary units, 585–588, 617–620

Lesson Essential Question, In every Student Edition lesson. Some examples are: 5, 37, 351, 383, 533, 637

Line graphs, 551–554, 571–574

Line plots, 533–536
  fraction operations with, 533–536

Lines
  parallel, 649
  perpendicular, 649

Liters, 611–614

Make a Table, 213–216, 617–620, 693–696

Make Connections, 6, 100, 152, 176, 182, 240, 266, 298, 318, 352, 358, 428, 440, 460, 492, 546, 670, 676

Manipulatives and materials
  analog clocks, 623–626
  base-ten blocks, 5, 8, 23, 99–102, 175–178, 181–184, 298, 300
  calculator, 220
  centimeter cubes, 663, 675
  Fahrenheit thermometer, 545
  fraction circles, 428
  fraction strips, 351–354, 357–360, 427, 491–494
  MathBoard, In every lesson. Some examples are: 7, 30, 132, 390, 427, 671
  number cubes, 4A, 350A, 532A
  protractor, 644
  ruler, 644
  square tile, 459
  unit cubes, 663–666, 669–672

MathBoard, In every lesson.
  Some examples are: 7, 30, 132, 390, 427, 671

Math in the Real World, 3, 85, 149, 231, 289, 349, 419, 489, 531, 583, 635

Mathematical Practices
  1) *Make sense of problems and persevere in solving them,* In some lessons.
    Some examples are: 14, 254, 312, 536
  2) *Reason abstractly and quantitatively,* In some lessons. Some examples are: 20, 386, 435, 599
  3) *Construct viable arguments and critique the reasoning of others,* In some lessons. Some examples are: 40, 170, 359, 548
  4) *Model with mathematics,* In some lessons. Some examples are: 90, 430, 594
  5) *Use appropriate tools strategically,* In some lessons. Some examples are: 152, 494, 637
  6) *Attend to precision,* In some lessons. Some examples are: 89, 474, 497, 640
  7) *Look for and make use of structure,* In some lessons. Some examples are: 133, 397, 562, 646
  8) *Look for and express regularity in repeated reasoning,* In some lessons. Some examples are: 170, 500, 645, 655

Math Idea, 11, 106, 637, 655

Math on the Spot Videos, In every lesson. Some examples are: 58, 154, 320, 514, 652, 684

Math Talk, In every lesson. Some examples are: 5, 30, 365, 391, 604, 700

Measurement
  capacity, 591–594
  conversions, 585–588, 591–594, 597–600, 603–606, 611–614, 623–626
  customary units, 585–588, 591–594, 597–600
  length, 29, 169, 189, 251, 271, 297, 401–402, 459–462, 477–480, 585–588, 644–645
  metric units, 611–614, 617–620
  multistep problems, 603–606
  time, 309, 329, 623–626
  volume, 675–678, 681–684, 699–702
  weight, 597–600, 604–606

Mental Math, 17–20, 29–32, 219, 364, 409, 598

Meters, 611–614

Metric units
  capacity, 611–614
  converting, 611–614, 617–620

length, 585–588

Mid-Chapter Checkpoint, 35–36, 111–112, 187–188, 263–264, 315–316, 381–382, 457–458, 509–510, 557–558, 609–610, 661–662

Miles, 586–588

Milligrams, 611–614

Millimeters, 611–614

Millions, 11–14
  place value, 11–14

Minutes, 623–626

Mixed numbers
  addition of, 381–382
  comparing, 465–468
  multiplication of, 459–462, 465–468, 471–474
  renaming as fractions, 390, 471–474
  subtraction of, 381–382, 389–392

Modeling
  decimal addition, 175–178
  decimal division, 239–242, 245–248, 317–320
  decimals, 175–178, 181–184, 317–320
  Distributive Property, 18–20, 50–51
  division of whole numbers, 50–51, 99–102, 137–140, 297–300, 309–312, 491–494
  fraction addition, 351–354
  fraction multiplication, 427–430, 433–436, 439–442, 451–454
  fraction subtraction, 357–360
  measurement, 585–588, 591–594, 597–600
  multiplication of decimals, 239–242, 251–254, 265–268
  multiplication of whole numbers, 239–242, 245, 251–254
  place value, 5–8, 11–14
  place value and rounding, 157–160, 169–172
  three-dimensional figures, 663–666, 675–678, 681–684, 693–696
  two-dimensional figures, 649–652

Modeling using bar models, 137–140, 585, 591, 597, 600

Modeling using base-ten blocks, 5–8, 23, 175–178, 181–184

Modeling using decimal models, 151–154, 175–178, 181–184, 239–242, 251–253, 265–268

Modeling using fraction strips, 351–354, 357–360, 427–430

Modeling using number lines, 363–366, 624–625

Modeling using place-value charts, 11–14, 157–160

Modeling using quick pictures, 100–102, 175–178, 182–184, 195–198, 240–241, 309

Modeling using Venn Diagrams, 4, 584, 650

Money
addition and subtraction of, 213–216
division of, 304
estimate, 112
multiplication of, 257–260, 277–280

Months, 623

Multiplication
Associative Property of, 17–20, 693–696
by decimals, 265–268, 271–274, 277–280
decimals by whole numbers, 239–242, 245–248
with expanded form of decimals, 251–254
Distributive Property, 18–20, 252, 471–474
draw a diagram, 257–260, 497–500
estimation, 37, 272
fraction modeling explained,
of fractions by fractions, 439–442, 451–454
of fractions by whole numbers, 427–430, 433–436
as inverse operation, 49–51, 94
inverse relationship to division, 49–51, 491–494, 511–514
mixed numbers, 459–462, 465–468, 471–474
models, 239–242, 251–253, 265–268
money, 257–260, 278
multistep problems, 603–606
by one-digit numbers, 37–40, 491–494
order of operations, 67–70, 73–76
patterns, 24, 29–32, 233–236
place value, 157–160, 233–236, 245–248, 251–254, 271–274
by powers of 12, 23–26, 29–32, 330
problem solving using, 55–58, 257–260, 497–500
properties of, 17–20
related to division, 49–51, 491–494, 511–514
by two-digit numbers, 29–32, 43–46
with zeros in the product, 277–280

Multistep problems,
measurement, 603–606
Go Deeper problems, In most lessons.
Some examples are: 46, 172, 320, 447, 494, 683

Nonagons, 637

Number lines
adding fractions on, 363
dividing unit fractions on, 491
estimating decimal sums and differences with, 190–192
estimating fraction sums and differences with, 363–366
to find elapsed time, 624
multiplying fractions on, 446–447, 466

Numbers. *See* Decimals; Fractions; Mixed numbers; Whole numbers
compatible, 113–116
expanded form of, 11–14, 157–160, 251–254
standard form of, 11–14, 157–160
word form of, 11–14, 157–160

Number system, base ten, 5–8, 11–14, 23, 233–236, 291–294

Numerical expressions, 17–20, 61–64, 67–70
evaluate, 67–70, 73–76

Numerical patterns, 395–398, 559–562, 571–574

Obtuse triangles, 643–646

Octagonal prisms, 655–658

Octagons, 637–640, 655

On Your Own, In most lessons. Some examples are: 13, 30, 391, 409, 639, 689

Operations
inverse, 49–51, 94, 202, 401, 491–494, 511–514
order of, 67–70, 73–76

Ordered pairs, 539–542, 571–574

Ordering
decimals, 163–166

Order of Operations, 67–70, 73–76

Origin, 539–542

Ounces, 597–600, 604–606

Parallel lines, 649–652

Parallelograms, 649–652

Parentheses ( ), 62–64, 67–70, 73–76, 407

Partial quotients

two-digit divisors, 105–108, 303–306

Patterns

on a coordinate grid, 571–574

with decimals, 207–210, 233–236, 291–294

in division, 113–116, 291–294

exponents, 23–26, 291

find a rule for, 565–568, 571–574

with fractions, 395–398

multiplication, 24, 29–32, 233–236, 252, 271–272

numerical, 559–562, 571–574

place value, 5–8, 12, 246, 252, 291–294

relate two sequences, 395–398

Pentagonal prisms, 655–658

Pentagonal pyramids, 656–658

Pentagons, 637–640

Period, 11

Perpendicular lines, 649–652

Personal Math Trainer, In every chapter. Some examples are: 3, 85, 149, 198, 248, 280, 319, 338, 354, 436, 448, 500, 514, 542, 568

Pint, 591–594, 603

Place value

decimal addition and, 195–198, 219–225

decimals, 157–160, 195–198, 201–204, 219–225, 233–236, 245–248, 251–254, 271–274

decimal multiplication and, 157–160, 233–236, 245–248, 251–254, 271–274

decimal subtraction and, 201–204, 220–222

expanded form and, 11–14, 157–160, 251–254

to hundred millions, 11–14

millions, 11–14

order decimals, 163–166

patterns in, 5–8, 12, 233–236, 246, 252, 291–294

round decimals, 169–172

standard form and, 11–14, 157–160

to thousandths, 151–154, 157–160

whole numbers, 5–8, 11–14, 245–248, 251–254

word form and, 11–14, 23–26, 157–160

Plane Figures, 637. *See also* Polygons; Two-dimensional figures

Polygons, 637–640, 643–646, 649–652, 655

congruency, 638–640, 643–646, 655–658

decagons, 637–640, 655

heptagons, 637–640

hexagons, 637–640, 655

nonagons, 637

octagons, 637–640

pentagons, 637–640, 655–656

quadrilaterals, 637–640, 649–652

regular and not regular, 638–640

triangles, 643–646, 655–656

Polyhedrons, 655–658

Pose a Problem, 96, 184, 210, 320, 430, 462, 520, 600

Pounds, 597–600, 604

Powers of 10 23–26, 29–32, 291–294

Practice and Homework

Guided Practice, Share and Show, In every lesson. Some examples are: 7, 30, 352, 376, 645, 689

Independent Practice, On Your Own, In most lessons. Some examples are: 13, 30, 391, 409, 639, 689

Practice and Homework, In every lesson. Some examples are: 53–54, 179–180, 313–314, 437–438, 615–616, 703–704

Problem Solving • Applications, In most lessons. Some examples are: 154, 192, 386, 494, 645, 666

Prerequisite skills

Show What You Know, 3, 85, 149, 231, 289, 349, 419, 489, 531, 583, 635

Prisms, 655–658

classifying, 655–658

defined, 655

rectangular, 655–658, 675–678, 681–684, 687–690, 693–696, 699–702

triangular, 655–658

volume of, 675–678, 681–684, 687–690, 693–696, 699–702

Problem solving

addition and subtraction, 213–216, 401–404

customary and metric conversions, 617–620

division, 55–58, 137–140

using multiplication, 55–58, 257–260, 497–500

Problem Solving • Applications, In most lessons. Some examples are: 154, 192, 386, 494, 645, 666

Problem solving applications. *See also*

Cross-Curricular Activities and Connections

Go Deeper, In most lessons. Some examples are: 46, 172, 320, 447, 494, 683

Independent Practice. *See* On Your Own

Investigate, 5, 99, 151, 175, 181, 239, 265, 297, 317, 351, 357, 427, 439, 459, 491, 545, 663, 669, 675

Math on the Spot, In every lesson. Some examples are: 58, 154, 320, 514, 652, 684

Personal Math Trainer, In every chapter. Some examples are: 3, 85, 149, 198, 248, 280, 319, 338, 354, 436, 448, 500, 514, 542, 568

Pose a Problem, 96, 184, 210, 320, 430, 462, 520, 600

Sense or Nonsense?, 8, 20, 178, 268, 494, 574

Think Smarter, In every lesson. Some examples are: 40, 122, 306, 494, 646, 684

Think Smarter+, In every chapter. Some examples are: 177, 198, 248, 280, 319, 338, 354, 268, 436, 448, 500, 514, 542, 568

Try This!, In some lessons. Some examples are: 11, 68, 252, 364, 396, 644

Unlock the Problem, Real World, In some lessons. Some examples are: 11, 29, 363, 389, 649, 693

What's the Error?, 14, 172, 192, 236, 300, 326, 442, 548

What's the Question?, 64

Problem solving strategies

draw a diagram, 213–216, 257–260, 497–500, 517–520, 605

guess, check, and revise, 477–480

make a table, 213–216, 617–620, 693–696

solve a simpler problem, 55–58, 565–568

work backward, 335–338, 401–404

Projects, 2, 348, 530

Properties,

Associative Property of Addition, 17–20, 219, 407–410

Associative Property of Multiplication, 17–20, 693

Commutative Property of Addition, 17–20, 219, 407–410

Commutative Property of Multiplication, 17–20

Distributive Property, 18–20, 50–51, 55–58, 251–252, 472–473

Identity Property of Addition, 17–20

Identity Property of Multiplication, 17–20, 465–466

Protractors, 644

Pyramids,

classifying, 656–658

defined, 656

Q

Quadrilaterals, 637–640, 649–652

classifying, 649–652

comparing, 649–652

defined, 649

parallelograms, 649–652

rectangles, 649–652

rhombuses, 649–652

squares, 649–652

trapezoids, 649–652

Quarts, 591–594, 603, 617, 619

Quick pictures, 23, 176–178, 182–184, 195–198, 240–241, 309

Quotients, *See* Division

R

Reading

Connect to Reading, 392, 588, 658

Read the Problem, 55–56, 137–138, 213–214, 257–258, 335–336, 401–402, 477–478, 497–498, 565–566, 617–618, 693–694

Visualize It, 4, 86, 150, 232, 290, 350, 420, 490, 532, 584, 636

Real World

Unlock the Problem, In most lessons. Some examples are: 11, 29, 360, 401, 593, 699

Reasonableness, 93–112, 195–198, 201–204, 239, 247, 253, 258, 363–366, 375–378, 472, 480

Rectangles
properties of, 649–652

Rectangular prisms,
properties of, 655–658
volume of, 663–666, 669–672, 675–678, 681–684, 687–690, 693–696, 699–702

Rectangular pyramids
properties of, 655–658

Regrouping
decimal addition, 175–178, 195–198, 213–216
decimal subtraction, 181–184, 201–204
division, 87–90, 93–112
multiplying, 37–40, 43–46

Regular polygons, 638–640

Relationships, mathematical
graphing, 571–574
multiplication to division, 49–51, 491–494

Remainders
in division 88–90, 93–112
interpreting, 125–128
writing as a fraction, 125–128

Remember, 12, 43, 88, 105, 189, 271, 291, 317, 364, 407

Renaming
fractions, 352, 389–392, 471
mixed numbers, 389–392, 471

Review and Test. See Assessment
Chapter Review/Test, 79–84, 143–148, 225–230, 389–288, 341–346, 413–418, 483–488, 523–528, 577–581, 629–634, 705–710
Mid-Chapter Checkpoint, 35–36, 111–112, 187–188, 263–264, 315–316, 381–382, 457–458, 509–510, 557–558, 609–610, 661–662
Review Words, 4, 86, 150, 232, 290, 350, 420, 490, 532, 584, 636
Show What You Know, 3, 85, 149, 231, 289, 349, 419, 489, 531, 583, 635

Rhombuses, 649–652

Right triangles, 643–646

Rounding
decimals, 169–172, 189–192, 272
fractions, 363–366
place value, 169–172

Scalene triangles, 643–646

Science
Connect to Science, 192, 332, 554, 646

Sense or Nonsense?, 8, 20, 178, 268, 494, 574

Sequences
addition, 207–210, 395–398, 559–562
pattern in, 207–210, 395–398, 559–562
relate using division, 560–561
relate using multiplication, 559–562
subtraction, 208–209, 396–398

Shapes. See Geometry

Share and Show, In every lesson. Some examples are: 7, 30, 352, 376, 645, 689

Show What You Know, 3, 85, 149, 231, 289, 349, 419, 489, 531, 583, 635

Simplest form
products of fractions, 433, 435–436, 452–453, 472–473
sums and differences of fractions and, 351–354, 357–360, 375–378, 408–409
sums and differences of mixed numbers and, 381–382, 389–392

Social Studies
Connect to Social Studies, 102

Solid figures. See Three-dimensional figures

Solve a Simpler Problem, 55–58, 565–568

Solve the Problem, 55–56, 137–138, 213–214, 257–258, 335–336, 401–402, 477–478, 497–498, 565–566, 617–618, 693–694

Spheres, 656–657

Square pyramids, 656–658

Squares
properties of, 649–652

Standard form, 11–14, 157–160

Strategies. See Problem solving strategies

Student help
Math Idea, 11, 106, 637, 655
Remember, 12, 43, 88, 105, 189, 271, 291, 317, 364, 407

Subtraction
of decimals, 181–184, 201–204, 208–210
estimation and, 189–192, 202–203, 363–366, 386, 389–390

of fractions with unlike denominators, 357–360, 376–378, 396–398
inverse operations with addition, 202, 401–403
of mixed numbers, 381–382, 389–392, 396–398, 401–404, 408
of money, 189–192, 213–216
patterns, 208–210, 396–398
with renaming, 389–392, 401–404

Summarize, 392

Synthesize, 175, 181

T

Table of Measures, H37

Tables and Charts. *See* Graphic Organizers
data, 14, 17, 20, 31, 46, 51, 64, 96, 140, 154, 160, 163, 166, 172, 192, 213–215, 222, 242, 248, 294, 306, 326, 268, 386, 424, 545, 547, 548, 551, 552, 553, 560, 561, 562, 565, 566, 567, 568, 614, 699, 700
Make a Table, 213–216, 617–620, 693–696
for measurement conversion, 586, 592, 598, 617–619, 623
place value, 5–7, 11–13, 152, 157–159, 163–165, 169–170

Talk Math. *See* Math Talk

Technology and Digital Resources
Go Digital, 4, 86, 150, 232, 350, 420, 490, 532, 584, 636
*i*Tools, 352, 359, 440
Math on the Spot Videos, In every lesson. Some examples are: 58, 154, 320, 514, 652, 684
Multimedia *e*Glossary, Access through the interactive Chapter ePlanner. 4, 86, 150, 232, 290, 350, 420, 490, 532, 584, 636

Temperature, 545, 546, 551

Term, 207–210, 395–398

Test. *See* Review and Test

Think Smarter problems, In every lesson. Some examples are: 40, 122, 306, 494, 646, 684

Think Smarter+ problems, In every chapter. Some examples are: 177, 198, 248, 280, 319, 338, 354, 268, 436, 448, 500, 514, 542, 568

Thousandths
model, 151–154

read and write, 157–160

Three-dimensional figures
base, 655–658
cones, 656–657
cubes, 635, 663–666, 675–678
cylinders, 656–658
identify, describe, classify, 655–658
prisms, 655–658
pyramids, 656–658
spheres, 656–657
volume, 663–666, 669–672, 675–678, 681–684, 687–690, 693–696, 699–702

Time
elapsed, 623–626
units of, 623–626

Tons, 598–600

Trapezoids, 649–652

Tree maps, 150, 532

Triangles
acute, 643–646, 657
classifying, 643–646
equilateral, 638, 643–646
isosceles, 643–646
obtuse, 643–646
right, 643–646
scalene, 643–646

Triangular prisms, 655–658

Triangular pyramids, 656–657

Try Another Problem, 56, 138, 214, 258, 336, 402, 478, 498, 566, 618, 690, 700

Try This!, In some lessons. Some examples are: 11, 68, 252, 364, 396, 644

Two-dimensional figures
classifying, 637–640
congruency, 637–640
comparing, 649–652
polygons, 637–640
properties of, 637–640
quadrilaterals, 649–652
triangles, 643–646

U

Understand Vocabulary, 4, 86, 150, 232, 290, 350, 420, 490, 532, 584, 636

Unit cubes, 663–666, 675–678

Unit opener, 1–2, 347–348, 529–530

Unlike denominators
adding, 351–354, 375–378, 381–382, 395, 397–398
subtracting, 357–360, 376–378, 389–392, 396–398

Unlock the Problem, In most lessons. Some examples are: 11, 29, 360, 401, 649, 699

Unlock the Problem Tips, 57, 403, 695

Venn diagram, 4, 584, 650

Visualize It, 4, 86, 150, 232, 290, 350, 420, 490, 532, 584, 636

Vocabulary
Chapter Review/Test, 79, 143, 225, 283, 341, 413, 483, 523, 577, 629, 705
Chapter Vocabulary Cards, At the beginning of every chapter.
Mid-Chapter Checkpoint, 35–36, 111–112, 187–188, 263–264, 315–316, 381–382, 457–458, 509–510, 557–558, 609–610, 661–662
Multimedia eGlossary, 4, 86, 150, 232, 290, 350, 420, 490, 532, 584, 636
Understand Vocabulary, 4, 86, 150, 232, 290, 350, 420, 490, 532, 584, 636
Vocabulary Builder, 4, 86, 150, 232, 290, 350, 420, 490, 532, 584, 636
Vocabulary Game, 4A, 86A, 150A, 232A, 290A, 350A, 420A, 490A, 532A, 584A, 636A
Vocabulary Preview, 4, 150, 350, 532, 584, 636
Vocabulary Review, 4, 86, 150, 232, 290, 350, 420, 490, 532, 584, 636

Volume
comparison of, 675–678, 693–696
composed figures, 699–702
cubic unit, 675–678
estimate, 681–684
formula, 687–690, 693–696, 699–702, 681–684
of rectangular prisms, 663–666, 669–672, 681–684, 687–690, 693–696, 699–702
unit cube, 663–666

Weight
converting customary units, 597–600, 604–606

What If, 31, 57, 68, 127, 166, 175, 181, 214–215, 246, 251, 252, 259, 271, 337, 398, 403, 478, 479, 567, 591, 603, 619, 682

What's the Error?, 14, 172, 192, 236, 300, 306, 326, 442, 548

Whole numbers
divide decimals by, 297–300, 309–312
divide unit fractions by, 511–514, 517–520
divide by unit fractions, 491–494, 497–500, 517–520
dividing, 87–90, 93–112, 99–101, 105–108, 119–122, 125–128, 131–134, 137–140
multiply fractions by, 427–430, 433–436
multiplying, 37–40, 43–46, 239–242, 427–430, 433–436
place value, 5–8, 11–14, 195–198, 201–204, 245–248, 251–254
relate multiplication to division of, 49–51, 491–494
standard form, 11–14, 157–160
word form of, 11–14, 157–160

Word form of numbers, 11–14, 23–25, 157–160

Work backward, 335–338, 401–404

Write Math, In every Student Edition lesson. Some examples are: 7, 269, 294, 366, 593, 621, 625, 702

Writing
Write Math, In every Student Edition lesson. Some examples are: 7, 294, 366, 593, 625, 702

x-axis, 539–542, 546
x-coordinate, 539–542, 545–548

Yards, 585–588
y-axis, 539–542
y-coordinate, 539–542, 545–548

Table of Measures

METRIC	CUSTOMARY

Length

1 centimeter (cm) = 10 millimeters (mm)	1 foot (ft) = 12 inches (in.)
1 meter (m) = 1,000 millimeters	1 yard (yd) = 3 feet, or 36 inches
1 meter = 100 centimeters	1 mile (mi) = 1,760 yards,
1 meter = 10 decimeters (dm)	or 5,280 feet
1 kilometer (km) = 1,000 meters	

Capacity

1 liter (L) = 1,000 milliliters (mL)	1 cup (c) = 8 fluid ounces (fl oz)
1 metric cup = 250 milliliters	1 pint (pt) = 2 cups
1 liter = 4 metric cups	1 quart (qt) = 2 pints, or 4 cups
1 kiloliter (kL) = 1,000 liters	1 gallon (gal) = 4 quarts

Mass/Weight

1 gram (g) = 1,000 milligrams (mg)	1 pound (lb) = 16 ounces (oz)
1 gram = 100 centigrams (cg)	1 ton (T) = 2,000 pounds
1 kilogram (kg) = 1,000 grams	

TIME

1 minute (min) = 60 seconds (sec)

1 half hour = 30 minutes

1 hour (hr) = 60 minutes

1 day = 24 hours

1 week (wk) = 7 days

1 year (yr) = 12 months (mo), or
about 52 weeks

1 year = 365 days

1 leap year = 366 days

1 decade = 10 years

1 century = 100 years

1 millennium = 1,000 years

SYMBOLS

$=$	is equal to	$\overleftrightarrow{AB}$	line AB
$\neq$	is not equal to	$\overrightarrow{AB}$	ray AB
$>$	is greater than	$\overline{AB}$	line segment AB
$<$	is less than	$\angle ABC$	angle ABC, or angle B
$(2, 3)$	ordered pair (x, y)	$\triangle ABC$	triangle ABC
$\perp$	is perpendicular to	$°$	degree
$\parallel$	is parallel to	$°C$	degrees Celsius
		$°F$	degrees Fahrenheit

FORMULAS

	Perimeter		**Area**
Polygon	P = sum of the lengths of sides	Rectangle	$A = b \times h$, or $A = bh$
Rectangle	$P = (2 \times l) + (2 \times w)$, or $P = 2l + 2w$		
Square	$P = 4 \times s$, or $P = 4s$		

Volume

Rectangular prism $V = B \times h$, or $V = l \times w \times h$

B = area of base shape, h = height of prism